THE CLASSICS
OF **WESTERN**
SPIRITUALITY

THE CLASSICS OF WESTERN SPIRITUALITY
A Library of the Great Spiritual Masters

President and Publisher
Lawrence Boadt, C.S.P.

EDITORIAL BOARD

Dominican Penitent Women

EDITED, TRANSLATED, AND INTRODUCED BY
MAIJU LEHMIJOKI-GARDNER

WITH CONTRIBUTIONS BY
DANIEL E. BORNSTEIN AND E. ANN MATTER

PREFACE BY
GABRIELLA ZARRI

PAULIST PRESS
NEW YORK • MAHWAH, NJ

Cover art: The image of Saint Dominic surrounded by Dominican penitent women is used with the permission of Biblioteca Comunale Intronati, Siena, from MS B.VII.5, folio 11r.

The Scripture quotations contained herein are from the New Revised Standard Version Bible, copyright 1989 by the Division of Christian Education of the National Council of the Churches of Christ in the U.S.A. and are used by permission. All rights reserved.

The Legend of Giovanna of Orvieto
Paoli, Emore and G. G. Ricci, eds. *La* Legenda *di Vanna da Orvieto* (Spoleto: Centro Italiano di Studi sull'Alto Medioevo, 1996), copyright Centro Italiano di Studi sull'Alto Medioevo, Spoleto. Used with permission.

Thomas of Siena: *The Legend of Maria of Venice*
Sorelli, Fernanda, ed. *La santità imitabile: "Leggenda di Maria da Venezia" di Tommaso da Siena,* in Deputazione di storia patria per le Venezie, Miscellanea di studi e memorie 23 (Venice: Deputazione Editrice, 1984), copyright Fernanda Sorelli. Used with permission.

Thomas of Siena: The *Libellus* concerning Catherine of Siena (Part One)
Cavallini, Giuliana and Imelda Foralosso, eds. Thomas Antonii de Senis "Caffarini," *Libellus de Supplemento. Legende prolixe Virginis Beate Catherine de Senis* (Rome: Edizioni Cateriniane, 1974), copyright Centro Nazionale di Studi Cateriniani, Rome. Used with permission.

Book design by Lynn Else
Cover and caseside design by A. Michael Velthaus

Library of Congress Cataloging-in-Publication Data

Dominican penitent women / edited, translated, and introduced by Maiju Lehmijoki-Gardner, with contributions by Daniel E. Bornstein and E. Ann Matter ; preface by Gabriella Zarri.
  p. cm. — (The classics of Western spirituality)
  Includes bibliographical references and index.
  ISBN 0-8091-3979-0 (pbk. : alk. paper)
  ISBN 0-8091-0523-3 (cloth : alk. paper)
  1. Christian women—Italy—Religious life—History. 2. Penitents—Italy—History. 3. Christian women—Italy—History—To 1500. 4. Dominicans—Italy—History. 5. Italy—Church history. I. Lehmijoki-Gardner, Maiju. II. Bornstein, Daniel Ethan, 1950– III. Matter, E. Ann. IV. Series.

BX2353.D57 2005
271'.972045—dc22

              2004020872

Published by Paulist Press
997 Macarthur Boulevard
Mahwah, New Jersey 07430

www.paulistpress.com

Printed and bound in the
United States of America

Contents

CONTENTS

Editor of This Volume

MAIJU LEHMIJOKI-GARDNER is lecturer in the Department of Theology at Loyola College in Maryland and fellow in the Department of Church History at the University of Helsinki, where she also directs a research project entitled Gendered Practices in Medieval Mysticism. She is author of *Worldly Saints: Social Interaction of Dominican Penitent Women in Italy, 1200–1500* (1999) and coauthor (with Tuomas Heikkilä) of *Keskiajan kirkko* (2001), a history of religious orders in the Middle Ages. She has produced several articles and editions concerning Dominican lay life and other aspects of medieval religious culture, including "Writing Religious Rules as an Interactive Process—Dominican Penitent Women and the Making of Their *Regula*," published in *Speculum 79* (July 2004).

Editor of Thomas of Siena: *The Legend of Maria of Venice*

DANIEL E. BORNSTEIN is professor of history and coordinator of religious studies at Texas A&M University. He is author of *The Bianchi of 1399: Popular Devotion in Late Medieval Italy* (1993) and a score of articles on the religious culture of medieval Europe, and co-editor (with Roberto Rusconi) of *Women and Religion in Medieval and Renaissance Italy* (1996). His translations of medieval Italian texts include Dino Compagni's *Chronicle of Florence* (1986) and Bartolomea Riccoboni's *Life and Death in a Venetian Convent: The Chronicle and Necrology of Corpus Domini, 1395–1436* (2000).

Editor of Lucia Brocadelli: *Seven Revelations*

E. ANN MATTER is professor and chair of the Department of Religious Studies at the University of Pennsylvania. She studies the history of Christian spirituality and biblical interpretation. Her published work includes *The Voice of My Beloved: The Song of Songs in Western Medieval Christianity* (1990), and she has co-edited books of essays on Italian women in the Middle Ages and Renaissance and on the medieval liturgy, including *Creative Women in Medieval and Early Modern Italy: A Religious and Artistic Renaissance* (1994). She has also produced critical editions of Latin and Italian religious works. With Maiju Lehmijoki-Gardner and Armando Maggi, she edited the Italian manuscript of the *Seven Revelations*, translated here. She was elected a Fellow of the Medieval Academy of America in 2003.

Author of the Preface

GABRIELLA ZARRI is professor of early modern history at the University of Florence. She has written several books and articles on medieval and early modern religious women's active and contemplative lives. Her publications include a collection of articles entitled *Le sante vive: cultura e religiosità femminile nella prima età moderna* (1990). The main article of this collection, "Living Saints: A Typology of Female Sanctity in the Early Sixteenth Century," was translated into English in *Women and Religion in Medieval and Renaissance Italy* (1996). She is also the author of *Recinti: donne, clausura e matrimonio nella prima età moderna* (2000), a collection of essays concerning early modern women's religious lives in monasteries and in the world. She is the editor of several publications, including *Women and Faith: Catholic Religious Life in Italy from Late Antiquity to the Present* (co-edited with Lucetta Scaraffia, translated into English in 1999).

To Eero, Lauri, Marja, and Anni, rakkaudella —M.L.-G.

In memory of Faye B. Matter—E.A.M.

To three impenitent women:
Jane Bornstein, Laura Bornstein, and Toby Bornstein —D.B.

Preface

This book could have been named *Catherine of Siena within Her Context*. Those who have known the Sienese saint through her *vitae* and her writings may now look at the novelty and significance of her message within a broader picture of penitent women who preceded or succeeded her. The penetrating work of Maiju Lehmijoki-Gardner draws attention to the institution and way of life of Dominican penitents in medieval Italy. While numerous scholars have addressed the evolution of the Franciscan penitent order and its various and notable contributions to medieval society and spirituality, the Dominican Order of Penance has hitherto been identified mostly through its great mystic, Catherine of Siena, and little attention has been paid to the movement at large. Already with her previous book, *Worldly Saints: Social Interaction of Dominican Penitent Women in Italy, 1200–1500* (1999), Lehmijoki-Gardner has shed light on the broader tradition and particular characteristics of the Dominican penitential life.

E. Ann Matter and Daniel E. Bornstein each enrich the present collection with a well-selected and thoroughly introduced translation. With their fine contributions Maiju Lehmijoki-Gardner examines spirituality within the framework of institutional developments of the Dominican penitent order. When the educated and influential masters general of the Dominican Order strove to strengthen the institutional position of Dominican penitent groups at the turn of the fifteenth century, one of their most effective tools was to disseminate an imitable model of penitent sanctity. This model was not the heroic sanctity of Catherine of Siena but the pious example of a Florentine widow or that of a young woman of the Venetian "bourgeoisie" who could not or did not want to enter a monastery. This model resonated the ideals of the *devotio moderna* that spread from the Low Countries to Italy through a distribution of codices, rules for religious life, prayer books, paintings and other images, and most important, through translations of *The Imitation of Christ* and Henry Suso's *Horologium* into Italian. In order to understand the quotidian nature of this spirituality, one may turn to Giovanni Dominici, whose writings centered on the theological virtue of charity, but his work also offered advice on how to lead peaceful communal life. Or one may read Anthony of Florence, whose writings were influenced by his duties as a pastor and by his focus on the sacrament of penance, but who at the same time exhorted mothers to instruct their children in Christian living by decorating their houses with images of holy virgins and other saintly youth.

This pious model of "imitable sanctity" promoted by the Dominicans had a profound impact on civic piety in fifteenth-century Italy. It particularly influenced women's religious lives and attracted new followers to lay groups associated with Dominicans, Franciscans, and other mendicant orders. Nonetheless, the *ideal* of women's sanctity continued to be shaped by the radical renunciation of the world through fasting and asceticism. Raymond of Capua's *Legenda maior* of Catherine of Siena was one of the most influential texts praising the ideal of holy women's extreme self-mortification. Fasting and eucharistic devotion were widely seen as the most significant external signs of laywomen's sanctity. These feats secured women's *fama sanctitatis*, even though the late fifteenth-century imitators of Catherine were more likely to identify themselves with Catherine's political involvement and her stigmata than with her strenuous self-renunciation.

The study of women saints has vastly expanded during the past two decades, thanks to an active interest in hagiographical texts and the history of spirituality, but *Dominican Penitent Women* remains in many respects a ground-breaking contribution to the field, not only because of the documents presented and commented in it, but because of the organization of its material. It is fruitful indeed to study the institutional history together with the history of spirituality and to place the hagiographic texts written by men within the context of women's own writing.

This volume succeeds in making a number of original observations and analyses. The collection takes a fresh look at the development of the Dominican penitent order by reexamining the history of the establishment of the Dominican penitent rule. The collection contains the translation and a study of the rudimentary original rule or the *Ordinationes* of Munio of Zamora, written in 1286, and hitherto unexplored by historians. This forgotten original rule of Munio brings new light to the institutional history of the Dominican penitent order and challenges the widely held claim that Munio wrote the formal rule for Dominican penitents. The collection also draws new attention to Catherine of Siena's role as a consolidator of the Dominican life of penance and examines in interesting ways the paradox of her model: Catherine became the paramount example of the Dominican life of penance, but her model of extreme self-mortification was not necessarily considered imitable or even an advisable model. And, yet again, while many hagiographers promoted imitable ways of quotidian sanctity, they still used Catherine as their point of reference, and the penitent women themselves reinvented Catherine—an ecstatic, a saint with stigmata, and a spiritual mother—by adjusting her model according to the demands of their own circumstances.

As it is the goal of this preface to provide the reader with a sense of the scope of work that follows, I shall not here delve deeper into examining the characteristics of Dominican penitential life during the Middle Ages. It remains to be said that thanks to the thorough work and expertise of the authors of this volume and to the interesting selection of texts here presented, we may now gain a deeper understanding of the *modus vivendi* of the Dominican tertiaries in medieval Italy and read about the variety of ways in which the inimitable has been imitated.

—GABRIELLA ZARRI

Introduction

Dominican penitent women made significant contributions to high and late medieval culture. During the early Middle Ages the centers of learning and religious writing were in monasteries, but from the twelfth century onward the rising urban centers became the loci of religious creativity and spiritual renewal. The itinerant preachers of the twelfth century moved from one urban center to another, targeting their religious message at merchants, craftsmen, and practitioners of other urban professions. From the thirteenth century, mendicant friars built their convents in town centers, preached in market squares and other public places, and counseled people at their homes. The beguines of central and northern Europe, the penitents of Italy, the *beatae* of Spain, and many other groups of laywomen throughout Europe looked to lead a disciplined life of devotion and penance. All these groups sought to strengthen the position of religion in secular life by advocating new forms of religious expression that did not demand a monastic withdrawal from the world.[1]

The existence of religious laypeople challenged neatly cut divisions between religious and secular states of life; the religious laity were not members of religious orders to the same degree as were professed monks or nuns, but their way of life was not entirely secular either. The church reacted by granting religious laypeople some ecclesiastical privileges but denied them the freedom from ecclesiastical and secular taxation that usually accompanied full membership in a religious order.[2] The church had no preemptive or systematic plan about the position of religious laity, however, and the status of lay groups varied greatly from region to region and era to era.

Religious lay life was particularly attractive to urban women who looked for social stability in religion amid the uncertainties of urban life, but who did not have enough wealth to secure a place in overcrowded monasteries. The life of penance presented urban

1

women an opportunity to work together in creation of semi-institutional systems of mutual assistance and shared lives of devotion.[3] Penitential life became a dominant feature of high and late medieval women's religious culture, and laywomen were among the most celebrated mystics.[4] For men, this semi-institutional life of devotion in the world was just one option among many, and it never dominated their religious culture to the same degree as it did that of women.[5] The Franciscan life of penance attracted considerable numbers of male disciples, but there was only a handful of Dominican penitent men, and the northern and central European beguines outnumbered by far their male counterparts, the so-called beghards.[6] The religious laymen continued to serve as lay helpers or *conversi* of the monasteries,[7] and some Franciscan penitent men and northern European beghards were venerated locally as saints for their patient service to others. Nonetheless, religious laymen seem not to have participated in the vibrant mystical culture that shaped the lives of their female counterparts. Laymen rarely attracted the attention of hagiographers and, unlike the beguines and penitent women, they did not leave behind a legacy of mystical texts.[8]

The confusing terminology concerning religious laywomen reflected the difficulty that medieval churchmen and ordinary people faced when they tried to classify the new phenomenon. The women were called religious women *(mulieres religiosae)*, religious virgins *(virgines religiosae)*, chaste women *(mulieres continentes)*, pious women *(devotae)*, beguines *(beguinae)*, *beatae*, bearers of the habit *(vestitae* or *mantellatae)* or *pinzochere*. The term *penitent (soror de penitentia)* was customarily used in reference to laywomen who operated under the auspices of Franciscan and Dominican orders. The term *tertiary (soror de tertii regulae)*, which in the modern era has come to denote the lay members of mendicant orders, was, in fact, rarely used during the Middle Ages.[9]

Franciscan and Dominican penitents were most densely concentrated in towns of central and northern Italy, where new religious ideas spread fast and women had a need for flexible systems of support amid the difficulties of urban life. *Dominican Penitent Women* focuses thus on Italy, but the Dominican penitents of Italy will be viewed in the context of laywomen's pan-European religious movements.[10]

INTRODUCTION

Sources

Dominican penitent women of Italy come forth in a wide range of sources. They appear in donation charters, testaments, chronicles, and necrologies. They were recipients of religious rules *(regulae)*, papal privileges, and indulgences. The most important sources for the lives of penitents were hagiographies. The lives of saints *(vitae)*, miracle collections, and canonization records portrayed the life of the exceptional few. Although these narratives were heavily shaped by a-historic hagiographic conventions, they nevertheless provide valuable information concerning penitential practices and religious ideals. Hagiographic sources concerning almost twenty medieval Dominican penitent women have survived, although only one of these women—Catherine of Siena (1347–80)—has been formally canonized. The reader may find the names, relevant dates, principal sources, and suggested secondary readings of known Italian Dominican penitent *beatae* in the Appendix.

Only a few Dominican penitent women knew how to write or had access to a scribe, but the letters and the mystical writings of these few help balance the idealized, sometimes formulaic, hagiographic point of view. Catherine of Siena's *The Dialogue* is considered one of the classics of Christian spirituality. The writings of less known Dominican penitent authors, Colomba of Rieti, Osanna of Mantua, Stefana Quinzani, and Lucia Brocadelli, also show that penitent women closely followed the events of their time and were well versed in Christian theology.[11]

The collection of translations presented here brings together different types of sources concerning the Dominican life of penance. The first section consists of two penitent rules. The *Ordinationes* of Munio from the late thirteenth century and the formal penitent rule of the early fifteenth century show how penitents were expected to enter the order, how they were supposed to structure their daily devotional lives, and what were their social obligations.

The second section of the book is dedicated to hagiographic sources. The *vita* of Giovanna of Orvieto is one of the earliest surviving lives of Dominican penitent women. The *Miracoli* of Catherine of Siena is the only hagiographic source written during

Catherine's life, and it opens a view to Catherine before her cult was taken over by the Dominicans. A section from the *Libellus* of Thomas of Siena focuses on Catherine of Siena's childhood and complements Raymond of Capua's portrayal of Catherine in the well-known *Legenda maior*. The *Legend* of Maria of Venice illustrates how a group of Dominican friars and penitents worked together to refashion the Dominican life of penance according to the example laid out by Catherine. The last text in this section is a notarized account of Stefana Quinzani's theatric imitation of Christ's passion.

The third and last section of the book is dedicated to penitent women's religious writing. Osanna of Mantua's letters to Francesco Gonzaga, Marquis of Mantua, show a court prophet in action; she was a determined advocate for the poor, but she was also a practical woman who used her spiritual powers to promote the interests of her own family. The *Seven Revelations* of Lucia Brocadelli of Narni, recently discovered by E. Ann Matter, is a visionary account of the heavenly court inspired by the writings of Pseudo-Dionysius and Girolamo Savonarola. The texts translated here present an overview of Dominican penitent women's literary production that complements the writings of Catherine of Siena, already available in English.

The Organizational Structure of Penitent Congregations

The relations between Dominican friars and penitent women varied from place to place. Some friars were enthusiastic supporters of laywomen's penitential life. A few acted as laywomen's confessors and publicized women's religious experiences in their *vitae*.[12] The close interaction between some mendicant friars and saintly penitent women even created a new genre of religious writing within which a friar celebrated the religious experiences and vernacular teachings of a female mystic.[13] Yet not all Dominican friars responded with enthusiasm to laywomen's efforts to dress in the Dominican colors of black and white. Some were concerned about the order's limited resources and believed that spiritual care of nuns and religious laywomen derailed friars from their main responsibility, preaching. Dominican superiors feared that close interaction with women jeopardized the friars' reputations and subjected them to unnecessary temptations.[14] Therefore, the order considered the spiritual direction of women as an activity that was suited only for some friars and required a special license from the order's master general.[15] In practice, confessors rarely sought such a license, but the ruling speaks of the order's efforts to discourage unsupervised interaction between friars and penitent women.

In most places, penitent groups arose from women's efforts to create meaningful religious and social alternatives for themselves. Women wore the Dominican habit of penance and frequented Dominican churches long before the order perceived them as a part of its institutional structure or had a coherent plan about their religious life. Moreover, a penitent's decision to seek supervision by the Dominican Order rather than by the Franciscans did not necessarily mean that she held an articulated preference for Dominican spirituality but rather that she lived in the vicinity of a Dominican convent.

The histories of the Dominican penitent order, almost exclusively written by Dominican friars, have tended to represent friars as the driving force in the creation of penitential life.[16] *Dominican Penitent Women* argues, on the other hand, that women played a more active role in the creation of the institutional foundations of their form of life than has been hitherto presumed. Women were not passive recipients of ecclesiastical legislation but actively sought ordinances and privileges that supported their way of life and protected them against accusations of heresy.[17]

Gilles Gerard Meersseman's *Dossier de l'ordre de la Pénitence* has had a deep impact on the ways in which the institutional foundation of the Dominican penitent life has been perceived. He established the argument that the formal Dominican penitent rule was written in 1285 by Master General Munio of Zamora (1285–91).[18] The formal rule that Meersseman regarded as the Rule of Munio offered detailed guidance concerning the taking of the habit, liturgical and devotional observances, and organization of penitent congregations. Perhaps most important, the rule created an official bond between the Dominican friars and the penitents, stating that penitents were to receive their habits from a Dominican master and be guided only by Dominican friars. Meersseman concluded that the formal penitent rule's detailed stipulations showed the Dominican friars' early commitment to the supervision of Dominican penitent groups.[19] Nonetheless, the argument that Munio authored the formal penitent rule was based on weak grounds, because the first reference to the rule came more than a hundred years after its supposed writing in the 1280s. The text of the formal penitent rule was first published in Thomas of Siena's *Tractatus* of the Dominican Order of Penance that was drawn up in 1402 but completed only after 1407.[20] Thomas aimed to show that the Dominican Order of Penance had a long institutional history, and to that end he claimed that the formal penitent rule was written by Munio of Zamora in 1286 (not in 1285 as Meersseman later claimed). Meersseman and many other historians of the Dominican Order of Penance accepted Thomas's claim. However, Martina Wehrli-Johns has criticized their reading of the sources and convincingly argued that the first version of the penitent rule could not have been written more than a few years before Pope Innocent VII approved the rule in his bull *Sedis apostolicae* on June 26, 1405.[21]

Dominican Penitent Women supports the conclusion that the formal penitent rule was not written by Munio but was produced more than one hundred years later. My discovery of a forgotten original penitent rule, the *Ordinationes* of Munio here translated, in the Biblioteca comunale of Siena supports the conclusion that Munio was not the author of the formal penitent rule.[22] The *Ordinationes* of Munio was written to penitent women of Orvieto in 1286 (just as Thomas claimed in his *Tractatus*), but it was not the penitent rule found in the *Tractatus* but merely a rudimentary set of guidelines intended for local use in Orvieto.[23]

On September 18, 1289, Nicholas IV, a Franciscan pope, confirmed the Franciscan penitent *regula* with his bull *Supra montem*.[24] When Thomas of Siena and modern historians claimed that Munio of Zamora wrote the formal penitent rule in 1285 or 1286, they strove to show that the Dominicans intended to incorporate penitents into their order at the same time that the Franciscans formalized their relationships with their penitent associations.[25] Thomas claimed that Munio tried to gain papal approval for his rule (which historians supposed was the formal rule), only to see his efforts rejected by the Franciscan pope, who favored the appeal of his own order.[26] However, there is no direct evidence of Dominican friars' efforts to stabilize their relationships with penitent women in the 1280s or to seek papal approval of a penitent rule. Once we accept that Munio did not write the formal rule and are aware of the rudimentary nature of his *Ordinationes*, it is indeed unlikely that the Dominicans tried to incorporate penitents at the same time as did the Franciscans. Whereas Saint Francis of Assisi and his followers identified with lay piety, the Dominican Order of ordained priests was slow to establish formal bonds between the order's clerical members and penitent groups.

Dominican penitent women in Italy were at times so loosely connected with the Dominican Order that it is not helpful to equate them with their institutionally more stable Franciscan counterparts. One should instead compare them to the independent beguines of central and northern Europe. The churchmen's better relations with the penitents of Italy have been explained on the basis of penitents' presumably close links with the friars, but a critical look at the relationships between the Dominican friars and penitent women does not support such a conclusion. Penitent women's integration in their surrounding culture seems to offer a more plausible explanation. Whereas the beguines assumed independent roles in economic production and created autonomous religious centers, the penitents of Italy blended in with the family-based social system and operated within the context of economic production led by men.

Until the writing of the formal rule and its approval by Pope Innocent VII in 1405, Dominican penitent associations sustained their institutional framework with various ecclesiastical privileges, indulgences, and such limited rulings as the *Ordinationes* of Munio. Such documents protected the penitent way of life but did not offer an institutional position within the order.[27]

Raymond of Capua's (ca.1330–99) support of Catherine of Siena's ascetic piety and intense mysticism opened a new phase in relations between the Dominicans and penitent women. Raymond was Catherine's confessor from about 1374 to her death in 1380. Within a few weeks after Catherine's death, Raymond was chosen as the master general of the Dominican Order, and while in this position he wrote Catherine's *vita*, the so-called *Legenda maior*.[28] Raymond's support of Catherine's sanctity and their shared interest in the reform of the church created a new model of intense cooperation between Dominican friars and penitent women. In an effort to legit-imize Catherine's mission and Dominican friars' interaction with her, in his *Legenda maior* Raymond claimed that Dominicans had estab-lished a formal bond with the penitents already in the early thirteenth century. The formal penitent rule was clearly not yet written during Raymond's time, because Raymond spoke of Munio's "rule" in a way that referred to the *Ordinationes* and not the formal rule that Thomas of Siena later introduced as the Rule of Munio.[29]

Raymond of Capua created an ideology of a new kind of Dominican life of penance, but the actual efforts to gain papal approval for the Dominican penitent way of life began in earnest only at the turn of the fifteenth century in Venice, where Thomas of Siena was based and where there was an active and affluent group of Dominican penitent men and women. The existence of penitent men of Venice represents one of the only known cases of men's involvement in Dominican life of penance, but it was their seamless cooperation with Thomas of Siena as well as their financial resources and good contacts at the papal curia that finally made possible the creation of a formally approved Dominican Order of Penance. Intense negotiations between the papal curia and Dominicans concerning the papal confirmation of the Dominican penitent order took place between 1402 and 1405. Thomas of Siena acted as the chief propagator of the new life of penance, but the documents that survive in the *Tractatus* show that penitents were actively involved in the negotiations and made significant contribu-tions to cover the costs the Dominicans accumulated at the curia.[30]

States of Life

Penitential life was particularly popular among urban widows, who had to redefine their social positions after the deaths of their husbands. Widowhood was understood as a continuous state of mourning. Thus, penitential life responded to medieval images of widowed women's duty to mourn, but it also answered to women's need to solidify their positions in the world.[31] The penitential way of life also attracted single women who did not have the means to get married or join a monastery, or who did not want to do so for religious or other reasons. The reputations of young single women were a particular concern for the older penitents, who did not want to tarnish their association's reputation with sexual scandals.[32] The Dominican friars shared these fears, but they nevertheless favored the membership of virtuous young girls. Most of the penitent women the friars represented as saintly were virgins who responded to the wider religious prototype of the sacred value of virginity.[33] Married women were allowed to join the penitent order with written approval from their husbands,[34] but their membership was rare, and they lacked the obvious social motivation of unmarried and widowed women.[35]

For some, the life of penance was only a temporary solution. It served as a respectable transitional status for a recently widowed woman who was not yet ready to settle into another marriage. The penitential life functioned also as a passage from the secular world into a monastery. For others, the penitential life meant a permanent commitment to a chaste life of daily prayer and other religious observances. At the turn of the fifteenth century, the formal penitent rule made penitential status irrevocable.[36]

The life of penance offered women a less costly alternative to monasteries, which toward the later Middle Ages demanded dowries that were beyond the means of even the wealthy middle class and lower nobility. Some penitent women came from the ranks of the urban poor and supported themselves as domestic servants or workers in lesser trades. Giovanna of Orvieto and Stefana Quinzani belonged to this social class. Giovanna worked as a dressmaker and, apparently, as a servant of a wealthy woman from Orvieto, Ghisla. Stefana Quinzani also earned her living as a domestic servant, but her fame eventually enabled her to leave her host family and found a community of Dominican penitent women in Soncino in 1519.

Yet, poor women like Giovanna and Stefana were not typical among penitent women. Penitent groups recruited from the ranks of well-to-do urban families. In surviving fourteenth-century membership lists of Dominican penitents in Siena, most women were listed as *dominae*, a term that implied a high social rank.[37] The hagiographic material supports this evidence: some penitents came from the urban middle class (Catherine of Siena belonged to a well-to-do family of cloth-dyers), but many came from the lesser nobility. Such was the case with Maria Sturion of Venice, Osanna Andreasi of Mantua, Colomba Guadagnoli of Rieti, and Lucia Brocadelli of Narni. Penitent groups controlled their membership, and, because their rules required mutual financial support among members, the groups seem to have favored women who were financially independent and were not likely to create a financial burden for others.[38]

Penitent women's semi-religious status offered fairly few tangible benefits. The penitents did not enjoy freedom from ecclesiastical or secular taxation, for example.[39] Penitent women's most important privilege came at their deaths: they had the right to be buried in their penitent habit in the presence of their fellow religious, who prayed for their souls.[40] These arrangements eased the penitent women's fear for the destinies of their souls and thus had high spiritual value.

Living Arrangements

Medieval Dominican penitents lived primarily in private homes. Unmarried women, such as Catherine of Siena, typically lived in the homes of their parents or other relatives. Home-dwelling unmarried penitents were often placed last in the domestic pecking order. They occupied themselves with servile tasks and commonly had their rooms in the attic or in other less desirable parts of the house.[41] Poor women, such as Stefana Quinzani, were rarely able to stay with their biological families but lived at the homes of their benefactors or patrons.[42] Married penitents, such as Lisa Colombini, Catherine of Siena's sister-in-law, pursued their religious life in homes that they shared with their husband, children, and in-laws.[43] Widowed penitents commonly returned to the homes of their parents or sought to live independently in their own houses. For many widows independent life brought social and financial uncertainty and destitution, but for wealthy widows life spent in their own houses could grant considerable social liberty and religious autonomy.[44]

The penitents who pursued their religious lives in private houses operated within the context of ordinary family life. Many penitents had little privacy or respect, but life at home still enabled them to support themselves without needing to beg in the streets. Medieval churchmen were hostile toward women's mendicancy and considered begging a privilege that was limited to mendicant friars and other established male religious groups. Thus, the churchmen were supportive of the penitential life that did not depend on people's charity but was based on women's own work or their previous wealth.[45]

Nonetheless, not all penitents found a place within the family system, or they preferred to leave the world behind for religious and other reasons. Such women could emulate eremitical or communal forms of religious life. While the Dominicans cherished the ideals of humility, simplicity, and ascetic rigor that they associated with the lives of the desert fathers, they did not favor seclusion from the world. They associated the eremitical life with religious radicalism, and they saw it as a burden on limited charitable resources. In Siena, for instance, penitents were forbidden to live as hermits.[46] Nevertheless, the Dominicans did not entirely close off this form of life, and a few of their saints earned their reputations as urban recluses.

Dominican penitents could not form official penitent communities before the approval of their rule in 1405. Nonetheless, they created domestic religious communities long before 1405, groups within which penitent women informally shared a house (typically that of a wealthy widow) and followed a regimen of daily devotions. The evidence concerning women's domestic religious communities is scarce: they were not official religious houses and thus did not receive ecclesiastical privileges, donations, or leave behind chronicles. Yet some archival and hagiographic sources open a view to these communities. Giovanna of Orvieto stayed nine years at the home of her mistress and prioress, Ghisla. They were joined by Ghisla's chambermaid and apparently some other women. These women followed a disciplined life of devotion, and Ghisla even arranged presentations of Giovanna's ecstatic experiences.[47] At times Catherine of Siena stayed extended periods at the home of her fellow penitent Alessia Saracini.[48] Dominican friars were not favorable toward penitent women's shared housing, but the anonymous author of the *Miracoli* of Catherine of Siena did not share these reservations and underscored Catherine's communal life with other penitent women.[49] Women's domestic religious communities and their places within the landscape of medieval urban piety are unexplored topics that, it is to be hoped, will attract more attention in the future.

Dominican penitent women could establish formal penitent communities after papal approval of the Dominican Order of Penance in 1405, but communal life became popular among Dominican penitents only at the end of the century, when Colomba of Rieti, Stefana Quinzani, Lucia Bartolini Rucellai, Lucia Brocadelli of Narni, and some other penitent women secured donations that enabled them to create religious houses.[50] Some of these communities suffered from meager resources, but a few of them became flourishing religious centers. Colomba of Rieti's penitent house in Perugia had close to fifty members.[51] Lucia Bartolini Rucellai's penitent community in Florence housed daughters of leading families of the town, including some from the Medici.[52] One of the community's members, Plautilla Nelli (d. 1587/88), was a well-respected painter of religious art and portraits of contemporaries.[53]

The daily regimen in these communities resembled the monastic routine: women slept and ate in shared living quarters, and they worshiped together in the community's chapel. Nonetheless, penitent women were not cloistered from the world initially, nor did they take monastic vows. Instead, they worked outside their houses and kept their private property.[54] The communal form of life made it necessary to adjust penitent practices and create regulations concerning the practical framework of the community. For this purpose, Colomba of Rieti wrote a *forma vitae* for her community of penitent women in Perugia around 1497.[55] A few years later the penitents of Florence turned to the Dominican friar Roberto Ubaldini to write a new set of directions that complemented the formal penitent rule as affirmed in 1405.[56] The *forma vitae* of Colomba and the *direttorio* of Ubaldini emulated the spiritual ideals of monastic life within which daily life circled around the collective celebration of the seven canonical hours.

In the sixteenth century the Dominican supporters of penitent communities responded to a wider religious trend of cloistering religious women. In 1510 Pope Julius II granted communal Dominican penitents a right to take the three monastic vows of poverty, chastity, and obedience, but the penitents were still not expected to observe cloister or sing the entire Divine Office.[57]

Nonetheless, the papal constitution *Circa pastoralis* (1566), published in the aftermath of the reformist Council of Trent (1543–63), formally established that all members of nunneries and penitent communities were obliged to observe strict cloister, shared property, and the three religious vows.[58] For some communities, seclusion from the world strengthened their religious status and enabled them to attract prosperous donors, but for many others strict observance of cloister rules brought poverty when the inhabitants were no longer able to earn their living by working outside their spiritual community. Economic pressure forced many communities to close or to seek a privilege of mitigated encloisterment. Some simply ignored the papal stipulations, which made women vulnerable to criticism and risked the future of their community.[59]

Devotional Practices

Dominican penitent women delicately balanced private devotions with collective liturgical worship and neighborly service. The christocentric and affective spirituality of Dominican penitent women mirrored wider currents apparent in their contemporary culture, but their celebration of these spiritual ideals through a blend of private devotions and collective worship produced a devotional culture with some distinctly Dominican features.

Dominican penitent women produced a series of techniques that enabled them to introduce religiously satisfying routines to their daily lives. They celebrated the seven canonical hours of the day, but as members of the laity they were not expected to sing the whole Divine Office. Instead, they commemorated the hours by reciting sets of simple prayers, such as the *Pater Noster*.[60] The Dominicans emphasized this aspect of devotional life, and they demanded greater numbers of prayers than did, for instance, the Franciscans. Franciscan penitents were required to recite twelve *Pater Nosters* at Matins and seven at all other hours, whereas the formal Dominican penitent rule from the beginning of the fifteenth century called for twenty-eight *Pater Nosters* at Matins, fourteen at Vespers, and seven at all the other hours.[61]

One of the particular aspects of Dominican spiritual guidance was the emphasis on the cult of the Virgin Mary, seen in the recitation of the *Ave Maria* and other Marian prayers. Indeed, the formal Dominican penitent rule seems to contain one of the first normative instances within which the *Ave Maria* was presented as a prayer that automatically accompanied the recitation of the *Pater Noster*.[62] Such a systematic emphasis on the recitation of Marian prayers foreshadowed the Rosary, established by the Dominicans during the second half of the fifteenth century. The Dominicans subsequently fostered the creation of confraternities dedicated to the Rosary and other Marian celebrations, and Dominican penitents widely participated in these Marian observances.[63]

Penitent women's recitation of prayers was accompanied by ascetic practices, such as wearing a hair shirt, disciplining oneself with a metal or leather scourge, restricting one's sleep, and, most notably, fasting. Dominicans encouraged moderate asceticism, but the penitent rules warned that any excessive form of penance had to be approved by prelates.[64] Saintly Dominican penitent women took their asceticism to great lengths, however. The most celebrated Dominican penitent ascetic was Catherine of Siena, whose denial of food and other bodily comforts challenged the moderate ideals present in the penitent rules. She did not keep herself to the prescribed abstinences and periods of fast but observed a perpetual fast and eventually sustained herself with only water and some vegetables. Whereas the penitent rules required penitents to observe Matins only at the times of Advent and Lent, Catherine kept vigil all night to pray for the souls of her fellow Christians. Catherine's asceticism set a new standard for future generations of saintly penitent women, but the ordinary penitents adhered to the more moderate forms of penance seen in the *regulae*.

Another devotional tool used by the Dominicans was pious images of Jesus and the saints. These images, which offered concrete support for the life of prayer, had both emotional and cognitive importance for the penitents. The author of the *Miracoli* of Catherine of Siena wrote that Catherine recognized the persons of her visions on the basis of ecclesiastical art.[65] The Dominicans also supported the use of portable images of saints. Thomas of Siena wrote in his *vita* of Maria of Venice that Maria ordered a small image of Catherine of Siena in order to anchor her dedication to Catherine to a tangible instrument of devotion.[66] This focus on devotional images may be viewed within the context of Dominican emphasis on pious role models. Such emphasis was seen in Jacobus of Voragine's *Golden Legend* and in other Dominican narrative sources that presented Christians with excerpted selections from the lives of saints.[67] By supporting the use of images of saints and by preaching on the lives of saints, the Dominicans advanced a religious culture that focused on concrete inspirational models. Ordinary penitents were not expected to reach the perfection of the saints, but saints' models offered concrete points of reference that guided the penitents in the varying circumstances of their lives.

The private devotional techniques of penitent women, ranging from the recitation of the *Pater Noster* and the *Ave Maria* to ascetic practices and use of devotional images, contributed to the sanctification of domestic and secular space. Penitent women recited their prayers amid their daily tasks and saw such activities as cleaning and cooking as opportunities for meditation.[68] The defenders of penitent piety argued that religious life in the world tested spiritual strength but also offered many fruitful opportunities for spiritual growth. They saw that spiritual perfection in the world was even of greater worth than life in monasteries and hermitages, precisely because penitent women were constantly forced to test their spiritual prowess. Raymond of Capua, for instance, saw special virtue in the fact that Catherine reached her spiritual heights at her home. He wrote: "As you, dear reader, may notice, this daughter of Abraham [Catherine] achieved greater degree of perfection in her abstinence than anyone of these [the previous generations of saints], not in a monastery or in the desert, but in the house of her own father, without anyone's help, and even while being hindered by all her family members."[69]

Penitent women's private devotional practices were complemented by their collective and liturgical worship. Penitents convened at local Dominican churches, where they attended Masses, heard sermons, and, once a month, listened to the reading of their religious rule.[70] These moments of worship added flavor to penitent women's domestic devotional lives and created a bond between them and the friars. This collective worship played a more prominent role in the lives of communal or regular penitents, who were inspired by monastic spiritual culture, and, not unlike nuns, regular penitents convened at their community's church to sing the seven canonical hours. They also followed the monastic practice of monthly or weekly, sometimes even daily, chapters of faults, within which the penitents convened to confess their sins and discuss the matters of the community.[71]

Penitent women's domestic devotional life, marked by visits to the local churches and the homes of other penitents, made them visible to their fellow townspeople in ways that cloistered nuns never were. Penitent women's mystical experiences became public spectacles that contributed to the later medieval sense of God's presence in all human affairs. Catherine of Siena fell into ecstasy on the streets of her native town.[72] Giovanna of Orvieto's *Legend* suggests that people came to view her ecstasies at the home of her mistress, Ghisla.[73] Stefana Quinzani's imitations of Christ's passion at the homes of her patrons were well-attended public spectacles as well.[74] These public displays of the extraordinary and the miraculous shaped later medieval popular piety and turned penitents into local celebrities, but women's public piety also attracted sharp criticism. Jean Gerson and many other later medieval theologians ridiculed the religious experiences of the likes of Catherine of Siena and saw their popularity as a sign of the end of time.[75]

The Imitation of Christ

The spiritual practices and mystical life of Dominican penitent women centered on the humanity of Christ.[76] Dominican penitents celebrated all stages of Christ's life. They cherished the cult of the baby Jesus. One of the most touching examples of their devotion to the infant Jesus comes from the *vita* of Maria Mancini (ca. 1350–ca.1431), who lived as a penitent before she settled in the strictly cloistered monastery of Saint Dominic in Pisa. When Maria nursed her infant baby boy during Matins, she imagined herself as the Virgin Mary cuddling the baby Jesus.[77] Penitents also saw themselves as the brides of Christ. Catherine of Siena, Osanna of Mantua, Colomba of Rieti, and many others received a mystical ring from Christ and had other mystical experiences that explored their betrothals to Christ.[78] Even penitent women's neighborly serv-ice was pictured in christocentric terms, as the penitents saw their beneficiaries as representatives of Christ on earth.[79]

The imitation of Christ culminated in the commemoration of his sufferings on the cross. Dominican penitent women imitated Christ's passion, they contemplated his suffering, and they had visionary experiences of his wounds and pains. One of the most important ways for them to commemorate Christ's sacrifice came through the celebration of the Eucharist. Even though the penitent rules expressed reservation concerning frequent communion,[80] Dominican penitent saints wanted to consume Christ's body every day. They saw communion as a spiritual and bodily union with the suffering Christ. Catherine of Siena's consumption of the Eucharist was often followed by raptures that incapacitated her for hours while her mind rested on the sweetness of Christ's presence.[81]

The meaningfulness of penitent women's ascetic lives of penance rested on their imitation of Christ. The penitents did not deprive themselves of sleep, food, or other comforts only because they wanted to discipline themselves or prepare for greater perfec-tion. They practiced their discipline in the memory of Christ's suf-fering. In their fasting and self-flagellation penitent women reenacted Christ's sacrifices offered for the sake of humanity. Penitents did not conceive of their pain as an ordinary affliction, but they represented it rather as a preparation for the greater glory associated with Christ's resurrection and the world to come. The ascetic life of penance thus gave women an opportunity to celebrate Christ's victory over death and victoriously transcend the limits of their bodies in the anticipation of the life to come.[82]

The extreme concreteness with which Dominican penitent women celebrated Christ's passion set them apart from many other religious lay groups. Two manifestations of this tangible imitation of Christ's passion were of particular importance: the stigmata and the-atric performances of Christ's crucifixion. While the Franciscans saw the stigmata as a special heavenly privilege reserved for Francis of Assisi, the Dominican Order did not share the Franciscan predilec-tion but publicized the stigmata of the order's own members.

In a fascinating traversal of boundaries, the Dominicans saw the stigmata as a specifically female religious experience. They celebrated the stigmata of nuns, such as Helen of Hungary, but most of all, they presented the stigmata as a spiritual gift found in Catherine of Siena and other penitent women.[83] According to Raymond of Capua, Catherine of Siena received her stigmata in the spring of 1375, while she was praying in a church in Pisa.[84] The Dominican devotion to Catherine's stigmata generated a bitter fight with the Franciscans, who regarded the stigmata as their privilege. Nevertheless, the Franciscans failed to stop the Dominican veneration of their own stigmatized saints.[85] Catherine inspired other penitent mystics in their contemplation of the wounds of Christ, and the late fifteenth-century penitent saints Colomba of Rieti, Osanna of Mantua, Stefana Quinzani, and Lucia Brocadelli of Narni reputedly received the divine favor of Christ's five wounds.

The symbolic value of the stigmata as the ultimate confirmation of Christ's presence made stigmatized penitents into celebrities. One of the most dedicated political supporters of stigmatized Dominican penitent women was Ercole d'Este (d. 1505), duke of Ferrara, who successfully plotted to move the stigmatized Lucia Brocadelli from Viterbo to Ferrara and who wrote a pamphlet praising the stigmata of specifically Dominican penitent saints.[86]

The cult of the stigmata and of the passion of Christ may be viewed within the context of the Dominican practice of bodily prayer postures. Dominican penitent women were certainly familiar with the mid-thirteenth-century text *The Nine Ways of Prayer of Saint Dominic*, with its celebration of bodily postures of prayer. According to the text, one of Saint Dominic's favorite positions of prayer was to pray extended in the shape of the cross: arms elevated on the sides, feet placed as if they were nailed together.[87] Giovanna of Orvieto meditated upon Christ's passion in this position. She extended herself in the shape of the cross with such petrifying force that it was impossible to move her for hours.[88] Some penitent women relived entire sections of Christ's passion. Stefana Quinzani's imitations of Christ's suffering were public spectacles in which Stefana reenacted Jesus' interrogation, his flagellation, and his being nailed on the cross.[89] These theatrical performances of the scenes of Christ's passion sought to deepen the understanding of his sacrifice through bodily imitation of his experiences. The performances also prepared ground for the devotional practice of the Stations of the Cross, which through the course of the sixteenth century developed into a popular technique to commemorate the stages of Christ's passion.[90]

The Active Life

The Dominican conception of penitential life was essentially devotional and liturgical. Hagiographers praised penitent women's social service and presence in the world, but they still saw the life of active service or the *vita activa* as subservient to the *vita contemplativa*, the life of prayer and inner perfection.[91] The Franciscan penitent rule encouraged service to the urban poor, and the Franciscans supported the work of such saints as Margaret of Cortona (d. 1297), who founded the hospital of Santa Maria della Misericordia in her hometown.[92] In the Low Countries, beguines were involved in works of charity, teaching, and manufacturing.[93] By contrast, Dominican penitents were not expected to get involved in the institutions that cared for the sick and the poor. We do not know of a single Dominican penitent who worked in an institutional setting comparable to the hospitals of the beguines or the Santa Maria of Margaret of Cortona. Dominican penitent rules only established social obligations among members of the association. If a member of a penitent group fell ill or was reduced to poverty, the other penitents were expected to provide for her.[94] When a member of the association died, the others were expected to attend the funeral and to pray for the deceased person's soul.[95]

The Dominicans did not, of course, directly deny the value of neighborly love. Thomas of Siena praised Maria of Venice's spirit of neighborly love, but all of his examples of Maria's neighborly service involved members of her family or her religious order.[96] One of the ways in which God praised Lucia Brocadelli in her *Seven Revelations* concerned her spirit of neighborly love, but we do not learn of any concrete actions of her service from the text.[97] Even in the case of a saint like Catherine of Siena, Raymond of Capua and other Dominicans represented her neighborly service more as a test of her patience and humility than as a socially virtuous deed. Moreover, the patients she nursed were either members of her family or of her penitent order, and thus her service exemplified a restricted understanding of neighborly service.[98]

The Dominicans had an appreciation for the life of the mind, and their system of values was reflected into the spiritual ideals of the Dominican laity. Formal education was limited to the friars, and apparently only a few penitent saints were literate. Nonetheless, penitent women had access to sermons and conversations with their confessors, and they learned about the teachings of the church at the monthly meetings of their group.[99] As a result, penitent women displayed sophisticated theological ideas through their mystical experiences. For instance, Catherine of Siena's mystical treatise *The Dialogue* shows the ease with which she used the terms and ideas of Augustine, Thomas Aquinas, and other theologians.[100] Lucia Brocadelli's *Seven Revelations* displays her awareness of the celestial hierarchies of Pseudo-Dionysius and the apocalyptic *Compendium* of the prophetic Dominican reformer Girolamo Savonarola.[101] These women practiced what Bernard McGinn has fittingly termed "vernacular theology." Women did not write in Latin, the traditional language of learning, nor did they claim to have any formal education, but they wrote or dictated to their scribes in their native tongues and they discussed God as they had experienced him in their personal encounters. Their writings were often filtered through the pens of their male scribes and confessors, but their experiences should still be seen as a form of theology that left a deep impact on Christian thought.[102]

Women could not occupy official positions of teaching (they could not teach *ex officio*), but as perceived saints some of them were allowed to teach by the grace of God *(ex beneficio)*. Penitent women served their neighbors as spiritual guides and prophetic teachers. They acted as *magistrae*, spiritual teachers, who offered private guidance to their followers.[103] Giovanna of Orvieto received advice-seekers at the home of her mistress, Ghisla.[104] Catherine of Siena's home was often bombarded by crowds of visitors looking for spiritual help, so much so that she sometimes escaped her home and looked for solitude at the home of her companion, Alessia Saracini.[105]

Prophetic counseling by Dominican penitent women gained a particular prominence at the turn of the sixteenth century.[106] After the dramatic execution of the Dominican visionary and prophet

Savonarola as a heretic in 1498, both the ruling families and the common people of Italian city-states sought spiritual advice from Dominican penitent women. Savonarola died as an enemy of Pope Alexander VI, but his spirit of ecstatic and eschatological reform lived on in the women who were inspired by his message and supported by the same families who a few years earlier had been guided by Savonarola himself.[107] Colomba of Rieti, Osanna of Mantua, Stefana Quinzani, and Lucia Brocadelli of Narni enjoyed prophetic authority that granted them positions of trust. They were asked to pray for their patrons in times of need, and they were sought out for spiritual and practical guidance. Duke Fredrick Gonzaga of Mantua even asked Osanna to take care of his wife and children at the time of his absence from Mantua.[108]

Penitent women instructed, counseled, and comforted in private. Only rarely did they teach in public. Catherine of Siena's *Legenda maior* presents a few cases in which Catherine acted as a public teacher who even addressed an audience of cardinals.[109] However, such examples of teaching were exceptional even in narrations concerning Catherine of Siena. They did not appear in the lives of other Dominican penitent saints.[110] Nonetheless, in the medieval world the boundaries between formal and informal or public and private were not drawn as they are in the modern world, and penitent women's roles as *magistrae* and spiritual guides granted them an opportunity to influence the affairs of their time. When we remember that the Dominicans emphasized the value of example and understood that presenting an example was a way to teach, Dominican penitent women were able to embrace the Dominican legacy that underscored the value of teaching by representing it as the highest form of the active life.[111]

Toward New Directions

Catherine of Siena is among the most studied of medieval saints, yet her fellow Dominican penitent women have attracted comparably little attention in the English-speaking world. Nevertheless, their way of life created an important alternative for women who sought religious perfection in the world. *Dominican*

Penitent Women presents an overview of the spirituality, religious practices, and ways of life of Dominican laywomen during the Middle Ages. Many questions concerning these women remain unanswered. The institutional aspects of the penitent way of life and the development of a penitent rule require further examination. It would also be of interest to study what impact the papal approval of the Dominican penitent order in 1405 had on the practical social and religious status of Dominican penitent women. Such a confirmation has been seen as a definite change in the status of the penitent women, but later fifteenth-century documents suggest that penitent women continued to feel the need to reaffirm their position by seeking new confirmations from the directors of the Dominican Order, bishops, and popes.

Traditionally, Italian penitents and central and northern European beguines have been viewed as two related but institutionally distinct movements. It has been presumed that penitents of Italy enjoyed a stable position within Franciscan and Dominican orders. If we are prepared to accept that Dominican penitent women of Italy did not, in fact, have an institutionally solidified position within the Dominican Order, it will be necessary to examine why the penitents created less controversy in Italy than did the beguines of central and northern Europe. I have suggested that the fairly peaceful integration of Italian penitents into society did not result from their presumed institutional status with the Dominican Order but from their firm embedding in family-based social and economic structures. These hypotheses will need to be investigated further.

The cooperation between a male hagiographer and a female mystic has produced several interesting studies, but the network of support that existed between a group of women and a saint has not attracted due attention. The cults of saintly penitent women were furthered not only by male hagiographers but also by these women's fellow penitents who took the initiative in attracting the attention of their contemporaries to the saint. The *vitae* of penitent saints and other writings concerning them contain valuable evidence of women's networks and their efforts to promote the fame of their fellow penitents. A close study of these systems of mutual support would certainly provide valuable information concerning women's social strategies and their exercise of power.

INTRODUCTION

It has long been acknowledged that Lucia Brocadelli of Narni, Colomba of Rieti, Stefana Quinzani, and many late fifteenth-century and early sixteenth-century penitent saints were profoundly inspired by the Dominican visionary Girolamo Savonarola. The topic has produced some noteworthy articles, but one would welcome more studies concerning penitent women's involvement in the Savonarolan movement and their appropriation of the friar's prophetic religious role.

The amorphous quality of the penitent way of life and its institutional ambiguity tell of the difficulty that medieval laywomen experienced when they tried to secure a position for themselves within a hierarchical church led by male clerics. Yet, the very indeterminateness of the penitent way of life may also be seen as one of its strengths. This institutionally loose religious way of life adapted to the varying circumstances that laypeople faced in the world. It allowed women to exercise fairly autonomous control over their own ways of life.

Note on Translation

The texts translated here were originally written in Italian or Latin, which posed some difficulties concerning the translation of personal names. The Italian form of personal names has been used throughout the book, with the exception of Catherine of Siena, Raymond of Capua, and a few other persons whose anglicized names are well known. Names of towns and institutions have been rendered in English. While the translations aim to preserve the unique styles of the different authors, the long sentence structures have been broken down when necessary for readability. Personal names or such appellations as "the virgin" or "the girl" replace personal pronouns when the excessive use of personal pronouns in the original texts would have made it difficult to follow the translation.

Acknowledgments

Many colleagues have read particular passages of the manuscript, and I shall thank them for their insights in the appropriate places. This collection was made possible by Bernard McGinn, who provided the venue to present these texts for the first time in translation and whose thorough review greatly improved the manuscript. The breadth of material presented here was made available by the valuable contributions of Daniel E. Bornstein and E. Ann Matter. I am indebted to my husband, Christopher K. Gardner, whose constant interest in the book and insightful comments on the translations and the essays further enriched the project. I would also like to thank the Academy of Finland, which supported my work with generous research fellowships between 2000 and 2003. The colleagues at my two home departments—the Department of Church History at the University of Helsinki and the Department of Theology at Loyola College in Maryland—created a pleasant and supportive working environment.

Notes

1. For religious lay movements within the context of the transformation of the religious culture during the twelfth and thirteenth centuries, see Herbert Grundmann, *Religious Movements in the Middle Ages: Historical Links between Heresy, the Mendicant Orders, and the Women's Religious Movement in the Twelfth and Thirteenth Century, with the Historical Foundations of German Mysticism*, trans. Steven Rowan (Notre Dame, IN: University of Notre Dame Press, 1995); André Vauchez, *The Laity in the Middle Ages: Religious Beliefs and Devotional Practices*, ed. Daniel E. Bornstein, trans. Margery J. Schneider (Notre Dame, IN: University of Notre Dame Press, 1993); and Brenda Bolton, *The Medieval Reformation* (London: Edvard Arnold, 1983), esp. 55–66, 80–93.

2. On definitions in canon law concerning religious status of the laity, see Ronald J. Cox, *A Study of the Juridic Status of Laymen in the Writing of the Medieval Canonists* (Washington, DC: The Catholic University of America Press, 1959), esp. 26–38. Elizabeth Makowski has studied canon lawyers' attitudes toward religious laypeople. I thank her for allowing me to consult the manuscript of her upcoming book, *A Pernicious Sort of Woman: Quasi-Religious Women and Canon Lawyers in the Later Middle Ages*, to be published by the Catholic University of America Press.

3. On religious lay life within the context of the wide range of urban women's social and religious needs, see Anna Benvenuti Papi, *"In*

INTRODUCTION

castro poenitentiae": *Santità e società femminile nell'Italia medievale* (Rome: Herder, 1990).

4. On laywomen's significance for high and late medieval mysticism, see Bernard McGinn, *The Flowering of Mysticism: Men and Women in the New Mysticism, 1200–1350* (New York: Crossroad, 1998), 153–98; Michael Goodich, "Contours of Female Piety in Later Medieval Hagiography," *Church History* 59 (1981): 20–32; and André Vauchez, *Sainthood in the Later Middle Ages*, trans. Jean Birrell (Cambridge, England: Cambridge University Press, 1997), 207–12.

5. On religious lay life as a women's movement, see Brenda M. Bolton, "Mulieres Sanctae," in *Sanctity and Secularity: The Church and the World*, ed. Derek Baker (Oxford: Basil Blackwell, 1973), 77–95; and Bolton, *The Medieval Reformation*, 80–93.

6. Franciscan penitent men have been the subject of many conferences organized by the Historical Institute of the Capuchins. See, for instance, *L'Ordine della penitenza di San Francesco d'Assisi nel secolo XIII*, ed. O. Schmucki (Rome: Istituto Storico dei Cappuccini, 1973); and *Il Movimento francescano della penitenza nella società medioevale*, ed. Mariano d'Alatri (Rome: Istituto Storico dei Cappuccini, 1980). On beghards and their connections with beguines, see Ernst McDonnell, *Beguines and Beghards in Medieval Culture, with Special Emphasis on the Belgian Scene* (New Brunswick, NJ: Rutgers University Press, 1954), 246–65. At the turn of the fifteenth century Venice had a group of influential Dominican penitent men, but this group represents one of the only known cases of men's involvement in Dominican penitent life (see Maiju Lehmijoki-Gardner, "Writing Religious Rules as an Interactive Process—Dominican Penitent Women and the Making of their *Regula*," *Speculum* 79 [2004]: 676–83.

7. On the practical duties and religious life of the *conversi*, see Duane J. Osheim, "Conversion, *Conversi*, and the Christian Life in Late Medieval Tuscany," *Speculum* 58 (1983): 368–90. On *conversi* and *conversae* in Dominican convents and monasteries, see Raymond Creytens, "Les Convers des Moniales Dominicaines au Moyen Âge," *Archivum Fratrum Praedicatorum* 19 (1949): 6–47.

8. On the practically oriented sanctity of laymen, see André Vauchez, "Lay People's Sanctity in Western Europe: Evolution of a Pattern (Twelfth and Thirteenth Centuries)," in *Images of Sainthood in Medieval Europe*, ed. Renate Blumenfeld-Kosinski and Timea Szell (Ithaca, NY: Cornell University Press, 1991), 21–33. On the differences between clergymen's perceptions of laymen's and laywomen's sanctity, see John Coakley, "Friars, Sanctity, and Gender: Mendicant Encounters with Saints, 1250–1325," in *Medieval Masculinities: Regarding Men in the Middle*

Ages, ed. Clare A. Lees (Minneapolis: University of Minnesota Press, 1994), 91–110.

9. For the wide variety of terminology concerning religious laypeople, see Romana Guarnieri, "Pinzochere," in *Dizionario degli istituti di perfezione*, ed. Guerrino Pelliccia and Giancarlo Rocca (Rome: Edizioni Paoline, 1974–), 6:1721–49, esp. 1723–24. Her focus is on penitential movements in Italy, but her mapping of various forms of lay life is helpful for understanding the fragmented geography of medieval lay piety. See also Alfonso Pompei, "Terminologia varia dei penitenti," in d'Alatri, *Il Movimento francescano della penitenza*, 11–22 (with particular focus on Franciscans); and Gilles Gerard Meersseman, *Dossier de l'ordre de la Pénitence au XIIIe siècle* (Freiburg: Editions Universitaires Fribourg Suisse, 1961), 20–23.

10. For an introduction to penitents and other religious lay groups in medieval Italy, see the articles in *Women and Religion in Medieval and Renaissance Italy*, ed. Daniel E. Bornstein and Roberto Rusconi, trans. Margery J. Schneider (Chicago: The University of Chicago Press, 1996); and Giovanna Casagrande, *Religiosità penitenziale e città al tempo dei comuni* (Rome: Istituto Storico dei Cappuccini, 1995).

11. On Dominican penitent *beatae*, see Maiju Lehmijoki-Gardner, *Social Interaction of Dominican Penitent Women in Italy, 1200–1500* (Helsinki: Suomen historiallinen seura, 1999). See also M.-C. de Ganay, *Les Bienheureuses dominicaines (1190–1577) d'après des documents inédits* (Bar-le-Duc: Imprimerie Comte-Jacguet, 1926). For the devotional life of the Dominican penitent women at the turn of the sixteenth century, see Gabriella Zarri, *Le Sante vive: Cultura e religiosità femminile nella prima età moderna* (Turin: Rosenberg & Sellier, 1990), especially the article "Le sante vive," 87–164. The article is translated into English as "Living Saints: A Typology of Female Sanctity in the Early Sixteenth Century," in Bornstein and Rusconi, *Women and Religion in Medieval and Renaissance Italy*, 219–303. The anthology *Scrittrici mistiche italiane*, ed. Giovanni Pozzi and Claudio Leonardi (Genua: Morietti, 1988), brings together a useful selection of texts by or concerning Italian female mystics. Among them are Dominican penitents Benvenuta Bojanni (Boiani), Vanna (Giovanna) of Orvieto, Villana de' Botti, Catherine of Siena, Stefana Quinzani, Lucia Brocadelli of Narni, and Osanna Andreasi.

12. John Coakley has written several articles on the positive interaction between mendicant friars and religious laywomen. See especially "Friars as Confidants of Holy Women in Medieval Dominican Hagiography," in *Images of Sainthood in Medieval Europe*, ed. Renate Blumenfeld-Kosinski and Timea Szell (Ithaca, NY: Cornell University

INTRODUCTION

Press, 1991), 222–46; and "Gender and Authority of the Friars:
Significance of Holy Women for Thirteenth-Century Franciscans and
Dominicans," *Church History* 60 (1991): 445–60. Some scholars have questioned the reciprocity of the relationship between male hagiographers and
female mystics. See the articles in *Gendered Voices: Medieval Saints and Their
Interpreters*, ed. Catherine M. Mooney (Philadelphia: University of
Pennsylvania Press, 1999). Siegfried Ringler, Ursula Peters, and a number
of other German literary scholars have been skeptical about the literary
cooperation between friars and saintly women and have regarded the depictions of "spiritual dialogues" as mere hagiographic topoi. For a summary of
the debate that Ringler's and Peters's arguments generated among German
scholars, see Frank Tobin, "Henry Suso and Elsbeth Stagel: Was the *Vita* a
Cooperative Effort?" in Mooney, *Gendered Voices*, 125–28 and 236–37 n. 33.

13. McGinn, *The Flowering of Mysticism*, esp. 12–30.

14. For the Dominican order's reserved stance toward the spiritual
direction of women and their incorporation in the order, see Micheline de
Fontette, *Religieuses à l'age classique de droit canon: Recherces sur les structures
juridiques des branches féminines de ordres* (Paris: Librarie Philosophique J.
Vrin, 1967), 89–127; and Gertrude Jaron Lewis, *By Women, for Women,
about Women: The Sister-Books of Fourteenth-Century Germany* (Toronto:
Pontifical Institute of Mediaeval Studies, 1996), 176–99.

15. See Lehmijoki-Gardner, "Writing Religious Rules as an
Interactive Process," 666.

16. Meersseman, *Dossier de l'ordre de la Pénitance*, esp. 143–56; M.-
H. Laurent, "Introduzione," in Thomas of Siena, *Tractatus de ordine
fratrum et sororum de penitentia Sancti Dominici*, ed. M.-H. Laurent, in
Fontes Vitae S. Catharinae Senensis Historici, vol. 21 (Siena: University of
Siena, 1938), v–vi; Raymond Creytens, "Costituzioni domenicane," in
Dizionario degli istituti di perfezione 3 (1976): 190–97; and William A.
Hinnebusch, *The History of the Dominican Order*, 2 vols. (New York: Alba
House, 1965), 1:400–404.

17. On Dominican penitent women's involvement in the writing of
their rules, see Lehmijoki-Gardner, "Writing Religious Rules as an
Interactive Process."

18. Meersseman, *Dossier de l'ordre de la Pénitance*, esp. 143–56.

19. Ibid., 23–24.

20. For an edition of the rule, see Thomas of Siena, *Tractatus de
ordine fratrum et sororum de penitentia Sancti Dominici*, 38–44. Thomas of
Siena is also known as Caffarini in modern scholarship, but the name did
not appear in medieval documents concerning him and will thus not be
used here.

27

21. Martina Wehrli-Johns, "L'Osservanza dei Domenicani e il movimento penitenziale laico: Studi sulla 'regola di Munio' e sul Terz'ordine domenicano in Italia e Germania," in *Ordini religiosi e società politica in Italia e Germania nei secoli XIV e XV,* ed. Giorgio Chittolini and Kaspar Elm (Bologna: il Mulino, 2001), 300–303.

22. Siena, Biblioteca comunale T.II.8.a. ff. 1r–8v. Giuseppe Pardi described the manuscript in 1924 in an article that addressed the membership list of Sienese penitents presented in the manuscript (see Giuseppe Pardi, "Elenchi di Mantellate Senesi," *Studi Cateriniani,* anno 2 [1924–25]), no 2: 44–49). Indeed, the membership list has attracted the attention of numerous scholars. Yet, the manuscript's significance for the history of the Dominican penitent rule has been ignored.

23. See the *Ordinationes* of Munio of Zamora, herein.

24. Meersseman argued that the Franciscan penitent rule approved by the pope was based on a version that Franciscan friar Caro wrote in 1284 (Meersseman, *Dossier de l'ordre de la Pénitance,* 75, 128–38, 156). Scholars working with the history of the Franciscan penitent order have recently proven that Meersseman's account was mistaken by showing that the Franciscan penitent rule was directly based on the *memoriale,* a version of the penitent rule already written in 1221. See Lino Temperini, *Carisma e legislazione alle origini del terzo ordine di S. Francesco* (Rome: Editrice Franciscanum, 1996), 111–16; and articles in *La "Supra Montem" di Niccolò IV (1289): Genesi e diffusione di una regola* (Rome: Editrice Franciscanum, 1988).

25. Meersseman, *Dossier de l'ordre de la Pénitance,* esp. 2–38.

26. The historians of the Dominican order have not only concluded that Pope Nicholas IV rejected the Dominican penitent rule, but they have also claimed that the presumed controversy over the penitent rule explained the pope's deposition of Munio from his position as the master general of the Dominican Order in 1291. See R. P. Mortier, *Histoire des Maitres Généraux de l'ordre des Frères Prêcheurs,* 3 vols. (Paris: Alphonse Picard, 1905), 2:278–93; and Hinnebusch, *The History of the Dominican Order,* 1:227. Peter Linehan has shown that Mortier's and Hinnebusch's accounts of Munio's deposition were undocumented and simplistic (see Peter Linehan, *The Ladies of Zamora* [Manchester: Manchester University Press, 1997], 98–107).

27. Lehmijoki-Gardner, "Writing Religious Rules as an Interactive Process."

28. Sophia Boesch-Gajano and Odile Redon, "La Legenda maior di Raimondo da Capua, construzione di una santa," in *Atti del Simposio Internazionale Cateriniano Bernardiniano,* ed. Domenico Maffei and Paolo Nardi (Siena: Accademia senese degli Intronati, 1982), 15–36.

29. On Raymond's role in creating a new ideology for the Dominican life of penance, see Lehmijoki-Gardner, "Writing Religious Rules as an Interactive Process," 674–75.

30. On Thomas of Siena and the penitents of Venice, and on their roles in the creation of the formal Dominican Order of Penance, see ibid., 676–83.

31. For widowed women's ambivalent social and religious position, see P. Renée Baernstein, "In Widow's Habit: Women between Convent and Family in Sixteenth-Century Milan," *Sixteenth-Century Journal* 25 (1994): 787–807. The article focuses on the sixteenth century, but it offers a perspective to medieval widows' religious and social options analogous to earlier eras. In hagiographies and other religious texts widowhood was represented as liberation from yokes of marriage and motherhood (see Clarissa W. Atkinson, *The Oldest Vocation: Christian Motherhood in the Middle Ages* [Ithaca, NY: Cornell University Press, 1991], 168–87).

32. Penitent rules contained particular stipulations concerning the conservation of young penitents' chastity (see the *Ordinationes* of Munio, chap. 11; and The Dominican Penitent Rule, chap. 13).

33. Maiju Lehmijoki-Gardner, *Worldly Saints*, 52.

34. The Dominican Penitent Rule, chap. 1.

35. Chaste marriages and spiritual ideals associated with them have been studied by Dyan Elliot in *Spiritual Marriage: Sexual Abstinence in Medieval Wedlock* (Princeton, NJ: Princeton University Press, 1993).

36. The Dominican Penitent Rule, chap. 22.

37. See *I Documenti*, ed. M.-H Laurent and Francesco Valli, in Fontes Vitae S. Catharinae Senensis Historici, vol. 1 (Siena: Università di Siena, 1936), 11–12, 22–24, 47–49.

38. The *Ordinationes* of Munio, chap. 10 and The Dominican Penitent Rule, chap. 15.

39. The Dominican Penitent Rule, chap. 10.

40. The *Ordinationes* of Munio, chap. 14; and The Dominican Penitent Rule, chap. 16.

41. On social problems that religious laypeople faced in their homes, see Alessandro Barbero, *Un santo in famiglia: Vocazione religiosa e resistenze sociali nell' agiografia* (Turin: Rosenberg & Sellier, 1991). Caroline Bynum has suggested that religious life in the world made women vulnerable to the pressures of misogynistic medieval society, whereas women who lived in religious communities encountered less criticism and hence enjoyed higher self-esteem. See Caroline Walker Bynum, *Holy Feast and Holy Fast: The Religious Significance of Food to Medieval Women* (Berkeley and Los Angeles: University of California Press, 1987), 26–28.

42. For saintly domestic servants and their position in their host families, see Michael Goodich, "Ancilla Dei: The Servant as Saint in the Late Middle Ages," in *Women of the Medieval World*, essays in the honor of John F. Mundy, ed. Julius Kirshner and Suzanne F. Wemple (Oxford: Basil Blackwell, 1985), 119–36; and Benvenuti Papi, "*In castro poenitentiae*," 263–303. On poor single women's limited social options, see Susan Mosher Stuard, "Single by Law and Custom," in *Single Women in the European Past, 1200–1800*, ed. Judith M. Bennett and Amy M. Froide (Philadelphia: University of Pennsylvania Press, 1999), 106–26.

43. On the spiritual strategies of married penitent women, see Papi, "*In castro poenitentiae*," 171–204.

44. Christiane Klapisch-Zuber, *Women, Family, and Ritual in Renaissance Italy*, trans. Lydia Cochrane (Chicago: The University of Chicago Press, 1985), 121.

45. Churchmen commonly labeled women's mendicant life heretical (see Robert Lerner, *The Heresy of the Free Spirit in the Later Middle Ages* [Berkeley: University of California Press, 1972], 45–60).

46. Siena, Biblioteca comunale, T.II.8.b.f.2v.

47. See chap. 7 of *The Legend of Giovanna of Orvieto*, herein.

48. Raymond of Capua, De S. Catharinae Senensis (the *Legenda maior*), in *Acta Sanctorum* April III (Paris/Rome: Palmé, 1866), 918 (par. 228), and 929 (par. 272).

49. See chap. 8 of *The* Miracoli *of Catherine of Siena*, herein.

50. On Dominican penitent communities, see Lehmijoki-Gardner, *Worldly Saints*, 146–65. Franciscan penitents, who had a stronger institutional foundation than did Dominican penitents, formed religious houses as early as the thirteenth century. See the articles in *Prime manifestazioni di vita comunitaria maschile e femminile nel movimento francescano della penitenza (1215–1447)*, ed. R. Pazzelli and L. Temperini (Rome: Commissione Storica Internazionale T.O.R., 1982).

51. Giovanna Casagrande, "Terziarie domenicane a Perugia," in *Una santa, una città*, ed. Giovanna Casagrande and Enrico Menestò (Spoleto: Centro Italiano di Studi sull'Alto Medioevo, 1991).

52. Giuseppe Richa, *Notizie istoriche delle chiese fiorentine divise ne' suoi quartieri*, 10 vols. (Florence: Pietro Gaetano Viviani, 1709), 8:278–84 (la chiesa e monastero di Santa Caterina da Siena).

53. Ibid., 282–83. See also Chris Petteys, *Dictionary of Women Artists* (Boston, MA: G. K. Hall & Co, 1985), entry "Plautilla Nelli"; and Giovanna Peirattini, "Suor Plautilla Nelli pittrice domenicana," *Il Rosario-Memorie Domenicane* 55 (old series) (1938): (2) 82–87, (3) 168–71, (4)

INTRODUCTION

221–28, (5) 292–97, and (6) 323–34. I thank Tamar Herzig for bringing the last-mentioned article to my attention.

54. On laywomen's semi-monastic communities during the later Middle Ages, see Katherine Gill, "Open Monasteries for Women in Late Medieval and Early Modern Italy: Two Roman Examples," in *The Crannied Wall: Women, Religion, and the Arts in Early Modern Europe*, ed. Craig A. Monson (Ann Arbor, MI: University of Michigan Press, 1992), 15–48; Joyce Pennings, "Semi-religious Women in Fifteenth-Century Rome," *Medelingen van Het Nederlands Institut te Rome* 47, n.s. 12 (1987): 115–40; and Gabriella Zarri, *Recinti: Donne, clausura e matrimonio nella prima età moderna* (Bologna: Il Mulino, 2000), 43–143.

55. Colomba of Rieti's *forma vitae* is edited in "Terziarie domenicane a Perugia," in Casagrande and Menestò, *Una santa, una città*, 142–47.

56. Raimondo (Raymond) Creytens, "Il Direttorio di Roberto Ubaldini da Gagliano O.P. per le terziarie collegiate di S. Caterina da Siena in Firenze," *Archivum Fratrum Praedicatorum* 39 (1969): 127–72 (the edition of the *Direttorio*, 145–70). The *Direttorio* of Ubaldini was a rather direct adaptation of the constitutions of the Dominican friars. For the Dominican constitutions, see Raymond Creytens, "Les constitutions des Frères Prêcheurs dans la rêdaction de S. Raymond de Penyafort (1241)," *Archivum Fratrum Praedicatorum* 18 (1948): 29–68.

57. Creytens, "Costituzioni domenicane," 197.

58. Raimondo (Raymond) Creytens, "La Riforma dei monasteri femminili dopo I Decreti Tridentini," in *Il Concilio di Trento e la riforma tridentina: 2 vols.* (Rome: Herder, 1965), 1:45–79. The constitution *Circa pastoralis* renewed and strengthened the stipulations that had already been outlined in the constitution *Periculoso*, published by Pope Boniface VIII in 1298. On *Periculoso*, see Elizabeth Makowski, *Canon Law and Cloistered Women: Periculoso and Its Commentators 1298–1545* (Washington, DC: The Catholic University of America Press, 1997). *Periculoso* failed to force nuns into a strict cloister (see Katherine Gill, "*Scandala*: Controversies Concerning Clausura and Women's Religious Communities in Late Medieval Italy," in *Christendom and Its Discontents: Exclusion, Persecution, and Rebellion, 1000–1500*, ed. Scott L. Waugh and Peter D. Diehl [Cambridge: Cambridge University Press, 1996], 177–93).

59. On the negative impact of enforced cloister on penitent women, see Gabriella Zarri, "From Prophecy to Discipline, 1450–1650," in *Women and Faith: Catholic Religious Life in Italy from Late Antiquity to the Present*, ed. Lucetta Scaraffia and Gabriella Zarri, trans. Keith Botsford (Cambridge, MA: Harvard University Press, 1999), 83–112.

60. On the relationship between collective liturgical worship and private devotional practices, see Jonathan Black, "The Divine Office and Private Devotion in the Latin West," in *The Liturgy of the Medieval Church*, ed. Thomas J. Heffernan and E. Ann Matter (Kalamazoo, MI: Western Michigan University, 2001), 45–72.

61. For the canonical hours within Franciscan penitential tradition, see The Franciscan Penitent Rule, chap. VII, in Temperini, *Carisma e legislazione*, 140–41. For the practice among the Dominican penitents, see The Dominican Penitent Rule, chap. 6.

62. I have studied the selection of penitent rules in Meersseman's *Dossier de l'ordre de la Pénitence* and a number of penitent rules edited elsewhere, but I have not yet encountered another penitent rule that required the saying of the *Pater Noster* and the *Ave Maria* side by side, as does the formal Dominican penitent rule.

63. On the history of the Rosary and Dominican involvement in its promotion, see Anne Winston-Allen, *Stories of Rose: The Making of the Rosary in the Middle Ages* (University Park, PA: Pennsylvania State University Press, 1997).

64. The *Ordinationes* of Munio, chap. 12; and The Dominican Penitent Rule, chap. 11.

65. *The* Miracoli *of Catherine of Siena*, 90 and 93, herein.

66. Thomas of Siena, *The Legend of Maria of Venice*, 138–39, herein.

67. Jacobus de Voragine, *The Golden Legend: Readings on the Saints*, trans. William Granger Ryan, 2 vols. (Princeton, NJ: Princeton University Press, 1993).

68. Lehmijoki-Gardner, *Worldly Saints*, 92–102.

69. Raymond of Capua, *Legenda maior*, 878 (chap. 64). Translation mine.

70. The *Ordinationes* of Munio, chap. 16; and The Dominican Penitent Rule, chap. 20.

71. Casagrande, "Terziarie domenicane a Perugia," in Casagrande and Menestò, *Una santa, una città*, 130–37.

72. On the public dimension of Catherine of Siena's religious experiences, see Karen Scott, "Urban Spaces, Women's Networks, and the Lay Apostolate in the Siena of Catherine Benincasa," in *Creative Women in Medieval and Early Modern Italy: Religious and Artistic Renaissance*, ed. E. Ann Matter and John Coakley (Philadelphia: University of Pennsylvania Press, 1994), 105–19.

73. See the introduction to *The Legend of Giovanna of Orvieto*, herein.

74. See *Stefana Quinzani's Ecstasy of the Passion,* herein.

75. Dyan Elliot, "Seeing Double: John Gerson, the Discernment of Spirits, and Joan of Arc," *American Historical Review* 107/1 (2002): 26–54.

76. On the celebration of Christ within the medieval Dominican Order, see the collection of articles in *Christ among the Medieval Dominicans: Representations of Christ in the Texts and Images of the Order of Preachers,* ed. Kent Emery, Jr., and Joseph Wawrykow (Notre Dame, IN: University of Notre Dame Press, 1998).

77. Seraphino Razzi, *Vite dei santi e beati del sacro ordine d' Frati Predicatori, cosi huomini, come donne* (Palermo: Giovanni Antonio de Francheschini, 1605), 653.

78. Gabriella Zarri's study on bridal mysticism in the Middle Ages and the Early Modern era includes a discussion of Catherine of Siena's mystical espousal (see Zarri, *Recinti,* 251–388).

79. Lehmijoki-Gardner, *Worldly Saints,* 102–10.

80. The *Ordinationes* of Munio, chap. 9; and The Dominican Penitent Rule, chap. 8.

81. Raymond of Capua, *Legenda maior,* 939–44 (pars. 311–29).

82. Caroline Bynum has examined the positive functions of medieval women's asceticism, arguing that asceticism enabled women to transcend social and religious limits imposed on them by men (see Bynum, *Holy Feast and Holy Fast,* esp. xiv–xv, 219–96).

83. One of the most outspoken advocates of the stigmata of the members of the Dominican Order was Thomas of Siena. He wrote an elaborate treatise on the topic (see *Libellus de supplemento: Legende prolixe virginis beate Catherine de Senis,* ed. Giuliana Cavallini and Imelda Foralosso [Rome: Edizioni Cateriniane, 1974], 121–266).

84. Raymond of Capua, *Legenda maior,* 910 (pars. 194–95).

85. Giacinto d'Urso, "L'Ultimo testo hagiografico caterininano e il problema delle stimmate," *S. Catarina da Siena: Rassegna di ascetica e mistica* 26 (1975): 219–27; and Antonio Lupi, "I due stimmatizzati: S. Francesco e S. Caterina," *Nuova rivista di ascetica e mistica* 2 (1977): 216–25. I thank F. Thomas Luongo for helping me locate these articles.

86. For Ercole d'Este's treatise and his patronage of Lucia Brocadelli, see E. Ann Matter, "Prophetic Patronage as Repression: Lucia Brocadelli da Narni and Ercole d'Este," in Waugh and Diehl, *Christendom and Its Discontents,* 168–76; and Tamar Herzig, "The Rise and Fall of a Savonarolan Visionary: Lucia Brocadelli's Forgotten Contribution to the *Piagnone* Campaign," *Archiv für Reformationsgeschichter/Archive for Reformation History 2004,* 95 (2004): 34–60.

87. An English translation of *The Nine Ways of Prayer of Saint Dominic* may be found in *Early Dominicans: Selected Writings*, trans. and intro. Simon Tugwell (New York: Paulist Press, 1982), 98–99.

88. *The Legend of Giovanna of Orvieto*, 68, herein.

89. *Stefana Quinzani's Ecstasy of the Passion*, herein.

90. On the history of the Stations of the Cross, see Herbert Thurston, *The Stations of the Cross: An Account of Their History and Devotional Purpose* (New York: Burns & Oates, 1906).

91. On medieval discussions concerning the spiritual value of the *vita activa* and the *vita contemplativa* and on the medieval tradition of placing the contemplative life higher in the spiritual hierarchy, see Mary Elizabeth Mason, *Active Life and Contemplative Life* (Milwaukee, WI: Marquette University Press, 1961); and Giles Constable, *Three Studies in Medieval Religious and Social Thought* (Cambridge: Cambridge University Press, 1995), 99–130.

92. Lehmijoki-Gardner, *Worldly Saints*, 110.

93. For the *vita activa* of beguines, see Walter Simons, *Cities of Ladies: Beguine Communities in the Medieval Low Countries, 1200–1565* (Philadelphia: University of Philadelphia, 2001), 61–90.

94. The *Ordinationes* of Munio, chap. 10; and The Dominican Penitent Rule, chap. 15.

95. The *Ordinationes* of Munio, chap. 14; and The Dominican Penitent Rule, chap. 16.

96. See *The Legend of Maria of Venice*, 131–38, herein.

97. Lucia Brocadelli, *Seven Revelations*, 226, herein.

98. Lehmijoki-Gardner, *Worldly Saints*, 104–5.

99. Katherine Gill has studied laywomen's involvement in the late medieval production of religious literature. She has persuasively argued that women were not just passive recipients of clergymen's religious guidance. Women took part in theological discourse by making specific requests concerning the kind of advice they needed, and their responses as an audience shaped the theological writing of their confessors (see Katherine Gill, "Women and the Production of Religious Literature in the Vernacular, 1300–1500," in Matter and Coakley, *Creative Women in Medieval and Early Modern Italy*, 64–104).

100. Giuliana Cavallini, *Catherine of Siena* (London: Geoffrey Chapman, 1998); and Suzanne Noffke, *Catherine of Siena: Vision Through a Distant Eye* (Collegeville, MN: The Liturgical Press, 1996).

101. See the Introduction to Lucia Brocadelli, *Seven Revelations*, herein.

102. McGinn, *The Flowering of Mysticism*, 19–24.

103. The prohibition that the women were not to teach in public or to hold official positions of authority derived in part from the Bible, but it was further developed by such medieval churchmen as Gratian and Thomas Aquinas. They claimed that teaching was a clerical task that was to be exercised only by men. Women could, however, teach as prophets, and they could teach in private as mothers, abbesses, and spiritual advisors. See Nicole Bériou, "The Right of Women to Give Religious Instruction in the Thirteenth Century," in *Women Preachers and Prophets through Two Millenia of Christianity*, ed. Beverly Mayne Kienzle and Pamela J. Walker (Berkeley and Los Angeles: University of California Press, 1998), 134–45.

104. See chaps. 7 and 8, *The Legend of Giovanna of Orvieto*, herein.

105. On Catherine of Siena's roles as a teacher, see Karen Scott, "St. Catherine, 'Apostola,'" *Church History* 61 (1992): 34–46. On Catherine's prophetic mysticism within the context of Dominican tradition, see Richard Woods, *Mysticism and Prophecy: The Dominican Tradition* (Maryknoll, NY: Orbis Books, 1998), 92–108.

106. Gabriella Zarri, *Le Sante vive*, esp. 51–85; and idem, "Potere carismatico e potere politico nelle corti italiane del Rinascimento," in *Poteri carismatici e informali: Chiesa e società medioevale*, ed. Agostino Pravicini Bagliani and André Vauchez (Palermo: Sellerio Editore, 1992), 175–91.

107. On Savonarola's impact on the religious lives of Dominican nuns and penitent women, see Lorenzo Polizzotto, "When Saints Fall Out: Women and the Savonarolan Reform in the Early Sixteenth Century," *Renaissance Quarterly* 46 (1993): 486–525; and idem, "Savonarola, Savonaroliani e la riforma della donna," in *Studi savonaroliani, verso il V centenario (Savonarola 1498–1998)*, ed. Gian Carlo Garfagnini (Florence: SISMEL edizioni del Galluzzo, 1996), 229–44. For studies on Dominican women as prophets inspired by Savonarola, see Adriana Valerio, *Domenica da Paradiso: Profezia e politica in una mistica del rinascimento* (Spoleto: Centro Italiano di Studi sull'Alto Medioevo, 1992), 21–56; Tamar Herzig, "The Rise and Fall of a Savonarolan Visionary"; and Claudio Leornardi, "Colomba come Savonarola," in Casagrande and Menestò, *Una santa, una città*, 291–97.

108. Giuseppe Bagolini and Lodovigo Ferretti, *La Beata Osanna da Mantova, terziaria domenicana* (Florence: Tipografia Domenicana, 1905), 119.

109. Raymond of Capua, *Legenda maior*, 935–36 (par. 296) and 945–46 (par. 334).

110. Studies concerning the teaching and preaching roles of other medieval religious women support the observation that women principally taught in private. Rose of Viterbo and Birgitta of Sweden were known to have taught successfully in public, but even in their cases opportunities for public teaching were rare. See Darlene Pryds, "Proclaiming Sanctity through Proscribed Acts: The Case of Rose of Viterbo," in Kienzle and Walker, *Women Preachers and Prophets*, 159–72; and Claire L. Sahlin, "Prophetess as Preacher: Birgitta of Sweden and the Voice of Prophecy," *Medieval Sermon Studies* 40 (fall 1997): 29–44.

111. Mason, *Active Life and Contemplative Life*, 94–97.

The
Penitent Way
of Life

Munio of Zamora:
The *Ordinationes*

Editor's Note: The existence of the *Ordinationes* of Master General Munio of Zamora (1285–91) challenges the standard representations of the institutional history of the Dominican Order of Penance.[1] The *Ordinationes* of Munio of Zamora, written in 1286 to the penitent women of Orvieto, was not the formal penitent rule hitherto attributed to Munio, but a set of simple, and at times awkwardly organized, guidelines.[2]

The *Ordinationes* offered rather detailed guidance concerning the reception of Dominican penitents or *vestitae* into their association. It also discussed at length penitent women's liturgical and devotional observances, and their social obligations toward their sisters. Other aspects of the text were less clearly defined. Most important, the relationship between the friars and the *vestitae* was not outlined with any precision and the duties of the prioress were discussed only summarily. The discussion of the correction of the faults was sketchy at best. The *Ordinationes* showed that Master General Munio favored the *vestitae* of Orvieto by granting them the privilege of confirming their way of life, but he did not intend to create a universal order of Dominican penitents.

The *Ordinationes* of Munio survives in a fourteenth-century manuscript in the Biblioteca comunale deqli Intronati of Siena.[3] Gilles Gerard Meersseman and other historians of the Dominican

---

Note: This translation is made from the unedited Latin manuscript Biblioteca comunale deqli Intronati, Siena, T. II. 8.a.,ff. 1r–8v. I have edited the text in Maiju Lehmijoki-Gardner, "Writing Religious Rules as an Interactive Process—Dominican Penitent Women and the Making of Their *Regula*," *Speculum* 79 (2004): 683–86. I thank Renzo Pepi and other personnel of the Biblioteca comunale in Siena for their generous help during my stays at the library. Thanks to Thomas Izbicki for discussing the translation with me.

penitent order were apparently not aware of the text, or if they were, they chose not to discuss it. They argued that Munio of Zamora was the author of the elaborate, formal, penitent rule that was approved by Pope Innocent VII in 1405.[4] The sources they used in support of their argument, however, do not stand up to critical scrutiny. The first reference both to the existence of a formal penitent rule and to Munio's authorship came at the turn of the fifteenth century when Thomas, also known as Caffarini, of Siena (ca. 1350–1434) published his history of the Dominican penitent order, the *Tractatus*.[5] He strove to create historical continuity for the Dominican life of penance by claiming that the idea of a formal Dominican *order* of penance existed already in the thirteenth century. Meersseman and other modern historians of the Dominican penitential life were critical of Thomas's work for many reasons, but they nevertheless accepted his claim concerning Munio of Zamora's authorship of the formal penitent rule.[6] Munio was thus credited with the creation of the formal Dominican Order of Penance, although he in fact wrote only a set of simple *Ordinationes* at the request of the *vestitae* of Orvieto and seems not to have patronized them in any other significant way.

Munio of Zamora: The *Ordinationes*

In the name of the Lord. Amen. These are the *Ordinationes* done by the venerable Fra Munio, master [general] of the Order of Friars Preachers, for the sisters bearing the habit of the order.[7] The aforementioned venerable father, master general of the order, commands that these *Ordinationes* do not bind the sisters under the pain of sin.[8]

[Chapter 1] On receiving the sisters

Nobody is received except by the permission of the prior or his vicar and the prioress, and with the consent of the elder sisters (appointed by the prior or his vicar and the prioress); and she should be of catholic faith, honest habits, honest life and fame; and she should be asked whether she wishes to follow the regular observances of the sisters, and she should have made a firm promise to follow them.

[Chapter 2] On the habit of the sisters

The habit of the sisters is made of black and white cloth. It should not be too costly as to its color and value, as may be expected of true and humble handmaids of the Lord. The mantle should be almost black and the tunic white.[9] The tunic does not quite cover the tunic underneath, and its sleeves come up to the thumb. These tunics are short so that they do not drag on the ground, and they are fastened with a belt.[10] The wimple or veil should be white and made of linen or hemp.

[Chapter 3] On the blessing of the vestments

The prior or his vicar blesses the vestment in the following way: "Show us your mercy, O Lord, etc. The Lord be with you etc." Let us pray: "The Lord Jesus Christ, you who lowered yourself to be draped in our mortal garment, we plead that in the abundance of your immense generosity, you bless these vestments, which the holy fathers established should be worn for innocence and humility, so that dressed in this your handmaid would be worthy to be clothed with you, Christ our Lord."[11]

Holy water will be sprinkled on the vestment and the sister. After this, the [other] sisters take the blessed habit and put it on her apart from the rest, give her a tonsure, and lead the vested sister to the steps of the altar where she genuflects.[12] The prior, or the one he commissions, stands and says: "Come Holy Spirit," and the friars who assist him continue the hymn to the end. Then it is said: "Lord have mercy upon us. Christ have mercy upon us. Lord have mercy upon us. Our Father etc. Send forth your spirit etc. Save your handmaid etc. The Lord be with you etc." Let us pray: "God who taught the hearts of the faithful by the light of the Holy Spirit, grant that, in the same Spirit, we may relish what is right and always rejoice in his consolation."

Another prayer: "Lord, hold your handmaid in the presence of your heavenly help, so that she attends you with her whole heart and develops into your worthy postulate. Through Christ our Lord." In response: "Amen." He sprinkles her with holy water. All the sisters receive her with a kiss of peace.[13]

[Chapter 4] On the institution of the prioress

The convent's prior or his vicar, on the advice of the confessor and the elder sisters, appoints the prioress.[14] She should be mature, discreet, and religious. Her duty is to take care of the sisters, admonish them, and correct them if they commit an offense.

[Chapter 5] On the saying of the Hours

When the sisters are healthy, they say all their daily hours: Matins, Prime, Terce, Sext, None, Vespers, and Compline. For Matins twenty-eight *Pater Nosters*, for Vespers fourteen *Pater Nosters*, and for all the other hours seven *Pater Nosters*.[15]

[Chapter 6] On blessing of the meal and giving thanks

For the blessing of and giving thanks for the meal the sisters say one *Pater Noster* before eating. When they are finished, they give thanks with another *Pater Noster*. Those who know the psalm *Miserere mei Deus* [Ps 50 in the Vulgate] always say that after the meal. The sisters who know the *Credo* say that at the beginning of Matins, before Prime, and after Compline. For the hours of the Blessed Virgin, the sisters say as many *Pater Nosters* at all the afore-mentioned hours as were assigned above for each canonical hour.

[Chapter 7] [Times] when it is necessary to get up for Matins

During the *Quadragesima* [Lent] of Saint Martin, the sisters wake up for the Matins on Sundays and solemn feasts. From the

Advent of the Lord to the feast of the Resurrection they wake up every night in their rooms or they go to the church with good company when it is not dangerous to go.[16]

[Chapter 8] On manual labor

On major feasts and Sundays the sisters cease to do manual work and other such works that are not commonly performed during holy days.

[Chapter 9] On confession and communion

Confession is done at least once a month. Communion is taken ten times during the year, namely, on the Nativity of the Lord, at the Lord's Supper,[17] at the Resurrection of the Lord, on Pentecost, at the four feasts of the Blessed Virgin,[18] on the feast of Saint Michael, and on the feast of All Saints.[19] On all these days, whenever it is possible, everybody should try to receive communion together in the Church of San Domenico.

[Chapter 10] On sisters who are sick

The sisters who are sick are visited frequently. They are lovingly provided with their needs if they fall into poverty.

[Chapter 11] On the social engagements of the sisters

There should be no unnecessary and curious wandering around the town. The sisters, especially the younger ones, do not move around alone. The sisters do not attend wedding banquets, dances, or any mundane or indecent feast. They never attend any worldly spectacles. They absolutely do not leave the town without a license from the prior or his vicar, or, at least, their prioress, even in the case of a pilgrimage.

[Chapter 12] On fasting

From Advent to the Nativity of the Lord, the sisters fast daily, and the same is done from the *Quinquagesima* to Easter Sunday.[20] They always fast on Fridays. They observe all the solemn fast days that have been instituted by the church. If they wish to fast more, they may do so with a license from their confessor.[21]

[Chapter 13] On the use of meat

Meat may be consumed only on Sundays, Tuesdays, and Thursdays. On other days the sisters abstain from it, unless they are ill, very weak, or have been bled.[22]

[Chapter 14] On death of a sister

When someone dies, everyone who learns about her death convenes at her grave. They burn candles and everyone says a hundred *Pater Nosters* for the deceased sister. They say eight *Pater Nosters* every day for all the deceased sisters.

[Chapter 15] On the silence of the sisters

When the sisters convene for services in the church, they observe silence, unless it is necessary to break it, as is expected of women religious. Anyone who breaks the silence fasts one day on bread and water.

[Chapter 16] On the coming together of the sisters

On the first Friday of the month the sisters convene in the Church of San Domenico. They are to listen both to the Mass and to the sermon, and afterward they listen to the reading of these *Ordinationes* in the same place. Anyone who is absent without permission fasts one day on bread and water.

[Chapter 17] On correcting the sisters

If sisters are careless or negligent in their actions, or if they commit a sin, they are to be corrected in the following ways:

If a sister is caught in suspicious intimacy and is several times admonished by the prior and prioress but does not mend her ways, she is excluded from the chapter and the company of other sisters. Or, she may be stripped of her habit, if the prior and the prioress, who consult the discreet friars and elder sisters, see it as expedient.

Furthermore, if a sister is caught addressing other sisters or someone else with opprobrious or otherwise shameful words, or if she hits someone in rage, or if she presumes to go into a prohibited area, for any fault of this kind she fasts for three days on bread and water.

Furthermore, if a sister decides to disobey the prior or the prioress, or if she knowingly says a lie, for these faults she fasts for one day on bread and water.

Furthermore, if a sister commits one of the capital sins, she fasts six days on bread and water and accepts any other penance that the prior and the prioress see as fitting.

[Chapter 18] On reverence to the parish priests

The sisters should attend the churches in whose parishes they dwell. They should show reverence to the priests of that parish and pay all their dues.[23] In all the aforementioned matters the prior or his vicar, and also the prioress, together with the aforesaid [elder] sisters, have the right to grant dispensations when necessity demands it.

The aforementioned sisters requested that the venerable father, Fra Munio, master general of the Friars Preachers, would ratify everything listed above and would see it fit to attach his seal to the *Ordinationes* presented here. On the pious insistence of the said sisters, I, the aforementioned master, attach my seal on the presented rules.[24]

In Orvieto on the Feast of Saint Ambrose [December 7], in the year 1286 of our Lord.

The Dominican Penitent Rule

Editor's Note: Pope Innocent VII approved the formal Dominican penitent rule with his bull *Sedis apostolicae* on June 26, 1405, thus granting the Dominican penitents an official position within the order. The penitent rule has traditionally been attributed to the sixth master general of the Dominican Order, Munio, but a critical examination of sources and the rediscovery of the original Rule of Munio, the *Ordinationes*, suggest that the formal rule was written only during the first years of the fifteenth century. It is not known who wrote this rule or when exactly it was produced, but it is probable that the first drafts were written around 1402, when Thomas of Siena made the first known reference to the existence of a formal Dominican penitent rule in his *Tractatus*.[1]

The surviving manuscripts of the *Tractatus* contain a copy of the formal penitent rule, one that is identical with the rule confirmed by the pope. Martina Wehrli-Johns has suggested that it is not clear whether the formal penitent rule was included in the first part of the *Tractatus* when it was handed to Master General Thomas of Firmo in October, 1402, as the Dominicans launched their campaign for papal approval for the penitent order, or whether the rule was added to the book after the rule's confirmation by the pope in 1405.[2] It thus remains unclear to what degree the formal

---

Note: This translation is based on the edition of the formal Dominican Penitent Rule found in the *Tractatus* of Thomas "Caffarini" of Siena (see *Tractatus de ordine fratrum et sororum de penitentia Sancti Dominici*, ed. M.-H. Laurent, in Fontes Vitae S. Catharinae Senensis Historici, vol. 21 [Siena: Università di Siena, 1938], 38–44). The edition of the rule may also be found in Gilles Gerard Meersseman, *Dossier de l'ordre de la Pénitence au XIIIe siècle* (Freiburg: Editions Universitaires Fribourg Suisse, 1961), 143–56. I thank Thomas Izbicki for his valuable comments concerning this text.

Dominican penitent rule as we know it reflects Dominican legislation, and to what degree it was shaped by the papal curia.[3]

Whereas the *Ordinationes* of Munio established only a loose bond between the Dominican friars and penitent women, the formal penitent rule created an institutional foundation for Dominican cooperation with its female religious laity. Dominican penitent groups were to be guided by the friars, and, like the full members of the order, they swore loyalty to the Dominican master general.[4] The formal rule also expected the penitents to go through a full profession within a year of their vestment. The practice of profession elevated the religious status of Dominican penitent women, lifting them from an informal association of religious laywomen into a proper religious order.

Although Dominican penitent groups consisted almost exclusively of women, the formal penitent rule was directed to both men and women. The naming of both men and women as recipients of the rule made it possible to publicize the rule as a universal document. Mention of both men and women also reflected local circumstances in Venice, where Thomas of Siena was based and led the efforts to institutionalize the Dominican life of penance. Venice had one of the only known groups of Dominican penitent men. It was, of course, in their interest to promote a rule that encompassed both men and women. The penitent men's financial contributions and their contacts at the papal curia between 1402 and 1405 helped the Dominicans to secure papal approval of the penitent rule in 1405. The group of penitent men of Venice left their mark on the rule, but they seem not to have inspired other laymen to take the Dominican habit. Women were thus left as the only ones practicing the newly established rules.[5]

The Dominican Penitent Rule

Here begins the rule of the brothers and sisters of the Order of the Penance of Saint Dominic, the founder and the father of the Order of the Friars Preachers

Chapter 1: On the reception of new members and their condition

To begin with: It is known that the continuous and perpetual growth of the order is dependent most of all on the reception of well-disposed persons. Thus, we demand and declare[6] that the new members should be received only by a master or a director[7] and the prior of the brotherhood in question, or with their permission. It is also necessary that the majority of the professed members of the brotherhood[8] of the same place give their consent to the reception. The person in question is to be examined carefully, and it should be determined that he has followed an honest way of life and enjoys good repute and is not suspected of any form of heresy. This way, like a true son of Saint Dominic in Christ, he will be a dedicated defender of the truth of the Catholic faith to the best of his ability.

Before the person receives the habit of this order, he pays back all that he owes to others and makes peace with his neighbors. He also draws up a testament upon the advice and orders of an experienced confessor.[9]

The same examination is done to women who want to enter the order. Married women can join this brotherhood only if they have a public instrument that proves their husband's permission and consent.[10] The same applies to married men, unless the advice of wise counselors determines that they have a legitimate reason to be exempted.

Chapter 2: On the habit of the brothers and sisters

Both the brothers and sisters of this brotherhood should dress in white and black cloth, the color and material of which should be of no value, as is fitting to honest servants of God.[11] The mantle should be black, and similarly the capuche of the brothers should be black. The tunics should be white, and their sleeves should reach the palms of the hands. The sleeves are to be cut narrow. Only leather belts should be worn, and the belts of the sisters should be fastened under their tunics.[12] Burses, shoes, and other such things should not show any signs of worldliness. The veil and wimple of the sisters are to be made of white linen or hemp.

Chapter 3: On the benediction of the habit and on reception into the order

The one who is to be received is received in the meetinghouse of the brotherhood or in front of the altar in a local church of the Preaching Friars by the master or the director mentioned above or by his vicar. The one who is to be received humbly kneels in front of the master in the presence of some friars, the prior of the brotherhood or his vicar, and other members of the brotherhood. The master first blesses the habit of the one who is to be received. He does it this way: "Show us your mercy, O Lord etc. The Lord be with you etc. Let us pray. The Lord Jesus Christ, you who lowered yourself to be draped in our mortal garment etc." After this benediction of the habit and clothing with it in a separate place, the one who is to be received returns to the steps of the altar and kneels in the front of the master. The master begins "Come, Holy Spirit" and the friars who are assisting him join in. Together they sing to the end. This is followed by: "Lord have mercy upon us etc. Christ have mercy upon us etc. Our Father etc. Send forth your spirit etc. Save your servant etc. The Lord be with you etc. Let us pray: God who taught the hearts of the faithful by the light of the Holy Spirit etc. Hold your servant etc." And as a response: "Amen." The master sprinkles holy water on the newly clothed member.[13] Afterward all the brothers of the brotherhood receive the new member with a kiss of peace. The women are received in the front of the altar in the same way as the brothers.

Chapter 4: On profession, that is, on the way in which one is professed

After a year, or before, the new member may be professed if the master or the prior discussed above, or his representative, and the majority of the professed brothers agree that the candidate is fit for the profession.[14] The profession is done in the following way: "In the honor of God, the Father, the Son, and the Holy Spirit, and the Blessed Virgin Mary and Saint Dominic, I [*Name*] profess in front of you [*Name*], master or the prior of the Brothers of the Penance of Saint Dominic in [*Place*] that from now until my death I wish to follow the form of life and the rule of the said order of the Penance of

Saint Dominic."[15] The women profess in the same way in the front of the master or the prioress, or their representative.

Chapter 5: On the permanence of this state

We declare that the brothers or sisters of this brotherhood and order are not allowed to exit the order to return to the world after they have given the above profession.[16] However, they are allowed to move to any approved religious order within which the three solemn religious vows are observed.[17]

Chapter 6: On the saying of the canonical hours

The brothers and sisters will recite the canonical hours every day, unless illness prevents them.[18] For Matins the brothers and sisters are to say twenty-eight *Pater Nosters*, for Vespers, fourteen, and for all the other hours, seven. In honor of the Blessed Mary Ever Virgin there should be said as many *Ave Marias* each canonical hour as *Pater Nosters*.[19] The brothers and sisters bless their meal with one *Pater Noster*. When they rise from the table they give thanks by saying one more *Pater Noster*. Those who know the psalms *Miserere mei deus* [Ps 50 in the Vulgate] and *Laudate* say them instead.[20] In addition, all those who know the Apostles' Creed, namely, the *Credo in deum*, always say that at the beginning of Matins, before Prime, and at the end of Compline. Those who know and say canonical hours in the same way as the clergy does are not obliged to say the *Pater Nosters* and *Ave Marias* discussed above.[21]

Chapter 7: On rising for Matins

Within the period from the feast of All Saints[22] to the feast of the Resurrection of Christ, everybody rises for Matins on Sundays and all feast days.[23] During Advent and Lent everybody wakes up every night. Those who are involved in daily manual labor may say all the hours up to Vespers in the morning. In the evening they say Vespers and Compline at the same time.

Chapter 8: On confession and communion

Everybody makes a careful confession of sins and devotedly receives the sacrament of the Eucharist at least four times a year, namely, on the feast of the Nativity of Christ, at his Resurrection, at Pentecost, and at the Assumption or at the Nativity of the Blessed Virgin, unless a confessor has a good reason to prohibit someone from doing so. Someone who devoutly desires to receive communion more often in the course of the year has God's blessing to do so after he has petitioned for and received permission from a prelate.[24]

Chapter 9: On observing silence in church

During the celebration of the Mass, the singing of the Divine Office, or the preaching of the sermon, everybody in the church is to remain silent and pay close attention to the prayers and the Divine Office. Only in a case of necessity may one quietly say a few words.

Chapter 10: On showing respect to parish priests and their churches

The brothers and sisters should try to visit their own parish churches, as is commanded by canon law and good custom. They are to pay deep respect to their prelates, that is, to bishops and other members of clergy. The brothers and sisters should pay all their dues, including tithes and other customary oblations, without any reductions.[25]

Chapter 11: On fasting

From the first Sunday of Advent to the Nativity of Christ, the brothers and sisters fast every day. The same is done from the Sunday of *Quinquagesima*[26] of the celebration of the Resurrection of Christ. Everybody fasts on Fridays and other fast days instituted by the church. Those who want to fast more often, or perform other forms of austerity, may do so with the permission of their prelate and according to the discretion of their confessors.[27]

Chapter 12: On eating meat

The brothers and sisters of the brotherhood may use meat on Sundays, Tuesdays, and Thursdays. On the other days of the week they are to abstain from meat, unless they are ill, very weak, or they have been bled, or it is a solemn feast day, or they are traveling.

Chapter 13: On moving in public

The sisters and brothers do not wander aimlessly and curiously around the town. The sisters, especially the younger ones, should not move around alone. Nobody goes to weddings, dances, licentious and worldly celebrations, or useless shows. Nobody leaves his or her hometown or village without special permission from prelates or the aforementioned masters of the brotherhood, not even in the case of a pilgrimage.

Chapter 14: On how brothers should not possess weapons

Brothers do not carry weapons, unless they are acting in the defense of Christianity or have other justifiable reasons and have permission from their prelate.[28]

Chapter 15: On visiting and caring for the sick

The prior names two brothers who are responsible for paying a visit to any member of their brotherhood who becomes ill. They should do so immediately after one of them hears about the case. Before these brothers do anything else, they should encourage the patient to receive the sacrament of penance and other relevant sacraments.[29] If the patient needs care, the brothers should help him in the ways that are available to them. If the patient is poor, the brothers will provide for him from their personal or collective means in ways that they see appropriate. The sisters do the same with their patients.

Chapter 16: On the passing away of a brother or a sister, and on suffrage for their souls

When one of the brothers passes away from this world, the other members of the brotherhood of the given town or village are called together to be personally present at the funeral rites until the completion of the burial. The same should be done for deceased sisters. Within eight days of the funeral, all friars and sisters recite the following kinds of prayers for the soul of the deceased: the priests celebrate a Mass, those who know the Psalter recite fifty psalms, and the illiterate say *Pater Noster* one hundred times. At the end of each prayer they add "Rest eternal grant them, etc."

Finally, each year three Masses should be celebrated for the souls of the brothers and sisters, both living and dead. Those who know the Psalter say it. The others say five hundred *Pater Nosters*.

Chapter 17: On instituting priors and prioresses

When the prior of a brotherhood dies or is removed from his position, the master or the director of the brotherhood consults the elders of the brotherhood and establishes the new prior. Once a year, during the Octave of the Resurrection of Christ[30] or at another time, the master consults the elders of the brotherhood whether the prior should be removed or confirmed. The master may confirm or remove the prior according to the counsel of the elders.[31] In the same way, the prior may appoint the subprior or the vicar of the brotherhood after he has consulted with the master and some of the oldest members of the brotherhood. The prior may confirm or remove the subprior and the vicar on the basis of what the master and the elders recommend. The prior may decide how wide the powers he grants to the subprior and the vicar. The institution and removal of the prioresses and the subprioresses of the sisters follow the same pattern.

Chapter 18: On the duties of the prior and the prioresses

It is the duty of the prior to follow diligently everything that the rule prescribes and to ensure that the other members of the brotherhood do the same. If the prior finds transgression and negligence among the brothers, he should lovingly correct them and lead them to amend their ways. If he sees major transgressions, he may ask the master or the director of the brotherhood to rectify the issue.

It is the duty of the prioress to visit the church regularly and to encourage other sisters into regular observance. Moreover, she should personally, and with the help of some sisters whom she has assigned for the task, ensure that nothing in the activities, habits, or clothes of the sisters threatens their reputation. The prioress especially takes care that the sisters, notably the young ones, do not have interaction with any men, from whatever background, unless the man is their relative within the third degree by blood and follows a respectable way of life.

Chapter 19: On the correcting of brothers and sisters

When somebody is found to have suspicious relationships and a prelate has warned the offender three times, the offender is expelled for a time from the chapter and the company of the other members. If the offender does not rectify his behavior, then on the advice of discreet brothers the offender should be publicly expelled from the company of the others. He will not be accepted back unless all the brothers agree that he has amended his behavior.

When somebody swears at another member of the brotherhood or at somebody outside the brotherhood, and his words can be seen as blasphemous, or if he becomes enraged and hits somebody, or he goes to a prohibited place, or he is disobedient in some other way, or he is caught intentionally lying to his prelates, he is to be put on a diet of water and bread, or he is excluded from the chapter and the company of the other brothers. The degree of the punishment is dependent on the condition of the offender and the gravity of his offense.

When somebody commits a mortal sin, the majority of the professed brothers of that place determine the severity of the punishment on the basis of the offense and the offender's condition. The punishment will also serve as a warning to the others. When the offender refuses his punishment, on the advice of the wise members of the brotherhood let him be expelled from the order. The sisters who need to be corrected are subjected to all the same terms as the brothers.

Chapter 20: On the convening of the brothers and the sisters, and on instituting masters or directors for them, and on the total subjection of this form of life to the master general and provincial priors of the Order of the Friars Preachers

Once a month, on a chosen day and hour, the aforementioned master or his vicar assembles all the brothers to a church of the Friars Preachers so that everybody can hear the word of God and, if the time is convenient, attend Mass. Afterward, the master will read this rule to the brothers and explain it. He offers advice, and he corrects and emends the negligent brothers, and he leads them to the good as seems fitting according to God and this rule of life. On the first Friday of each month[32] the sisters are to convene in a church of the Friars Preachers. They too hear the word of God and attend the Mass. The master, who is assigned for their service, reads and explains this rule and corrects the sisters' mistakes.

We wish that brothers and sisters of each town or village have an honorable ordained friar from the Order of the Friars Preachers as their master or director, one who is either chosen by the brothers or sisters and presented to the master general or the provincial prior of the given province of the said order, or appointed by the said master general, the provincial prior, or their representative. Moreover, we will and declare that for their continuity and advancement all the brothers and sisters of the Penance of Blessed Dominic, wherever they are, be totally subjected to the direction and correction of the master general and provincial priors of the aforementioned order in all the matters that are covered in their way and form of life.[33]

Chapter 21: On dispensations in the case of legitimate reasons

The prior of the brotherhood together with brothers, or the prioress together with the sisters, or the master or the director who acts together with them, have the right to grant dispensations from abstinences, fasts, or other practices described in the preceding chapters, if they see that there is a legitimate and understandable reason to do so.

Chapter 22: On the obligation of this rule and form of life

Finally, we will and declare that any constitutions and ordinances of this rule or form of life, beyond the divine and ecclesiastical precepts and statutes, do not bind the brothers and sisters under pain of sin, but only under pain of penance, just as is stated in the constitutions of the Order of the Friars Preachers.[34] When a prelate or a master imposes penance for an act of transgression, let the transgressor humbly and promptly receive it and execute it with the help of the grace of our Lord and Redeemer Jesus Christ who reigns with the Father and the Holy Spirit now and forever. Amen.

Penitent Women as Subjects

The Legend of Giovanna of Orvieto

Editor's Note: Giovanna, also known as Vanna, of Orvieto was one of the first Dominican laywomen to be venerated as a *beata*. She was born around 1264 in Carnaiola, near Orvieto. She died on July 23, 1306, in Orvieto, where she had lived as a Dominican penitent or, as her *Legend* addresses her, *vestita* for about twenty-two years. Not unlike many other religious laywomen, she came from a troubled background: she had lost both her parents by the age of five, and at twelve she was forced to support herself after she had escaped from relatives who plotted to marry her against her will. Giovanna earned her undoubtedly meager living as a dressmaker and as a domestic servant. Yet, her association with other religious laywomen and her saintly fame saved her from the life of destitution that awaited many poor and single women. As a Dominican *vestita*, Giovanna lived for several years in the upper floor of the home of her wealthy mistress, Ghisla, and many of her supporters came from wealthy families of Orvieto.[1]

Giovanna's *Legend* draws a portrait of a saint whose life was shaped by various corporal manifestations of sanctity. She enacted physically the passions of Christ and the early martyrs. Her encounters with the devil left her with broken bones and a bruised eye. The

Note: The translation is based on Luigi G. G. Ricci's edition of the *Legend* in Emore Paoli and Luigi G. G. Ricci, *La* Legenda *di Vanna da Orvieto* (Spoleto: Centro Italiano di Studi sull'Alto Medioevo, 1996), 137–76. I thank Stefano Brufani, the director of the Centro italiano di studi sull' alto medioevo, for granting the right to translate Giovanna's *Legend*. I also wish to thank Luigi G. G. Ricci for discussing the edition of the *Legend* with me and offering his generous advice concerning some unclear references in the text. I am grateful to E. Ann Matter and Armando Maggi for their help in finding the right forms of some of the complicated personal names mentioned in the text.

warmth of the Holy Spirit made her sweat so profusely that she was unable to wear clothes during her prayers, and the rich sweetness of the heavenly gifts made her body round and beautiful. Her sanctity was also manifested in various sweet fragrances both at her death and at the translation of her body. The anonymous writer of the *Legend* was focused on the extraordinary aspects of Giovanna's sanctity, but we also learn that Giovanna was venerated for her humble disposition, neighborly service, and spiritual advice.

Giovanna enjoyed saintly fame during her lifetime and immediately after her death, as may be seen not only in her *Legend*, but also in surviving civic documents.[2] The *Legend* has been traditionally attributed to the Dominican friar Giacomo Scalza (d. ca. 1343), but such attribution has recently been questioned, so both the author and exact date of the *Legend* remain unsettled issues.[3] Given Giovanna's popularity in Orvieto at the time of her death, it would not be surprising if her *Legend* were written soon after her death or at least during the first half of the fourteenth century.[4]

Giovanna was a *vestita* at a time when women sought Dominican guidance but the Dominican life of penance had not yet been institutionally established and penitent women did not have an official position within the order. The sixth master general of the Dominican Order, Munio of Zamora, wrote his set of simple religious guidelines, the *Ordinationes*, for the *vestitae* of Orvieto in 1286. This *Ordinationes* supported the religious practices of the Dominican penitents of Orvieto, but it did not yet establish a formal bond between the Dominican friars and the penitent women.[5] It is probable that Giovanna was among the women of Orvieto who received Munio's *Ordinationes*, but it is difficult to determine what impact the text had on the religious life of Giovanna or her fellow penitents. In fact, the penitent women in the *Legend* seem to have been independent religious women who wore Dominican colors and were inspired by Dominican spirituality, but received only minimal guidance from Dominican friars.

At the end of the fourteenth century, Thomas Caffarini of Siena translated Giovanna's *Legend* into Italian and presented her as a role model for subsequent generations of Dominican penitent women.[6] Whereas the *Legend* had implied only a loose connection between *vestitae* and Dominican friars, Thomas flavored his translation with a few small but significant changes that drew an anachronistic image of the existence of a formal Dominican Order of Penance during Giovanna's lifetime.[7]

The Legend of Giovanna of Orvieto

The **Legend** *of the Blessed Vanna, that is, Giovanna, a virgin from Orvieto*

Here below are the titles of the chapters of the *Legend* of the Blessed Vanna, that is, Giovanna, a virgin from Orvieto. She belonged to the sisters of the Penance of Saint Dominic,[8] who was the founder and the father of the Order of Friars Preachers:

[1] On the name, homeland, and parents of this virgin, and a few words in praise of her sanctity. The first chapter, which begins: "Our God, the creator of everything, etc."

[2] On the signs of a saintly future that this virgin manifested at an early age. The second chapter, which begins: "The virgin was, etc."

[3] On the virgin's fervent affection for and preservation of her virginity, as well as on its divine protection. The third chapter, which begins "As the virgin grew, etc."

[4] On the taking of the habit of Saint Dominic, which the virgin had desired for a long time, on the tasting of divine blessings, and on the significance of the said habit. The fourth chapter, which begins "When the girl saw, etc."

[5] On her exceptionally fervent ardor for prayers and contemplation, and on the miracles and rewards that for this ardor brought about and that were conveyed through her.

The fifth chapter, which begins "From the time the virgin began, etc."

[6] On the singular providence the Lord showed toward the virgin through presentation of both sacramental and corporal food and feeding her both corporally and spiritually. The sixth chapter, which begins "Let us consider, etc."

[7] On the singular praiseworthiness this virgin acquired through her numerous virtues and especially through her profound humility and admirable patience. The seventh chapter, which begins "Lest the wind of vainglory, etc."

[8] On the virgin's spirit of prophecy that was manifested in several clear cases. The eighth chapter, which begins "This saintly woman, etc."

[9] On the various injuries and persecutions the virgin suffered under diabolic spirits. The ninth chapter, which begins "So great a woman did not, etc."

[10] On the revelation the virgin received concerning her death, on her death, and on her burial in the church of the Friars Preachers of Orvieto. On the miraculous and various odors that emanated from her corpse and reflected her various virtues. Also, on some explanations concerning her extraordinary humility and patience and burning love. The tenth chapter, which begins "After a great deal of agony, etc."

[11] On her glorious death and the many manifestations of her glory that surrounded her passing away. The eleventh chapter, which begins: "God revealed, etc."

[12] On many extraordinary miracles, which happened after her glorious death by her sepulcher, or by invoking her name, or by touching her relics or the vestments that had belonged to her. The twelfth chapter, which begins: "After her death, etc."

[13] On the miraculous translation of the virgin's body, which was found totally preserved and emanating a sweet odor, as well as on many other miracles that occurred at her sepulcher, or by invoking her, or by touching the virgin's

relics, or through her legend. The thirteenth chapter, which begins: "Fra Simon, etc."

Here begins the compendious Legend of Blessed Vanna, that is, the virgin Giovanna of Orvieto. She belonged to the sisters of the Penance of Saint Dominic,[9] who was the founder and the father of the Order of Friars Preachers.

[1] On the name, homeland, and parents of this virgin, and a few words in praise of her sanctity. The first chapter.

Our God, the creator of everything, and the Lord, Jesus Christ, takes care of his own for eternity and shows to his chosen ones the glorious gifts of his grace already in mortal life. And he wants to declare these chosen ones to the world, according to the variety of his graces and his immense mercifulness, by distributing certain gifts of the Holy Spirit. Some are given the utterance of wisdom by the Spirit, others the gift of healing, and still others the spirit of prophecy. These various kinds of gifts of the Spirit are distributed to each person according to the choosing of the Holy Spirit [1 Cor 12—14].

But now our minds turn to the memory of someone to whom God distributed abundantly almost all kinds of gifts of celestial grace. This person is Giovanna, a most holy virgin, the memory of whose glorious life we recall every day.

She who shines like a heavenly star was from a village called Carnaiola, which is in the Diocese of Orvieto. Her parents were old, honest, and, in worldly terms, rather rich, but the frequent blows of war drove them into poverty and great need.[10] As an infant she was already vested with an admirable simplicity and with the wisdom of a serpent [Matt 10:16], and she faithfully preserved the innocence of her baptismal vestments until the day of her death. Hence, dressed in the bridal gown for her celestial and royal wedding, she was not rejected, but she happily entered perpetual peace.

Let us, therefore, follow her way and keep her in front of our mental eyes as a path laid out to us.

[2] On the signs of a saintly future that this virgin manifested at an early age. The second chapter.

The virgin was three years old when she lost her father and five when she lost her mother. At such a young age, that is, when she was five years old, she began to show the signs of her future sanctity. At her young age she pronounced that she did not want to have a mother or father on earth. Once some girls of her age said to her: "Giovanna, you don't have a mother." She led them to a certain church, showed them an angel painted on the wall, and stated: "Know that this angel is my mother."

[3] On the virgin's fervent affection for and preservation of her virginity, as well as on its divine protection. The third chapter.

As the virgin grew older, she became a young woman of a considerable physical beauty. When she reached the age of discretion, she began fervently to love the virginity of her body and soul, and she pleaded for their preservation in her prayers and sighs directed to the Lord. She considered that there was no better way to unite with the God, who is the supreme purity, than through virginal purity. "Immortality brings us near to God [Wis 6:19]."

Because idleness is the root of sensual desire, she wished that the devil would always find her in some kind of an occupation, and thus she wanted to engage in manual work.[11] Therefore, she placed herself with a female dressmaker to learn the art of dressmaking.[12]

She fought with all her might to keep her chastity, the incomparable treasure of the soul, intact and fled from anything that could have even slightly tarnished it, as if that thing were lethal. Thus God, who from the heavens saw her determination, used his mercy to keep her always intact. He removed everything that stood in the way of her chastity.

One time when the blessed virgin was almost twelve and was returning from her mistress, who taught her the art of dressmaking, back to the place where she was staying,[13] she encountered an impudent man on the street who gazed at her with lustful eyes. The trembling and fearful virgin prayed to God that he would preserve her from sin. She fled, and soon after the miserable man passed away from this world.

Another time, when the virgin was returning home from the place of the same mistress and did not know that the aforementioned man was dead, she took a more hidden street, on which she encountered another man who was burning with the wretched flame of lust, but she forcefully fled in the same kind of terror. Soon after, he passed away from this world. Everyone should understand that those who try to offend or molest the saints and friends of God are not allowed to go without punishment.

[4] On the taking of the habit of Saint Dominic, which the virgin had desired for a long time, on the tasting of divine blessings, and on the significance of the said habit. The fourth chapter.

When the girl saw that it was not safe to live among scorpions [Ezek 2:6], she began to think how she could reject the world, not only in her heart, which she had already done, but also through external acts. Guided by Divine Providence, she set out to take the habit of the *vestitae* of Saint Dominic, who was the founder and the father of the Order of the Preachers.

When her relatives realized what she had chosen to do, they tried in their ignorance to force her into wedlock and promised her to a handsome young man. The holy girl took along one of her friends and fled to a certain village,[14] wanting to serve the Lord in her virginal purity. There she subjected her body to fasts and vigils. She spent her nights praying to God and poured out humble prayers to the Lord for the preservation of her chastity.

God, to whom "the prayers of the humble and meek are always pleasing" [Jdt 9:16],[15] fulfilled even her smallest petitions. As she persevered in her prayers and holy meditations, she was enraptured with the bliss of divine consolations.

After she had tasted the sweetness of God, she despised all the pleasures of the world. The grace of Jesus Christ protected her, and she was granted the aforementioned and long-desired habit, in which she steadfastly served the Lord for twenty-two years to the day of her death.[16] It was appropriate that she was dressed in the white-and-black habit of the Friars Preachers, because the white signifies the purity of the mind and the black the mortification of the flesh.

[5] On her exceptionally fervent ardor for prayers and contemplation, and on the miracles and rewards that this ardor brought about and that were conveyed through her. The fifth chapter.

From the time the virgin began to live among the sisters, she shone like a guiding star wrapped in all virtues. She was the elected one of the Divine Goodness: vested in simplicity, blooming in her mental and corporal virginity, tender in her humility, constant in her patience, content in her obedience, remarkable in her way of life, miraculous in her opinions, bashful in her speaking, far-reaching in her charity, profoundly merciful for those afflicted and burdened, and in all her manners mature and well-ordered.[17] She spread the aroma of her virtues over other people.

She adhered ardently to fasts, prayers, vigils, abstinences, saintly meditations, and celestial contemplations. Bearing the weight of her flesh with sorrow, all she desired was to take part in the hymns of the angelic choir.

The soul that loves God finds peace only in him. Thus, she loved God as perfectly as is possible in this world, and, more than anything, she loved to contemplate eternity, where the mind finds peace. So that she could achieve this in the best possible way and then hold firmly onto it, she totally dedicated herself to assiduous prayer. Hence, beginning from the time she took the religious habit, every day she remained in prayer without moving from morning until Sext or None.[18]

During prayers and celestial contemplations, the virgin's heart burned so intensely that she could not wear clothes. Therefore, when she wanted to reach the height of prayers and contemplation, she went to her usual place of prayer, a cell located in the attic of the house in which she lived.[19] There she took off all her clothes, during both the summers and the harsh winters (when the cold could have hindered her from her rigorous practices). Dressed only in a simple sack, she remained steady without moving. Divine love created such a heat in the virgin's mind that her entire body was overcome by extreme sweating. She always had to have at hand a cloth with which she frequently dried the sweat that surfaced. All this was fitting: divine fire burned inside her, and therefore she could not have stayed outwardly cold.

This blessed virgin was in the habit of staying in such continuous contemplation and spiritual meditation that when she heard stories concerning Christ's love or passion, or those concerning the saints, her spirit was immediately raptured or elevated. She did not lack the crown of the sufferings of the martyrs, because when she heard of the way in which a martyr had suffered, she focused her mind on meditating on the passion of this martyr, so that her body stayed impassive and immobile in the position in which the martyr was subjected to his or her torments.

During the feast of the princes of the apostles, Peter and Paul, the virgin occupied herself with meditation on their passions. She first evoked the memory of Peter's passion. She experienced an immediate rapture, and her body was fixed immobile in the same way that the apostle was suspended on the cross. Afterward, she reflected on the passion of Paul, and she was raptured in the same way so that her body lay prostrate and her neck stretched out, just as Paul had been stretched out when he was beheaded.

As the virgin's soul received these gifts, her body lay lifeless so that if she would have been seen by someone who did not know, the person would have deemed her dead. She did not move or feel anything. Just like a corpse, she did not breathe. During such a time, one could see swarms of mosquitoes move freely on her uncovered and unmoving eyes, which she always kept half-open. Any other person would have been extremely distressed by stings of these numerous aggressive insects. Her eyes did not seem to belong to a living person, but to a one who had just died.

The Lord's passion and the cross of Jesus, the Lord and the Savior, were so firmly imprinted on her devoted mind that when she reflected on them, and when she even heard them mentioned, the torments of her beloved melted her heart and she burst into tears. She constantly bore the cross of mortification on her body for her suffering love.

On Good Fridays, during which holy mother, the church, calls for devotion to the passion of Christ (which for the sake of our misery the Son of God for love of our salvation, so to speak, bore like an inebriated man), the virgin annually went through an intense meditation of Christ's brutal suffering. As her mind was absorbed in the bitterness of the Passion, she did not have control over her senses, and her body was extended in the shape of the cross. Her body remained rigid, pale, and insensible in the same way that the body of the Lord had been when it was attached to the cross for ridicule.[20]

Those who happened to be present could hear that this painful stretching of the body resulted in what seemed to be such a powerful collapse of the bones that her limbs were loosened. One foot was placed on the top of the other, and the members of her body were stretched out in such forceful immobility that it would have been easier to cut or break them than to move them. The members of her body felt notably sharp suffering, pain, and weakness. In imitation of Christ she stayed fixed on the cross until dusk. She experienced these pains every year on this day during the last ten years of her life, except once, when she was suffering from a high fever and, we believe, God wanted to save her from such pains and suffering.

Often on Holy Saturday and on the day of the Lord's resurrection she meditated on the glory of the resurrection, and she was instantaneously enraptured to such a degree that there was no doubt she was given the gift of tasting the glory of the Savior. Indeed, her face appeared translucent and her eyes shone.

Once, on the day of the Assumption of Mary, the Mother of God,[21] she heard a reading concerning Mary's assumption. The virgin was reflecting upon it with a joyous heart when she began slowly to be raptured and her body was elevated off the ground. She was stationed in the air, her body elevated above the ground by about a cubit, and her hands were raised toward heaven like those of somebody who was praying while lying on the ground. She stayed for a long time in this elevation of spirit, and, with the same kind of lightness with which her body had been elevated in the air, she returned back to the ground.

On the feast of the holy virgin Catherine of Alexandria, when the virgin heard a reading of her life,[22] her heart and mind were filled with joy and she burst out with these words: "Raise, Saint Catherine." Immediately after these words she was freed of her bodily weight, and for a while she was elevated in the air.

Once, as she was longing for the love of her Beloved and in the fervor of holy inebriation, she said with an anxious mind: "Ah, how amazing and distressing it is that I cannot speak to my Beloved!" She said these words because as soon as she began to speak of or hear about Christ, her mind was drawn into ecstasy.

Every day her soul received so much sweet refreshment from contemplation that afterward she hardly cared for corporal food. As a way to speak consolingly, she used to say: "Why would eating not be tedious to someone who takes no pleasure in consuming food?" She said this, as she herself explained, because after she began to taste divine consolations and draw pleasure from God's sweetness, all delicacies tasted to her like garbage. This is not surprising, because a person despises the flesh after he or she has tasted the fruit of the spirit.

[6] On the singular providence the Lord showed toward the virgin through presentation of both sacramental and corporal food and feeding her both corporally and spiritually. The sixth chapter.

Let us consider how this virgin lived under the providence of the Lord, who chose to refresh her not only mentally but even corporally.

Once the virgin suffered from an upset stomach, and she became quite weak from profuse vomiting. She stayed in constant divine meditation, and in the middle of a night a person appeared to her carrying a vessel of wine. After she drank the wine that was offered to her, she immediately felt better as she recovered her strength and her stomach was healed. Thus, as she said afterward, the taste of the wine of the miracle beat all terrestrial wines. At the gentle urging of Lady Ghisla, her prioress,[23] Saint Giovanna said, just as lovers' secrets can only be forced out with sweet violence: "I was surrounded by a heavenly light and in the middle of the light I saw a golden cross, because Christ is indeed the true light. Amen."

Once when the virgin was suffering from her corporal illness, she was not able to join the others in the church in order to consume the body of Christ on the day of the Nativity, as is the practice among believers and especially among the sisters of her religious state. On the day after the feast a most miraculous light, sent from heaven, shone above her. As she was looking at it with intensity and delight, a pure white host emerged from the light and entered her mouth. She immediately consumed it. The Divine Goodness, who is the true light, and who said "I am the light of the world [John 8:12]," did not allow that on such a special day the virgin whom he had chosen as his special one and the recipient of his graces would have been deprived of the sacrament when she was unable to attend communion with the others.

Another time, when the blessed virgin was at the altar when holy communion was being celebrated, she sensed a strong odor that filled her soul with a most sweet delectation. Once when she was not able to join the others in the church for communion because of her illness and was most upset about it, the Blessed Mother of the Lord, the Virgin Mary, appeared to her carrying the child Jesus in her hands. The child said to her: "Giovanna, although you did not receive me today in the sacrament of the altar and you were not able to take the communion, you will always have me." Filled by his joyous aspect and mellifluous words, from the depths of her heart she exhaled every mundane and temporal trouble that was in her heart to him whom she saw before her.

Dear brothers,[24] what would one think all these blessings meant were they not signs that the Merciful God was preparing her for his glory?

I should also not remain silent concerning the following. She was so filled out, fleshy, and attractive that anybody who saw, but did not know her, would have thought that she had lavished herself with baths and many bodily delicacies. But one should not be astonished, because she did not live from an abundance of corporal delicacies, but she frequently tasted the sweetness of spiritual and celestial goods.

As has been shown, the virgin focused her mind's eye every day on the celestial contemplation of God, whom she loved with all her heart. Her mind was saturated with celestial food that tasted of honey; it filled her entire body even to her outward lips. When she descended from the heights of the mountain of contemplation, she returned with such a burning and glowing face that nobody doubted that she was coming from the furnace of the divine fire found in the celestial Jerusalem [Isa 31]. It is also true that many people testified that a fire was often seen during the night on the top of the roof of the house in which the holy virgin lived. When a household member asked her in a friendly way about the apparition of the fire, she immediately replied with a joyous and firm voice: "It is God." Did a prophet not testify that our God is a consuming fire?

[7] On the singular praiseworthiness this virgin acquired through her numerous virtues and especially through her profound humility and admirable patience. The seventh chapter.

Lest the wind of vainglory snatch her from herself, the virgin hid these gifts of grace as long as she could. She kept them to herself for twelve years without anybody else knowing about them, because she was afraid to submit what was done for Christ to human praise. But just as "a city built on a hill cannot be hid [Matt 5:14], or a burning lamp should not be put under a bushel basket [Mark 4:21]," her sanctity could not be hidden but would be revealed for many.

When she realized that she could no longer hide away, she turned to her prioress, with whom she had lived for nine years. The virgin begged and pleaded with the prioress by saying: "I beg you, Mother Prioress, and put in your judgment the fact that when I experience the graces of celestial consolations you do not reveal this to others." But the prioress said: "I am your prioress, and therefore I can let the others see you or do with you anything I choose to do." The virgin responded: "Nonetheless, Mother, I repeat what I just said to you."

Although she was strong in the virtues, she wanted to keep herself in the cellar of profound humility so that she would not be carried away by the waves of vainglory. Thus, she often called herself miserable, sinner, the worst of all women, or the devil. Once a group of women who were preparing to venture on a pilgrimage came to her to ask for her blessing for their undertaking, but she vehemently resisted them and said that they had come to ask for the blessing not from a saint but from the devil. When somebody called her a lady, she responded: "Watch out, because I am not a lady."

Let us then venerate, my beloved,[25] this saint whose glorious example shone like rays of sun that spread their light on our pilgrim's path.

Let us walk in the light of this virgin who, as we believe, lacks none of the virtues. She was angelic in her appearance, sweet in her speaking, untouched in her body, saintly in her works, catholic in her faith, patient in her hope, and general in her charity. She was a saintly virgin, a prudent virgin among the most prudent virgins, virgin of modesty, and a radiant soul. She was unwavering in her faith, radiant in her mind, devoted in her virginal love, always ready to obey, respectful in her works of humility, calm in tribulations, mentally compassionate with the sufferings of Christ, effective and kind in her saintly exhortations. When the suffering and anguished turned to her for consolation, they immediately became consoled and joyous.

What more could be said about her patience than that sometimes she was ill and weak for six years, sometimes two, four, or six months, but she never burst out with impatient words or with complaints?

[8] On the virgin's spirit of prophecy that was manifested in several clear cases. The eighth chapter.

This saintly woman of so many virtues excelled also in clear signs of prophetic spirit; she received many divine revelations during her contemplations and prayers. When the Friars Preachers of Orvieto were without a prior and were about to elect one, the virgin said to her prioress: "Lady, our friars are going to have such and such as their prior." What she said was proven true by what actually happened. The friar whose name the virgin had secretly mentioned to her prioress was elected the prior of the brothers. After he arrived, the virgin pointed him out, even though she had never seen him before. This prior, named Giacomo of Bevagna, was a man of great sanctity and an exceptionally religious way of life. He is buried in the convent of the Friars Preachers in Bevagna; there he rests, famous and radiant in many miracles.[26]

Once the venerable father Dom Francesco, the bishop of Orvieto, granted the congregation of sisters of the Order of Preachers an indulgence of one hundred days.[27] The prioress of the sisters, in her turn, promised the bishop that each sister would do one hundred genuflections on his behalf. After some while the virgin called the prioress to her and said: "Mother, you and certain other sisters have fulfilled the prayers you promised to the bishop, but this sister and that other did not render them all." When the prioress carefully examined the matter, the accusations of the virgin proved to be true.

A noble lady named Toscha, whose son was ill, sent a messenger to ask the virgin to pray for the son. After the prayers were completed, the saint sent the lady a message: "Know that your son is healed." When the mother set out to find out about the matter, she found her son totally cured.

A woman named Saracena was worried about her in-laws because of a certain imminent danger they faced, and she sent a messenger to the saint, asking her to pray to God for them. After the prayer was done, the saint said to the messenger: "Do not be afraid, because they will be saved from imminent danger." The liberation of the in-laws confirmed the truthfulness of the prophecy.

A young boy named Giacomo had the tertian fever, for which some barley water was being prepared. The blessed Giovanna took the water from the fire where it was cooking, and, lifting it up, she said: "You will no longer drink this water." Her words were proven true by the healing that followed.

Once on the most Holy Saturday before the resurrection, the virgin's mind was elevated to the glory of the Lord's resurrection. Her face and eyes shone with great flames, and she emitted bright rays of light. All of a sudden her face turned pale and with a weak voice she said: "Ah, poor dead one." And soon she added, "the justice of God." When she was asked on the following day what she saw, she said: "Did somebody die yesterday?" When the bystanders inquired why she said such a thing, she added: "God's justice was being done." When careful investigations were carried out, it was found out that at the hour the virgin had been in ecstasy and let out the words of lamentation, a man had met his miserable death without showing contrition and without taking communion or other sacraments of the church. Her distressed words made it clear that she saw his damnation.

It is especially miraculous that she saw in her life the miracles that she was going to perform after her death. Once when the virgin had completed her usual prayers, she said to her matron: "I see that I shall be three times in such-and-such a man's house," mentioning the man's name. After she passed away, three miracles were performed in a wondrous way through her divine powers in that very room. We may thus understand that after her death she came spiritually to the room that she had never visited corporally. These are clear evidence of her virtues, the commendations of her sanctity.

[9] On the various injuries and persecutions the virgin suffered under diabolic spirits. The ninth chapter.

So great a woman did not avoid the devil's plots and persecutions. When Satan saw her ascending in humility to the place from which he had been cast down in pride, he sought to pull her away from prayer by blows and by threatening her.

When the virgin was focused on her usual prayers, the devil transformed himself into the appearance of his friend the serpent and presented himself under the eyes of the praying virgin.

Another time, when the town of Orvieto was suffering from a great dissension,[28] as the virgin prayed for the town the ancient enemy of man assaulted her by hitting her on the shoulders with such a bodily force that she fell on the ground. One other time, when the saint had celebrated her usual vigils and wanted to rest her body, the enemy of man approached her and hit her so forcefully in the eye that the sound of the beating woke up the members of her household. They found her with a severely bruised eye.

The devil frequently appeared to her disguised as a religious woman,[29] or as an Ethiopian, or as a handsome young man who wore decorated clothes and was girded up with a golden belt and many other accessories. He tried to tear her away from the fulfillment of her saintly intention, but the saint was not moved by this, and she persisted in her usual meditations, intense prayers, and vigils.

[10] On the revelation the virgin received concerning her death, on her death, and on her burial in the church of the Friars Preachers of Orvieto. On the miraculous and various odors that emanated from her corpse and reflected her various virtues. Also, on some explanations concerning her extraordinary humility and patience and burning love. The tenth chapter.

After a great deal of agony and virginal sweating from her faithful labors in the Lord's vineyard, in the sight of the Most High the time was drawing near when the Lord Jesus Christ would reward "her work with pay" or the *denarium*, that is, her daily wage [Matt 20:2]. He revealed to the virgin her death. She called the prioress after the prayer and said: "Mother, I am dead." In a piercing pain the prioress replied: "Ah, daughter, what are you saying?" The virgin said: "Mother, I am totally dead."

Immediately on the same day the weakness that she had almost all the time got more intense. She fortified her death by devout reception of the body and the blood of our Lord Jesus Christ. On Saturday, July 23, after she most devoutly received the sacraments of the church, the holy virgin's soul, freed from the flesh, hastened to its heavenly triumph. There the virgin, happily inebriated with the embraces of her sweet spouse, Jesus Christ, gained strength from the superabundance of peace and rest. Having borne the fruit a three-hundredfold reward,[30] she entered the Lord's realm.

Thus, in the year 1306 of the Lord at the age of forty-two years, she was buried amid popular veneration in the Church of San Domenico at the convent of the Friars Preachers of Orvieto.

An abundance of divine miracles showed that God acknowledged her precious death. As her inanimate holy body lay on the bier, there was such a sudden abundance of marvelous odor that it spread over all people, none of whom could remember having ever smelled anything of such intensity and quality. Indeed, that odor was superior to any other fragrance. The Lord wanted to declare with the odor of sanctity that the odor of virginity, which she had possessed in life, was fittingly paired with another odor. Through this we can learn that as her body lay there alien to any worldly stench, she had offered herself to the Lord as a living host of sweet odor.[31] It is most wonderful to speak about or to witness how the crowd standing by the virgin's bed had the most diverse sensations of the kinds of odors that emerged from the one and the same virginal body at the same moment. Some stated that they sensed the odor of lilies, some the odor of violets, and many others a mixture of aromas.[32] What else could these various odors signify if not a variety of virtues? The whiteness of a lily expresses virginal purity, and thus it showed the virginity of this glorious virgin, who flourished in both mental and corporal integrity, not violated even by the illusions of dreams. What else than humility could be signified by the violet, which is lowest of all the flowers and keeps always close to the earth? This virgin radiated such a profound humility that she saw herself as inferior to everyone, worse than anyone else, and the lowest of all.

This friend of humility abhorred arrogance so much that if she saw any kind of pride in another person, she shut her nostrils tightly as if she smelled a terrible stench. Or, when somebody praised her or called her "lady," her soul suffered and lamented, just as proud people are distressed in a similar way when their honors are taken away. When somebody offended her, her soul rejoiced and intensely celebrated to such a degree that great internal joy spread to her face. She also poured out prayers and pleas to the Lord for the salvation of the one who offended her.

When a wretched, reviling woman once offended her, the virgin said in anguish that due to a severe bodily distress, she was unable to pray for the soul of the offender as much as she wanted. But, so that she would not be ungrateful for the gift of offense that she highly valued, she said two hundred *Pater Nosters* for the soul of the offender. Thus, she rendered the sacrifice of praise to the Lord. Someone summed up her actions in the proverb: "When somebody wants to be aided by your prayers and suffrages, he should trample you under with rough injuries."

At another time when she and another religious woman were insulted, the saint said to the woman: "We have been blessed with a beautiful gift today, let us not be ungrateful." What else was the pressed and strong mixture of aromas,[33] a result of various fragrances, if not the diversity of the virgin's abundant virtues of charity? The more she was afflicted by illnesses, tribulations, and insults, the greater the odor of her patience, found in God. This mixture of virtues was grafted into her soul and all the celestial gifts were given to her by the grace of God.

Her charity was so inflamed that anybody who was once touched by her words was wounded by divine charity and set on fire. By the power of her loving eloquence, many were also guided away from the restless waters of this world to the soul's tranquil harbor found in the religious way of life.

[11] On her glorious death and the many manifestations of her glory that surrounded her passing away. The eleventh chapter.

God revealed the virgin's death and glory to many.

When a certain devout and religious man was praying in the Church of Sant'Andrea, he had a vision of John the Baptist in the air waving a banner. The man saw Christ Crucified on the banner. When he looked closely, he saw that at the feet of the Crucified was the most blessed Giovanna. He heard a voice saying: "This is made and given as a sign, just as at the time of Moses the people were given the sign of a serpent in the desert" [Num 21:7–9]. After these words the banner and the saint were received in heaven, and the vision disappeared. The man checked the time and the hour, and came to the home in which the still-unburied body of the saint was laid out. He found out that his vision happened at the same time that the saint had been freed from her body.

A certain nun fell asleep for a short while. The blessed virgin Giovanna appeared to her during her sleep carrying lilies in her right hand. When the nun wanted to smell the lilies, the holy hand immediately withdrew. This happened several times, and the nun continued to enjoy great delight. When the others called for her, the indignant nun said: "May God almighty have mercy on you, sisters. Why do you want to draw me back so soon and take me away from this great delight?"[34] When the sister was telling about her vision, a messenger came to announce that at that same hour the saint was freed from the bond of her flesh.

When another religious and devout woman on the evening of the day on which the saint had fallen asleep in the Lord heard that the saint had expired (it was almost the time for Vespers when the saint passed away), she gravely lamented that she had not been able to be present at the virgin's death. As she was thinking about this, she fell asleep for a while. The saint appeared to the sleeper in the habit that she had worn during her life. When the woman saw the saint, she said: "Oh, Vanna, how is the pain on your side?" She said this because during her life the saint had suffered for a long time from pains in her side. The saint replied: "Know that all my pains have been taken away." After these words, the saint vanished from her sight.

When another woman, who was the chambermaid of the lady in whose house the saint had lived,[35] refreshed her body with some sleep, she saw with her mind's eye Giovanna, who was wearing the most beautiful jewels, walking with great glory and extreme brilliance. She was carrying in one hand lilies and in the other flowers of ruby color. She who was having the vision said to the saint: "Oh, Giovanna, who are the people in your company?" The saint responded: "Do you not see that I am with a multitude of saintly priests?" Then the woman with a keen mind saw a multitude of priests who both preceded and followed the saint in a bright light and glory. They were all about to celebrate a solemn Mass. As the woman was looking at them, the vision vanished from her sight.

When another devout and religious woman was sleeping after her prayers, God showed her the following kind of vision. She felt that she was standing by the sepulcher in which the saint was laid. When she let her eyes wander in the sky, she saw in the air two eagles who stood in their places without moving. As she was admiring the sight, her eyes went back to the tomb in which the saint rested. And behold, from it emerged the most blessed virgin, who was, as it seemed, dressed in light. She rested on a radiant cloth pallium. Four friars from the Order of Friars Preachers held its four splendid corners, each holding one corner with his hands. One of these four friars, at that time still alive, was a man who was gifted with an admirable innocence and sanctity of life.[36]

As the woman was looking at this vision, she saw how the virgin was being lifted toward the heavens to the eagles standing there. She asked: "Oh, Vanna, how is it possible for you to pass through the canopy?" She was saying this because the virgin's sepulcher was placed under a timbered canopy. The saint responded: "What are you saying? Would I not be able to pass through a few planks after I have passed through nine heavens?" After this the saint continued to be lifted higher. As the woman watched, she shouted with admiration: "Oh, Vanna!" The saint responded: "Do not call me Vanna, because in the heaven everybody calls me the Most Beautiful, not Vanna." After this, the vision disappeared.

[12] On many extraordinary miracles, which happened after her glorious death by her sepulcher, or by invoking her name, or by touching her relics or the vestments that had belonged to her. The twelfth chapter.

After her death, the virgin became known for her extraordinary miracles.

A sick boy was standing by the bier on which the still-unburied saint lay. On the suggestion of his mother, he touched the virgin's hand. He was immediately freed from his illness.

There was a certain paralyzed woman whose extremities were constantly shaking and had totally lost their strength. A few devout persons made a vow on her behalf to the saint Giovanna and the extremities of the woman's body recovered their strength and were totally healed.

A man named Aldebrandino, called Rella, suffered from the tertian fever. After he made a vow to the saint, he recovered his prior health.

When a certain religious man was having an intense pain after fracturing his foot, he devoutly invoked the saint's name and was at that moment freed.

A person who was ill in his stomach invoked the saint's name and was immediately freed.

A man named Cecco suffered from a strong pain in his feet. When he made a vow to the saint, he was immediately restored to his prior health.

A man named Pietro suffered from an illness called lethargic fever. He was mortally ill, and the doctors had lost hope of saving his life. The people who stood by him made a vow to Giovanna on his behalf and he immediately gained perfect health.

A religious sister named Rosa suffered from a strong fever. When she placed the saint's veil on her own head and invoked her name, she was given perfect health.

Another woman, named Sibilla, who was ravaged by a continuously strong fever for a year, invoked the virgin's name and was totally healed.

A certain man, who was worn out by pain in his entire body, dressed in the saint's clothes and immediately his health was restored.

A woman named Riccha, who was in the hospital of San Domenico of Orvieto, suffered from an eye problem. After she made a vow to the virgin Giovanna, her eyes totally recovered their ability to function.

A boy from the same hospital suffered from a poisonous disease that left ulcers on him. He was about to die. He made a vow, and his prior health was totally restored.

A *conversus* of the same order, that is, of Preachers, had an inguinal hernia and had great pain as a result of the descent of his intestines and an external tumor in the area.[37] He made a vow and called the name of the saint and was totally freed from his illness.

Lord Nerius of Ugolino Buonconte, a canon of the Church of San Costanzo of Orvieto, was weakened by fever. After he touched the vestments of the saint, he was at that moment freed from his illness.

There was a man named Sceus Savino Salamari with whom the doctors had lost their hope and who was so near his death that everybody thought he was dead. When his wife saw him in that condition, she said in a feeble voice: "Saint Giovanna, help me and give my husband back to me." After this, the saint's relics were placed on the patient's head, and he was immediately freed from all his illnesses.

A certain Giovanni Gratia had brought back a falcon from a forest, but when the falcon refused to eat, he threw it twice on a piece of wood and killed it. His wife lamented the bird's death, invoking Giovanna with a weak voice and saying: "Oh, virgin Giovanna, restore this falcon back to me so that I can sell it and buy some bread for my family. I will give you my vow." The bird immediately returned to life and to good health.

A woman called Morbida suffered from a persistently high fever that seemed to drive her out of her mind. She was approaching her death when she touched the relics of the virgin and offered a vow and was freed from her illness at that moment. A certain woman who had an ailing son called Chola prayed for his health in front of the virgin's sepulcher. When she returned home, she found her son freed from his illness. A boy of eighteen months fell from the height of fourteen feet onto a seat and then onto the ground. As his sister saw what happened, she commended his soul to Giovanna. When the family examined the boy, they found that he had remained untouched because of the virgin's virtues. A certain woman suffered from a severe illness in one of her breasts, and she was afraid that it was going to be cut away, which is what the doctors had determined to do. After she made a vow to the saint, she was immediately and completely freed from her illness.

A man named Cecco Cerfallo suffered from a cruel fever. He made a vow to the saint and totally recovered his health. A certain woman had a son who was suffering bitterly from spasms. He meticulously followed all the prescriptions assigned by the doctors, but he was making no progress. After a vow to the virgin, he was completely freed from his illness.

A religious and devout woman named Roccha, the daughter of Sinibaldo Pepi Sinibaldo, suffered from a cruel illness in her eye, which is called cataract. After making a vow and tracing the sign of the cross with the saint's garments over the ailment (from which a drop of deep black blood fell on the ground), she received the gift of perfect health. A boy named Paolo, who suffered from a most intense bodily pain, was draped by his mother in one of the virgin's mantles. When the mother invoked the virgin's name, he immediately recovered his health. A woman named Mattea had been afflicted by a pain in her foot for several months. After the invocation of the saint's name, she was healed.

A woman named Margareta suffered fevers and endured a swollen ulcer on one knee. When she prayed to the virgin for her healing, she was immediately freed from the ulcer. As she persisted in her prayers, asking for the alleviation of her fevers, she fell asleep. In her sleep she saw the blessed Giovanna, who was wearing her religious habit richly decorated. The virgin said: "Go and let my prioress know about the gift of grace that you received." When she did this, the fever was suddenly gone and the woman was fully cured. A girl named Benedetta, who was at the end of her life and was pronounced dead by the doctors, lay on the bed. Her tearful mother invoked the blessed Giovanna on behalf of her daughter. When the girl was touched with the vestments of the saint, she opened her eyes, and, totally healed, she rose up.

A woman in religious life named Bartolomea had a cruel pain in her tooth, and in her dream she invoked this glorious virgin. She saw in her dream that the saint touched the sick tooth with her vestments. When the woman woke up in the morning, she found herself totally cured. Oh, what a wonder: when she looked in her purse a few days later, she found a piece of these vestments, given to her in her sleep. She was not sure whether the piece was real or not, but, nonetheless, decided to keep it.

After some time, the mother of the said Bartolomea, named Theodora, suffered from a strong pain in her eyelids. She placed the relics, which her daughter had kept, for a brief moment on the place in which she felt the pain, and she was completely healed. Theodora's son, named Ciuccio, endured an almost intolerable pain in his fractured foot. The mother fetched the piece of saint's vestment that her daughter had received in her sleep and kept with great veneration. She made the sign of the cross with it above the fractured foot and invoked the saint's name, and the son was immediately healed from his illness.

[13] On the miraculous translation of the virgin's body, which was found totally preserved and emanating a sweet odor, as well as on many other miracles that occurred at her sepulcher, or by invoking her, or by touching the virgin's relics, or through her legend. The thirteenth chapter.

Fra Simon, a member of the Order of the Continent[38] and an inhabitant of Montefiascone, had a vision of Saint Giovanna, who appeared during Matins in a bright light and in the company of two virgins. She said to him: "Go to my matron[39] and tell her that I am not content in staying here in the ground, because the secular ladies rant on about venial and mortal sins here, something which is painful for me to hear.[40] Therefore, tell her to go to Fra Ildebrandino,[41] the penitentiary of the supreme pontiff, to discuss preparations for my sepulcher."[42]

Fra Pietro, the provincial prior,[43] and Fra Nicola, the convent's prior,[44] together with other friars decided to move the virgin on the Octave of Saint Martin.[45] This translation was observed by Fra Pietro, the provincial prior, Fra Nicola of Perugia, the convent's prior, and four friars of their order, as well as by Paolo, the abbot of San Severo with three of his friars, and by Lady Ghiscila with three of her *vestitae*.[46]

When they began to dig the grave, such an odor emanated from it that—as Ghiscila testified—all the bystanders were astonished. As they reached the body, they found it totally preserved, and from the head and feet emanated such a flow of oil that the head was soaked in it. Her body was found covered in manna, and her feet and hair had not moved from the position in which she was first laid in the sepulcher. Her habit was folded in several pleats by her side, and some blood had soaked through all the pleats.[47] Her body was like hardened wax. When the women who were present touched the body, they sensed a strong odor on their hands that lasted for several days. Many people were astonished by this odor. Many miracles happened at the time of this translation: demoniacs were freed; the bodies of the lame were straightened; and many were immediately freed from their different kinds of illnesses.

A certain woman named Andrea, from the region of San Lorenzo de Arari, suffered from a grave illness of having pains in both her legs. She made a vow to Vanna to free her from that grave illness. After she had given her vow, she was totally healed.

A girl from the quarter of Santa Maria Nuova, named Mita, suffered from an unheard-of illness that began on the feast of Saint Gregory, then celebrated on the Tuesday following the second Sunday of Lent, and lasted until the following Sunday.[48] Little stones, coals, and pieces of wood flew frequently into her eye. Although they were invisible, they caused sensation and were painful. She was freed from her illness through the merits of the blessed Vanna.

A man named Andrea Giacobi from the quarter of San Cristoforo was struck by an illness under his armpits that people call *duragnum*.[49] After he made a vow to the blessed Vanna, he was healed.

A young girl from the Fonte family from the quarter of San Giovanni lost her speech for three days when a rock accidentally fell on her head. She was able to signal that she should be taken to the sepulcher of Saint Vanna. Her mother carried her there, and after the girl knelt there for just a moment, she was totally freed from her illness. A certain boy had a hole in his throat because of the tumor he had in it. After he made a vow to Saint Vanna, he was completely healed. A son of Duccio Berardino Claudi[50] was bathing in the River Paglia when the water pulled him under. He began to sink toward the bottom and was about to drown. When his mother heard what was happening, in an anguished state she made a vow to the blessed Vanna to save her son from the danger of death. He was pulled out of the water almost lifeless, but after a while he returned back to health.

A man named Matteo Crasso,[51] who lived in the plateau of Sant'Egidio, was kicked by his own mule. He was in extreme pain and at the brink of death. He made a vow to the blessed Vanna for his liberation, which she heard. He recuperated and gained back his prior health. A man named Vanni di Nuto from the quarter of Santa Maria Nuova had such a lethal wound in his stomach that one could see his viscera. After a vow to the blessed Vanna, he escaped the danger of death. Vanni, a son of Master Giovanni Vanni, who was overcome by an extreme fever and a tumor in his body, rose up all of a sudden and said that at that moment the blessed Vanna, a daughter of Saint Dominic, had freed him from his illness.

The Lady Morbida from the order of the *vestitae* of Saint Dominic had impaired vision from two piles that grew in front of her eye.[52] One night the head of the blessed Vanna appeared to her, and in the morning Morbida found herself totally cured. Lady Nera, the wife of Sembianto of Orvieto from the region of San Leonardo, testified in the Church of San Domenico that she had fallen fifteen feet down the stairs that lead to the loft of her house. She was so thoroughly shaken that she could not move herself at all. She pleaded to the blessed Vanna and made a vow to her, and after two days she was totally cured, even of the pains that had earlier given her notable trouble.

Lotto di Andreotti Frascambocca rode with his horse into a certain river. He thought he had found a firm and good place for crossing, because he saw marks of other people crossing from the same place. But suddenly the horse was covered in water that reached the rider up to the waist. Lotto made a vow to the blessed Vanna that if she would free him from the peril, he would bring or send her a wax image. When his petition was heard, he did as he had vowed to do.

A man called Rella from the region of Ripa dell'Olmo suffered from an abscess on his thumb, which gave him such a pain that he was unable to rest or to sleep. He placed a holy relic of the saint on the place of the injury, and he was completely freed from his illness.

In the village of Gili there was a twelve- or thirteen-year-old girl who was alone in her room on the day of the annunciation of the Lord when the whole room began to shake. She was so extremely frightened by this that her face was totally distorted. However, the memory of the blessed Vanna soon came to her mind, and after she made a solemn vow to the saint,[53] she was freed. A man called Sacceo, a son of a certain Guido de Camera, from the quarter of San Stefano, suffered from a serious pain that reached from his chest to the top of his head. He called Saint Vanna for help. Soon after he made the vow, he was freed from his illness. Giovanni, a brother of presbyter Stefano, from the quarter of Santi Apostoli, as well as his wife, both suffered from a severe illness that people call paralysis. They both made a solemn vow to the blessed Vanna and prayed that for her merits they would regain their health after such an extreme illness. Soon after they made their vow, they returned to their prior health.

A person suffered a hernia in the area of his genitals and was in great pain. He solemnly commended himself to the blessed Vanna and made a vow to her. Her merits brought about his healing. Lady Jacoba, the wife of Muscato from the region of San Leonardo, had totally lost her memory after a grave illness. After a vow was made on her behalf to the blessed Vanna, she was totally freed.

Lady Benvenuta, the wife of Pietro from the region of San Leonardo, had been blind for three years. After she made a vow to Saint Vanna, she was healed.

When a certain notary placed the *Legend of Saint Vanna* on his face three times, he smelled a miraculous odor three times.[54] This is recorded in a public instrument. A young son of Cecco di Vannuccio della Terza[55] fell down the stone steps of a certain loft where he was staying. He was considered dead beyond doubt. When a vow was made to the blessed Vanna, he was immediately restored to his prior health.

There was a man in Orvieto who was held alone as a prisoner in a tower, where there were numerous fleas and bugs. He was continuously attacked so forcefully by them that to fight against their bites and the torment they brought, he asked for a small fire in which to destroy them. The fire spread to the hay, and the man nearly died from the smoke from it. When he made a vow to the blessed Vanna, she appeared to him in a great splendor and said: "My son, rest assured: you will soon be totally freed." On the following day he was brought out from his captivity, and he did not suffer any damage from the smoke.

Sister Ghiscilla, a daughter of Cecco Facietti from the *vestitae* of Saint Dominic, was suffering from blindness that had resulted from an accident.[56] When she heard that Vanna had freed many men and women from their various illnesses, she made a vow to her and placed Vanna's relics on her eyes. She fell asleep for a while. When she woke up that night, she found herself suddenly totally freed.

The year of the Lord 1396. The person who carried this *Legend* from Orvieto to Venice said that he and his companions avoided serious dangers in their journey. The said master attested that this happened through the merits of the saint whose *Legend* they were carrying.[57]

The end. Praised be the Lord. Amen.

The Miracoli *of*
Catherine of Siena

Editor's Note: The Miracoli *of Catherine of Siena* (ca. 1347–80), written by an anonymous author from Florence between early summer and October 1374, provides a contemporary testimony of Catherine's life. It offers a view of Catherine as a young woman who was already known locally for her visions, asceticism, and patient service to the poor and the sick. However, Catherine's public and itinerant mission for the restoration of the papacy in Rome, for a crusade against the infidels, and for the unity of the church began only after the *Miracoli* was completed.[1]

The identity of the author of the *Miracoli* remains unknown. We know that he learned of Catherine through her companions when Catherine was in Florence during the meeting of the Dominican General Chapter in May 1374. Judging by the author's use of the vernacular, his simple and unassuming style, and avoidance of theological expositions, he probably was a layperson.[2]

The reasons for Catherine's stay in Florence are still debated. It has often been claimed that Catherine was there to be examined by the Dominican General Chapter. The *Miracoli* has been used as evidence that such an examination was arranged, but, in fact, the text does not necessarily support such a reading.[3] Moreover, no existing source suggests that the Dominicans suspected Catherine

---

Note: The translation is based on *I miracoli di Caterina di Iacopo da Siena di Anonimo Fiorentino,* ed. Francesco Valli, in Fontes Vitae S. Catharinae Senensis Historici, vol. 4 (Siena: Università di Siena, 1936), 1–25. I wish to thank F. Thomas Luongo, who has generously shared with me his thoughts and research concerning Catherine and her fellow penitents. His critical and insightful analyses have helped me to set the *Miracoli* in its historical context and to appreciate the number of ways with which the text challenges standard representations of Catherine's life of penance.

of such a serious problem that she would have been called to appear before the order's supreme leaders. Nevertheless, it is clear that Catherine's life changed during, or soon after, her stay in Florence. Raymond of Capua was assigned as Catherine's confessor around the time of the meeting of the General Chapter.[4] Catherine's public mission began under Raymond's guidance. Raymond became one of the leading reformers of the Dominican Order and the Latin Church, and in May 1380, just weeks after Catherine's death, he was chosen as the master general of the Dominican Order. A few years after Catherine's death, between 1385 and 1395, Raymond wrote the *Legenda maior*, the canonical *vita* of Catherine.

The particular nature, and value, of the *Miracoli* may be best understood when it is compared with Raymond of Capua's *Legenda maior*.[5] It took Raymond more than ten years to write his massive *vita* of Catherine. Raymond offered striking details about Catherine's life of self-mortification, he staunchly defended Catherine's activities as a public prophet, and he used her life as an opportunity to create an ideal of a specifically Dominican way of penitential life. Catherine's *Legenda* was instrumental in Raymond's efforts to redefine the Dominican life of penance, to reform the entire order, and to promote the glory of the Roman papacy during the schism of the Western church.[6]

By contrast, the *Miracoli* is a short account concerning a few extraordinary aspects of Catherine's life up to 1374. It may well be that this text, like so many other vernacular lives of female saints, was intended to be used as edifying reading for female audiences.[7] But beyond this, the author of the *Miracoli* did not seem to have high ambitions for his text. In fact, the inner contradictions and some vague references in the text suggest that it was a spontaneous and unrevised collection of oral testimonies. Yet it is precisely this spontaneous nature of the text that makes it valuable for readers interested in the development of Catherine's cult. Whereas Raymond's account offers a polished interpretation of Catherine's mysticism, asceticism, and public deeds, the *Miracoli* captures the mixture of doubt and enthusiasm that people must have experienced as they tried to understand the extraordinary person who lived among them.

The *Miracoli* and the *Legenda maior* narrate several events in common. In both legends we read, for instance, about Catherine's first vision as a young girl, Catherine's difficulties in defending her decision to take the penitential habit, Catherine's strenuous asceticism concerning food, her generosity toward the poor, and her healing miracles during the summer of 1374, when plague hit Siena.[8] However, Raymond seems not to have known the *Miracoli,* written several years before he began his version of Catherine's life. The similarities between the *Miracoli* and the *Legenda maior* may be explained on the basis of shared sources. Both authors knew Catherine personally, although the relationship between the author of the *Miracoli* and Catherine was certainly less formal and intense than that between Raymond and Catherine. Both authors also relied on Catherine's female companions and their testimonies. Moreover, it seems that the author of the *Miracoli* was familiar with the notes that Tommaso della Fonte, Catherine's first confessor, kept of her early years. Raymond also used Tommaso's notes.[9]

Nevertheless, the *Miracoli* and the *Legenda maior* differ considerably in their presentation of chronology and details of the events in Catherine's life. For instance, the author of the *Miracoli* wrote that Catherine took her habit when she was twenty-three years old, whereas Raymond gives the impression that Catherine was much younger at the time of her vesting.[10] Raymond wanted to represent Catherine's vocation as a youthful determination and the entrance in the penitential order as a decisive and clearly defined moment, but the account in the *Miracoli* may, in fact, capture better the unstructured quality of the penitential way of life at the time. The *Legenda maior* was in part written as an effort to redefine the Dominican way of religious lay life, whereas the author of the *Miracoli* was unconcerned by the independence of Catherine and her fellow penitents.

The *Miracoli*

[Chapter 1] In May 1374 a *vestita* of the *pinzochere* of Saint Dominic, Catherine, a daughter of Jacobo of Siena, came to Florence at the same time that the General Chapter of the Friars Preachers was summoned there by the order's master.[11] She was twenty-seven years old and had the reputation of being a holy servant of God.[12] She was guarded by three *pinzochere* of her habit.[13] When these women told me about her, I wanted to see her and befriend her. She came a few times to my house. As I began to understand her way of life, I yearned to learn as much as possible about her. In her praise and for the strengthening of my spirit, I am writing down a few things that I learned concerning her life.

[Chapter 2] When this girl was a child, she always wanted to go to churches and other sacred places. When she was seven years old, her mother said to her: "Catherine, go to your married sister, take with you your older brother, and give your sister this thing from me."[14] On the journey there was a totally unsettled area. While the girl and her brother were returning home through this unsettled area and the brother was walking a few steps ahead of her, she lifted her eyes to the sky. Suddenly, she saw in the air, only a little bit above the ground, a fairly small open gallery that was full of light. Inside she saw what appeared to be Christ dressed in totally white clothes. He looked like a bishop who was prepared for a solemn ceremony, and he had a pastoral staff in his hand. He looked at the girl with laughing eyes and directed a ray of light that was rather like a sunbeam toward her. Behind Christ there were some saints, all dressed in white, and, on the basis of some paintings that the girl had seen in churches, she recognized the saints Peter, Paul, and John.[15] As the girl stood, her eyes fixed on this wonder, her brother turned back and saw her standing still on the path. The brother urged her to follow him, but she continued to stare at the marvel without answering him. The enraged brother yelled at her, cursed her, and called her to move on. At this point, she turned and in great turmoil she shouted at her brother: "Go away, I do not want to follow you." But when she turned back, the luminous marvel had vanished. The girl was left with a great fear. Feeling deeply tormented, she followed her brother. At home, she did not tell her father or her mother or anybody else what she had seen. From this moment, she was always tormented from inside, fearful, conscientious, and afraid of falling into sin, as much as was possible for a girl of her age.[16]

[Chapter 3] As the girl grew older, she became increasingly conscientious, and she tried to find ways of life that would least offend God. Whenever she could hide from her father, mother, and other members of her household, she sought solitude to say her *Pater Nosters* and *Ave Marias.* Her desire to live a solitary life grew so intense that one time she escaped her home and left Siena. Outside the gate of Sant'Ansano, where there are, I believe, some low valleys and hidden caves, she found a cave in which she could not be seen or heard by other people. Catherine knelt down and, full of devotion, prayed to the Mother of Christ. In her youthful innocence she asked to be espoused to her son, Jesus. As the girl was praying, she sensed that she was being lifted above the ground. The Virgin Mary appeared carrying her son in her arms. He espoused the girl with a ring. Immediately afterward he vanished, and the girl found herself back on the ground. She returned to Siena and to her home.[17]

[Chapter 4] Sometime after these events, the girl's married sister, of whom we have spoken above, died. As is commonly done, a friar of the Order of Preachers, Tommaso della Fonte, came to console the mother and other women who had gathered in the house. The girl asked her mother for permission to confess to the friar. In her confession she told about the vision we have just discussed. The friar encouraged her to turn her back to the world and stay with God. He urged her to steer away from the vanity and lasciviousness of her deceased sister and other young women. The friar took his leave, but the girl remained deep in her thoughts. As she prayed, she tried fervently to do as the friar had taught her, and suddenly the following sentence emerged in her soul and mind: "My Lord, Jesus Christ, I promise to give you my virginity forever and you will be the guardian of my purity." She had never heard of such a vow. Nevertheless, at the age of seven, she made this solemn vow.[18] From this moment she always tried to escape the company of her father, mother, and other family members. She looked for solitary places inside her home. As the girl grew older, she went step by step further in her continuous avoidance of sleeping on a bed or drinking wine. She also showed that she hated meat and all other delicious foods. She sneaked out of the house early in the morning to go to a church that was fairly close to her home and confessed frequently to the friar.[19] Her father, mother, and brothers caused her much trouble and affliction. They wanted her to give up her way of life and to marry. But the more she was attacked, the stronger she persisted on God's path.

[Chapter 5] The girl grew up. When she was fifteen and her father had already died, her mother and brothers made all possible efforts to marry her.[20] In fact, the girl often overheard her mother and brothers discuss the fact at home. But she prayed even more fervently that God would preserve her virginity and would allow her to keep the vow she had made. In her increasingly frequent confessions to the friar discussed above, she asked him to pray for her and to give her counsel on the problem. The friar answered her: "Go and cut your hair." She returned home, but when she was thinking how to begin, she was disturbed whether she should let her mother know. On the one hand, she wanted her mother's approval, but on the other hand, she said to herself "my mother will not approve." She was tormented for many days, but eventually she took the scissors and forcefully cut off all her hair. Then she covered her head as well as she could so that her mother would not discover the deed. She had already developed a habit of staying alone in one section in the upper part of the house. Only rarely, if ever, did she come down to spend time with the others. Thus, it was not difficult to hide the deed from her mother.[21]

[Chapter 6] One day a female relative of the family came to visit the mother. The girl was called down. The mother was complaining that the husband of her deceased daughter had taken a new wife too soon. This led the mother to say that she wanted Catherine to marry. But the visitor said: "What are you saying! Catherine does not want a husband." The girl confirmed that this was the case, but the upset mother threatened her: "In that case I shall lay my hands in your hair and pull it out in great quantities." The girl hastened to reply: "You can pull my hair as much as you like." Then she uncovered her head. Her mother let out a scream so loud that it is difficult even to imagine it. The girl climbed up to her habitual place. She decided to make her decision clear to her brothers, which she did. She said that they should forget all thoughts of trying to make her live in the world. She concluded: "I am not going to ask you to spend money on me. I only ask for bread and water. Let me stay on my own and follow my own way." Her mother and brothers now believed in the girl's decision and let her adhere to it. After this, the girl stayed in the upper part of the house in a room that was appointed to her. She remained enclosed for about seven years, and she performed rigorous penance.[22] She did not sleep on a bed, or eat any meat, or drink wine. She only ate bread and water, and occasionally legumes and herbs. From this day she never ate more than once a day, and as each day went by she imposed further limits and restrictions upon herself.

[Chapter 7] The girl persevered on her path. One day she had a vision. A crowd of people appeared to her in a place that seemed to be far removed from this world. The people made all kinds of movements and confused gestures, and she could not understand what was happening. She had to walk through the crowd, but she did not have the strength to do so. As the frightened and terrified girl was standing in the midst of the people, she heard a voice speaking to her: "If you want to pass through this crowd, you will have to hide yourself under something white." As she lifted her head toward the voice, she recognized Saint Dominic, whom she had seen depicted in paintings in the church.[23] He said: "Come and receive my habit." When she started to move forward, she saw a pair of sisters,[24] disreputable, beautiful, and embellished women, who began to follow her. They pulled her clothes with all their might. She turned to them and hit them to set herself free. She was so forceful that she managed to escape the hands of the women. As she continued alone she saw that the crowd had taken hold of the two sisters, but she passed through safe and without hurting herself.[25]

[Chapter 8] The girl revealed this vision to her confessor, and she decided immediately to become a *pinzochera* of Saint Dominic, which she did. In fact, she did not take the habit alone but was joined by her mother.[26] She continued to follow a life of strenuous asceticism at her home. Her desire to serve God increased every day. Every morning, around Terce, she wanted to consume the body of Christ.[27] She had now reached twenty-three years of age, or around that. She had begun her practice of fasting and persevered in it, but she wanted to stop eating even the small amounts of corporal food that she still consumed. This she did from around 1370. After taking communion, she is always overcome by such a powerful fervor of the Holy Spirit and is so inflamed toward God that she cannot move from her place. She is enraptured to the heights, and it seems as if she would be emptied of the spirit of life. Her body and all her limbs, with the exception of her face, are numb and cold. She remains this way for around two hours every morning. It seems to be almost the hour of None before she recovers.[28] Because she is always accompanied by one to three women of her habit, she sits down to the table with them, not for her own sake, but for the comfort of her companions. Her companions do not eat meat, but they use herbs, legumes, fruits, bread, wine, and other such simple things, which they eat either cooked or raw. She always puts in her mouth some offerings of the table. She might eat a piece of bread, smaller than a size of a nut, a leaf of an herb, a bean, or an almond, or other similar things, but always in these small quantities. However, she never swallows anything that she puts in her mouth. Instead, after she has chewed the food, she immediately spits it in a bucket that she has placed at her feet. She frequently washes her mouth with a gulp of water, but she swallows the water only occasionally. She eats like this once a day, soon after None. To pass the time that she spends around the table and to give her companions time to finish their meals, she speaks about God and paradise, or she reads about the deeds of the saints.[29] If all the things that she puts in her mouth during the meal would be put together, the amount would not be more than a size of a walnut.

[Chapter 9] After the meal Catherine spends the rest of the day guiding people on the path of God, or she is in contemplation, or in similar raptures like the ones discussed above, or in reading holy books. She cherishes the time of contemplation the most, but she is often kept away from it by the people who want to see her and learn from her example and teaching.[30]

[Chapter 10] Catherine's habit is lowly, worn out, and full of patches. On her flesh she always has a woolen hair shirt that is tied with an iron chain, and almost never are her sides free of pain. In the night she sleeps with her clothes on, and she rests on a wooden board or on a sack of straw. She stays up most of the night and spends her time in prayer, in contemplation, in pious thoughts, or in meditation until it is almost one in the morning. Then she falls asleep, and she normally sleeps until the dawn. She gets up and, even if she suffers a violent pain in her sides, she always spends her time in some kind of good and pious work. At Terce she goes to the church to hear Mass and to receive communion.

[Chapter 11] This young woman is so full of charity that she lovingly receives anybody who comes to ask her for prayers, and willingly she promises to pray for them. When she prays for the people who have come to her, she not only prays fervently, but often, especially during the nights, she does such rigorous penance on behalf of these people that she draws blood.[31] Once somebody asked her how it was possible for her to pray for all those who turned to her when she did not know them personally and they were so many. She replied: "When a servant of God is filled with devotion and a burning desire for the salvation of sinners, and when she prays to the Eternal Majesty, he rewards her with a mental eye with which she sees all those for whom she is praying."

[Chapter 12] Another time somebody asked why she wanted to take communion every day, even though Saint Augustine wrote that daily communion is not to be praised or condemned.[32] And the holy church recommends that all Christians should receive communion once a year, but not necessarily more often.[33] The person said: "Your desire to receive communion every day seems thus to be excessive." She responded: "It would not be enough for me to be good only once a year or once a month or once a week. Instead, I rejoice and am comforted by being good every day. Saint Augustine is right when he says that the practice should not be condemned."[34]

[Chapter 13] After Catherine receives communion and falls into raptures that leave her cold, rigid, and stiff, she sometimes or even several times raises herself up on her feet or on her knees and crosses her hands or her arms in front of her. Her face is glowing red and covered with sweat. She pronounces words of jubilation, some of which are hard to interpret. The words make manifest that her mind had ascended to heaven, where she sees exceptional happiness and celebration. When she kneels with humble meekness, she slowly bows her head to the ground as if she would be receiving a commission or a license from a great lord. After a little while, she returns to herself, but she seems to be totally out of breath. When she is finally back together, she asks a friar or somebody else who might be able to answer her: "What feast day is it today?" She might be told: "Today it is nobody's feast day." Or, she might be told: "Today is a feast day of such and such saint." Or, she might be told only about the feast days of those saints whose feasts are incorporated in the holy church's calendar and who should be celebrated in this world. However, she is not told about the many saints who are not celebrated in the calendar but who still have their feast days. She replies: "I am certain that today is the feast day of such and such saint." After this, Catherine asks friars or somebody else to check the martyrology of the church, which proves that the day was dedicated to the saint that she mentioned by name. This shows that Catherine sees with an inner eye things that happen in paradise.[35]

[Chapter 14] When the rulers of Siena were thrown over, Catherine's brothers were enemies and opponents of the party that was stronger and emerged as the winner of the upheaval.[36] The enemies of her brothers came after them, wanting to kill them or hurt them, which is what they did to some others. A close friend of the family came to their home. With great agitation he said: "A company of your enemies is coming in this direction, and they are after you. You have to take your leave immediately and follow me to the Church of Sant'Antonio (which was close to their home) where you will be safe and where others have taken refuge as well." Catherine was present, and after the friend finished speaking, she stood up and said to him: "Those who go there are not going to survive, and I grieve for them." She asked the friend to go in God's peace. After he left, Catherine put on her mantle and said to her brothers: "Come with me and do not be afraid." She walked in their midst and she took them directly through the *contrada* of their enemies.[37] As they walked through, people bowed respectfully to her, and they passed safely through. She took her brothers to the Hospital of Santa Maria in Siena, where she left them with the hospital's lord.[38] She said to her brothers: "You must stay here for three days, but after these days are over you should come home and you will be safe." This happened. In the evening of the third day, peace returned to the region. All those who had taken refuge in Sant'Antonio were either dead or taken hostage. As the outrage calmed down, Catherine's brothers were sentenced to pay a fine of one hundred *fiorini* of gold, which they did, and they survived.

[Chapter 15] A close friend of Catherine told her that here in Florence people, not only the laity but the religious as well, were complaining about her extraordinary life. She responded: "That is what I am looking for—to be tormented during my life. Do not worry, and let them say what they want. I am not sorry for myself but for them."

[Chapter 16] I have heard that, in Siena, Catherine was approached by a religious who at first had honest intentions and who wanted to become friendly with her. He truly cherished and admired her life of holiness. But after a while, he was tempted by the devil. He turned away from his noble goals and was burned by a perverse love. However, she continued in her path of holiness, and she was always pure and saintly in her dealings with him. The man's torments increased every day. One day he decided to kill her when she was in a church. When he was moving toward her in order to commit his deed, it was God's will that another man in the church saw what was going to happen and stopped the malefactor. After a few days the religious left the order and gave up his habit and retreated to his house, which was in a village far away from Siena. There he lived in desperation. Catherine knew of his departure, and she prayed God to have mercy on his soul. While she prayed for him, demons appeared above her screaming and wailing at her: "You are trying to steal that soul from us." And they attacked her by choking her and striking her, but she continued to pray. The man persisted in his desperate way of life until finally he hanged himself.

[Chapter 17] Once a *pinzochera* of Catherine's habit, who was perhaps envious of her virtues or who might have been out of her mind, went around to complain about her, to belittle and to defame her. But when the *pinzochera* suddenly was overcome by a terrible illness, she sent for Catherine so that she could pray to God for her. Catherine remained with the *pinzochera*, serving and helping her during the illness. She stayed until the *pinzochera* recovered.

[Chapter 18] In Lecceto, only four miles away from Siena, is a place for the hermits of Saint Augustine. An English friar called the Bachelor of Lecceto has lived there for more than twelve years. He is a venerable man of great wisdom, sanctity, and solitude. He often lives in the wilderness where he has found caves in remote and harsh areas. He carries books with him so that he avoids conversation with people. He goes to church and then returns to his place. He is a man of mature counsel; he is a friend of God, and a man of great exemplarity. He avoids speaking unless the situation makes words necessary. He has never seen Catherine, or she him, but they are connected by the Holy Spirit and speak of each other with great devotion and respect.[39]

[Chapter 19] In Siena, not long ago, an execution was going to take place in front of Catherine's house. Two malefactors were carried in a cart, their flesh being torn with red-hot pincers. Perhaps because of the pain or for some other reason these two ungodly men cursed God and the saints. With loud voices they called for the devil. The people in Catherine's house ran to the window, and she alone was left behind in the room. When those who had run to the window saw the cruel events, they asked Catherine to join them and to see what was going on. She moved toward the center of the room, where she heard and understood the meaning of the desperate shouting that she had already heard in her room. She did not move on to the window. Instead, she returned to the room to pray in front of a painting of the Madonna. She prayed for the souls of the malefactors with such devotion, love, burning charity, and flowing tears that it is difficult to find words to describe her action. She said to the Crucified: "My Lord, Jesus Christ, the fountain of mercy and forgiveness, cure these hearts that you have created and redeemed with your martyrdom. Please give them to me." After this, she turned to the Madonna: "You are the advocate for all sinners, the Virgin and the Mother of the Son of God. I am praying to you for the malefactors so that you may liberate their souls and let me bear all the torments that you want them to suffer." She continued to pray in this way as the cart moved on to the place of the execution. The malefactors started to shout in a clearly new way and with joyful faces: "Here you are, Catherine—praised be the Lord and his mother, the Virgin Mary. We are sinners and we have deserved these and all other punishments. Our Lord, have mercy on our souls." As the men said these words of devotion and contrition, they were led to the gallows.[40]

[Chapter 20] In Montepulciano there is a monastery for women, which has the holy body of one of its nuns whose name was Agnes.[41] Although Agnes has been dead for sixty years, her whole body has been preserved, and it looks as if she has died just recently. Catherine went to the monastery to leave there a girl whom the monastery accepted as a favor to her. After Catherine had completed her task, the nuns wanted to show her the corpse of the saint. They uncovered the body, and, full of devotion and reverence, Catherine knelt before the saint's feet. She prayed for a while, and all the nuns were respectfully gathered around the holy body. When Catherine had completed her prayers, she moved toward the saint's body in order to kiss the saint's foot. As she bent over the foot, people saw that the holy foot lifted to meet her mouth. Each and every one should see how important this moment of devotion was for the nuns.[42]

[Chapter 21] Once, when Catherine was in a church in the region of Camporegio in Siena and was waiting to hear the Mass a poorly dressed pauper came in and walked straight to her.[43] The pauper asked her for a piece of clothing and said that he was freezing to death. She saw that he was half naked. She replied: "Please wait!" She asked one of her companions to bring a knife and secretly to tear her sleeveless undergarment from her shoulders. She slipped the tunic out from under her dress and gave it to the pauper. The pauper received the tunic, but he did not leave. Instead he said: "But, my lady, I beg you that for the love of God you give me a shirt with which I can cover myself." The companion, who had cut Catherine's undergarment from the shoulders and seen her give it to the pauper, started to reproach the pauper and send him away. But Catherine said to her: "Let him stay." To the pauper she said: "Please wait here!" She went back to her house, which was close to the church, to get a shirt. She then secretly gave it to the pauper. But the pauper still looked unsatisfied. He said: "But, my lady, would you have a pair of sleeves that I could attach to the tunic? I ask you for them in the name of Christ's love." She returned to her home again and tore away a pair of sleeves from a gown that belonged to one of her brothers. She brought the sleeves to the church and gave them to the pauper. But the pauper still did not take his leave. Instead he said: "My lady, you have done well and

God will reward you, but I would be very grateful if you could still give me a bottle of wine that I could take to my family." Once again she said humbly: "Please wait!" She went to her house and took one of the biggest wine bottles, hid it under her mantle, and gave it to the pauper. Finally, the pauper gave her ample thanks and, totally contented, he left in God's peace. The day after, Catherine was praying in the solitude of her room. Suddenly a man appeared to her and asked: "Catherine, do you recognize me?" She looked at him and replied:" I think you look like the pauper who yesterday morning came to ask me for a piece of clothing." After she had said this to him, he disappeared and she was left with a sense of great marvel. Later she told her companion who had reproached the pauper about the apparition.[44]

[Chapter 22] There were some years when there was not enough wine in Siena. During one of them, when the grape harvest was still far away and Catherine's family had only one barrel of wine left, every day she gave some wine to the paupers who came to ask for it. Her brothers scolded her. They asked her to remember that there was only a little wine left, the harvest was still far away, and the family was poor itself. She replied that she would remember, but still she did not stop giving out wine in the same manner. She perhaps gave out even more wine than she used to. Eventually, the barrel was so empty that just a few drops could be poured out. However, the drops did not lose the taste or the color of wine. The wine lasted until it was time to harvest the new wine.[45]

[Chapter 23] Catherine left Florence on the feast day of Saint Peter [June 29] in 1374 and returned to Siena where a great many people were dying.[46] She and her mother returned to their home, where there were eleven children of her deceased brother.[47] Eight children out of the eleven soon followed their father. She buried all these eight children herself and rejoiced: "I shall never lose them again."

[Chapter 24] A friar who was given to Catherine as one of her spiritual guides suddenly fell ill.[48] He bore all the signs of the fatal pestilence, but before reaching the state when he would be bed-ridden, he went to meet Catherine. He said to her: "I am in a bad state, and I ask you to help me. If God now wants to call me to him, I am not suggesting I would resist his will. But, if you think that you can help me, I pray you do so." She immediately put her hand on his head and lifted her eyes to the heavens. She stayed like this for a while. It seemed as if she was somehow outside of herself. When she revived, she said to the friar: "Go, you have been healed." He took his leave. He was totally recovered and free of all the signs of plague that had overtaken him.

[Chapter 25] In a few days another friar, a friend of the healed one, fell ill.[49] He had the same mortal signs as the first friar. He lay down to rest and tried to cure himself with all the possible medicines, but he continued to get worse. The friar who had been healed by Catherine wanted to help and went to Catherine. He said: "So, are you going to let my companion and your other confessor die? His state is fatal, and I ask you to have compassion for him. You know that he has great devotion for you and he trusts you. He is turning to you in the name of Christ so that you pray for him." She then fell into her usual sleeplike prayer, and when she revived, she said to the friar: "Go and tell the friar that he should trust God, who is going to make him well." The friar took his leave and returned to the bedside of his companion. When the friar had left, the companion was desperate for his life, but now the friar found the companion comforted. The companion started to get better immediately. In a short while he was freed from all his ailments.

[Chapter 26] Then Messer Matteo, rector of the Hospital of Misericordia in Siena, fell ill with all the fatal signs of the poisonous pestilence. He was a greatly respected man who led a good and holy life. The whole of Siena was grieving at the prospect of losing him.[50] The doctors came to see him. They found the mortal signs of plague in him, but none of their cures worked. A devout religious went to Catherine and asked her: "Are you, servant of God, going to allow the death of one of the best men in Siena, who has helped and been merciful to the paupers of Christ? I beg you in the name of God and for his mercy that you turn to God so that the city will not be hit with this loss." The man took his leave. Catherine and one of her female companions went to see the ailing man. She comforted him with beatific words that Christ Crucified inflamed in her mind. Before she left, she said: "Rest with a peaceful mind; I trust that God will make you well." Catherine returned to her home. After a while, the religious who had gone to meet Catherine and asked her to pray to God for Messer Matteo went to him without knowing about Catherine's visit. The religious found Matteo back on his feet. The next day Matteo was so much better that he sat at table with his usual companions and this religious and consumed the same bread, wine, and food that was prepared for the others.[51]

[Chapter 27] On the feast of the Assumption of Our Lady in the middle of August 1374, Catherine herself fell mortally ill.[52] However, she did not have any signs of the plague. She became totally numb, not in the manner when in contemplation she was enraptured to the heavens, but through an illness of the body. The pains of her illness became so severe that she felt faint and close to dying. When she sensed that she was leaving her body, she was filled with an immense joy. The thought of entering eternal life filled her with an extremely deep joy and jubilation. However, soon after she started to feel that the spirit of life was returning to her and her sudden suffering was ending. She became melancholy, filled with sadness and pain. She called for the most glorious Virgin Mary and prayed that these signs did not mean that she was to continue living on earth. Our Lady appeared to her and said: "Catherine, my daughter, can you see all the people who stand behind me?" She replied: "Yes, my Lady, I see them all." The Virgin continued: "Now, listen. It is a time for you to choose. My Son wants that you continue to live, and he wants you to guide all these people to eternal life, and they will join the ones you have already saved. This means that you will still need to wait for your death. If you want to die now, my son will not give you the lives of these people. You may now choose between these alternatives." Catherine replied: "My Lady, you know that I do not have my own will. I only want what your Son Jesus wants." The Lady responded: "Be comforted. My Son has given you the lives of all these people you see in front of you, and they will join the ones that were given to you before. When my Son thinks it is the time, he will call you to him." Then Our Lady vanished in the air. Catherine was totally freed from her illness and the all-embracing pain. In due time Catherine revealed the vision to a person of her choice. This person asked: "Would you recognize these people who were shown to you by Our Lady?" Catherine responded: "Yes. When I see them, I will recognize each of them."

[Chapter 28] For about four years that preceded this vision, Catherine swallowed no food. She only put a little bit of food in her mouth. Then she spat it on the ground. Afterward she drank a few gulps of water to rinse her mouth. But after the day of the Assumption of Our Lady in August 1374, she even stopped drinking water. She also refrained almost completely from her habitual chewing of the food. As a result, Catherine presently does not eat or drink. Only on the feast of the Lady in September 1374 did Catherine make an exception.[53] She said that she wanted to celebrate. On that day she put a few pieces of fruit in her mouth in her habitual way and had a gulp of water. This was the last time she ate or drank.

[Chapter 29] I have heard these miracles from well-respected people and have written them down on different occasions over the course of time. On October 10, 1374, I heard another miracle that left me with a great sense of wonder. It goes as follows: Before Catherine came to Florence, a woman of her habit, that is, a *pinzochera* of Saint Dominic, had a wound in her chest.[54] The smell was so disgusting and nauseating that nobody was able to help the woman or even to come close to her. She was abandoned by everybody. Nobody helped her, and she could not get up on her own. When Catherine learned about the situation, she went to meet the woman. Seeing the woman's misery, Catherine decided that she would not abandon her. She stayed with the woman and diligently helped her with all her needs. Catherine worked especially hard at treating the wound on the woman's chest; she cleaned the wound, washed it, medicated it, and did everything that was of help. She stayed with the patient for a long time. It often happens that ailing people attack those who help them, and such happened with this ill woman as well. She turned against Catherine and began to criticize her. The patient soon complained about everything and accused Catherine in all kinds of ways. Catherine suffered everything patiently and continued to treat and serve the woman in all her needs. One day, when she was treating the wound, she smelled a smell so repulsive that she had never sensed anything like it before. The smell made it impossible for Catherine to continue her task. She escaped to the other part of the house. When she thought about what had happened, her conscience began to blame her for leaving the woman, and she immediately returned. She prepared the wine, which was used to clean the wound, in a cup, took a stick, and directed the smelling pus into the cup. She was heard to say [to herself]: "So, Catherine, you abandoned the patient who cannot help herself and you abhorred the pus? I will pay you back with the pus." She lifted the cup on her lips and drank it empty. After that she continued to treat the patient in her usual way, if not even better, and she no longer felt any nausea. On the following night, Christ appeared to Catherine. He said: "I will espouse you, because you are willing to do a thing like that for the love of me." He put a ring on [her finger] and then vanished.[55]

Deo gratias. Amen.

Thomas of Siena:
The Legend of Maria of Venice

Introduced and Translated by Daniel E. Bornstein

Editor's Note: Tommaso di Antonio da Siena—Thomas, son of Anthony, from Siena—is often referred to as well by the surname Caffarini, though there is no evidence that he or his contemporaries ever used it. He was born in the Tuscan city of Siena around 1350 and entered the Dominican order there at the age of fourteen. He left no trace in the documentary record until 1373, when he appears as belonging to the chapter of the Sienese friary of San Domenico in Camporegio, where he also held the post of teacher of logic. Over the next twenty years he circulated through Tuscany—Pisa, Florence, Prato, and, above all, Siena—with stays in Bologna and Genoa as well, figuring as a teacher, preacher, spiritual guide, and, occasionally, prior of a friary. In short, when he landed in Venice in 1394 on his way back from a year-long trip to the Holy Land, he was well established in a career that showed no sign whatsoever of any intellectual, literary, or administrative distinction.

In Venice Thomas found both a home for the rest of his long life, until his death around 1430, and a mission: the spiritual guidance of the groups of penitent women loosely associated with the Dominican Order and the promotion of their way of life. In recent

Note: The translation is based on Fernanda Sorelli's edition of the *Legend* in *La santità imitabile: "Leggenda di Maria da Venezia" di Tommaso da Siena*, in Deputazione di storia patria per le Venezie, Miscellanea di studi e memorie 23 (Venice: Deputazione Editrice, 1984), 150–225. I thank Fernanda Sorelli for granting permission to do the translation on the basis of her edition.

years these penitent women have attracted considerable attention, both from scholars intent on recovering an important element of women's history and expression of female piety, and from spiritual seekers looking for possible models of a lay life of Christian charity and devotion. At the time, however, direction of these small groups of women was anything but a prestigious task, and certainly not the sort of thing that would have appealed to a friar intent on making his way in the order, the church, and the world. If it was entrusted to someone of Thomas's modest abilities, it was surely because nobody else particularly wanted it.

Thomas approached his task from two angles, institutional and literary. From 1396, by appointment of the master general of the Dominican Order, Raymond of Capua, Thomas acted as director of the Dominican penitents in Venice. At the same time he began acquiring texts about female penitent saints. Four years later Thomas embarked on a literary campaign designed to furnish exemplary models for the penitential life and secure for it official approval. He translated from Latin the *vitae* of two Dominican holy women from the late thirteenth and early fourteenth centuries, Giovanna of Orvieto and Margherita of Città di Castello.[1] He prepared an abbreviation of[2] and a supplement to[3] Raymond of Capua's monumental life of the greatest Dominican penitent, Catherine of Siena, and arranged for the first official inquiry into her sanctity, held in Venice between 1411 and 1416.[4] He wrote a history of the Dominican penitents in Venice,[5] in which he invented for them a formal constitution—the so-called Rule of Munio, supposedly written in 1285 or 1286 by the master general of the order, Munio of Zamora—that they had never in fact enjoyed; and he finally secured for them papal approval of that constitution with the bull *Sedis apostolicae* of June 26, 1405.[6]

It was in the context of these efforts that Thomas drafted his most ambitious hagiographical text: *The Legend of Maria of Venice*. Thomas's subject, Maria Sturion, was born around 1379 to a well-to-do, though not noble, Venetian family, and grew into a proper young lady with a normal interest in worldly display. At the age of fifteen or so, she married a man of similar social background, Giannino della Piazza, and moved into the house of her husband's family. The marriage, however, was not a great success; Maria's husband soon went off to the wars near Mantua, abandoning her to the care of his father. Unhappy with this arrangement, Maria returned to her family home. It was at this point that she began to frequent the Dominican Church of Santi Giovanni e Paolo, where she passed her time listening attentively to the sermons of our Thomas of Siena, who became her spiritual director and eventually robed her in the habit of a Dominican penitent. She did not get to wear it for long; her short life came to an end when she died of the plague in 1399, only twenty years old.

Out of this unpromising material Thomas crafted a model of sanctity that would be not just admirable in his readers' eyes but applicable to their lives. In standard hagiographical fashion Thomas briefly sketched the basic biographical features of his subject and then proceeded to describe at far greater length her many virtues, organized in thematic chapters: her devout attendance at Mass and dedication to her prayers; her mortification of the flesh; her assiduous practice of confession and communion; her observance of the religious vows of poverty, chastity, and obedience; her charity for God and neighbor; her great desire to receive the habit of a Dominican penitent; her patience in illness and suffering; and her joyous acceptance of death. In Thomas's presentation Maria was modest and humble, chaste and obedient. She was pious, but not heroically so; one of the greatest signs of her holiness, according to Thomas, was that she always arrived early at the church where he was to preach and stayed awake throughout his interminable sermons. She renounced her youthful worldliness, stripped her clothing of every superfluous ornament, and devoted herself to charitable activities, though always with the moderation urged by her spiritual advisor. Thomas credited her with the virtuous performance of everything she intended to do for God and neighbor, even if she didn't actually do it because her confessor—Thomas—advised against it out of concern for her health and safety, so that *not* doing these pious works became evidence of her great virtue of obedience. And he persuaded Maria to "become poor" by turning over all her possessions and property rights to her parents, with whom she continued to live; the family lost nothing of its patrimony, while she continued to enjoy all the comforts of home.

In Thomas's carefully crafted biography, Maria served a dual purpose. She transmuted into imitable form the inimitable sanctity of her own model, Catherine of Siena.[7] In Thomas's presentation, *anyone* could be a Sister of Penance, with minimal effort and no great personal sacrifice. In place of Catherine's extravagant self-mortifications, Maria performed measured austerities; instead of being rapt in ecstatic visions, she walked to church with modestly downcast eyes. In short—and this was Thomas's second point—she exemplified the way in which any pious woman could live by the rules governing the Dominican Order of Penance, which Thomas was eagerly promoting in the very years that he was counseling Maria and writing her biography. Anyone who wanted to know what the rule's precepts meant in practice could turn to Thomas's *Legend of Maria of Venice* and find there a living exemplar of decent, well-bred, and nondisruptive piety. All in all, Maria seems to have been quite an ordinary young woman, but this very ordinariness made her an extremely ductile and easily generalized model for the penitent way of life.

Thomas's interest in Maria was not strictly utilitarian, however, and one of the striking features of this *Legend* is how openly he expresses his emotional responses. Passage after passage reveals with transparent clarity the barely sublimated feelings of this man in his late forties, at the mid-point of a not particularly distinguished career, for a young woman in her late teens who showed every sign of being exceptionally impressed by and devoted to him—and who was, moreover, extremely attractive, as he says repeatedly. Even more, perhaps, Thomas's identification with Maria gave him a vehicle for voicing, through the longings of this young woman for her celestial spouse, his own emotional commitment to the God he served all his life long. This, it seems to me, is the sense of the elaborate speech in Chapter 11, in the very center of the *Legend*, in which Maria professes her love of God directly to God in words that are very obviously those of a scholastically trained preaching friar.

Something, at least, of what Maria meant to Thomas, in both practical and personal terms, should be clear by now, but what did she get out of their relationship in return? At the most basic level, her involvement with the Dominicans gave her something to do when her marriage collapsed and she returned to her parents' home. Maria heard about the excellent preaching of the friars from her mother, who attended their sermons regularly, and her desire to hear these sermons for herself gave her an excuse to get out of the house. It also gave her license to move quite freely throughout the city, tracing as she went the geography of her pious attachments. She began by shuttling between her home in the heart of the city, between Piazza San Marco and the Rialto Bridge, and the nearby Dominican Church of Santi Giovanni e Paolo. Indeed, one might guess that her spiritual affiliation was as much an accident of geography as anything else; if her parents had happened to live near Santa Maria Gloriosa dei Frari, she would probably have become a Franciscan penitent. But she also roamed the city more widely: to hear Thomas preach at San Barnaba, across the Grand Canal; to talk with the nuns at the Dominican convent of Corpus Domini, on a spit of land at the farthest edge of Venice; and to visit her friend and fellow penitent Caterina Marioni at her house near Santa Maria della Carità. Young women of good family did not normally wander about like this, imperiling their safety and honor. Maria's desire for religious services gave her a socially acceptable reason to venture forth, and her religious identity and devout bearing protected her as she moved through the winding alleys of Venice.

Assuming a religious identity also did something to restore her damaged honor. Her parents were making the best of a bad situation when they brought her back home to live with them, in what could not have been a happy household. The atmosphere must have been heavy with doubts, misgivings, and at least implied recriminations on the part of both Maria and her parents, to which would be added the wondering looks and critical whispers of her siblings. Maria's growing religious identity and involvements gave her some leverage in the moral economy of the family and household—and got her out of some distasteful chores.

Outside the household, as well, Maria's ostentatious piety allowed her to feel morally superior to those around her who might sniff or sneer at her awkward social situation, embarrassingly abandoned by her feckless husband. Thomas does indicate that there were people who wondered who she thought she was to be putting on such airs. These detractors remain shadowy, faceless, and name-

less, in contrast to the well-defined circuit of her friends and asso-
ciates. Maria's religious devotions brought her into regular contact
with like-minded people, often female and almost always
Dominican: the Dominican friars with whom she never spoke,
admiring them from a discreet distance; the Dominican nuns of
Corpus Domini, who accepted her for burial and said they would
have accepted her in life; the Dominican penitents with whom she
circulated.

Thomas tells us the names of these penitents, and Fernanda
Sorelli's painstaking research in the Venetian archives has defined
their socioeconomic features.[8] A very few, such as Marina Contarini
and her husband, Antonio Soranzo, belonged to wealthy and distinguished patrician families. More typically, Maria's penitent circle
comprised people like Maria herself: those from families of shop-
keepers or local merchants who were fairly well off, but not exces-
sively so, and who did not belong to the patrician class (though they
were not without ties to it). Many of the women associated with
Maria as Dominican penitents also came from families newly
arrived in Venice, with weak and uncertain roots there. Their position on the edges of Venetian good society may explain why they
sought this form of association, and why they gravitated in particular to someone marked as a Tuscan outsider the instant he opened
his mouth.

Thomas initially wrote his *Legend of Maria of Venice* in Latin,
the language of official learning. He himself then translated it into
Italian to make it available to women who, like Maria, could read
the vernacular or, failing that, have it read to them. My translation
is based on the Italian version, not simply because of the quality of
Fernanda Sorelli's excellent critical edition, but because it was
intended for the use of other women like Maria who might aspire
to imitate her life.[9] However, I have also consulted the Latin version, especially for linguistic guidance: Thomas's Italian is often so
mechanically transposed from Latin that one can grasp his sense
most readily by turning back to the Latin original.[10] The content,
however, clings far less closely to that of the Latin original. As in his
borrowings from Thomas Aquinas and other Scholastic authors,
Thomas's borrowings from his own text are often loose and approx-
imate: he constantly employs two Italian near synonyms to render

110

one Latin word, drops or adds phrases, inserts similes or brief asides, and in other such small ways manipulates his source text. The vast majority of these alterations are insignificant, and I have made no note of them in preparing this translation. However, Thomas does make some major changes, both of omission and commission, dropping an occasional paragraph from the Italian and, more significant, adding several long didactic passages. These I have duly pointed out in the notes. On the other hand, while doing my best to render his meaning and even his style, I have silently pruned some of Thomas's verbal excesses, broken his long tendrils of sentences into units more acceptable in English, and ruthlessly excised innumerable manifestations of one of his more annoying verbal tics: the constant use of "the said," "the aforementioned," and "the aforesaid." In short, whereas Thomas's translation of his text from Latin into Italian was mechanical but not faithful, I have done my best to be faithful but not mechanical in rendering the Italian into readable English.

Thomas of Siena:
The Legend of Maria of Venice

This is the table of contents of the following Legend of a certain blessed Maria of the Sisters of the Order of Penance of Messer Saint Dominic in Venice

The prologue or preamble of the said Legend, which begins "Wishing, etc."

About the proper name of this blessed woman, and about her origins, and also her homeland and her relatives, and about their names and lineage: Chapter One, which begins "In the aforementioned year, etc."

About the conduct of this woman beloved [of God] during her childhood years, and how she was given in marriage by her parents and entered the household of her husband's father: Chapter Two, which begins "Despite being, etc."

About how this beloved woman returned to the home of her father and mother and resided there for a certain period of time, principally because of her husband's absence: Chapter Three, which begins "The new husband, etc."

About this beloved woman's remarkable, sudden, and genuine conversion to God; and about some holy signs and effects testifying not only to the authenticity of that conversion, but also to her future holy conduct: Chapter Four, which begins "Having returned, etc."

About this beloved woman's progress in the way of God, and about the perfect desire and pleasure she felt in hearing the word of God, especially in preaching: Chapter Five, which begins "This woman beloved of the Lord then, etc."

About this beloved woman's devout hearing of the Mass and the other divine offices in church, and about her devout recitation of her office in church and at home: Chapter Six, which begins "This beloved woman, etc."

About this beloved woman's austerity of corporal life, and about her mortification of the flesh concerning various things: Chapter Seven, which begins "With admirable fervor, etc."

About this beloved woman's devout confession and communion, and her assiduousness in reading and writing and keeping vigil in prayer: Chapter Eight, which begins "In order not only to obey, etc."

About this beloved woman's loving desire to fulfill and observe Christ's counsel—that is, all three of the vows of holy orders—even before she was robed in the religious habit: Chapter Nine, which begins "Not only did Christ's beloved delight, etc."

About this beloved woman's great charity for her neighbor: Chapter Ten, which begins "Finding herself as if transformed, etc."

About the perfection of this beloved woman's charity toward her God, and her full participation in all the other virtues: Chapter Eleven, which begins "Just as this beloved woman burned, etc."

About the singular devotion and affection that this beloved woman felt for the habit of Saint Dominic, and the persistent requests she made to have it, and how she begged for it and with the greatest festivity and solemnity received it: Chapter Twelve, which begins "Among the other things, etc."

About the physical infirmities that this beloved woman avidly and joyously bore for Christ; and how in the final one, which was the illness of the plague, she passed happily from this life to her desired Spouse: Chapter Thirteen, which begins "After this beloved woman converted, etc."

About the devout burial of this beloved woman: Chapter Fourteen, which begins "Since (as was said above) this beloved woman had passed away, etc."

About various things that happened after the said burial; and about certain visions, some of which occurred while this beloved woman was mortally ill, others after her burial, and one shortly after she took the habit of Saint Dominic: Chapter Fifteen, which begins "A few days after her burial, etc."

About the universal grace that this beloved woman generally had in life and in death and afterward, both in the eyes of God and those of persons of every sex, condition, and status: Chapter Sixteen, the last, which begins "How much grace, etc."

Here ends the table of the prologue and of all the chapters of this Legend.

Here begins the prologue of the Legend of the holy woman Maria of Venice, of the Sisters of the habit of Penance of Messer Saint Dominic. Thanks be to God. Amen.

Wishing, in keeping with the grace that the Lord shall grant, to tell the story of a woman who in recent times was exceptionally beloved by Messer Jesus Christ—that is, principally, her wonderful conversion and the commendable manner of her life thereafter and also her happy passing, doing this for the edification of all the faithful and as an example to be imitated by some people, especially those women who might wish to take or have indeed taken the decision to live in her manner and her habit, that of the penitents of Messer Saint Dominic—it occurred to me to begin with the saying of the apostle [Paul] in the first chapter of his First Letter to Timothy, where he says: "Fidelis sermo, etc." That is, "The saying is sure and worthy of full acceptance, that Christ Jesus came into the world to save sinners" [1 Tim 1:15]—and not only of both sexes, but also of every condition and status, since the apostle says in the second chapter of that letter that God "desires everyone to be saved and to come to the knowledge of the truth," in which complete and perfect knowledge rests our final beatitude and salvation [1 Tim 2:4].

Now, God has efficaciously provided and procured this truly desirable work of human salvation not only through his own self, whether by inspiration or by coming in the flesh, nor simply through the ministry of the angelic spirits, but even by means of mere men, his servants, from the beginning of the world right down to the present. That is, by means of the patriarchs and prophets, apostles and evangelists, doctors and preachers—and not only ancient ones, but also by means of those modern preachers sent by God in the fullness of time, who belong to that order of which Messer Saint Dominic was leader and triumphant patriarch. That order, the Order of Preaching Friars, acknowledges that it was instituted and ordained by Saint Dominic for this purpose—that is, for the salvation of sinful souls—as appears in the prologue to the constitutions of the said order.[11]

Of that order I, Brother Thomas of Siena, have been a least and unworthy part for nearly forty years. In 1395, having visited the Holy Sepulcher, I came with the Venetian galleys to Venice, to our friary of Santi Giovanni e Paolo.[12] I began to preach there starting that same year and subsequently exercised the office of preacher in many other places and churches of Venice. Since our friary of Santi Giovanni e Paolo and likewise our order's convent of Corpus Domini had been restored to a remarkably diligent observance of the rule, I found many people, men and women alike, put in a notably good and holy state of mind by the example of that regular observance and eager to hear the word of God.[13] My impression was shared by others, particularly the friars of our order, and above all by a special [spiritual] father of mine, Brother Giovanni Dominici, the leading zealot and promoter of the regular observance.

It so happened that, for the love of Christ, many of these well-disposed people dedicated themselves to leading a wonderfully austere life while still remaining in the world. Many others left the world entirely and gave themselves for Christ to the high and arduous observance of the religious life, even against the wishes of their families, so that they might more swiftly fly to and attain that celestial kingdom they knew and desired. To speak more plainly about these people, you should know that among those of masculine gender, so many took the habit of the preaching friars that within a short space of time our order received more than eighty friars in the friaries of Santi Giovanni e Paolo and San Domenico. More than a few of them attracted considerable attention and fame for their lives and learning and even, in some cases, for evidence of miracles. Some of this is recorded in a little book I composed that deals specifically with the way of life of the Brothers and Sisters of Penance of Messer Saint Dominic—a little book that I shall refer to from time to time in what follows, in a few chapters of this Legend.[14] Similarly, so many women fled not only from the secular world, but also from various other nunneries in Venice, and out of desire for their own salvation entered this convent of Corpus Domini, which Brother Giovanni Dominici organized and founded in 1394, that before the year 1398 was out the sisters in that convent of Corpus Domini had reached the number of eighty or thereabouts. Some of them have already gone to heaven, but many, many others have lived and continue to live right down to the present a life more angelic than human, about which it is inappropriate to elaborate any further here and now.[15]

In much the same way, many people, men and women alike, also received from me, with the authority of the master [general] of our order, the habit of the Brothers[16] and Sisters of Penance of Saint Dominic.[17] Nearly all of them have been persons of outstanding virtue and outstanding lives, as God is my witness (and also as one can see in that little book I mentioned just now, which discusses this). One of them was this woman especially beloved by God, whose story (as was said above, at the outset) we have gladly taken upon ourselves to recount separately in this Legend, to the honor and glory of our Lord, Redeemer, and Savior Christ Jesus and his saints. May Jesus with the Father and the Holy Spirit live and reign as God forever and ever. Amen.

With the prologue ended, here begins the Legend of the blessed Maria.

Chapter One: First, about her proper name and her origins, and also concerning her family and also their name and their lineage.

In the aforementioned year or rather in the year immediately following—that is, in 1396—while I was preaching in the said friary of Santi Giovanni e Paolo, among the other well-disposed persons I came into contact with a woman truly beloved by the Lord. She was born in the city of Venice and known by the proper name of Maria, or rather, Madonna Maria. She came from a fairly wealthy and prominent family. Her father was named Messer Nicolò, of the house of Sturion, a man very active in the spice trade and quite well known among the citizenry of Venice. Her mother was named Madonna Giacoma, a woman of exceptional prudence and outstanding honesty and reputation from a good and noteworthy lineage and family from the city of Verona.[18]

Chapter Two: About the conduct of this beloved woman during her childhood years, and how she was given in marriage by her parents and entered the household of her husband's father.

Despite being a girl or young lady of exceptional probity and honesty, adorned with good habits and certainly far more virtuous and well brought up than other girls, nonetheless when this beloved woman had grown to girlhood in the house of her father and mother, she still gave herself to, occupied herself with, and took delight in those vanities of bodily adornment in which adolescents commonly find pleasure. She was drawn all the more to these things in that she was better looking than other girls and young ladies; and on top of that she was encouraged and incited by her mother and father, who constantly urged her toward a worldly marriage. And so it finally came to pass that they married her to a young man named Giannino from a rather prominent family in Venice, named the house of Piazza, whose father was considered to be a very wealthy man.[19] Thus, after certain things that are customarily done between husbands and brides and their kin, this woman found herself led to and brought into the house of the father of her new husband, Giannino, when she was about fifteen years old.

Chapter Three: About how this beloved woman returned to the home of her father and mother and resided there for a certain period of time because of her husband's absence.

The new husband of this beloved woman was not just a little dissolute but very much so; and even though he had taken a wife, he nonetheless continued to indulge his vices. As a consequence, he got on very poorly with his father, just as he had before he took a wife. So it was that Giannino decided to leave his father and his wife and to set out from Venice toward Mantua, where war was expected or had already broken out between the lord of that city and the duke of Milan.[20] Having purchased horses and arms so that he could draw good pay and make a profit or win honor in the world's eyes, as is the custom with soldiers, he put into execution what he had planned. For this reason, his wife, unhappy with being left in his father's house and not being treated with the decency she deserved, departed from there on her mother's advice and in her company soon returned to her own house, that of her parents. All this was ordained by he who dispenses everything to his beloved and chosen ones and converts it all to good.

Chapter Four: About this beloved woman's remarkable and sudden conversion to God; and about some holy signs testifying not only to the authenticity of that conversion but also to her future holy conduct.

Having returned (as was said) to her parents' home, which was located near our friary of Santi Giovanni e Paolo, where I was preaching at that time, it happened that this beloved woman (who was then about sixteen years old) heard about our sermons from her mother, who attended them regularly. When this beloved woman began to give ear to this, she likewise started humbly and sweetly to beg her mother, even with a sort of holy wheedling, to please take her along to hear those sermons for the love of God. Her mother finally decided to grant her wishes and give her that consolation, taking her along with her to the sermon. Listening to it with exceptional attentiveness, all of a sudden she turned herself completely from the world and gave herself to God so marvelously that her mother and I (as those to whom this was more clear and more immediately manifest than to others) were amazed and stunned by it.

After her great and true contrition and her humble and complete confession, among the other signs of her true conversion and penitence from the outset was this one, which her mother (who deserves complete faith) once told me confidentially. That is, one day about the time of her conversion, this beloved woman returned home from the sermon with her mother as if she were completely absorbed in God. Leaving her mother and everyone else in the household, she went upstairs to the upper portion of their residence where her room was—in effect, a little chapel that had been granted to her and set aside for her use. Entering it, she took all her clothes and, with marvelous fervor of spirit, set about removing and cutting off all their vain and superfluous worldly ornaments. She had spent a good deal of time at this when her mother, wondering why she was taking so much longer than usual before joining the rest of the household, finally went up to look for her and, entering her room, found her and saw what she was doing so energetically. The mother was more than a little—in fact, quite a bit—upset by this so that bursting with indignation she began to scold her and say: "Young lady, what do you think you're doing? If you're not interested in these things, why don't you think about those around you, especially your sisters, who don't share your attitude? Couldn't these clothes be of some use to them?" This was quite true, since they had not only her two sisters, but also a goddaughter in the household, all of whom were looking to get married.

That notwithstanding, this beloved woman replied to her mother with the utmost humility and sweetness: "O sweet good mother, for God's sake don't get upset over this. I'm acting right now on this good impulse, both so that I might grow in it from good to better and so that I might cut off and remove from myself any occasion for future temptation that might befall me, of ever again tricking myself out in these trappings." The mother heard these words and was so struck within herself by the wisdom of this response that her mind was amazed. She quietly reflected on that reply, storing up in her heart not only her daughter's words but also her actions, and pondering it all with exceptional discretion and maturity. Though she was careful not to show anything openly, nevertheless within herself she remained full of the greatest admiration and edification.

Another sign of no less importance appeared subsequently in this beloved woman, evidencing and shedding light not only on her true conversion but also on her future life of good and holy conversation. That is that from then on she began to take such pleasure in spiritual and divine things that not only could she find no pleasure or delight in any worldly thing, but she despised them all and abhorred them as if they were excrement, like that true convert or *converso* Saint Paul.[21]

Chapter Five: About this beloved woman's progress in the way of God, and about the perfect desire and pleasure she felt in hearing the word of God, especially in preaching.

This woman beloved of the Lord then proceeded step by step in the way of God so virtuously that she finally came to be raised and drawn to the heights of perfection (as was shown by evident signs, which shall be clarified in what follows). Thus, having entered on her seventeenth year and begun to frequent our sermons assiduously, she was impelled with fervent desire to hear them without missing any. In order that she might better fulfill her desire, she begged her father and mother with such humble and sweet insistence that she finally convinced them to let her remove and set aside all her juvenile clothing and to wear instead the green mantle and other vestments of mature women. She was able to be all the more persuasive because in that time of pestilence two of her sisters had passed from this life, as had a thirteen- or fourteen-year-old brother, all of whom she sent before herself to the Lord with great gladness, having first taken every care to make sure that they all received and were armed with all the ecclesiastical sacraments.[22]

After this, her good disposition and fervor increased so much that she would eagerly and promptly set about putting into effect anything that she thought she might be able to do that would honor and please God, whether in church or at home or wherever she might find herself. Among the other things mentioned, there was this quite exceptionally commendable and marvelous one: for the whole period of four years and more after she decided to listen to our sermons, she always and without fail followed me to hear them wherever I might have gone to preach. She listened so attentively and with such eagerness of mind that she seemed to hear them longingly not just with the ears of her body; indeed, she seemed to ruminate and chew and savor and swallow every word of the sermon with an admirable intellectual and interior comprehension and took them right into the intimate recesses of her heart, laying claim to an inner jubilation and mental joy that matched her outer one. Every day she grew more ravenous and more avid for the word of God, and such was her persistence, perseverance, and vigilance that no one—neither myself nor anyone else—ever saw her doze off, or even begin to nod, however long she had to wait for the preaching or however long the sermon might be. Nor did she ever miss a sermon, either during or outside of Lent, howsoever inclement the weather or distant the place might be. On the contrary, she always arrived early and silently took her usual place or some other one better suited for hearing, and she never left the sermon on account of rain or bad weather. Indeed, the fouler the weather or more distant the sermon, she went to the sermon that much more joyfully.

When the Lenten season approached, her great thirst to hear preaching led her not just to get up before dawn, especially when she had to go some distance that morning, but sometimes, because of her overflowing desire, she even left the house before daybreak, at the faintest dawn. When she was told that for God's sake she should be more careful and more watchful, since she was young and especially attractive in body (as she was in mind), with her gracious humility she replied sweetly, saying that by the grace of her eternal spouse she would be in his good company and under his protection. She said this meaning a mental cell, about which she had received from me a certain written text that she copied with her own hand and studied carefully.[23] Wherever she went or stayed, she was placed in that cell mentally by intellectual meditation. She felt as if she were in the presence of Christ and the Queen of Heaven and all the angels and saints and the whole court triumphant and militant, whether she was physically alone or accompanied by other women and female companions making the pilgrimage of this life with her.

Also, when it happened that she needed to look after her father (because he was old and often suffered from gout and because he liked to have her wait on him), she performed that service so thoughtfully and sweetly that she then graciously asked her father and mother as well and obtained from them her devotion and her desire: to be able to go hear the sermon. This beloved woman knew so well how to humble herself to her parents in order to obtain this favor that sometimes her mother kindly agreed to remain home and look after the father in her stead, so that the beloved woman might receive the complete consolation of being able to go hear the word of God, which she so loved and desired. For this beloved woman was truly another Mary Magdalene, who would have been pleased to remain forever at the feet of the Lord Jesus in order to hear his words [Luke 10:39]. And also, for sure and certain, if she had lived at that time, she would have been among those devout Marys who followed Christ Jesus and provided for him out of their means, out of desire to hear his holy doctrine.

Nor did this great desire of hers to hear the word of God arise out of any curiosity for knowledge or any other vanity, but only to please God and also because she thirsted to know God's will for her and, knowing it, to fulfill it completely and to put it into effect in keeping with what she heard from the preacher, which she valued just as if it came from the mouth of God himself. Hence, sometimes when she was speaking with her mother, she would say: "O good sweet mother, if you only knew with what delight and pleasure I hear the word of God!" Then she would add: "Take it for certain, mother, that just as I desire and delight in hearing it, so I long to fulfill it; so that everything I hear, I want it all and want to fulfill it all." And with all her strength she strove to do just that, in conformity with her celestial spouse, who came to fulfill the law and the divine word, and in obedience to the apostle Saint James, who commanded and said in his epistle: "Be doers of the word, and not merely hearers" [Jas 1:22].

From this it followed that when this beloved woman saw that others heard the word of God eagerly, efficaciously, and devoutly as

121

she did, she was filled with joy—not only by herself and within herself, but openly sharing her joy and celebrating with her companions, just as she grieved and grew sad at the opposite. Also, when she was able to speak with me and hear the word of God after her sacramental confession or on some other occasion apart from the sermon, she received such refreshment and joy from it that even though she was physically worn and wasting away as a result of her fasting and other austerities, nonetheless she grew fat on it mentally—and even physically became all full, festive, and rosy, as if she had recently or just then risen from great bodily banquets and solemn wedding feasts. In conclusion, wishing to put an end to this chapter, I confess before God and men that I do not believe I have ever seen a woman of such condition who could match this one in her eager, fervent, and perfect attention to the word of God. In this she demonstrated perfectly clearly that she numbered among the women of God and among those of whom the incarnate Word said: "Beati quelli qui audiunt verbum Dei et custodiunt illud" [Blessed rather are those who hear the word of God and obey it—Luke 11:28].

Chapter Six: About this beloved woman's devout hearing of the Mass and the other divine offices in church, and about her recitation of her office in church and at home.

This beloved woman surpassed many others in devoutly hearing the holy Mass and the other divine offices; whether in her parish church or that of Santi Giovanni e Paolo or whatever other church she found herself (although she most often frequented that of Santi Giovanni e Paolo), however many Masses or offices she heard, she always heard them all kneeling and in silence, and all the while she either prayed or meditated or contemplated or said her hours. It was obvious that if on some occasions she might have been able to or it had been allowed, she would have stayed like that all day long; but remaining there only so long as the hour was decent and obedience allowed it, she always kept her face humbly lowered toward the ground. She did this in such a manner that from the very beginning of her conversion, before she wore the green mantle or received the habit of Saint Dominic—that is, while she still wore a little hood and cloak as is the custom of Venetian girls and young brides, although even then she wore everything with the greatest modesty and without slashes or other vanities, all of which she had removed (as described above in Chapter Four)—nonetheless there was not a single person who could ever look her fully in the face. And this was the case not only while she remained like this in church, but also outside of church, whether going or coming.

It is true that she was better able to do and achieve this after she started wearing the mantle mentioned, and subsequently the habit of Saint Dominic, both because of their veiling and because she adopted the practice of drawing part of the mantle's edge over her head. Since this beloved woman managed to keep her body all covered in this manner, she found herself all the more able to keep her mind entirely composed and tranquil, free from all distractions. She always occupied herself with her holy meditations, including that mental cell which the preceding chapter touched on briefly. In this respect this beloved woman was truly like a mirror and an outstanding example to all those who saw her walking or standing in the manner mentioned—and this not only for girls or adolescents or young ladies, but even for mature and elderly women, and for religious as well as worldly persons. Above all, those who had heard something about her were all greatly edified not only by her other devout actions but also by her composed and withdrawn bearing, even if some criticized it at first.[24]

Nearly every day this beloved woman recited carefully and devoutly the entire office of the Virgin according to the usage of the Preaching Friars, in church and at home. Likewise, each day she made herself better able and more ready to say the other office, that of our Lord and the other saints. To better accomplish this, a breviary according to the usage of the Preaching Friars was purchased in her name in the city of Siena. That breviary, together with some of her other things, is presently preserved and cherished by the Sisters of Penance of Saint Dominic in Venice, out of reverence for her.

Chapter Seven: About this beloved woman's austerity of corporal life, and about her mortification of the flesh concerning various things.

With admirable fervor, this woman beloved of God longed to act upon what she heard in holy sermons, and not only (as just said) by busying and occupying herself with hearing and saying the

Divine Office, but also concerning austerity of corporal life. She strove to observe not just the life of the Preaching Friars of Santi Giovanni e Paolo or their nuns of Corpus Domini in Venice; she even sought to follow, to the best of her abilities, the austerities of life of the blessed Catherine of Siena, Sister of Penance of Saint Dominic.[25] Thus, she never ate meat so long as she was healthy; even when she was ill, she would not eat it except by special command. By the same token, she never wore fur in any season and observed the greatest fasts; she always slept (when she slept) dressed and almost on her knees and out of bed, on some planks—except when she happened to be sick with some serious illness, and then on account of holy obedience. She also covered her flesh day and night not simply with clothing of wool or ordinary haircloth, but rather with especially coarse haircloth.

Sometimes I questioned her, saying: "Tell me, how can you wear such rough hair shirts so constantly?" With a face all happy and smiling, in her dovelike simplicity she answered me humbly and sweetly, saying: "Dear father, I tell you truthfully that I don't feel it at all, as if I were wearing none of these things." And indeed great things seemed very tiny to her, because of the superabundance of her fervor. Thus, when one of her and my sisters in Christ among these nuns secretly gave her a whip with bits of metal and a good thick brass chain, she often beat herself with that whip and bound herself with that chain, girding her flesh to the very end of her life. These objects—that is, hair shirts, chain, and whip—are preserved to this very day by the Sisters of Penance of Saint Dominic in Venice, out of reverence for her.

Here it should be particularly noted that the penitence and austere life of this beloved woman were all the more marvelous and commendable in that she was of youthful age and always nourished on and accustomed to sensual pleasures and delicacies. Moreover, she resided in the home of her parents, who led a particularly delightful life and by whom she was especially loved and coddled. Nonetheless, with admirable joy and admirable energy and the agreement of the entire household, she supported these hardships and used them to mortify her sensuality.

She also strove as best she could to maintain silence, not only in holy places and on the street or at set times, but even, having heard of the silence of the blessed Catherine mentioned above, taking it upon herself to maintain complete silence for an entire Lent, both at home and outside the house.[26] And so she did, despite often having to care for her father and do things around the house, using certain gestures and signs instead of words and for that whole time never speaking without special permission or command. This Lent was the one during which I preached at San Barnaba in Venice, where she could be found every day; afterward, during the summer immediately following, she passed to heaven.[27]

Chapter Eight: About this beloved woman's devout confession and communion, and also her assiduousness in reading and writing and vigilance in prayer.

In order not only to obey the commandments of God and the church, but also to accustom herself to observing those of holy religion, on the advice and instructions of me, her unworthy spiritual father, this woman, beloved of Christ, did not simply dedicate herself ever more each day to hearing and saying the office and performing these austerities: with the greatest desire she also craved and sought to refresh her spirit with the food of sacramental communion. With the benevolent consent of her parish priest and myself, she made use of that grace with great happiness and joy, receiving communion on the great feast days of the year—as the nuns of Corpus Domini are accustomed to do, and those friars of Santi Giovanni e Paolo who are not priests. She received communion with such devotion that it aroused great admiration in those persons who saw her when she communicated.

She approached sacramental confession in the same fashion, with truly exceptional humility and heartfelt contrition, especially when the time for her communion approached. She confessed in the way I had taught her, making her confession in few words with great wisdom, reciting explicitly that in which she felt she had particularly offended her celestial spouse between one confession and the next, and then implicitly including all her general offenses. Thus, she first confessed that in which she had especially sinned, whether in cogitation (that is, in whatever she might have spoken aloud) or in action (that is, in whatever else she might have actually done) or in omission (that is, in anything she might have neglected to do, whether internally or externally, that she felt specifically obliged to do).[28] Then she acknowledged in general her guilt for that in which she felt she had offended and was offending her Creator, such as ingratitude for God's many gifts, wasting time, and not seeing herself respond to and love God with everything, in everything, and for everything and especially above everything, as she knew she should have done, etc.

Here the devout reader should note that one can classify the ways which a person can offend God or oneself or one's neighbor in one or more of the aforementioned four principal modes, that is, cogitation, locution, operation, and omission. For once one has reached the age of the use of free will, a person can be guilty of some interior deed of thought, sensual pleasure, or consent to vice, and this may be in various ways. The first is by thinking, enjoying, or accepting some good thing (that is, *de genere bonorum*) or something morally indifferent, but with a bad intention or in some other wicked conditions. The second is by thinking (and so on) about some wicked thing *de genere malorum* (that is, about whatever sort of sin it may be), with either a good or bad intention or some other wicked circumstance. The third is when the person is guilty in both one way and the other. In addition to this interior act of cognition and so on, a person can also be guilty of another, exterior act, that of speech, and this likewise can be in the aforesaid three ways. Also, in addition to vicious [speech] acts, a person can be guilty of some other act done externally, by whichever sense or limb it may be other than the tongue, and this likewise can be in the aforesaid ways. In addition to all the aforementioned forms of acts of commission, a person can also be guilty of omission, either specifically or in general; that is, omitting to do that which a person is specifically obliged to do or that which in general is obligatory for all Christians. And this can be in three ways: the first is neglecting entirely that which one is obliged to do; the second is neglecting it in part; and the third is performing negligently or halfheartedly all or part of what one is obliged to do.

Thus, absolutely all the offenses that a person might commit either directly against God or against oneself or against one's neighbor, and all their gradations, are reduced or can be reduced to the aforesaid four principal modes and included in them. And the general confession that is commonly said was organized along these lines, to wit: "Confiteor Deo et beate Marie et beato Dominico et omnibus sanctis et tibi patri, quia peccavi nimis cogitaçione, locuçione, opere et obmissione mea culpa; precor te, ora pro me vel absolvas me."[29]

To further clarify the things mentioned, here one should also know that one can sin in one sort of guilt in all four of the aforesaid principal modes—that is, in the act of thinking, speaking, doing, and failing to do the virtuous deed rather than the vicious one, and the guilt is that much greater as it proceeds by the said acts and degrees. It is also greater insofar as the person deviates farther from rectitude or from the rule or order of reason, in any one of the said acts or in all of them together or in the omission of virtuous acts. It is also greater insofar as reason is disordered concerning a nobler object or a nobler end. The guilt is also greater insofar as it runs contrary to a greater virtue. It is also greater insofar as the circumstances are more detestable, and insofar as the person intends greater harm by his offense, and insofar as the person who offends or is offended may happen to be greater, and insofar as the said offenses may happen to be committed more voluntarily, deliberately, and consciously and with a more perverse will, and also when the offense happens to be committed more frequently or habitually, or even obstinately.[30]

This beloved woman was informed about all this, so that (as was said) she confessed fully and completely in few words between one sacramental confession and the next, exaggerating what she did or failed to do as if her offenses and guilt had been very serious indeed, whereas they were quite small and venial. And whoever reads this should be aware that from the conversion of this beloved woman right down to the end of her bodily life, in her confession I always found her to be as pure as if she were a four- or five-year-old girl or child, especially in matters of sensual concupiscence, to the point that she did not seem to be in the flesh. In effect, the entire sin of this beloved woman—if it can be called sin—amounted to this: the desire and wish to pass from this life, both so that she would no longer be able to offend her God and so that she would be able to love and praise him as she wished, immediately and entirely, without the slightest shortcoming, forever and ever.

In addition to this, since she knew how to read somewhat and kept learning to do so even better for as long as she remained in this world, not only did she read the Divine Office (as was said earlier), but she also devoted herself to other devout and holy lessons, according to what I had arranged for her. Since at first she did not know how to write at all, I gave her some instructions in this regard, and in a short time she learned how to write so well that later, with my permission, she wrote to certain Sisters of Penance of Saint Dominic in Pisa. She also wrote certain other devout things, some of which are now kept by the Sisters of Penance of Saint Dominic in Venice, with her hair shirts and other things.

Soon this beloved woman became so assiduous and vigilant in prayer that always, after the recitation of the Divine Office or when she had written or read for a while, she would give herself entirely to prayer—so much so that her mother, noting this and not wanting to be responsible for drawing her away from such good things, sometimes deliberately saw to it that she was not bothered with the physical chores of the household, even though this beloved woman was always as quick to obey her mother as she was me, receiving her instructions as coming from my vicar and lieutenant as well as her mother. I recall how her mother, speaking with me at times, told me that she considered it much better for the household that her daughter dedicate herself to prayer, to which she was evidently so drawn, than occupy herself with the physical tasks of the household. She further added that since she saw her so steadfastly inclined and drawn to prayer and to celestial and divine things, it must necessarily make her slow, remiss, and tardy about material and human things—if, that is, there did not happen to be some special obligation of piety or neighborly charity or (as was mentioned) the commandment of holy obedience did not intervene.[31] To conclude this chapter, when she suffered one of the infirmities to be discussed later (to wit, a great swelling of the knees), this was obviously judged to have befallen her because she remained on her knees almost constantly, whether she found herself in church or at home, as shall be narrated later, at the beginning of the thirteenth chapter.

Chapter Nine: About this beloved woman's loving desire to fulfill and observe Christ's counsel—that is, all three of the solemn vows of holy orders—even before she was robed in any religious habit.

Not only did Christ's beloved delight in the aforementioned acts, she also, as someone who sought constantly to grow in virtue, or rather from imperfect virtue to perfect virtue, desired to keep the three vows of holy and approved religious orders with such fervor that it seemed as if she would utterly exhaust herself. Insofar as the vow of poverty of spirit was concerned, even though she was not yet robed in any religious habit, she would have liked to give to the poor everything she owned actually and potentially, in order to remain completely poor and humble for Christ. Since she had given away some things with her mother's knowledge and some other things without her knowing about it, to achieve her goals while avoiding any scandal, on my advice and instructions she simply and joyously consigned into her mother's hands everything she owned and that belonged to her, and by this means she became poor in spirit. Her feelings and actions showed such joy at this that it was a marvelous delight to see her reveling so in the blessedness of holy poverty.

As for her devotion to the vow of chastity, what shall we say? Simply this: that from her conversion on I always found her to be like someone who had never known a man and with the holy intention that, if it were possible, she would never have known a man in the past nor wish to know one in the future. She assured her eternal spouse, Christ Jesus, that, if her corporal spouse were to pass from this life before her or if she could get him legally to set her aside while he was living, she would observe eternally the vow of continence and chastity.[32] To conclude this subject, this beloved woman achieved such a surpassing perfection of chastity that, while confessing to me at various times as described above, with great intensity she announced to me and said: "Take it for certain, dear father, that by the help of divine grace I feel myself to be of such disposition as if I were not made of flesh." It was almost as if she were claiming that, like the great Virgin Mary, her impetus (that is, her sensual inclination) was somehow extinguished or contained by a singular participation in grace. For this reason I was forced to speak with her as if she were completely virgin, never making mention of anything that pertained to sensuality. Moreover, once she converted to Christ, when she was living in her parents' house and it would have been appropriate for her to return to her husband's house, nonetheless she would never interrupt her holy intention (even if by the Lord's dispensation she did reside with her husband for a little while until he left Venice in such a way that thereafter she was never again in his company, returning to her parents' house).

As an example for married women, especially those of youthful age, I am constrained to explain here the commendable behavior of matrimonial chastity observed by this beloved woman. Despite having a young and dissolute man for her husband, when this beloved woman found herself in his company after her conversion for the time just mentioned, she nevertheless maintained and observed fully and boldly that chastity which is required by holy matrimony. As further evidence of her perfect chastity, I recall that once, when she and her mother were in my presence, she happened to say that before her conversion she had acted like a most sinful woman with her husband, almost like another Mary Magdalene. To this she added: "O dear father, if you only knew what a bad woman I've been!" Nonetheless, by the abundance of divine grace she reached such a point that it seemed like even the first stirrings of sensuality could find no place in her chastened flesh. And, reader, I do not want you to suppose that this beloved woman had been or was even reputed to be anything less than chaste in worldly terms, simply because she called herself a bad woman during the period when she was with her husband, since she was always of purest condition and excellent reputation. However, after her conversion she conceived such affection not just for true matrimonial or widowly chasteness, but even for virginity, that she considered any action that was even the slightest bit immodest to be an enormous sin.

And finally, as for her attachment to the vow of obedience, it was a wonderful thing to see the holy awe she felt for me and for not overstepping that which I might ordain or command, truly thinking of me as her God's vicar. Thus, she received everything from my mouth as if it had come from the mouth of God himself. For this reason, she hastened to perform with the greatest reverence and joy whatever I commanded or ordered, and when I told her to, she obeyed her mother in the same way. Hence, to conclude this

chapter, I declare that I found this beloved woman so truly obedient and so eternally disposed to holy obedience that I can honestly
affirm that I cannot recall that she ever consciously overstepped a
single one of my commandments. On the contrary, she desired with
all her strength to perform fully whatever I might command, in
such a manner that I do not think I have ever seen a woman of her
condition who matched her in this.

*Chapter Ten: About this beloved woman's great charity
for her neighbor.*

Finding herself as if transformed, through desire and affection
for the aforementioned virtuous acts and three solemn vows, into an
instrument suited to bring the soul to perfect fulfillment of the
divine commandments of charity for God and for neighbor [Matt
22:36–40; Mark 12:28–31; Luke 10:27], this true lover steadily grew
so perceptibly in that charity that it would be difficult for words to
explain it. Still, wishing to pursue that subject a bit here, concerning first the charity she felt for her neighbor, you should know that
she was so devoted and zealous above all for the salvation of her
neighbor that when she saw someone scorn his own salvation, she
suffered for it in the highest degree. The converse was equally true:
when she saw her neighbor, abandoned to vices, devote himself to
virtue, she showed a most exceptional delight and rejoicing. She
stood ready to do everything for the salvation of her fellow beings,
even to go everywhere preaching for that purpose—if only it had
been possible, fitting, and decent for her to do that.

To speak in more detail of the great charity she felt for her
husband, you should know that although he was (as was said earlier)
a dissolute young man who treated her badly in many ways, appre-
ciated her very little, and left her completely abandoned and for-
lorn, nonetheless she always carried in her heart the desire for his
salvation. At times, when certain persons expressed profound compassion for her misfortune in having been given away to such a husband, she responded to them humbly and sweetly, saying: "Dear
ladies, I want you to know that I feel much more grateful to God
for this, and also to my husband, than I might feel if he were different; because it is thanks to being abandoned by him and his other

strange actions that I feel myself united and find myself joined to my heavenly spouse and visited and loved by him in many ways, and as a consequence more freely called and promptly ready to serve my eternal spouse." For this reason she redoubled her prayers for the salvation of her husband, and with the greatest desire offered and presented him to God.

Her mother once happened to mention to me that this beloved woman sometimes had second thoughts about having received the habit of Saint Dominic (which shall be described later, in Chapter Twelve) while her husband was away from Venice. On the one hand, she placed her confidence in God, while on the other, she worried that if her husband returned, her receiving or having received this habit in his absence might give him reason to take offense with God. She lay mortally ill at the time; and hearing something about her husband's return, like a zealot for his salvation she called her mother to her in private and said to her: "O sweetest mother, behold now how well he who rules and governs all things has provided for me, since so far as I can see, it seems that the Lord wishes to call me to himself. And thus I have no more need to fear that I might now (or might have in the past or could in the future) give my husband an opportunity to take offense with God in any way on account of anything I might have done in order to please God. Rather, when he sees how I have dedicated myself to God's service and that whatever I have done has been for the love of God, he will realize how I have given him an opportunity for true contrition and compunction and a reason to leave his usual vices and give himself to holy virtues. For this reason, and even if it were for this reason alone, I feel bound to give eternal thanks to the Lord, and by his loving providence in my regard, I feel sweetly and joyfully called to depart from this troublesome pilgrimage and exile."

She loved her parents and other relatives with true charity, just as she loved her husband, loving them all first and foremost in God. Thus, her mother sometimes marveled that even though this beloved woman was a dearest daughter, she did not show her any filial tenderness or compassion upon the deaths of her other daughters (the sisters of this beloved woman, whom she truly loved in Christ in their lives as in their deaths, as described above in Chapter Five) or when any other unfortunate accident befell her. On the contrary, this beloved woman appeared joyous and glad at this divine dispensation, as if she had entrusted herself entirely to God and conformed herself to his will. When she realized her mother was astonished at this, she said to her with admirable prudence and sweetness: "You may be certain, dearest mother, that I love neither you nor any of our family in any way according to the flesh, but only according to the spirit. Loving you in this way doesn't mean I love you any less, but rather that much more completely and perfectly, just as the spirit is greater than the flesh."

According to what her mother told me, sometimes when this beloved woman was caring for her father, she would speak to him too in the same terms, to wit: "You should know, sweet father, that I don't love you at all according to the body or sensuality, but I love you entirely in Christ; and just as if it were Christ's person, so I serve you." Then she added: "I ask that you love me, sweet father, in the same way—that is, only in Christ and for Christ." As a consequence of this sort of love, sometimes this beloved woman strengthened her father and mother in God and (when she thought it appropriate) sweetly corrected them out of charity and with fraternal charity, with all respect and humility. She treated the other people in the household just as she did them. So long as her siblings lived, she charitably and sweetly taught them what she had learned from the holy sermons. This included not only those in her household, but even her other relatives as well, as far away as Verona, to whom she sent letters and messengers to strengthen them in Christ. She even (and especially after she had received the habit of Saint Dominic) wished to go to Verona in person so that she might further there the desirable goal of her neighbor's salvation, not only among her kin but among others as well, and multiply and increase the habit of Saint Dominic in keeping with her holy desire.

What, then, shall I say about myself, whom she loved in God so intensely, perhaps more than any other creature? That notwithstanding, she gave not the slightest thought to any bodily comfort or any earthly goods and worldly prosperity whatsoever that might come my way. Rather, she strove above all to give me refreshment and recreation with her holy prayers and virtuous life and other spiritual things, in keeping with what she thought should please me more, and wished with her whole heart to see me a true and great servant of God, a great proclaimer of the word of God, and a most fervent zealot for souls—even to the point of suffering every terrible martyrdom for Christ and for the salvation of souls.

Thus, her mother told me that sometimes she would chide her daughter, saying to her: "You are indeed a rude and thoughtless woman, since even though by God's grace we have an abundance of earthly goods, it doesn't seem that you ever think of sending some comforting thing to this spiritual father of yours, who toils day and night for you and other fellow creatures." She replied in her usual manner, all reverent and sweet, saying: "Sweetest mother, he to whom everything is clear and manifest knows well whether I think of him and love him. It is true that I don't want him to have these vile little things, which are suitable for servants and children, but I love for him to have those great things that pertain to the perfect, which is why I would wish he were a great martyr and were all chopped to pieces for Christ, just like his father Saint Dominic wished for himself, yearning like that for martyrdom and longing for it as a thirsty stag longs for the spring of living water [Ps 42:1].[33] I wish this would happen to my holy father not only in feeling, but also in fact, so that he might then receive in heaven the great reward that befits such great merit. These things, sweet mother, are something, and in comparison to them all others are nothing." When her mother heard all this with more than a little astonishment, she fell silent for the moment. But note how this woman truly understood our way of life, which is in a community, so that she knew that sending me alone any item of bodily comfort would have caused me more trouble than pleasure, if it were not in sufficient quantity that it could be shared properly with the entire friary of Santi Giovanni e Paolo.[34] Indeed, I cannot recall that either she or her mother ever (except for perhaps one or two times) sent or gave me something to eat or to clothe my body or for any other earthly use.

In addition, she was touched by exceptional charity for many other persons, just as she was for me, such as all the Brothers and Sisters of Penance of Saint Dominic; and likewise all those persons who had borne or demonstrated special affection, devotion, and reverence for the blessed Catherine of Siena (to whom she was especially devoted) and for the aforementioned persons of the Penance of Saint Dominic. So great was this charity that she took complete delight in being with the said sisters of the habit of Saint Dominic, just as they did in being with her. This was true both before she took that habit and after; she wished that this way of life might grow and multiply not only among men, but even more among women, for the honor of God and his saints and the edification of her fellow creatures, and she found the greatest pleasure in seeing it grow and multiply. The contrary was equally true; that is, its decline or lack of progress caused her terrible sorrow. Thus it happened that when a certain Madonna Sister Caterina, who was the first to receive the habit of the Sisters of Penance of Saint Dominic in Venice, passed from this life and was brought for burial at the convent of the women of Corpus Domini, this beloved woman was present at her burial and raised such a lament that nothing like it was ever seen from her before or since.[35] This was due both to the great tenderness of the love she bore for her personally and to the way her loss sapped the strength of this habit, since she felt exceptional compassion for her and for the other sisters who were thus left prematurely widowed and deprived of such a dear and special spiritual mother in Christ Jesus.

She likewise felt a very special charity for the women of Corpus Domini, with whom she acquired a special familiarity in Christ through me and the other sisters of the habit of Saint Dominic. Because of that special charity, with my permission she arranged to be buried among them upon her death, wherever she might happen to depart from this life, since that was a time of plague. As it happens, she passed on soon thereafter, as shall be recounted below in Chapter Thirteen.

In similar fashion, she felt such charity for all the Preaching Friars, especially those of the lesser and greater friaries of Venice,[36] that she considered them all to be her dearest brothers in Christ. This is truly an amazing thing to say, that even though she felt as much affection for the said friars as for angels, nonetheless she never got involved with any of them, nor with anyone from another order, and never even spoke with any of them except in my presence, as her spiritual father and her God's lieutenant in all things pertaining to her salvation. By the same token, before she confessed with me, she never had any conversation with any other religious person for any reason, except that after she came into contact with me, she spoke to some of us one or two times with my permission or in my presence. And during her illness, from which she passed to heaven, she declared in the presence not only of myself and my companion, but many other people as well, that everything had indeed been as stated here.

And even if, because of the exceptional affection she had for our friars, she took remarkable delight in hearing them sing the Divine Office or (as it might happen) in watching them preach or for some other reason, nonetheless she would never let her glance linger on any of them, except perhaps on me, an elderly man and her father in the Lord. Thus it sometimes happened that I realized she was watching me with a look full of admiration and reverence. She regarded me in this way as the vicar and spokesman of her God, whom she loved above all (as the following chapter will make clear); and so she loved me in and for God, being firmly and certainly of the opinion that I had been given and sent to her by God. For this reason, as was said, when I became aware of her devout regard for me, I sometimes felt so touched to the heart that my eyes shed real tears, as I reflected and pondered within myself with great amazement how God looked upon me through her with such devout affection and loved and cherished me with such sincere and perfect charity.[37]

Finally, just as she did with me and with certain other persons (as was said), so in accordance with the commandment of charity she reached out with affection to all, including those who had in some way insulted or injured her, and even including all unbelievers. Thus it was that she was always liberally prepared to make every effort for the physical or spiritual health of her fellow creatures by means of the corporal or spiritual works of mercy.[38] She promptly put into effect whatever she could properly do, not just offering financial support but even personally visiting the sick and tending them right through to their burial, doing many pious things—and she would have done many more, if I had not forbidden and prohibited it, which I did out of consideration not only for her sex, but even more for her youth and physical attractiveness. To conclude briefly, this beloved woman attained such perfection of charity for her fellow creatures that she would forget herself and her own solace, even that which she received from me, and she would have been glad to see me sent under obedience to various parts of the

136

world, even among the infidels, wherever this might be expected to bear fruit for my salvation and that of other beings, just as if perfect charity had made her the mother of all.

For this, then, is what perfect charity for one's neighbor requires. First, that it be true, loving the neighbor for the good of that neighbor. Second, that it be just, loving the neighbor principally according to the principal goods of his salvation. Third, that it be consecrated to God, loving one's neighbor out of charity in God and with the love for that neighbor reaching its end in God. And fourth, that it be active, loving the neighbor with the effect of assisting him.[39] This beloved woman observed all this completely, as one may recognize in the things said above, leading clearly to the sound conclusion that she felt great and outstanding charity for her fellow creatures. Moreover, charity for one's neighbor can be considered in three ways. First, concerning its extension, which should include not just family and friends, acquaintances and enemies, but even strangers and those far off. Second, concerning its intensity and affection, giving out of charity for one's neighbor not only one's temporal possessions but spiritual things as well, and not only individually but also collectively and universally.[40] Since this beloved woman demonstrated all these in some manner according to her capacities, it evidently follows how singularly fervent and ardent she was in her charity for her fellow creatures. Indeed, when one considers her perfect and persistent dedication to her fellow creatures, one could say of her that which is said about her eternal spouse's feeling for his disciples, when he was taken to his most holy passion. That is, that having loved his own who were in the world, he loved them enduringly to the end, and also loved them in God and for the chosen and desired end, and even in the end of his life showed them notable signs of love and affection.

So also this beloved woman, even when she was sick unto death, did not cease comforting in Christ not only those of her household, but all those persons, men and women alike, who visited her in her illness—and there were quite a few of them, even though she was ill with the plague. They did so because of a singular grace with which this beloved woman was endowed; that is, since she was (as is evident from what was said earlier in this chapter) moved by true charity for all people, so each person, and especially those who knew her best, was wonderfully drawn to her by notable charity and love (as appears in greater detail later, in the last chapter of this Legend). And thus this chapter should close.

It is true that if you, devout reader, should wonder why this chapter about love of neighbor is placed before the chapter about love of God, one might answer that even though the precept of love and charity for God precedes in dignity and perfection that of charity for neighbor, nonetheless love of neighbor precedes in some ways that for God, since imperfect things go before perfect ones and loving one's neighbor is not only a sign and indication of loving God, but also a way, a model, and a preamble to loving God. The glorious apostle Saint John says things to this effect in his epistle. That is, that if you do not love your neighbor whom you see, you cannot love God whom you do not see, etc. [1 John 4:20].[41]

Chapter Eleven: About the perfection of this beloved woman's charity toward her God, and her full participation in all the other virtues.

Just as this beloved woman burned with charity for neighbor, so was she fervent in charity for God—because of whom and in whom (as was said) she loved her neighbor so perfectly. You should know that once she was established in the foundation of the truth of the holy faith and accompanied by the certainty of holy hope, with the passage of time she so increased in the said holy charity of God that she found herself fully prepared in everything and for everything that she might be able to do for the love of Christ Jesus, including even suffering holy martyrdom. Thus, once when I was speaking with her and vigorously asking if she was ready to set forth against the Turks to receive holy martyrdom with me and many others, she replied to me and said: "O dear father, if only it could be so!" She was then swept up in such mental delight and joy and such fervor of heart that it suffused her appearance as well, turning her face all red the way a seraph's face is depicted.

In addition, having heard me preach in my sermons at Santi Giovanni e Paolo and elsewhere about the fervent and superabundant charity which that seraphic virgin, the blessed Catherine of Siena, felt for her eternal spouse, she was inflamed with much devotion for her.

Passing one time through the neighborhood of San Luca of Venice, where many painters are found,[42] she happened to see in one of their shops a panel on which that painter had depicted an image of the blessed Catherine, as the Lord had inspired him, which he intended to give to me, though I knew nothing about it.[43] Even though this was the situation and the master explained it to her, nonetheless this beloved woman was entirely set on having it, as if God had so ordained it, and she was able to plead with that master so sweetly that in the end she obtained it from him. When she had acquired that image, the beloved woman began joyously to wear a white tunic over her hair shirt, longing (if it pleased her heavenly spouse) to be dressed entirely in the complete habit of Saint Dominic for love of him, just like the blessed virgin Catherine. This desire developed until she eventually had herself depicted in another icon, wearing that habit among some images of saints of our order set before the image of the crucified Jesus, holding her heart in her hand and offering it always and in every way to the Lord Jesus, who had offered himself on the cross for her and other sinners.[44] When this desire swelled to the point that she could no longer resist it, it finally came to fruition when she received the habit in its entirety, as shall be explained in greater detail in the following chapter.

To summarize many words in just a few, you should know, devout reader, that both before and after she received that habit she was so fervent and so continuously inflamed with divine charity that she longed to pursue even impossible tasks for Christ. Her love was so extreme that she believed that even if she undertook and accomplished not just little things but truly great ones, she was doing very little or nothing. In her confessions, therefore, she would declare herself to be the guiltiest of all, considering herself to be the worst ingrate for not responding to God's charity according to her desire and what she thought she was obliged to do. I sometimes questioned her about this, saying: "Tell me, are you not ready to do every good thing you can for love of Christ? Have you not given yourself to Christ always and in every way and with everything and above everything, entirely and eternally? So why are you lamenting?" She then answered me in her dovelike simplicity and with a special gladness and mirth, saying: "Dear father, you can be certain that I have indeed given myself to him always and in every way and with everything and above everything and for all eternity, and that he knows it well."

She had heard me occasionally use this manner of speaking in my sermons and was taken with a tremendous desire to put it into practice. It was so strongly impressed on her mind that with the greatest delight she had gotten into the habit of adopting that mode of speech not only between the two of us, but even in the presence of others. As a consequence, in addition to the acts of the contemplative life and the exercises of her marvelous penance and of the active life, she also strove to seek out every other way and means by which she could do, or at least endure, something for love of Christ. So it was that when she had any bodily infirmity whatsoever, she rejoiced and celebrated as do those who obtain that which they have desired and awaited with great longing. What is more—and I can provide the whole world with clear and true testimony of this—I never saw her so joyous and festive as when the Lord granted her some infirmity of her body. She demonstrated this above all in her final illness, when, feeling herself stricken by the plague, she then went to heaven fulfilling her holy desire, as shall be explained more fully in Chapter Thirteen.

Another result of the aforementioned fervor was that for Christ she took it upon herself to visit without any distinction those women who were ill with the plague and tend them and even bury them when they died of that pestilence. And in fact she did just that to the limit of her ability, with exceptional gladness and mental and physical joy that she displayed especially toward female slaves as well as to those persons most forsaken and abandoned by others.

Here you should note, devout reader, that during that time of plague (which lasted in Venice for several years, growing more intense or abating from time to time), when I was preaching at the friary of Santi Giovanni e Paolo and throughout Venice to comfort people, I often used to say that all those persons who, finding themselves ill with the plague, accepted that illness willingly and patiently for Christ as atonement and for the salvation of their souls were just like martyrs for God; and this was all the more surely true the more joyously and gladly they accepted death from the plague, if God wished to grant it. The reasoning behind this was that through the great and terrible suffering of divine and expiatory justice, the souls of such persons remained so fully reconciled to God and justified and purged that when they passed from this life, they were freed not only from hell but even from purgatory as well, in all likelihood, and were carried to heaven by angelic spirits. For this reason, just as in the age of martyrs, when those who aided and comforted them at risk of their own lives acquired great merit with God alongside the martyrs, so we must believe that giving aid and comfort—especially aiding and comforting those sick with the plague—acquires more than a little merit with God, just like the ill who are martyrs for God.

I would say all this for the solace and consolation of the people and to encourage them to mutual charity, so that one would not abandon the other, contrary to charity's due, especially in these circumstances—since I heard from one or more persons that this had indeed happened, to the detriment of body and soul. With the help of God's special grace, these exhortations had such an impact on many people that dying from the plague, which previously had been so terrible and frightening, came to seem welcome, pleasant, and gracious. Sometimes I would shout and exclaim from the pulpit, crying: "Long live the good death!" For there is nothing that can be called better than a good and holy death resembling the precious deaths of Christ and his saints, by which every present misery comes to an end and all happiness and glory is received and acquired.[45]

Now, having heard me repeat these statements in my sermons on various occasions, each time this beloved woman was stirred in her heart by such joy that she displayed an exceptional delight and shared her joy with all those women that she saw stricken with the plague; as she saw the need, she graciously looked after and cared for them with all charity for Christ, right through to their burial, as I said earlier. A further consequence of this was that (as was said and shall be repeated) when the plague happened to strike her own self, she was as full of gaiety and happiness as if the desired martyrdom for Christ had befallen her, and all the more because no one bore any guilt for martyring or having martyred her.

As an additional sign of her singular charity in God, when she happened to find herself engaged in conversation with me, she always seemed to me to be in a genuine fervor of divine love. Divine and angelic words burst from her mouth as if she were a pot boiling away or pan bubbling over—words sweet "super mel et favum"[46] that gave voice to the tremendously great, heated, ardent, and holy desires of her heart. She offered herself always to all, without any exception, entirely and fully and in every virtuous way she could, all for love of her eternal spouse who with such generosity had offered himself entirely and fully for us, longing with all her strength to love him every day more immediately, fully, and totally.

Because of this strong desire, when she found herself alone, she often felt impelled to raise her bodily eyes to heaven along with the eyes of her mind, fulfilling that common saying that wherever one's heart or love goes, the eye will follow. Among other times, I happened to see her like this once when she was ill with the infirmity that caused her to pass to heaven. After she had taken a little food, she instructed her mother to leave her alone so that she might have some quiet and sleep. Her mother and I, after a certain period of time, went silently to check whether she was resting at all. Lifting the veil or curtain covering the bed, we saw her lying on her back, holding her eyes fixed unblinkingly toward heaven and moving her lips as if she had something sweet in her mouth, and every so often she would smile sweetly, with her face all angelic and rosy. Observing her like that for a while, her mother and I could not help but be moved to tears by a singular compunction and devotion.

As I shall explain more fully later, when she was alone, not only did she sometimes like to keep her eyes raised to heaven in the manner described, but at times would even shout or exclaim: "Up to heaven, up to heaven!" Thus, in addition to those many occasions on which I saw her do this, her mother told me about one time (among others) during that last illness when, having left her alone in this manner, the mother heard her speak and say: "Oh, look at this fine throng!"—almost as if she saw many beloved men and women appearing to her from heaven. Turning her face toward one among them, she spoke aloud: "O blessed Brother Niccolò, O blessed Brother Niccolò, how very much I loved you in God during your lifetime, even if I never spoke with you." And then, when the beloved woman had said these words and seen that heavenly multitude, she began to cry in a loud voice: "Up to heaven, up to heaven!"—as if they had invited her to a heavenly feast.

Here, devout reader, you should note and know that this Brother Niccolò had been the brother in the flesh of a certain

Master Andrea, a doctor who resided in the parish of Santa Fosca in Venice, and the brother of Sister Margherita, a nun in the convent of Corpus Domini of Venice belonging to the order of the Preaching Friars, and the son of Madonna Sister Lucia of the penitents of Saint Dominic.[47] When this Brother Niccolò was about nineteen years old or so, he left the world and with great fervor entered the Order of Preaching Friars in Venice; for his great virtues, he was eventually named prior of the friary of San Domenico of Venice. When he reached the age of twenty-seven or thereabouts, he passed on to heaven, having led the life of a friar with the greatest sanctity. Special mention is made of his holy life and learning in that little book referred to in the prologue and various other chapters of this Legend and elsewhere as well, so I shall not speak of him at length here. But at least I should say that never in my life did I see a friar as fervent as I saw him to be. Others understood this as well, considering his life as described in that little book and in certain works written by the hand of Brother Giovanni Dominici, whose name appears at various points in this Legend.[48]

What I have just said about this Brother Niccolò, I could say equally well about this beloved woman; that is, I never saw a woman of her condition of such fervor and such fervent words—which were matched by deeds. Because of this similarity, it was only reasonable that she should feel a special charity in Christ for this beloved man from the very first time she met him right to the end, so that when she heard that he had passed from this life, she immediately set off for San Domenico and his burial, and did not leave there until she had obtained a piece of his clothing as a special gift and relic. By the same token, since the Lord allowed Brother Niccolò to visit this beloved woman in her final illness, there is no need to marvel if (as I said) she called to him in particular with such sweetness of charity.

In effect, in her every word and mental and physical act and in every way, one could see the commandment of divine love fulfilled in this angelic and fervent beloved woman (as much as it is possible to see in the journey of this life); that is, to love God with all your heart, etc. [Deut 6:5].[49] Note that she had this commandment entirely impressed upon and diffused throughout every corner of her mind in such fashion that she was often heard to repeat it with her tongue and in her every deed, desiring to fulfill that commandment completely in every way she could. And thus in fact she fulfilled it, so that one could certainly call her what she was: a living mirror and lovely exemplar of the commandment of divine love, placed before the eyes of all the faithful wayfarers, especially those who knew her best and were most familiar with her.

I do not wish to omit one deed that demonstrates how this beloved woman felt about all this, however small it might seem. Accordingly, you should know, devout reader, how once, when this beloved woman looked at the image that she had had made of herself offering her heart to Christ and noticed that she only offered it with one hand, she immediately sank into holy sorrow because the painter had not portrayed her offering her heart to Christ Crucified with both her hands. This true lover wished to convey in this way that just as she had offered her heart to God in all and through all and with all, so she would have wanted that total offering of her heart to have been effected not merely with both her hands, but with all her organs and all her limbs and all her powers.[50]

To finish finally with this beloved woman's perfection of divine charity, it reached the point that her body was failing under such constant fervor and inflamed desires. On many occasions, and especially not long before her death, she spoke with me and told me that her only wish was to separate herself from her body in order to be with the spouse she desired above all things.[51] She lamented that because here on earth she did not see how she could love him as fully as she would have wished, on account of the many obstacles, she absolutely had to wish to be there where she could see and love her God at her pleasure among the other blessed spirits and without any impediments. The Lord, wishing to fulfill this desire, then granted her a death from pestilence in order that, dissolved and freed from the filthy burden of her body, she might be introduced to that direct vision and heavenly delectation for which she longed (as shall be explained at greater length in Chapter Thirteen).

The perfection of charity not only involves the removal of its opposite (that is, mortal sin), when this charity is found in beginners, and the removal of licit impediments and the fulfillment of vows and other holy exercises, when this charity is found in those who are making progress. When it is found in the perfect, this charity extends even to the actual and continuous fervor of divine delectation, from which follows and is born the desire that the body might dissolve in order to be with Christ.[52] And since all this was found in this beloved woman, as can be seen from what has been and will be said, it clearly follows that she was indeed of perfect delectation with respect to God. Furthermore, some people who are in charity at times desire bodily death in order to escape the many tribulations, miseries, and sufferings that surround them (as happens in beginners), and some in order to put an end to anything in them that offends God (as happens in those who are making progress), and some simply to remove any impediment to actual divine delectation (as happens in the perfect). Considering that (as appears from what was said earlier) this beloved woman wished to be deprived of bodily life in this manner in order to be with Christ, the same conclusion follows: this beloved woman was found to be perfect in divine charity and delectation.

So that she could speak boldly to the Lord Jesus Christ, repeating three times and more that which Saint Peter replied to him thrice, when the Lord Jesus asked three times whether he loved him—that is, "Lord, you know that I love you" [John 21:15–17]— this beloved woman might say something like this:[53] "Lord, you know that I love you not only according to the charity of beginners, but also of those who are progressing and perfect. My Lord, you know that I love you not only more than my things, but also more than my family and my own self. My Lord, you know that I love you not only in nourishing my neighbor for love, speaking of the meal of the example of holy conversion and holy life, but also the meal of holy doctrinal persuasion and even the meal of corporal subvention. My Lord, you know that I love you not only for myself, but also you for yourself and me totally for love of you. My Lord, you also know that I love you not only with all my heart (that is, with my entire intellect unmarred by any error), but also with all my soul (that is, with my entire will, unmarred by any contradiction), and with all my mind (that is, with my entire memory, unmarred by any forget-fulness). My Lord, you know that I love you not only with all my heart (that is, with an extremely intense love), but also with all my soul (that is, with a unique and singular love), and all my mind (that is, with an excellent and supernal love), and with all my strength (that is, with a constant and perpetual love), just as the true bride loves her true beloved spouse—who, to signify the four qualities mentioned, (first) wears the ring on the fourth finger, whose vein is linked to the heart, and (second) keeps only one ring, which (third) is of gold and (fourth) is circular in form, and thus without end.

"My Lord, you know that I love you not only with all my heart (that is, sweetly, so that nothing seems more sweet to me than your perfect love), but also with all my mind (that is, wisely, so that to me nothing is more prudent and wise than your perfect love), and with all my soul and my strength (that is, strongly, so that I find nothing stronger than your perfect delectation). My Lord, you know that I love you and have loved you with such sweetness of heart that no other thing has drawn me away from you, and also with such wisdom of mind that no falsehood has deceived me, and moreover with such strength of will that no adversity has overwhelmed me. My Lord, you also know that I love you not only with all my heart (that is, with every good intention), but also with all my soul (that is, with all good will, in conformity with yours), with all my mind (that is, with all good discretion and discernment), and with all my strength (that is, with all good constancy and perseverance). My Lord, you know that I love you not only with all my heart (that is, with the elicited action of the will informed by charity), but also with all my mind (that is, with the elicited action of the intellect governed by that will informed by charity), and with all my soul (that is, with the elicited action of feelings moved and governed by that will informed by charity), and with all my power and strength (that is, with the deeds of the motive and executive capacities to act, governed by the aforesaid will informed by charity).[54] My Lord, you know that I love you not only with all my heart (that is, with all the modes of the active life), but also with all my mind (that is, with the attention of the contemplative life), and with all my soul and powers (that is, with the whole of the mixed life, or mixture of active and contemplative together).

"My Lord, you know that I love you not only with all my heart (that is, loving you with all purity of heart, as holy virgins love you), but also with all my soul (that is, loving you through working for my salvation and the salvation and support of my kin and neighbors, just as holy confessors, members of religious orders, preachers, prelates, and pastors loved and love you), with all my mind (that is, with all my mental intelligence, just as the mental and angelic intel-

146

ligences love you), and with all my strength (that is, loving you constantly and perseveringly and by means of what suffering you wish to bestow upon me, just as all your beloved and glorious martyrs love you). My Lord, you know that I love you not only with all my heart (that is, in response to the love that you showed me in all your creation), but also with all my soul (in response to the love that you showed me in your protection and governance), and with all my mind (that is, in response to the delectation you showed me in all your redemption), and also with all my strength (that is, in response to the love that you showed me in all your glorification). And finally, my Lord, you know that I love you with a love without limit and without measure and without end—that is, with a perpetual, immeasurable, and infinite love and affection, both because you are infinitely lovable and because you have given me the desire to love the finite and the infinite forever and ever." And this properly and clearly concludes [this chapter] about the perfection of this beloved woman concerning divine charity, delectation, and love.

Next, wanting to say something further about the faith, hope, prudence, justice, fortitude, and temperance of this beloved woman, I declare that one could not easily expound on this in detail without a great prolixity of words. Wishing to avoid that prolixity in order to put an end to this chapter, let us simply say that what has been said and will be said about her should suffice, since those virtues shone in all her words and deeds. What is more, the perfection of her charity argues and demonstrates that in her was the perfection of all the virtues and Beatitudes and gifts and fruits of the Holy Spirit, which with the Father and the Son lives and reigns in that eternal Godhead forever and ever. Amen.

Chapter Twelve: About the singular affection that this beloved woman felt for the habit of Saint Dominic, and the persistent requests she made to have it, and how she begged for it and with the greatest festivity and solemnity received it.

Among the other things that demonstrate and confirm what has been said about this beloved woman's charity for God and neighbor, there is her singular and devout determination in wanting at all costs to receive the habit of Saint Dominic for God's honor and the edification of her neighbors, satisfying all worldly and carnal considerations and opinions and, with marvelous insistence, asking for it, begging for it, and receiving it as soon as she saw that she could do so licitly and virtuously.

Here you should know that this beloved woman was present together with her mother at Santa Maria della Carità in Venice, where, on the authority of the master of our order, I gave the habit of Saint Dominic with great solemnity to two venerable and virtuous women, the first sisters of this habit in the city of Venice: Madonna Caterina of the Marioni family, and Madonna Astrologia of the Verzoni family.[55] (This is described in that little book mentioned in an earlier chapter and also in the prologue of this Legend, and which should be in the keeping of the Sisters and Brothers of Penance of St Dominic in Venice.[56]) On that occasion, this beloved woman was so taken with devotion and holy affection for this habit that, for love of her heavenly spouse—who for love of us chose to cloth himself in the habit of our mortality, "habitu inventus ut homo" [being found in a human form—Phil 2:7–8]—she for her part would have taken that habit quite willingly that very moment.

As her desire for this grew (as was said in the previous chapter), she wore the habit underneath her outer garments; as it increased further, she had herself depicted in an icon entirely clothed in that habit and thus, by contemplating herself in her cell, she herself satisfied her desire as best she could. Finally, after a while, one time when she was praying and it was shown to her that even though she had a husband, she still could licitly and virtuously receive the habit without dissolving her marriage, the desire for it simply overflowed in her. All of a sudden she seized the opportunity, threw herself humbly at her father's and mother's feet, and so sweetly and prudently managed to plead and petition them that even though they were entirely of the opposite intention, wish, and opinion, and even though she still had a young husband (albeit an absent one), nonetheless she obtained their free and full consent that she be allowed to don this habit exactly as she desired. They considered that this would be pleasing to God, and it seemed to them that God was speaking to them through their daughter's mouth. Moreover, they felt unable to offer resistance or refuse her request, since they had the greatest reverence for the holy life that they had seen her follow and persevere in from good to better.

Now, when this beloved woman had obtained her parents' permission, she decided she wanted to obtain mine as well. On the morning of the vigil of Saints Peter and Paul she came to speak to me at Santi Giovanni e Paolo.[57] Not finding me there, since I had gone with Brother Giovanni Dominici to hear confessions at the convent of Corpus Domini, she was immediately taken by her companion, Madonna Sister Astrologia of the habit of Saint Dominic, to meet me at that convent. When I saw her panting as if from heat and fervor and with her face all flushed, I was struck with amazement and asked her why she had come. She replied humbly but with holy boldness that she had come because God had inspired her with the conviction that on that very day she should receive the habit of Saint Dominic that she desired so greatly, and that this was what God wanted. I began to chastise her sharply, explaining to her that this could not be done properly at that moment for various reasons, citing (among others) the repulsive character of her physical spouse, and her relatives; in effect, there was no way this could be done just now without greatly scandalizing her family and us friars.

She then answered all my objections quickly and easily. After replying to me, she threw herself at my feet and asked this favor of me with so many prayers and such insistence that I can't recall ever having seen the like; nor do I expect to ever see it again in this life. I can truly say that I cannot imagine a heart so hard that it would not have softened and melted at those prayers, which she made with such confidence in God, such humble and kindly insistence, and such promptness and effectiveness. Being unable to resist her any longer myself, I called upon my companion, Brother Giovanni, to help me, and with his reasoned arguments strive to temper this beloved woman's great heat and fervent desire for this deed. As it happens, neither he nor I could restrain her by any means. On the contrary, the more we struggled to calm her and contain her, the greater her fervor grew. Whatever we said, she answered more wisely and swiftly, pointing out first that I myself had given this habit to a certain Madonna Marina Soranzo, even though she was then married to Messer Antonio Soranzo—who himself, during his wife's lifetime, took this habit of Saint Dominic.[58] And so she argued boldly that having a husband did not bar someone from receiving this habit, to which she added that she could receive this habit much more easily than that other woman and with better reason: since her husband had departed from Venice and led a life that was less than good, she could reasonably don that habit in order to observe a better and more holy life, maintaining in this way the essence of the matrimonial bond.

She also argued that since her father and mother were worldly people of rigid and inflexible character and yet, as if by divine miracle, they had agreed to this, we ought to be all the more agreeable, being religious preachers and proponents of a virtuous and religious life. She further argued that her father had promised that he would answer for her to her husband and everybody and would see that they were all satisfied, since once he had granted her this favor, everyone else should be willing to accept it.

She presented these and many other reasons just like a great philosopher of Christ, until she had Brother Giovanni entirely persuaded and convinced (as I was) that it was impossible to offer resistance to he who spoke in her. If I had not objected to it, he would have agreed right on the spot to let the beloved woman receive the desired habit, since the nuns had tunics and mantles and everything that was necessary. Brother Giovanni would have done all this immediately, since he was generally of this temperament; that is, if he saw a person disposed to serve God, he really did not like making her wait but recommended that a good impulse should be acted upon without delay. And you can be sure that this good woman would have been as quick to receive as Brother Giovanni was immediately inclined to give, if I had given my consent.

In the end, in order to avoid any grounds for disturbance, I begged the beloved woman to return home, since I thought that her business might be settled around Vespers; I said this thinking that in the meantime I would speak with her father and her relatives, to seek their advice about what should or should not be done about this affair. And so, since I had asked her to leave, she humbly left and went with her companion, Sister Astrologia, to the house of the other woman mentioned above, Madonna Sister Caterina, who had been the first woman in Venice to receive the habit of Saint Dominic. She resided at Santa Maria della Carità, and when they found her, they took her with them to the beloved woman's house and there, they and her mother put in order the habit and everything else that was needed for this. Then, near Vespers, they all came to Santi Giovanni e Paolo.[59]

Now, Brother Giovanni and I had set out from that convent for our friary of Santi Giovanni e Paolo a little after None.[60] I wanted to go speak with the beloved woman's family, as I had proposed, but passing by our church, I found all the aforementioned women together with the beloved woman, prepared with everything needed in order to receive the habit. Throwing herself at my feet like the Magdalene before Christ [John 11:32], in the presence of so many others this beloved woman begged me even more insistently than she had at the convent that I might concede her this favor without further delay, pressing her request with as much constancy as if God had not simply inspired her but revealed as certain that in that day her present petition must be granted. I explained that even though I believed that everything she said to me was true, I absolutely wished to speak with her father and mother for my greater clarity and certainty before I would agree to this. In the presence of the other women, she replied that there was no need for me to speak with her father, since he was more than happy with all this and (as was said earlier) had not only given her his permission but had also promised her that he would defend her against everyone if she took this holy habit—and if he was pleased with this, then every other person ought to be left satisfied. Then she added that her mother was equally happy with this decision and should be there shortly, since she had gone to fetch certain women of the Mocenigo family who were connected with them, "so that they might accompany her here to see me receive this favor that I have desired for so long."[61]

Right then, as I was speaking with her, her mother arrived with the women just mentioned and with two other noblewomen on her other side: one was Madonna Madaluccia Morosini and the other the aforementioned Madonna Sister Marina Soranzo of the habit of Saint Dominic, both intimate friends in Christ Jesus of this beloved woman. I went to meet her mother and drew her aside to speak privately. When I repeated everything her daughter had told me, she assured me it was all true and that she had come with these women for this very purpose. Upon hearing this, wishing to go along with her, I said: "Well, now, mother, what do we know? Perhaps this beloved woman must soon pass on to the Lord"—not knowing what I was saying, since I desired the contrary, for God's honor and the salvation of souls.[62] Therefore I added: "It is good that we give her this consolation and grant the devout and holy request of a daughter like this." At that moment it also occurred to me that just as God had inspired Saint Ursula and Saint Costanza, the lady of Santi Giovanni e Paolo, with complete faith that their virginity would be preserved even if they consented to take corporal husbands, so this woman joined in matrimony, as if truly inspired by God, had full confidence in the Lord that even though she was requesting this habit without her husband's permission, nonetheless nothing inappropriate would follow from it. Rather, it would encourage virtue in herself and in her husband as well—or at least he would be preserved from any scandal, as in fact happened, even if the Lord could have arranged the same result by infinite other means.

When I had heard, considered, and grasped all these things—not without great astonishment—as if compelled and constrained on every side, I took the libretto and convoked certain friars. Together with all the aforementioned persons, we entered the chapel of San Domenico, which is in that Church of Santi Giovanni e Paolo, just as the first call to Vespers was beginning to sound. I placed myself before the altar of that chapel with my face turned toward the choir. This woman came and knelt before me, holding in her hands the habit that she was to wear and presenting it to me so that I might bless it. I did indeed bless it and then gave it to her so that she could put it on in private.

She received it with such fervor and joy of spirit, continuously laughing and delighting in the great celebration, that it moved me and all the people present to tears and cries of devotion. When she had donned the said habit and returned to her previous position, kneeling before me with (if I remember correctly) a white candle lit in her hand, we recited the *Veni Creator Spiritus* and the other prayers used when bestowing that habit. The beloved woman readily gave me her promise to preserve and keep the habit so long as she lived. Having finally received the benediction from me, like someone totally drunk with joy at the fulfillment of her most praiseworthy desire, she left me and turned toward her mother before any of the other women. She flung herself around her neck, embracing her and giving her the kiss of peace for the gift received, and magnificently gave thanks first to God, Saint Dominic, and the blessed Catherine of Siena, and then to her father and after that to her mother. Then she did likewise to all the sisters of the habit who were present there, embracing them and giving them the kiss of holy brotherhood, and then she turned in similar fashion to all the other women. This was such a fine game that while this beloved woman was doing all this, she was always laughing and almost as if clapping her hands for the great joy and happiness she felt. All the rest of us were equally unable to contain ourselves; we wept and cried out, moved by exceptional devotion and amazement, and there certainly could not be a heart so hard that, had it been there, it would not have been similarly touched. As for myself, in fact, I can't recall ever having seen or read of behavior like this on such an occasion, nor do I expect to see or read of the like.

Here you should note, devout reader, that I feel not the slightest doubt that this beloved woman would have set her hands with all joyous fervor not only to receiving the habit like this, but to all things she recognized to be more acceptable to God and of greater perfection. Consider it certain that, if it were not for the tie with her husband, her excess of fervor would have led her to enter the convent of Corpus Domini. That is exactly what happened with another woman both she and I held exceptionally dear in Christ, a widow named Sister Zanetta dalle Boccole, who mentioned to me the habit of penitence of Saint Dominic because she thought she would not be able to get into that convent of Corpus Domini; nevertheless, when she obtained admittance through my intercession, she immediately left her children and the whole world and flew in there with the greatest fervor and festivity.[63] And as I said, that, in all likelihood, is what this beloved woman would have done.

Even if she were kept from entering the convent, if she had lived longer, she seemed fully inclined to follow in the footsteps of that seraphic virgin, the blessed Catherine of Siena, to whom she was especially devoted, since she was a most extremely fervent zealot for the honor of God and the salvation of souls. In effect (to conclude this section), I declare that considering this beloved woman's great fervor and burning desire for the things of God, if she had lived in the time of the persecution of martyrs, without fail she would have been among the number of those beloved virgins and holy women of youthful years who with such fervor, joy, and celebration raced toward holy martyrdom as happy, festive, laughing, and joyful as if they were going to their weddings.

Now, in order to bring this chapter to an end, you should know that when this beloved woman received the habit of Saint Dominic in the manner described, it aroused considerable admiration and provided a holy example for those around her. As a consequence, everyone now held her in even greater devotion and reverence for her virtues than they had before. Thus, in those days, a recently married young woman of the Contarini family fell sick of the plague; when she heard how this beloved woman had taken this habit, she immediately sent for her. She went to her with my permission and was received by her with the greatest devotion and warmest welcome and with assurances that she too wished to share her habit and her life in all circumstances. And since she became entirely convinced that she must pass from this life, she demanded to have in her hands the habit of Saint Dominic—that is, of this beloved woman—and this was done. In effect, wherever this beloved woman went or stayed dressed in her holy habit, it seemed that she inspired everybody with a special devotion to her, being gracious to all and by each loved and blessed in Christ, as shall be explained in greater detail in the last chapter of this Legend.

Chapter Thirteen: About the physical infirmities that this beloved woman bore with great joy for Christ, and how in her final illness, which was the plague, she passed happily from this life to her desired eternal Spouse.

After this beloved woman converted to God and approached the end of her pilgrimage, she suffered from numerous infirmities. The first was a swelling of her knees, which afflicted her for more than a month. Everyone, including the doctor, thought that this misfortune befell her because she stayed so assiduously on her knees in church and at home, day and night. Whatever the case may be, she always remained notably happy and festive until she was freed from it. Even though her mother and other people worried that this might present a serious danger, she was always happy and smiling; moreover, she would have liked to maintain the rigor of her usual austerities despite this infirmity, if the commandment of holy obedience had not intervened.

When she had been freed from that infirmity and had taken the habit of Saint Dominic in the manner described in the previous chapter, this beloved woman incurred another defect of bodily infirmity. She kept it hidden, enjoying it secretly for Christ, but I noticed a few outward signs of it and commanded her under obedience to tell me the truth. She was thus compelled to reveal it to me, which she did with remarkable happiness and joy, and I judged within myself that the Lord would soon call her to him. So it happened, though not only for the defect mentioned, but for the third infirmity, which befell her later, that is, the plague. When it struck her on July 19, she immediately came to me and announced it to me with remarkable joyousness and both outward and inner expressions of happiness.[64] When I heard this, I felt completely shaken; it seemed to me terribly bitter (in a good and holy respect, of course) that she must depart so soon. She, however, reveled in this just the way brides commonly celebrate when the time has come to go to that most welcome husband they have long desired. When she went on to tell me many things, I was so upset that I could hardly pay attention, so that all she said left only an impression of her manner of speaking, which was something like this: "Dear father, when I said this to you and told you that, etc."—always in the past tense, just like a person who recognized that she must soon depart from this life. And so, when she had left me and I went off to Vespers for the vigil of Saint Mary Magdalene, she remained there like this for Vespers and then returned home with her companion, Sister Astrologia.[65]

After she left me, I turned over in my mind what was said earlier, and also what I had said about her when she was about to receive the habit, and also her boundless lament at the burial of Sister Caterina of the Marioni family, as if she were saying to her: "O beloved mother and sister, I should not remain here after you, etc." Considering all these things, I came to the conclusion in my mind that she almost certainly must soon pass to heaven. I was strengthened in this conviction by the memory of certain things she had said to me not long before, such as: "O dear father, you should know that I feel myself dissolving like salt in water." When I asked her why, she humbly answered me as reported above in Chapter Eleven: "Because of the desire to love fully this God; since when I see myself so impeded, held back, and delayed from this, I seem to feel as if my body and mind are entirely dissolving from the ache of this desire." This was so in fact, since I always found this beloved woman to be in genuine fervor; just as when she suffered from that swelling due to constantly remaining on her knees, so I believe that it was because of her excessive desire and fervor that she incurred her second ailment, to which the Lord then added the third—that is, the plague—to give fulfillment to this excessive desire of hers. And pondering all these conjectures like this, I thought I could presume that she must soon depart from here—even if right up to the end I still remained somewhat hopeful, wishing in all things to render the honor to God, as I should.

When the next day came and I had preached at the convent of the Celestia in Venice about Saint Mary Magdalene, most fervent lover of Christ Jesus, I went to see what was happening with this beloved woman who had accepted the illness of the plague with great reverence and pleasure, as something given to her by God's special grace. In fact, I found her in such good spirits and with such laughter and celebration that I had never seen her like that, so that she seemed unable to contain or restrain herself. What is more, when I looked at her in amazement and scolded her for such excessive festivity, the more I scolded her, the greater her laughter and celebration seemed to grow, and she would have come all too willingly to my sermon if her mother had permitted and allowed it. I left there thanking the Lord and saluting her in Christ together with her mother and all the other women, but still reflecting within myself that all this joy could be a sign that she must go to the eternal feast. I went off to the Church of Santa Agnese, where I joined many devout people at the burial of someone named Bianco the Gesuate from Città di Castello, who had been known as an exceptionally fervent servant of God.[66] I then went to the place of the Gesuates, which is right near there, and after giving them some comfort in Christ through preaching and conversation, I returned to the friary, since it was quite late.

The following morning I returned to the house of this beloved woman and found her laid out in bed by the high pestilential fever. She was somewhat comforted by my visit and by my words of counsel, and when I had left her (according to what her mother later reported to me), she drew up her will. Declaring herself to be entirely and in all ways dedicated to God, she then forbade and prohibited what she had forbidden in the past, indicating that her body should not be placed in the sepulcher of her earthly kin but rather interred at the friary of Santi Giovanni e Paolo (since the Sisters of Penance of Saint Dominic did not yet have their common sepulcher there, as they later did), or else that she should be buried at the convent of Corpus Domini, where her spiritual mother and sister in her habit (that is, Sister Caterina of the Marioni family) had been buried, and that this should be done with only four candlesticks and with the priests and clergy of her neighborhood.

Next she left her entire engagement gift and dowry in the hands of both her parents to distribute, commending to them especially (among other things) the aforementioned convent. She also urged her mother to arrange things so that five ducats be given to the friary of Santi Giovanni e Paolo every year in perpetuity in celebration of the holy memory of the blessed virgin Catherine of Siena, to whom she was particularly devoted, whose memorial and commemoration is held every year in that convent on the first Sunday after the feast of our Saint Peter Martyr of the Order of Preaching Friars.[67] All this was done exactly as she specified.[68] Shortly after her death, in fulfillment of the promise made by this beloved woman, her mother had a pair of fine vestments made in honor of the blessed Catherine, which along with many other things are in the keeping of the Sisters of Penance of Saint Dominic in Venice. In addition, the father of this blessed woman left three hundred ducats to the convent of Corpus Domini when he died the following year.[69]

After she had made these arrangements, this beloved woman's illness worsened so much that the night following the feast of Saint James the Apostle [July 25], feeling overwhelmed, she sent for me. In the meantime, while she was as if totally withdrawn into herself, her mother (who was there beside her) heard her say: "O, look at this fine throng!" "Dear daughter," said her mother, "whom are you talking about?" This beloved woman replied to her, saying: "O mother, can't you see all these fine servants of God?" Then she immediately added: "O dear beloved blessed Brother Niccolò, O blessed Brother Niccolò, how very much I loved you during your lifetime, even if I never spoke with you." Having said this, as if these blessed souls had invited her to the heavenly nuptials, she started to cry out in a loud voice: "Up to heaven, up to heaven!" and so on, as was recounted earlier in Chapter Eleven. Next, since by then I had reached her side, with great urgency and eagerness she asked me for holy communion and wanted to be armed with all the sacraments of the holy church. When I had confessed her and sent to have the parish priest bring the sacraments, with the utmost devotion she received the sacrament of the body of Christ in the presence of us all, and then she received that of extreme unction with as much devotion and concentration as I have ever seen anybody receive it.

Here it is particularly noteworthy that even though she had heard about the seven sacraments and their formulas (among other subjects) quite some time earlier—to be precise, in the sermons I preached the previous Lent in San Barnaba—nonetheless it seemed as though she had the formulas of those sacraments so impressed in her memory and present that, when it came time to give her extreme unction, she strove with all her faculties to utter those formulas for the unction along with the priest who was anointing her according to what she had heard me preach, whereas the priest said them according to the usage of his church. I was quite amazed that she could recall these formulas so accurately, considering how long ago it was and also her physical weakness, difficulty breathing, and the pain in her head. I can certainly say that of all the people I ever saw at a sermon, she seemed the one who listened most attentively by far; what she heard, she took in avidly and stored up within herself so that, as she went through life, she came to be wonderfully able to share it abundantly with others.

Now, after receiving those holy sacraments, as though fortified with a divine garrison or as a bride all adorned and prepared to ascend to heaven for the wedding feast with her desired spouse, her sole occupation was to sing loudly the divine praises, sighing and saying: "Up to heaven, up to heaven, since it is open."[70] Many times thereafter she cried and shouted in that same loud voice, saying: "In manus tuas comendo spiritum meum, in manus tuas comendo spiritum meum" [Into your hands I commend my spirit—Luke 23:46, quoting Ps 31:5]—as if she expected at any moment to pass on to those heavenly nuptials, in fulfillment of her desire. But the Lord disposed otherwise, whether for her further purification or to multiply further her merits or to amplify still further her holy desires, since he prolonged her bodily life for three days more. As she endured those three days, her whole refreshment consisted principally in and of spiritual things, while bodily things were such a burden to her that her body would hardly take any comfort, except as commanded.

Because of the singular and holy affection she felt for the habit of Saint Dominic and also for me, she tried to persuade her parents both through others and directly herself that they should receive that habit for the salvation of their souls and take me as their spiritual father and humbly obey me for Christ, as she had done. She did the same thing with that Madonna Madaluccia Morosini named earlier, a widow and a special friend in Christ of both hers and mine; she urged her lovingly to receive completely for Christ the habit that she wore under her other clothing, to which she replied that she was not prepared to do so for the moment. When this beloved woman heard this, she immediately perceived—as if moved by a prophetic spirit—that this woman would never in her life receive that habit (or so her mother later told me). And that indeed is what ensued, as appears in the little book cited earlier at various points, in which for a certain reason the passing of that Madonna Madaluccia is mentioned in the appropriate place.[71]

She also urged this habit on Madonna Isabetta of Lucca, the wife of Gherardo Burlamacchi, when she visited this beloved woman; in my presence, with great joy, she gladly indicated to her that she intended to do so, if her husband would allow it or if he should pass from this life before her.[72] When her husband died shortly thereafter, she received from my hands the habit of Saint Dominic in the chapel of Saint Ursula, with the greatest solemnity and devotion.[73] Some time later, this Madonna Sister Isabetta went to Lucca and Pisa, taking with her (with my permission) that dearly beloved woman Madonna Astrologia, whose name appears here so often. After a few months the two of them, along with two daughters of Sister Isabetta, all entered as nuns the convent of San

Domenico of Pisa. That convent was the model for the convent of Corpus Domini of Venice, of the Order of Preaching Friars; its prioress was a respectable lady of holy life, Sister Chiara, the daughter of Messer Pietro Gambacorta of Pisa, who had been a great nobleman in the eyes of the world.[74]

In addition, while this beloved woman was so ill, she and her mother would sometimes speak just between themselves and she would tell her various things, including about one special divine providence; that is, that in calling her to himself, the Lord was providing for the salvation of her husband by removing any occasion for scandal and giving him reason to follow a virtuous and holy life (as was recounted above, in Chapters Ten and Twelve).

Many persons visited this beloved woman, men and women alike, especially those who wore her habit, such as Messer Antonio Soranzo and his wife, Sister Marina, and others who bore for her a special affection in Christ. She comforted them all in Christ Jesus and spurred them all to God's service with such amiable, sweet, and gracious good humor that they all felt moved to holy sorrow and inspired to dedicate themselves eagerly to every good thought, word, and deed.

In fact, one moment she wanted to pass to heaven lying on the bare ground like Saint Martin, and the next she wanted to sing hymns, devotional songs, and divine offices and to hear them sung. One moment she would be speaking of her divine Spouse and of heavenly things, invoking and referring to all these things as her dearest medicine, and then either contemplating or praying, especially when she was left alone (as was recounted earlier in Chapter Eleven). Finally, in the presence of her mother and me and of Sister Astrologia and many other persons, she heaved great sighs and uttered some loud cries because of her great physical pain and the bursting of her heart—resembling in this and in various other things Christ her husband, who, when he was about to expire on the cross, cried out in a loud voice several times [Matt 27:46, 50; Mark 15:34, 37; Luke 23:46].

A bit later, toward the hour of Matins,[75] this beloved woman was lying on her back at the foot of her bed, on a little cot set up in her loft, with her face turned now toward heaven and now toward me. My companion and I were proceeding with the office for the soul that is approaching death, and had come to that prayer which begins: "Suscipe Domine animam serve tue in loco sperande salutacionis, etc."—which means "Receive, O Lord, the soul of your servant Maria in the place of hoped-for salvation. Amen." This prayer then ends: "Libera Domine animam serve tue Marie sicut liberasti tuam beatissimam Teclam"—that is, "Free, O Lord, the soul of your servant Maria; as you freed your most blessed virgin and martyr Thecla from three atrocious torments, may you deign to free the soul of this your servant Maria and bring her to enjoy with you the heavenly rewards." This beloved woman sweetly responded together with my companion, saying "Amen"—which was her last word, after having already announced many times: "In manus tuas commendo spiritum meum" [Into your hands I commend my spirit—Luke 23:46, quoting Ps 31:5]. And so that blessed soul, dissolved from the flesh in fulfillment of its desire, entered into the wedding banquet to which it had been invited—that is, into those celestial storerooms full of the knowledge, delectation, and enjoyment of the divine face; and introduced therein, it savored and received fully in that homeland that for which it had so thirsted and longed along the way.

This beloved woman passed from this vale to the celestial mountains toward morning on July 28, 1399, being twenty years of age or thereabouts. The Lord signified by that early morning hour that he had introduced his bride, according to his vow, into the dawning of full and beatific divine cognition. As was said, among those present at her happy transit was Sister Astrologia, who, like Sister Caterina Marioni, never abandoned this woman in her infirmities, neither by day nor night, neither in life nor in death, right down to her burial, like a most loyal and dear companion in Christ. She deserves special commendation and praise for the exceptional charity bestowed upon her by the Lord.

When I had completed the entire office for the commendation of the spirit, and this beloved woman had passed on as described, her mother suddenly threw herself on the ground. Kneeling at my feet, in front of Sister Astrologia and all the other women who were present there, she humbly commended herself to me and—as her saintly daughter had wished and willed—offered to obey me fully, with promises to follow in her daughter's footsteps as best she could.

When I saw her holy disposition, I graciously received her, raising her from the ground and comforting her. I gave her and the other women my blessing, and having bid them farewell and comforted them in Christ, I took my leave of them. Descending to the floor below, where the father of this beloved woman was weeping sadly at the departure from his side of such a daughter, I remained with him for a certain while and consoled him somewhat. Just as his wife had done, so he too out of his goodness offered himself to me in any way he could, as his saintly daughter had requested that he do, except that for the moment he did not feel inclined to accept the habit for various reasons. I gave him thanks for all his humility and courtesy, bid him farewell in Christ, and parted from him around sunrise, and so I returned to the friary both thoroughly sad and thoroughly joyous and happy all at the same time. Thanks be to God.

Chapter Fourteen: About the devout burial of this beloved woman.

Since (as was said above) this beloved woman had passed away toward morning, when day came arrangements were made for her burial. Around the hour of Terce[76] her body was carried to the convent of Corpus Domini in Venice with great devotion and a large retinue of people, men and women alike, and with the clergy of her neighborhood and candles, as she had stipulated. Nearly all the people who had been at the burial of Sister Caterina were there, including Messer Antonio Soranzo and some other Brothers and Sisters of Penance of Saint Dominic and many other persons of every walk of life, moved to be there by the exceptional devotion they felt for her. In addition, there were several of our Preaching Friars, including the father Brother Giovanni Dominici, whose name has been mentioned earlier, and I myself, who celebrated and performed the office, and the nuns as well, singing some verses. Words cannot easily express the devout solemnity with which this burial was celebrated, since you would have seen some people weeping for the special tenderness and sweetness of spirit, some sighing, some contemplating her in a daze, and some groaning— even though her entire holy way of life and its holy end were nothing but an occasion for spiritual pleasure and celebration, as one treats the death of saints, which is precious and festive in the sight of God and of his church triumphant and militant.[77] And in the end, when these exequies had been completed with wonderful devotion and spiritual consolation for all, the blessed and holy body of this blessed beloved woman was buried and laid to rest in that convent, in the sepulcher of the nuns, as she had wished.

Now, when the office of this devout burial was entirely completed and the consecrated remains[78] laid to rest, I hastened to the sorrowing and afflicted mother and the other women lingering with her in the church outside the convent, to bless them and let them know that they should return home. The mother, coming toward me, once again threw herself on her knees at my feet, telling me the same thing that she had said that night, when after Matins that beloved woman had passed to the Lord. I ordered her to rise up and comforted her somewhat along with the others and then sent her home, saying that I hoped to visit her after None.

After this, before I left the convent, I was told that the bearers of the blessed body wished to report (with more than a little admiration and devotion) that while they were carrying it to the convent, they had sensed it giving off a singular fragrance and aroma, the like of which had never happened with anyone else.[79] Just then one of the nuns in that convent—a noble marquise known in name, as she was in fact, as Sister Onesta[80]—told me that when the blessed body was brought and presented to them inside the convent for burial, the sight of it aroused such devotion in her and likewise in all the other nuns that, if it had been permissible, by no means would she have allowed it to be placed inside the sepulcher, at least for that day.

Later, as I had promised, after the hour of None I went to visit the mother, with whom were some women wearing the habit of Saint Dominic and quite a number of other devout women. I spoke about the virtues of this beloved woman and consoled these women, and likewise the father and the men who were with him, and then bid them all farewell in Christ. I returned to the friary joyous and glad indeed for the glory of this beloved woman, but also more than a little sad to see myself bereft, widowed, and deprived of such a welcome, true, and amiable companion on the pilgrimage and road that remained to me of this mortal life. I had often thought and even hoped that for the great honor of God and Saint Dominic and for the salvation of many souls, this beloved woman could be expected to outlive me by quite some time, and yet she had gone to glory before me, young in age but old in virtue and wisdom, leaving here behind her in the present misery this poor fellow, weak and elderly in age but young in wisdom and virtue. Thanks be to God.

Chapter Fifteen: About various things that happened after the said burial and about certain visions, some of which occurred while this beloved woman was mortally ill, some after her burial, and one shortly after she took the habit of Saint Dominic.

A few days after her burial, a certain Messer Antonio (that Brother of Penance of Saint Dominic referred to earlier, who was present at the burial of Sister Caterina and at that of this beloved woman) reported to me in private how he had visited Sister Caterina during the illness from which she passed from this life. Seeing her ready to please the Lord with such sweet patience and happiness, he was filled with such compunction and devotion that he decided he would no longer sleep in a bed regularly from that time onward. In the same way, having felt a special affection for the beloved woman during her holy life, visited her many times during her illness, and been present at her burial, he felt himself drawn so powerfully by the odor of her sanctity that he intended never again to eat meat regularly from then onward.

Also, a few days after this beloved woman was buried, I went to her mother's house and gathered up various whips, hair shirts, chains, and writings done by her hand and kept in some little pouches or sacks. I had all these placed in a chest kept by the Sisters of Penance of Saint Dominic, as a holy remembrance of this beloved woman.

Next, the aforementioned Madonna Isabetta of Lucca, who was deeply attached to this beloved woman on account of her virtues, put into effect what she had given her to understand she would do during her illness; that is, the Lord permitting, she would take the habit of Saint Dominic (as was said above in Chapter Thirteen). When she happened to be left a husbandless widow not long after the passing of this beloved woman, soon thereafter she not only took that habit but a little later proceeded to enter the convent of San Domenico in Pisa, together with her two daughters and with Sister Astrologia, changing their names from Sister Isabetta to Sister Cristina and from Sister Astrologia to Sister Teodora. There they have pursued a life of remarkable perfection and holiness.

Also, several days after the burial of this beloved woman, five women of honest conduct and reputation came to see me at the friary of Santi Giovanni e Paolo of Venice on their own initiative, as if inspired by God. I knew nothing of why they felt it necessary to come see me or of what they had to say to me. They came to report to me a vision that had appeared to a certain virgin named Orsa or Orsolina, thirteen years old or so, who had been ill from the pestilence at the same time that this beloved Sister Maria was ill; a few days after Sister Maria passed on, this Orsolina also went to heaven. One of these women was Orsolina's mother, another was the mother's mother, others were friends or neighbors, and one was the mother of a certain Sister Maria in the Dominican convent of Corpus Domini in Venice.[81] As it happened, when all five of them were seated at my feet, they humbly told me the course of that vision in these terms, to wit: "You should know, dear father, that on the octave of the recent feast of Corpus Christi, this Orsolina was at San Pietro of Castello, where a special solemnity and celebration of the sacrament of the body of Christ was held.[82] Christ Jesus appeared and said: 'Know, Orsolina, that you shall never have any other spouse but me.'" Accepting this with great delight, she decided firmly that for all eternity she would never want an earthly husband, even if her mother might still have some thought of giving her away to a husband.

Now, after this it happened that the said Orsa fell ill with the pestilence on the day of the vigil of Saint James the Apostle[83]— which was the night when, toward Matins, this beloved Sister Maria had received all the ecclesiastical sacraments and cried aloud and groaned "Up to heaven, up to heaven, since it is open, etc.," believing at the time that she would pass to heaven that morning (as was explained above in Chapter Thirteen). And so, when the morning of that feast of Saint James arrived, in just the same way this Orsa urgently wanted to receive communion and did so. Staying as if she were kneeling, she received the sacrament of the body of Christ with her hands clasped and with such devotion that, when she had taken it, she remained in that position as if she were rapt from her senses.[84] She stayed like that from morning until after Vespers, in such a state that until that hour she could not be roused, nor could she hear or speak, nor could she be given any food, nor could anything be gotten from or understood of her, except that while she was remaining like that with her hands clasped, sometimes she would make some gestures of special reverence, either with her hands or with some other movements of the body, as if she had been summoned into the presence of some great monarch and was seeking to obtain a favor from him.

Now, when the hour of Vespers had passed and Orsa had (as it were) awakened from a long sleep, she immediately called her mother with great joy and asked how her mother's mother was. These two women answered her sweetly, and right away they and the other women mentioned earlier were by her side, along with many other people. Then, in front of them all, this Orsa began to speak and to say: "Do not marvel, dear mothers, if I have been like this until this hour, since this morning, when (as you saw) I had received the venerable sacrament of the body of Christ, all of a sudden I was raptured and led into a most beautiful, spacious, and lofty place. Saint Peter the Apostle appeared to me, whose face I recognized easily not only from having seen him depicted in churches, but also from having embroidered it at times"—since she had mastered that art. "Saint Peter opened a gate for me, and entering by it I saw paradise, all golden and larger than a thousand worlds would be, and in it I saw a glorious and magnificent throne, on which the Lord was seated in triumph above all the angels and all the saints.[85]

"On one side I saw Saint Ursula, my special patron, with a banner in her hand and accompanied by all her holy virgins; on the other I saw the Queen of Heaven, whom I took as my mother quite some time ago now, similarly holding a banner in her hand and accompanied by a great number of virgins and holy women, and she was kneeling as she entreated the enthroned Lord to have mercy on sinners. Then this queen looked toward me and said: 'Know, Orsolina, that you and your fasts have been welcome and agreeable to me, and that soon you will be seated among these virgins, and you will not have to suffer any pains other than those of your present illness.' While that queen was saying this, the other virgins and holy women spoke to me and said: 'Orsolina, be careful to show proper reverence in the presence of such majesty.' Hearing these things with tremendous joy and wishing to carry out what had been said to me, and also longing to see clearly the glory of these saints, I struggled to open my eyes with my hands and to make every gesture of reverence I could, physically as well as mentally, as you could see by my expressions and the movements I made during the time I was in that rapture. And while I struggled to make those gestures, I saw and heard my little brother who had died a few days earlier from the pestilence, who spoke to me and said: 'Know, dear Orsolina, that you can never see these things truly clearly and fully until you are entirely separated from your body.'

"When he had said this, I saw a most beautiful throne, and, marveling at its glorious decoration and its extraordinary beauty, I heard a voice that spoke to me thus: 'This very throne has been made ready and prepared for this Madonna Maria of the habit of Saint Dominic.' And raising my eyes I saw that sister, dressed in a beautiful habit of Saint Dominic, who came and seated herself upon that throne which was so lovely and so glorious. I was very amazed within myself at what I had heard and seen, and it seemed to me that this provoked and caused in me a holy sorrow that this sister would go before me and precede me and would be received on so noble and beautiful a throne, whereas I would have wanted it for myself, and I would have longed to go before any other person to that beatific glory. And so, when all these things had been shown to me, I was suddenly restored to my senses and came to myself, as you see."

Now, when this virgin had recounted all these things to these women, one of them, named Madonna Cataluccia or Madaluccia, who had a daughter named Sister Maria in the Dominican convent of Corpus Domini who was sick at that time, asked Orsa: "My sweet Orsa, that Sister Maria wearing the habit of Saint Dominic whom you saw go to such glory, would she be my daughter, since she is ill and is named Sister Maria and is a nun in the convent of Corpus Domini and robed in the habit of Saint Dominic?" Orsa replied: "It is not her, but another woman whom I have seen and know well." And so, with no little amazement on the part of all the people surrounding her, this Orsa stopped speaking for the moment and took a little food from the hands of these women for the sustenance and comfort of her body.

When three days had passed after that feast of Saint James when Orsa had the vision reported above, it happened that this blessed woman Sister Maria Sturion passed to heaven toward the hour of Matins as Monday, July 28, was dawning (as was narrated earlier, in Chapter Thirteen). Hence, when news of her passing spread through the city that day and reached the ears of this virgin Orsa, she immediately began to cry out and exclaim loudly, saying: "This is that Sister Maria! This is the very hour! And the third thing is that on the day of the feast of Saint James, when I was in that rapture, I saw her enter heaven to receive the glory prepared for her! This is she, since I know her and I have known her for a long time, and look how she has even preceded me to that glory. Thanks be to the Lord. Amen."

Now, although I initially mentioned this virgin Orsa here because of the vision described above that she had of Sister Maria Sturion, nonetheless I should conclude the tale that those five women told me about this virgin Orsa with her death—and this because I assure you it will prove to be both useful and edifying for any devout persons who may read this Legend. To continue, therefore, you should know that on that Monday on which the body of Sister Maria Sturion was buried, Orsa had another rapture, in which she was shown the pains of purgatory. As a result, the desire to suffer every torment here and now, in order to be entirely free of the said pains of purgatory, grew so great in her that she asked this of the Lord with great urgency and as a special favor. The Lord granted her prayers in such fashion that, even though she was gravely ill with the pestilence, nonetheless, on top of that she broke out in pestilential boils all over her frail body. When she discovered herself to be so well supplied with them, she not only gave thanks to the Lord for granting her this, but even with singular festiveness delighted and gloried in them, as does a new bride who is about to go to her husband and finds herself all adorned with pearls or other noble and precious stones. Her mother, looking upon her with the deepest compassion, in the presence of her and all the other people around her, said with more than a little amazement: "Now what will God do to great sinners, when he inflicts such torments on a young virgin?" Hearing this, Orsa replied: "O good mother, don't say that, since the Lord has arranged to purge me of everything in this life and to give me no pains in the next. But it will not be like this with you, since you will have to go to purgatory."[86]

The following day was the octave of Saint Mary Magdalene, when Venice celebrates the feast of Saint Martha.[87] Since those boils were spreading over Orsa's frail body, her mother said to her: "O Orsa, commend yourself to this beloved Saint Martha, so that by her merits you might be freed from such torments." She immediately replied, saying: "Good mother, that I shall not do." Having said that, she prayed the Lord that if these sufferings were not enough, he should please add still further ones, so that, more quickly purged, she might more quickly go to him to enjoy and celebrate with him and with the other saints in his glory. After speaking these words and having rested somewhat in her mother's bosom—or rather, as if rapt—she began to sing a hymn never before heard, with such sweetness that all those present were dumbfounded. When she was later asked where she had learned such a beautiful song, she replied it was in her first rapture, when she was taken to see the heavenly glory. What is more, when all those who had been present at her singing were later asked what hymn this was or what it was about, they indicated that at the time they had been so absorbed in the sweetness of that song's melody that they had no idea what to answer—except for her mother, who said only this: that it seemed to her that the song was about the joys and happiness of the Virgin Mary.

Then, on the following day, which was July 30, around the hour of None, this Orsa began to talk to herself a bit about some past events. She said: "I remember how I heard Brother Thomas preach in Santi Giovanni e Paolo about the blessed Catherine of Siena, telling (among other things) about how when she was just a little child, she would honor the Virgin Mary with such devotion, effectiveness, and delight; yet I have grown old in my sins."[88] Then she added: "I also recall how I heard him preach about the virginity of that blessed Catherine, praising it in many ways, which was why I then prayed the Lord that by his grace he might give it to me, too, so that I might figure among the ranks of his holy virgins. Behold how he has deigned to grant me such a gift, for which may he be eternally thanked. Amen." As it was getting on toward evening and she had prayed almost the entire day, she began to say aloud repeatedly: "Iesu Christe fili Dei miserere mei,"[89] and "Sweet Virgin Mary, receive too my soul." And thus it was done, since while she lay on the straw of her bed as she expressly wished and in great faith was brought to her final moment, thinking that she saw the devil, she asked her mother to say the *Credo* and she said one as well. When she had said it, she added: "Dirupesti Domine vincula mea, tibi sacrificabo hostiam laudis" [Ps 116:16–17]—that is, "O Lord, thou hast loosed me and freed me of all my bonds; therefore I will offer to thee freely and fully the host and the sacrifice of divine thanksgiving."[90] When she had finished these words, that blessed virginal soul passed freely up to heaven to praise and bless her eternal spouse forever and ever. Amen. And the body of that virgin was carried to our Church of Santi Giovanni e Paolo and buried there with great devotion.

Returning now to the beloved woman who is our principal concern, Sister Maria Sturion, you should know that I came to hear not only about the vision described above but many others as well. One of them I heard from the mother of that beloved woman, who told me that several days after her daughter, Sister Maria, was buried, she appeared to her once in her sleep, dressed in the habit of Saint Dominic and all resplendent, joyous, and laughing. The mother received great consolation from seeing her like this, in such good state, almost as if she were sharing her joy. She marveled, looking at her fixedly and remembering the great sufferings this beloved woman had borne, and she asked her about her passing, saying: "O sweet daughter, wasn't the passage of death full of pain and sorrow?" "No, mother," she replied, adding: "Dear mother, the passage of death is indeed painful and sorrowful, but it wasn't so for me because of the close conformity of my will to that of God, and also because of my desire to reach him, as the ultimate and desired goal." The mother thought of asking her many other things, but her husband called her and when she replied, saying, "Here I am," this vision withdrew from her and disappeared. Even though she was unhappy about the interruption caused by answering her husband and was also mourning the loss of her daughter, nonetheless, having received this vision as described, she was left tremendously comforted and consoled. She asserted that she had never in her life had a vision or dream that gave her as much comfort and pleasure as this vision brought her.

This mother also reported to me that the priest of their parish of San Giuliano[91]—an elderly man of exemplary life who considered this beloved woman to be a saint because of her virtue, and called her a saint—told her father, Messer Nicolò Sturion, that she had appeared to him several times in a resplendent habit with her face all joyous and glowing; Messer Nicolò himself repeated this to me with great devotion.

In addition, this beloved woman's special companion in Christ—that is, the oft-mentioned Sister Astrologia, who was exceptionally endowed with sincere charity—told me in private on a number of occasions, before she left for Pisa, that she had appeared to her in her sleep many times, and always festive, splendid, and joyous. Also, several months after this beloved woman passed away, when I was at the convent of Corpus Domini to hear the confessions of those women, an elderly nun who stood out for her great sincerity and charity told me in confession how she had been affectionately eager to know what had become of one of their virgin nuns named Sister Marina Ogniben, who had passed from this life on the [twentieth] day of that month.[92] Once, when she was praying, this Sister Marina appeared to her all festive and happy, and at her side was that beloved woman, Sister Maria, dressed all in gold—that is, with her habit all gilded; yet, this Sister Maria had not yet departed from this life, though she was quite close to her passing. When this elderly nun who saw them wanted to ask Sister Marina about certain things, she answered and said: "You should know that I cannot linger with you just now. I must depart, because we have to get ready to hold a great celebration for and about this Sister Maria of the Penance of Saint Dominic, whom you see here below me praying so devoutly." And once she had said this, the vision vanished.

Later, when this beloved woman Sister Maria had passed to heaven, the virgin Sister Marina appeared another time to the elderly nun mentioned above, together with Sister Maria. She revealed to her what she had wanted to know—that is, to what extent her life and her virginity had been acceptable to God—and then she also spoke about her companion, and how meritorious and acceptable in the sight of God had been the life and the matrimonial chastity of this beloved Sister Maria, once she had converted to him. And then the vision vanished.

Here it should be noted that what God wished to demonstrate by this vision—that is, how and how much he approved of this beloved woman's matrimonial chastity—was not without a special motive and reason. As I recall, after this beloved woman's conversion, when she had to return to her husband's house and rejoin him, I instructed her that she should maintain and defend her holy matrimony so chastely and piously that she would not stain it in any way, despite any flattery or threats on her husband's part. She replied frankly and happily, saying: "Dear father, you can be sure that with the help of divine grace, I shall do just that." Indeed, she carried that out fully, not like some girl or damsel or adolescent (if you will), but like an entirely virile woman (according to what I later heard from her in confession, and also related earlier in Chapter Nine). [93]

That elderly nun mentioned earlier also told me how she was in prayer at the time when this beloved woman took the habit of Saint Dominic. This nun marveled that this beloved woman had taken the habit, considering her youthful age and the kind of husband she had, and also a father and mother of worldly condition and concerns. Worrying that this might lead to great scandal, she received the following answer: "Know that just like a great gust of wind will sometimes make a roof tile fall to the ground without suffering any damage itself or harming anyone, so this devout woman's taking the habit of Saint Dominic will cause no scandal, actively or passively, for herself or for others." Such, in fact, was the result— and much more, since in addition to the benefit this beloved woman derived from having received the said habit, she also offered tremendous edification and a holy example to other relatives, friends, and strangers.

I also heard later from some nuns in that convent that at the end of the year, when they came to open the sepulcher in which the body of that beloved woman had been placed in order to lay another one there, her body appeared the way it did when it was buried, without any whiff of noxious odor or stench. And in fact, to put an end to this chapter, this beloved woman has also appeared in my imagination—whether I may be sleeping or waking, going about or standing still, celebrating or praying—and always in the one same fashion, from the time she passed to heaven until the present, that is, entirely full of exceptional joy, exceptional delight, and exceptional glory. If she almost continuously appears to me like this, perhaps it is to denote that just as she followed me with such charity wherever I went to preach when she was alive in the flesh, so now, since she is confirmed in charity and a much more perfect and faithful sister and companion in Christ, it seems that she wants continuously to accompany me mentally and spiritually by dispensation of the grace of Lord Jesus Christ, to whom be thanks in all eternity for this and for his other innumerable gifts. Amen.

Chapter Sixteen, and last: About the universal grace that this beloved woman generally had in life and in death and afterward, both in the eyes of God and those of persons of every sex, condition, and status.

How much grace this woman universally had in the eyes of God and men, especially from her conversion onward, can be clearly seen from the things already said in the preceding chapters. Nonetheless, since this gift—of being gracious and considerate toward everyone— shone especially in her, it is fitting that it should receive special attention in a separate chapter, summarizing in it everything that has been said on this subject in the preceding chapters.[94]

Here you should know that she had such grace in the eyes of every person who knew her or even just heard of her, of whatever sex, condition, or status that person might be, that they all revered her highly and loved her in the Lord, to the point that many persons decided to receive the habit of Saint Dominic for love of her, both in her life and after her death, as appears in part in Chapters Eleven and Thirteen.

Also, she had such grace especially in the eyes of her parents that from the time of her conversion until her death, she never asked for anything that they did not graciously grant as she desired (as appears above in chapter after chapter), since they believed that Christ resided in their daughter by a special grace and consequently spoke through her. When she had passed to heaven, they wanted Sister Astrologia to live with them for at least a while in their daughter's place, because of the great and intimate charity that they had felt for each other; and so it was done, with my permission. After a year or so, when the father of this beloved woman came to his death, out of respect for Sister Astrologia and for his daughter, he left three hundred ducats to the convent of Corpus Domini and took the habit of Saint Dominic. The mother as well, after the death of her beloved daughter, growing in devotion and affection for her every day, made certain vestments in her honor (as was said above, in Chapter Thirteen). By the same token, she also hopes to do more things and eventually to take the habit of Saint Dominic, just like her devout and gracious daughter.[95]

Also, this beloved woman had such grace in the eyes of all our Preaching Friars that, even though she never conversed with any of them outside of my presence, nonetheless she was exceptionally accepted and welcome to them because of her virtues, just as they were to her, as was said above in Chapter Ten.

Also, she had such grace in the eyes of the nuns of Corpus Domini that they all would have gladly received her among them as a nun during her lifetime, just as they all gladly and graciously received her in among them in their own sepulcher after her death. When the body of this beloved woman was borne into that convent for burial, on the day of its burial all of the nuns regarded it with such devotion and esteem that putting it away forever that day of the burial seemed bitter to them, as was said in Chapters Ten and Fourteen.

Also, this beloved woman had such grace in the eyes of all the Sisters and Brothers of Penance of Saint Dominic who lived during her lifetime that she was loved in the Lord by all, women and men alike, more than any other person. I, too, was compelled in the same way—that is, to love her in Christ more than anyone else for her perfection of chaste goodness, the grace and virtue that shone more brightly in her than anyone else. This not only rendered her amiable and gracious to others but also spurred them to virtuous deeds, even when she lay ill and also dead (as was said above in Chapters Ten, Fourteen, and Fifteen).

Also, she had such grace in the eyes of her parish priest, an elderly man mentioned in Chapter Fifteen, that he considered her to be one of God's saints and reverently granted her every favor she asked of him, including permission to receive communion at her pleasure sometimes. It is true that after this beloved woman passed to heaven, Boniface IX granted two privileges to all the Brothers and Sisters of Penance of Saint Dominic, allowing them to receive communion freely and also to confess to the friars appointed to that task and at their places and friaries. These two privileges and various others are in the possession of the Sisters of Penance of Saint Dominic in Venice.[96]

This beloved woman had such grace in the eyes of a certain married woman named Franceschina, dear to us in Christ, that when she gave birth to a daughter sometime after this beloved woman's death, she wished to resurrect her name—that is, Maria—in her own daughter, and so she had her given the name Maria at her baptism. When she began to grow up and gave some signs of a good and holy life in the future, the mother credited this to the merits of this gracious beloved woman.

What is more, this beloved woman had such grace in the eyes not only of good people, but even worldly ones, that wherever she was or went through the streets, they especially revered and regarded her. They felt and displayed a striking devotion not just for her other holy and devout actions, but even for her bearing and her manner of going about all closed within herself (even if at first some people murmured and spoke ill of this, as was said above in Chapter Six).

Also, even though this beloved woman had been stricken with the pestilence, which is generally so horrifying to everyone that each person flees from the other (as sometimes happens even among people who are related), this beloved woman nonetheless had such grace in everyone's eyes that any person who was able to visit her during her illness, or see her or speak with her even a little, felt blessed. Those persons who by special grace were able to visit her came away from the encounter with much holy solace and holy spiritual consolation, as was said above in Chapter Thirteen.

What is even more noteworthy, even though this beloved woman died of the pestilence, whose victims are usually buried immediately for fear and terror of the corruption or infection, nonetheless with this beloved woman quite the opposite happened. She was so gracious even in death that when those nuns had her corpse in their convent for burial, their hearts could hardly bear to place it in the sepulcher, as was said earlier in this chapter and also in Chapter Fourteen.

To bring to an end this chapter and the entire Legend, this beloved woman was evidently endowed by God with such special grace that no person who spoke or preached and conversed with her could help but be inspired with singular affection and esteem for her; this was because of the abundance of that grace, which (as in the saints) is followed by an abundance of glory. That this beloved woman was held in such special grace by God can be seen in her genuine and perfect conversion to God and in her perfect charity for God and neighbor (as was declared above in Chapters Four, Ten, and Eleven). It naturally followed that she would make herself—as she was—extraordinarily gracious to all, both angels and men, the triumphant and the militant. For this reason, since this beloved woman in this manner found grace in the eyes of God and men, one can conclude that she must be similarly glorious in the eyes of God and men. And so we may fittingly and finally say of her that which is written of the great prophet Moses in Chapter 45 of Ecclesiasticus: beloved by God and man was this Sister Maria, whose memory is blessed[97] and who has been made like to the saints in glory by her eternal spouse Christ Jesus, who with the Father and the Holy Spirit lives and reigns forever and ever. Amen.

Here ends the aforesaid Legend, composed in Latin and translated into the vernacular by Brother Thomas of Siena of the Preaching Friars in the friary of San Domenico of Chioggia in 1403, finished and completed on the day of the octave of the Assumption of our Madonna Virgin Mary.[98] Thanks be to God. Amen.

Thomas of Siena:
The *Libellus* concerning Catherine of Siena (Part One)

Editor's Note: Thomas of Siena's *Libellus de supplemento,* or the *Supplement,* is a mosaic of various reports addressing Catherine of Siena's visions, stigmata, and other mystical experiences, her devotion to the Eucharist, and her death.[1] Thomas wrote his book as a supplement to Raymond of Capua's massive life of Catherine, the *Legenda maior;* and, in imitation of the tripartite division of the *Legenda maior,* Thomas divided the supplement into three loosely connected parts.[2] Nonetheless, the two books offer strikingly different portraits of Catherine. Raymond presented Catherine's life in the context of such wider political concerns as the Avignon papacy, the papal schism, and Dominican reform, whereas Thomas focused on Catherine's inner life of visions and prayer.[3]

It is evident that Thomas composed his *Libellus* in several sections over an extended period of time. The first of the three parts, translated here, and some other sections were probably completed by 1412, but the whole book was finished only around 1418.[4] The lengthy writing process reflects Thomas's style as a writer. It was typical for him to assemble various documents, piece them together with a (more or less fitting) narrative, dedicate lengthy sections to

Note: The translation has been done on the basis of Giuliana Cavallini and Imelda Foralosso's edition: Thomas Antonii de Senis "Caffarini" (Thomas of Siena), *Libellus de supplemento* (Rome: Edizioni Cateriniane, 1974). I wish to thank the late Professor Cavallini for granting permission to base this translation on the edition and for the generous advice she offered during our meeting in Rome.

themes that he saw to be of particular importance, and weave a loose hagiographic narrative to shelter the assembled materials.

Thomas had two intertwined objectives in his career. First, he sought recognition of the formal Dominican penitent rule. His efforts were rewarded in 1405 when Pope Innocent VII confirmed the rule with his bull *Sedis apostolicae*.[5] Second, Thomas wanted to see the canonization of Catherine of Siena, whose way of life had given the Dominican penitents a new inspiration and sense of focus. To this end, Thomas wrote several documents concerning Catherine's life, among others the *Libellus*.[6] Thomas was not, however, successful in his efforts to obtain papal recognition of Catherine's cult. She was canonized in 1461, thirty years after Thomas's death.

Part One of the *Libellus*, translated here, consists of two treatises. They focus principally, although not exclusively, on Catherine's childhood and youth. The first of the two addresses Catherine's dedication to the Dominican habit, the comfort she received from her reflection upon Christ's passion, and her miraculous ability to learn to write, which, Thomas claimed, was manifested in a few of her letters and some other shorter texts.[7]

The second treatise of Part One contains stories about Catherine's visions, during which she was accompanied by Christ and such saints as Mary Magdalene, Paul, and James the Great. This treatise is of particular importance because its style and subject matters suggest that it is a fairly close copy of a section from the booklets of Tommaso della Fonte, Catherine's first confessor and a friar at San Domenico in Siena.[8] Tommaso wrote several booklets concerning Catherine's youth, and both Raymond and Thomas extensively used his writings, which, however, seem to have vanished soon after their work was completed.[9] Perhaps Thomas discarded Tommaso's booklets after he estimated that he and Raymond had used all useful and acceptable information contained in them.[10]

Why, then, did Thomas decide to make such a close reproduction of a section from Tommaso's booklets? Thomas did not offer an explanation, and, for that matter, he did not even specify that he copied from Tommaso's booklets. However, the subject matters of the second treatise of Part One may offer a lead to understanding why Thomas felt an urge to complement Raymond's text and why he found Tommaso's testimonies a convenient way to do so. While

Tommaso's text included several revelations concerning the heavenly courts, these types of revelations do not appear in Raymond's *Legenda maior*, which focused on Catherine's christocentric mysticism. Moreover, Raymond emphasized Catherine's active involvement in the mystical encounters with the Godhead, whereas the revelations reported by Tommaso present Catherine in more passive terms. Raymond's reticence to discuss the revelations concerning heavenly courts suggests that he saw these kinds of visions as unnecessary additions, perhaps because they could have blurred the *Legenda maior*'s focus on Catherine's christological piety. Nonetheless, some letters of Catherine's contemporaries, solicited by Thomas in fact, prove that her supporters were not necessarily pleased to see that Raymond had excluded a number of visions that Tommaso's booklets had made available.[11]

Thomas of Siena's loyalty to Raymond's work made it impossible for him to voice these thoughts in his own name, but it is evident that he was supporting an image of Catherine that was more otherworldly and contemplative than the apostolic image promoted by Raymond.

Thomas of Siena: *Libellus* (Part One)

Here starts the first part of the *Libellus*, which corresponds with the first part of the *Legenda* of the virgin.[12]

Everything that I write about this virgin derives from her *Legenda*, written by the Reverend Raymond [of Capua], a master general of the Order of Preachers;[13] or, from the virgin's book that she dictated to several scribes in her native tongue during one of her raptures;[14] or, from her letters that were dictated in the same way as her book and sent to both men and women of various status and conditions;[15] or, from sermons, epistles, and letters that various persons wrote concerning this virgin;[16] or, from several booklets concerning the virgin's life that were written by her first confessor [Tommaso della

Fonte]. It is on the basis of these texts, as well as on the basis of oral testimonies of trustworthy persons, that I have supplemented the *Legenda* to which I have referred several times.[17] As was already pointed out in the preface, some additions have been made to the paragraphs and chapters of the *Legenda*, but this *Libellus* also comprises stories that may already be found in the *Legenda*.[18] It should not be judged that this results in excess, because here one kind of style is used and in the *Legenda* another kind. Moreover, it is important to note that in the *Legenda* the matters are narrated more completely, because Master Raymond was the last confessor of the virgin, given to her by the Virgin, the mother of the Lord, as was attested by the virgin and may be learned in the beginning of the third part below.[19]

Thus, he addresses the deeds and teachings of the virgin in a more complete and fuller manner than anybody else, although in a few matters relating these things there is a more complete treatment here than in the *Legenda*.

The material that I have gathered together from the aforementioned sources may be divided into two treatises, both of which can be traced back to the first part of the complete *Legenda*, as well as to that of the abbreviated legend.[20]

The first treatise of the *Legenda* focuses on some of the virgin's visions, dialogues with God, temptations, and some exceptional triumphs that were granted to her. This treatise is divided into ten chapters or paragraphs that follow the way in which the first part of the *Legenda* is divided into ten chapters. Thus, each of the ten chapters displayed here corresponds to a chapter in the first part of the *Legenda*.[21]

Chapter 1. Let it be known that when the virgin was about five years old, she was devoted to the Virgin, the Mother of God, and whenever she encountered an image of the Virgin, she said: "*Ave Maria.*" Sometimes when she was saying the words, she was elevated from the ground.[22]

Chapter 2. When the virgin was approaching her sixth year, she went with her younger brother to visit their sister. She saw in the air a most beautiful lodge, inside which there were three people: Christ, John, and Paul. She saw that the last two wore priestly vestments, while Christ wore a pontifical habit. She saw an intense brightness. Her brother called her when she was in this state, but she was enjoying the sight. Then, the Savior gave his benediction, and she received it with great reverence. She was so deeply absorbed in the vision that she did not respond to her brother. These first two events are explicitly discussed in the second chapter of the first part of the *Legenda*.[23]

Chapter 3. The virgin's confessor wrote that later, before the virgin received her religious habit, she had an apparition of Saint Dominic and Saint Francis. She heard Saint Dominic call her: "My daughter, you are to take and wear this habit." He showed her the habit of the Order of Penance of Saint Dominic. Saint Dominic also held in his hand a most beautiful lily that was inflamed with a miraculous fire that did not consume the flower. The virgin took the habit with great joy and devotion.[24]

Chapter 4. Before the virgin took the habit of Saint Dominic, she was one evening praying in front of an image of the Crucified when the devil appeared to her holding a silk dress in his hands. He tempted her to put on the dress, but she only ridiculed and mocked him and turned back to the image of the Crucified. The devil disappeared, but she was overcome by a horrible temptation to wear the pompous and beautiful dresses that brides wear. She prayed and said to the Crucified: "My sweet Spouse, you know that I have never wanted anyone else but you as my spouse. Please help me to overcome this temptation. I do not ask you to take it way, but grant me victory over it." Soon after, the Blessed Virgin appeared to the virgin and showed her a most beautiful dress that emerged from the wounded side of the Crucified. The Virgin had even decorated the dress with golden ornaments and gems. The Virgin dressed the virgin and said: "May it be known that the dresses that flow from the side of my Son are more beautiful than any other dress."[25]

This may be found at the end of the sixth chapter of the first part of the *Legenda*.[26]

Chapter 5. The virgin had just recently taken the habit when the Lord showed her the following vision. As the virgin wondered why people prefer the ruin of the world over the refreshment in Christ, she saw a most beautiful tree in front of her. It had the most beautiful and sweet fruits, but the long branches made it difficult to get to them. Under the branches was some brushwood. By the tree was also a hill of the empty chaff of a cork oak.

Then hungry people came running to the place and saw the sweet fruits of the tree. They began to approach it, but as soon as they saw the brushwood they backed off because they were afraid of the thorns. They turned to the hill and with great care and dedication they collected and ate all the chaff. But the chaff did not nurture people; instead, the people remained hungry and became ill. Some others who came to the tree made their way through the brushwood, but when they realized how long the branches were and how difficult the ascent, they retreated and turned to the hill and did the same the first group had done. However, a few brave and avid ones rushed forward. They did not fear the brushwood or the hardships of the ascent, but they climbed up the tree, tasted and ate its sweet fruits. They were healthy, content, and well fed.

The vision may be explained in the following way: The tree is the incarnate Word, its fruits are the virtues, the hill of bran is the world.[27] The first group was afraid of the painfulness of penance and virtues. The second was prepared to try, but the people did not persist and they returned to the world. Both of these groups are always spiritually ill because they are drawn to superficial and worldly things that do not refresh the mind. But the difficulties and adversities did not keep the third group of people away from the virtues. One may find this vision in the ninth chapter of the first part of the *Legenda*.[28]

Chapter 6. At the first stages of her temptations, the virgin experienced grave carnal temptations as the devil committed his indecent acts before her. She started to pray at the break of dawn and prayed until the third hour, saying: "I put my trust in the Lord, Jesus Christ." Then, at the third hour, the Crucified appeared to her. His face, hair, and whole body were soaked in blood. She was astonished and did not recognize him. When the Crucified lifted his right hand from the cross and called her: "My daughter Catherine, can you see what I have endured for your sake?" she froze from fear and threw herself face down on the ground. But Christ consoled her: "Be strong, because I shall always be with you."

All the demons dispersed. She was consoled and thanked the Savior. She told her confessor how sweet a sensation it was to hear Christ say: "My daughter Catherine." Always when she remembered this event, she was filled with great joy.

Chapter 7. At times of tribulation and temptation the virgin persevered in fervent prayers, because after tribulations always came consolation. She was deeply absorbed into the passion of Christ, and in the passion she found her consolation and refreshment. One time she was battling the devil and experienced a great deal of anxiety and pain. But when she afterward prostrated herself in prayer, she saw Christ on the cross through her corporal eyes. He showed his side to her and said: "My daughter, see what I have accepted for your sake! Be fierce, because I am with you." These words sounded so sweet to her that she was totally overwhelmed. She said: "My Lord, my troubles are nothing. I am ready to endure anything for you, because you endure everything for me." By preserving in her prayers, the virgin always overcame her enemies. She used to tell to people with whom she discussed how prayer should always be the shield against one's enemy and a source of consolation and nourishment for one's soul. The movements of the soul, which is nourished and sustained with this food, will not be tedious but full of joy. She was, indeed, in continuous prayer, because her heart was always with God.

The two above-mentioned narrations may be found in the section that begins in the middle of the eleventh chapter of the *Legenda*.[29]

Chapter 8. I learned from the aforementioned scribes that the virgin learned miraculously not only to read but also to write. Let it be known that one time this holy virgin got hold of a vase in which a scribe had placed and prepared sinoper[30] for writing and illustrating letters. She took the quill and a small sheet of paper. Although she had minimal training in writing, she sat down and began to write in clear letters in her vulgar tongue on the sheet of paper. Her writing was translated into Latin and it reads as follows:

"Holy Spirit, enter my heart. Your strength leads me to God and grants me love and fear of God. Christ, keep me away from all evil thoughts. Rekindle and inflame your sweet love in me so that all suffering will seem light to me. My Holy Father and my sweet Lord, assist me in all my necessities. Christ, the love, Christ, the love."

The style and the form of the text above were such that they produced a clear sign of a miracle. Similar results are normally produced only after long practice in spelling, calligraphy, and writing. A venerable father, Fra Girolamo of Siena, from the Hermits of Saint Augustine, kept the sheet of the virgin's miraculous writing as a special relic. After the virgin had passed away, he became a preacher in Venice. There, he donated the sheet as a special gift to a venerable presbyter, Dom Leonardo Pisani of Venice. Subsequently, Leonardo Pisani generously donated it to me as a special gift. This sheet of paper and a few other relics of the virgin are now held by the sisters of Penance of Saint Dominic in Venice.[31]

Chapter 9. It should be noted that before the virgin miraculously wrote the text discussed above, nobody had ever seen her write. I received, however, a few letters from a certain venerable man, Father Dom Stefano Maconi of Siena from the Carthusian Order, who was one of the holy virgin's scribes and her beloved son in Christ. He wrote to me in order to explain, among some other things, how the virgin learned to write miraculously. She rose up from her prayers and had a desire to write, and she wrote by her own hand a brief letter and gave it to this Dom Stefano. As a conclusion to the letter she wrote in her vulgar tongue a sentence that would translate in the following way: "Know, my dearest son, that this is the first letter that I have ever written."

I learned from the letters that the said father submitted to me that the virgin later wrote several other letters in his presence and also a few pages of her book that she composed in her vulgar tongue. He had deposited and kept these letters written by the virgin in the Carthusian house in Pontignano, close to Siena. Moreover, I read and understood from collections of the virgin's letters, transcribed by several of her scribes, that the virgin wrote by her own hand two letters to the Reverend Father, Master Raymond, the one who wrote her *Legenda* after she passed away. These letters intimated, among other things, that God miraculously formed in her mind the aptitude to write as a sign of divine providence.[32]

These two chapters on the virgin's writing may be found at the beginning of the third part of her *Legenda* and also at the end of the eleventh chapter of the first part.[33]

Chapter 10. One time when the virgin was petitioning the Lord to espouse her, Christ appeared to her during her prayer and carried a ring that was decorated with five stones. As he gave her the ring, she was so filled with an overwhelming devotion that she was hardly able to endure it. She always saw the ring in front of her eyes, and it continued to fill her with a new devotion and delight, except when she felt that she had committed some act of negligence. Christ appeared to her together with the Prophet David, who was carrying a Psalter, and Saint Dominic. This narration clearly pertains to the twelfth, that is, the last chapter of the first part of the *Legenda*.[34]

The second treatise concerns some visions, abstractions, divine allocutions, or revelations that the virgin received when she was thinking of God, contemplating or praying, standing or moving around. These things brought both bodily and spiritual consolation to her and others. She also received special graces that she asked for herself or for others. This treatise is divided into twenty-one sections that may to some extent be found in the first part of the *Legenda*, especially in the ninth chapter, which concerns the virgin's visions.[35]

Chapter 1. May it be known that the virgin once told her confessor that she saw God in such sweetness that she could only say that he was entirely good.

Chapter 2. Once when the virgin's soul was drawn to the delight of God in the way just discussed, she placed herself by a certain window to contemplate God. She heard a sublime and unusual singing of a deep joy that made her feel that she was not in the world but in eternity.[36]

Chapter 3. When she was in the company of her companions and attentively thought about God, she was filled with such overwhelming delight that when her companions touched her, they could not feel any pulse.[37] Afterward, she began such a loud singing that she seemed to be transformed into another person. All her companions drew such comfort from this experience that they did not want to eat for almost three days. Filled with the abundant showers of the Spirit, they constantly sang their prayers.

Chapter 4. When the virgin was in the church of the Friars Preachers, Saint Dominic appeared to her and comforted her in such a way that she wanted to die out of delight.[38] He accompanied her all the way back to her home.[39]

Chapter 5. When the virgin was praying in the church, she saw Christ and spoke with him. Such a great light emerged from his chest that it illuminated the entire church. She was greatly consoled. Afterward, he led her to the eternal life and kept her there for a long time. She did not want to return back to the world, but Christ said to her: "Go with my benediction." She returned to herself and realized that she was alone in the church. Immediately she returned back to her home, but she walked almost without knowing what she was doing. The virgin told this experience to her confessor when she was commanded to do so.

Chapter 6. When the virgin was praying in her room, she sensed some heaviness above her head and as she stood up she saw Christ and Saint Dominic. She began to sing, and they joined her. Christ was between the virgin and Saint Dominic, and all three of them sang together. She felt such a consolation that she wanted nothing else but to die.

Chapter 7. When the virgin was with her companions and she was contemplating God, her mind was suddenly drawn to the eternal life. She saw herself in the company of God and all the saints. Then she saw a lamb that was white as snow. All the saints followed the lamb and she joined them. Together they were singing a most beautiful song [Rev 5:13; 14:4; 15:3].

Chapter 8. The virgin was praying in her room, and she yearned for Christ's grace. She had just said "Let him kiss me with the kisses of his mouth" [Cant 1:2], when Christ appeared to her and offered her his kiss. She was so filled with delight that she asked him how she could always keep him with her. He answered that the right way was to focus always on spiritual goods. As the virgin heard these precious words, she asked Christ to take her soul away from this world. He responded that he did not want that to happen. He added: "On the contrary, I want that you take care of people and that your life will serve as a rule and example for many."[40]

Chapter 9. The virgin petitioned Christ to give her and her two companions vestments of purity. As she was praying, she saw Saint Mary and Saint Dominic in the company of Christ. Christ opened with his hands his side that was wounded on the cross. She entered the wound and with a great delight she received habits for herself and her companions.[41]

Chapter 10. The virgin was in prayer when an angel of God appeared to her and brought her a garland of lilies. He said: "I am giving this to you on the behalf of God as a symbol of your purity." The garland was so beautiful that the virgin did not know how to describe it, but when she reflected on its beauty, she was filled with such delight that she nearly died.

Chapter 11. The virgin was once so deeply absorbed in her mind that when her companions touched her, they could not feel any pulse. She saw that Christ held her in his arms. Christ held her and pulled her toward him in such a way that she did not touch the ground. This experience was granted her because she only wanted celestial goods and did not care for worldly goods, which she intensely despised as filth. She marveled at the ignorance of many people who loved and desired worldly things when they could have had celestial goods. Often she said: "O unknown Lord! Why do people not know you, good Jesus?" And, she said to people who were conversing with her: "Rejoice, rejoice in Jesus Christ, our father who is the consolation of the souls." And, when someone asked her how she was, she answered with a happy face: "I am doing very well, praised be my Lord, Jesus Christ." She was always happy, because she was engaged in good occupations and practiced spiritually worthy things. Her first confessor testified that he never saw her do anything else but pray, read, weep, sing, or some other spiritual practices. She was often in rapture and absorption of mind. She always had Christ in her heart and on her lips, and when she was on the streets she saw nothing else but Christ.

Chapter 12. One time the virgin prayed that she would be granted real virtues, that is, true charity toward both God and her neighbor. She prayed that her neighbor's well-being would give her a greater pleasure than her own good, and similarly, that her neighbor's suffering would cause her more pain that her own ill-fortune. As she was praying, Christ appeared to her and her companion all of a sudden. He said: "My daughter Catherine, I shall grant you the gift you requested. It will be directed to you and to anyone else you want." After she received the gift, she was in such fervor that for ten days she could not eat or drink. When she returned to herself, it was as if she had been sleeping. She said that she found herself in great peace and in extreme purity. She wanted to be with young children, and to give them kisses and embrace them.

Chapter 13. The virgin's confessor wrote that once one of the virgin's companions told him that as she and the virgin were conversing about God in the virgin's home, the virgin withdrew a bit apart.

She began to pray. After a while the virgin began to laugh loudly and to cry, both at the same time. The companion observed the virgin closely and saw her face turn totally red. When she touched the virgin, the virgin did not sense anything. As the virgin returned to herself, her companion asked her to tell what had taken place during the absorption. But the virgin refused to tell anything to her companion. She only wanted to speak to her confessor.[42] She revealed to him that when she was laughing, her soul was overcome by such an infusion of grace and divine bliss that her body was not able to endure them. She said that she was not able to explain her bliss. She only knew she had seen the humanity of Christ, who showed her the wound in his side. She told the confessor that after she got up, she went and found for herself a place in one of the quiet corners of the church. There she was overcome by such a sweet bliss that she was totally bathed in sweat from the labor of the prayer. She lamented to her confessor that she was unable to explain the depth of her bliss.

Chapter 14. When the virgin was praying in her room, the apostle James the Great and Saint Mary Magdalene appeared to her.[43] The virgin saw herself between the two and she was deeply consoled. Afterward she saw Christ, who had a birthmark on his face.[44] He embraced her so tightly that she felt he constantly touched her. She said: "The Lord loved us so much that he gave the one who he loved so much to us, rather than to the angels." She said to her confessor: "See, Father, how I am unable to converse with other people because I am so drawn to my spouse, Jesus Christ, that even my corporal senses are pulled toward him. Thus, I beg you to give me license to go somewhere else." She said this because sometimes her companions took her to a certain place to benefit and to learn from her teaching; because she spoke with a great fervor and in a miraculous way she attracted people to the fear and love of God.

Chapter 15. Sometimes the virgin suffered from bleeding from her sides, which she got from the violence she inflicted on herself at receiving the abundance of God's sweet and tender gifts.[45] She was drawn in such a way to God that she was unable to bear it and thus suffered from severe bodily illness. It happened, however, that when the virgin was in this state, Christ and Mary Magdalene appeared to her. She felt that they touched her, and immediately she was freed from her illness. She said that she almost felt the physical sensation of the touch. The illness returned several times, but God always freed her. She never consumed any kind of bodily medication, but, instead, she had in her soul Jesus Christ, the healer of all illnesses.

Chapter 16. The virgin was in the church of the Preaching Friars in Siena contemplating Christ's humanity, when she saw in Christ something even higher than his humanity. She saw in him such plenitude, charity, sweetness, pleasure, and so much beatitude that it was impossible for her to explain them in words. Thus, she asked her confessor: "Please petition God to open my mouth so that I could explain this beatitude to you. Help me to praise the Lord. My tongue is unable to express all the things that he performs in my soul."

Chapter 17. The virgin had to go with two of her companions to the monastery of Santa Bonda, which was not far from Siena.[46] She was very ill, with lower legs so swollen that it was difficult for her to move, but love made her to go on. She was going this way, but as soon as she left Siena behind, Saint Paul and Mary Magdalene appeared to her. Both of them walked with her and consoled her, and she began to walk so fast that her companions could not keep up with her. She walked half of the way with Paul and Mary.

Then the virgin suddenly saw Christ in front of her. He showed her his open side, and she began to go so fast that she was almost running, and her companions had to struggle even harder to follow her. She walked with her mouth open and so withdrawn into herself that she did not see the things around her. Moving in this way, she arrived at the monastery without her companions, who were unable to keep up with her. She entered a church and threw herself on the ground, but then she embraced Christ and placed her mouth to his side. She tasted such a divine sweetness that she did not know how to express it. She stayed this way for a long time. When her companions caught up with her, they found that she was totally alienated from her senses. Afterward, the virgin rose up and began to speak with the nuns in such a fervor and charity that everyone was astonished. Everyone gathered on the church choir and other places to see her.

Chapter 18. Two of the virgin's companions were once visiting her room, and they ate on the plank on which the virgin used to lie while she slept.[47] One of them said: "Oh, this is a holy table." The servant of God answered: "If you would know who was on this table, you would say even more." The companions asked: "Who?" The virgin answered: "Christ and Saint Mary Magdalene. One day when I was alone in the garden by the house, Christ and Mary Magdalene appeared to me, and I conversed with them the same way I do with my companions. After a short while I said to Christ: 'Master, I do not think it is good to stay here.' He replied: 'Daughter, go where you wish.' We came to my room, and Christ was on my one side and Magdalene on the other. Christ sat on one end of the table, I sat in the middle, and Mary stood leaning on the other end. We remained this way for a long while, and this is why the table is indeed holy."

Chapter 19. One year, on January 11, the virgin told her confessor that when she was in rapture she heard the singing and lauds of the saints on high.[48] Earlier she had not been able to understand the lauds, but on that day she did. She said that everybody sang together, but those who loved more ardently sang more clearly than the others. This is what her beloved Mary Magdalene and John the Evangelist did. The saints finished all their lauds with the acknowledgment that everything they had was as a gift of God's grace and mercy. She said to the Lord: "You make me think of those who, in the Apocalypse, follow the Lamb and then take off their crowns and throw them at the Lamb's feet" [Rev 4:10].

When she was telling this to her confessor she asked him: "Do you not hear these voices?" She wept out of profuse sweetness and continued to say: "Do you not hear Magdalene, who sings very strongly and has a unique voice?" She listened intensely, as if she would have heard the singing with her corporal ears. Then she said to her confessor: "Be prepared tonight, because I will send the Lord, Jesus Christ, to you." This indeed happened, although not corporally but rather through the change of heart of that confessor, as he himself testified.

Chapter 20. During Vespers of the vigil of a certain feast of Saint Lucy,[49] the virgin began to feel a great elevation of the spirit. She saw, not in a dream but while she was awake, that in heaven preparations for a feast were being made, but she did not know why and by whom. The bliss continued immediately after the virgin arrived at a church, and it was so solemn that the virgin felt that the church bells should have been sounded. On another occasion, God fulfilled the virgin's desire. One day there was stormy weather, and it looked likely that there was going to be some heavy rain. As is commonly done in her hometown in situations like this, the bells of not only one church, but of all the churches of the town were rung. This way the virgin's desire was fulfilled. Afterward, she saw that Vespers were sung solemnly in heaven and a multitude of virgins arrived in a choir. One virgin outshone all the others, and all the male and female saints showed their reverence to her. She had a golden clasp on her chest, and she was embellished with a marvelous beauty.[50]

Chapter 21. Once the confessor told the virgin that the following day would be the feast of the Blessed Margaret,[51] the virgin began to laugh. Afterward she explained why she rejoiced. For three years the demons fiercely fought against her on that day especially, and even on the preceding days. She saw many in her cell who tried to strike her, but they were helpless because God's strength shielded her. Nevertheless, she felt a lot of pain in her heart and was unable to cry. She then wanted to rise and to speak with a few people, but she heard a voice that asked her to sit down, which she did. And look! Saint Mary Magdalene appeared and came to her. The virgin started immediately to weep, and a fountain of tears broke out from her eyes. She felt such deep consolation and sweetness that she was unable to endure them. For this reason she begged her Lord, Jesus Christ, to take her away from this life.[52]

Some of the events discussed here may be found in the second part of the *Legenda*. However, most of them derive from the first part of the *Legenda*, just as has been described above.[53]

May this suffice for the first part of this *Libellus*, the part which corresponds with the first part of the virgin's *Legenda*.

Stefana Quinzani's Ecstasy of the Passion

Editor's Note: Stefana Quinzani of Orzinuovi (1457–1530) became an orphan when she was fifteen. Subsequently, she earned her living as a domestic servant.[1] Despite Stefana's humble situation, her dramatic ecstasies and imitations of Christ's passion granted her religious and secular authority as a spiritual guide who was consulted by leading magnates of her time. Some of Stefana's theatrical imitations of Christ's passion were attended by the ruling family of Mantua, the Gonzagas. Stefana even wrote religious exhortations to the members of the noble family.[2] She also met with another saintly protégée of the Gonzaga family, Osanna of Mantua (1449–1505), who attended one of Stefana's ecstasies.[3]

Stefana began her religious life as a home-dwelling secular penitent, but in 1512 she founded her own religious community for penitent women in Soncino. This foundation, dedicated to Saint Paul and Saint Catherine of Siena, was intended as a haven for poor women, but despite the fame of the foundress, the community suffered from poverty and lack of institutional support.[4] The difficulties that Stefana experienced in providing the means for her foundation show that people's fascination with Stefana and other female mystics did not necessarily imply consistent institutional support for these women's religious lives.

Note: The translation of this text, written in Italian, is based on Giuseppe Brunati's edition in his *Vita, o Gesta di santi bresciani*, 2 vols. (Brescia: Venturini, 1854–56), 2:55–62. An edition of the text may also be found in Antonio Cistellini, *Figure della riforma pretridentina: Stefana Quinzani, Angela Merici, Laura Mignani, Bartolomeo Stella, Francesco Cabrini, Francesco Santabona* (Brescia: Morcelliana, 1979), 194–97. Cistellini does not, however, include the valuable list of the twenty-one witnesses who signed the document. I am grateful to Tamar Herzig for her insightful comments concerning this text and its historical context.

The *Ecstasy of the Passion* is a detailed description of one of Stefana's physical imitations of Christ's passion, signed by twenty-one high-ranking witnesses. The event took place at the beginning of the Lenten season, on Friday, February 17, 1497, in the house of Stefana's master, GianFrancesco Verdello. This four-hour-long ecstasy spanned from the devil's attacks on Stefana to her imitation of Christ's crucifixion; it ended with Stefana's prayers for the church and with Christ's acknowledgment of her suffering.

Stefana's ecstasy may be viewed in the context of the later medieval cult of Christ's passion and, in particular, the Dominican tradition of imitating Christ's suffering through corporal prayer. According to a mid-thirteenth-century text, *The Nine Ways of Prayer of Saint Dominic,* one of Saint Dominic's ways of prayer was to extend his body in the position of a cross, a technique used by Giovanna of Orvieto as well.[5] Another religious practice that presented a context for Stefana's experience is the Stations of the Cross, a practice that began to take shape during the late Middle Ages and focused on the various stages of Christ's suffering.[6] The Christian pilgrimage to the sites of Christ's passion in Jerusalem became increasingly difficult during the late fourteenth century, and the practice was brought to an end when the Turks conquered Constantinople in 1453. Thus, Western Christians looked toward new ways to commemorate the scenes of Christ's sacrifice. Stefana's passion must have given her audience a comforting sense of being physically present in the places that were no longer accessible to Christians.

The Ecstasy of the Passion[7]

Jesus

In nomine Domini nostri Jesu Christi. Amen. In the praise and glory of the high and immortal God, in the strengthening of our holy Catholic faith, and in the edification of Christian believers. This document is to make manifest to all readers and listeners the events that happened this year, one thousand four hundred and ninety-seven years after the nativity of our Redeemer, Jesus Christ, in the noble land of Crema, part of which belongs to the Diocese of Piacenza and part to the Diocese of Cremona.[8] Crema is located in Lombardy and is ruled by the most illustrious *signoria* of Venice. In the house of GianFrancesco Verdello, a nobleman from Crema who lives in the parish of San Jacomo, there was a devout and holy woman called Sister Stefana Quinzani from Orzinuovi, which is in the Diocese of Brescia.[9] She wears the third habit of the sacred and divine order of Patriarch Saint Dominic.

Every Friday Stefana has powerful visions and divine revelations that are beyond description. During these visions the supreme and omnipotent God communicates to her all the mysteries of the passion of the Redeemer of the universe, Jesus Christ. This is what happens: Before dawn, this sister is tempted by various and diverse operations and manifestations of the devil, as can be understood from the words that she speaks during her rapture. The severest temptations concern the sacred faith and her fortitude. The devil claims that she cannot endure the heights of the passion, and he accuses her of vainglory: "Many people want to see you. You want them to call you a saint." All this happens within a period of half an hour. The saintly woman forcefully resists all the temptations and repulses the demon. In her ecstasy and rapture of the spirit, she speaks clearly and responds to all the attacks and temptations of the devil. With divine help, she thus prevails over the devil.

After [the temptations], her hands are tied above her head with insoluble but invisible straps, and her feet are tied as well. She is like Christ when he was tied to the pillar. Her visible bodily movements make it clear that she is being invisibly flagellated. Her whole body moves for half an hour, but her hands and feet are immobile, just as if they were tied with real cord to the pillar. Many of those who were present made efforts to separate the hands, but they did not succeed, even though many used great force. Indeed, it was not possible to move even a finger. She was tied to this position for almost an hour. Her torments and afflictions were so great, and she let out such weeping laments and sighs that it would not be possible for a human heart to think or to comprehend such pain unless one witnesses it with one's own eyes. And, even then, it is impossible to explain completely the pain in a human tongue. Then there was an interval of about half an hour. Then, as one can understand from the sister's deeply respectful gestures and pious words, Jesus Christ appears to her. He comforts her and strengthens her for the acceptance of the passion. He offers her his most holy passion. In ecstasy, filled with an intense fervor, she answers him: "Lord, I am not worthy of suffering this holy passion, but, Lord, may your sacred will always be done."

After she has spoken, her hands are tied in front of her with the same kind of invisible and unbreakable ties that were described above. When Pilate examined Jesus Christ, Jesus' hands were tied the same way. Then she opens her right hand, as if she would receive a reed and hold firmly onto it. While she is in her contemplation, Jesus Christ offers her the crown of thorns. She replies with great joy and humility: "Lord, be assured that I want it." She rises up, and, with great reverence and fervor, she receives the crown of thorns on her head. So great are her suffering, pains, torments, and trembling that it is not possible to explain her painful torments and corporal movements in human language. She stays in this intense torture and tearful lament for a quarter of an hour. She is covered in sweat from head to toe. Then her pains cease. Her body is immobile while her spirit is lifted in rapture. But if somebody even lightly touches her forehead with a finger or a small object, immediately the pains, cries, and aforementioned laments return, as was seen several times, because she feels the intense pain of her crown. Then she calms down and stays for half an hour in contemplation.

As Stefana prepares for the passion of the cross, her reason fights against her sensuality. The poor woman says: "Do not fear. Look at your Lord who is covered in blood from head to toe. If you fear the pain, look at the award. Let your reason reign." Then she sees the cross and stares at it with fixed, unwavering eyes. She says: "O you Great Redemption; O you Redemption of the humanity; O you Salvific Cross. I have longed for you for a long time." Then she moves to the cross and, with great devotion and joy, she embraces and kisses the invisible cross, as if she were in its corporal presence. Then her right arm is stretched on the side, and it is as if her hands were fixed with real nails. And, immediately, one sees how the joints are pulled and extended, the veins raised, and her hands become black. Just as if her hand were fixed with material nails, she lets out a terrible cry and a tearful lament. Then her left arm is extended the same way as the right one. Both her arms are stretched out and held above. Then her legs are stretched out and her right foot is placed on top of the left one. As the legs are pulled out, the entire body curves out. Only the hands rest totally immobile in the place that they were nailed, just as if they have been fixed on the cross with real iron nails. And on the right foot that is placed on the top of the left foot appears a red mark that looks like a *marcello*.[10] When her left hand is tied down, she lets out a similar cry and weeping lament to that she did when her right hand was tied down. She cries out and laments the same way also when her feet are tied down.

She remains extended on the cross in the likeness of Jesus Christ, the Crucified. After a short interval, she drinks sour wine and gall from the sponge, just as did Jesus. Then, after another brief interval, she trembles in such a violent way that her spirit seems to have left the body. She stays immobile for a while and then breaks into a great commotion of cries and prayerful laments. It seems that she is poked with a lance in her side. Afterward, she stays in a position that makes her look dead. The time that she spends on the cross is altogether about an hour. After that her right hand is freed, then the left, and then both feet. After the removal of the nails, it seems as if all her body parts discussed above are in great pain.

The sister's gestures and words show that Jesus Christ appears to her. She offers her deep thanks for the gift of the passion that he has given to her. She makes fervent prayers to Jesus Christ, and she prays for the souls of the people. She first commends her soul to God and then prays for the general well-being of the church. She makes special prayers for the state of all priests and asks the Lord to enlighten their minds so that they can tend well the sheep who have been given to their care. She prays particularly for the confessors who are responsible for her spiritual care and guidance. Most singularly she prays for the Order of Saint Dominic, which is unjustly attacked by many, and then she predicts trouble for those who speak against the order.[11] Then she prays for the Benedictine, Franciscan, Augustinian, and Carmelite orders, and then for all the orders in general and for the entire church, especially for the preachers so that their preaching bears fruit. She concludes: "If they do not bear fruit with their sermons, the Lord will not rest in their hearts, but in those of the crowds of the unrepentant sinners."[12] Then she prays particularly for the Order of the Third Habit of Saint Dominic by saying: "Lord, this holy habit is a hidden treasure that is not known by many, I pray that you protect it."[13] Then she tearfully prays for the well-being of Italy and for that of some particular regions, especially Crema and a few other ones. Moreover, she commends her soul to God, and she prays once again for the confessors who guide her and for all her benefactors. Then she prays for the sinners, especially for those who have offended her, and she asks Jesus Christ to forgive them and to illuminate their minds, because they do not know what they are doing.

Afterward she prays to Jesus Christ with great urgency: "Lord, I pray to you that you take away this visibly manifested pain and give me all the other sufferings, even greater ones, if only they are invisible. This way I will not be famous during my lifetime." She continues to say: "I do not regret suffering all kinds of pain for your love. I only do not want to be known for them. Thus, I pray to you, my beloved Lord, that you take away this visible suffering and passion, and give me all kinds of greater pains that happen in secret and do not make me known." Then with great modesty, devotion, and joy she rises and humbly asks for Jesus Christ's benediction. Having received it, she returns from the rapture to her natural bodily senses. Her suffering for the passion happened entirely in ecstasy. In the ecstasy she speaks and gestures in the way that is described above. *Per omnia benedictus Deus, qui in sexu fragili tam magna et mirabilia, ac non solum non videntibus sed etiam videntibus pene incredibilia temporibus nostris fecit et factit in persona prefate sororis Stephane et ostendit nobis.*[14] Amen.[15]

Penitent Women
as Authors

Osanna of Mantua: Letters to Francesco Gonzaga (a selection)

Editor's Note: Osanna Andreasi of Mantua (1449–1505) was a resourceful woman. She supported her younger siblings after the death of their parents, and she mastered a number of practical household responsibilities. She also negotiated positions of power for her family members and acted as a determined advocate for the weak and the poor.[1] While Osanna's hagiographers emphasized her inner life of prayer, visions, and mysticism, Osanna's letters to the Gonzaga family reveal that she was a woman acutely interested in the matters of the world.[2]

Osanna was a Dominican penitent and an imitator of Catherine of Siena's christocentric mysticism. It was not the Dominicans who secured Osanna's success as a saint, however. Rather, the ruling couple of Mantua, Francesco II Gonzaga (d. 1519) and his wife, Isabella d'Este (d. 1539), played the key roles in supporting Osanna during her life and promoting her posthumous cult.

Osanna advised Isabella d'Este in spiritual manners.[3] Isabella was a woman with a noted appreciation for learning and the life of the mind, and her support of saintly women like Osanna reflected contemporary ideals of courtly life. Isabella's father, Ercole I d'Este, shared her fascination with the mystical experiences of saintly

---

Note: The translation of Osanna's letters to Francesco Gonzaga is based on Giuseppe Bagolini's and Lodovigo Ferretti's edition in *La beata Osanna da Mantova, terziaria domenicana* (1449–1505) (Florence: Tipografia Domenicana, 1905), lxv-xcvj (appendix). The translated sixteen letters are selected from the surviving thirty-four letters that Osanna addressed to Francesco Gonzaga.

women and showed his support by patronizing Lucia Broccadelli, another Dominican visionary and the author of *Seven Revelations.*[4]

Osanna's interaction with Isabella's husband, Francesco Gonzaga, revolved around practical matters. Francesco was a military leader, a *condottiere*, who bounced from one political camp to another and even served in the army of the king of France, who originally had been the archrival of the Gonzagas and their allies. He was also a womanizer who was more known for his fine breed of horses than for love of culture and religion.[5] Francesco's morals were thus questionable and his worldliness evident. Nevertheless, Osanna was his devoted supporter. We learn from her letters that she fervently prayed for the success of his military campaigns and ensured that others did the same. She worried about Francesco's poor health and anxiously waited to hear from him. Osanna's protective and partisan dedication to Francesco and Mantua earned her the appellation *madre della patria*, or mother of the fatherland.[6]

Whereas many saintly women denounced the morals of worldly leaders and directed harsh criticism even at their own supporters, Osanna did nothing of the kind. She petitioned the marquis on behalf of her family and other people, but she never urged him to reform his worldly ways. Francesco needed the protection of Osanna's prayers, and he was ready to grant her favors in return, but it is evident that he had little use for spiritual advice and Osanna wisely stayed away from any language that might have suggested her possible spiritual or moral displeasure with the marquis.

The Gonzagas continued to support Osanna after her death, and they ensured the exceptionally swift production of her *vitae*, collections of letters, and other documents concerning her sanctity.[7] Osanna's *vita* by the Dominican Francesco Silvestri was ready only a few months after her death, and it was soon followed by another *vita* by an Olivetan monk Girolamo Scolari, Osanna's longtime confessor.[8] As quickly as 1515 Pope Leo X granted the right for local celebration of Osanna's *dies natalis* or feast day.[9]

Osanna of Mantua: Letters to Francesco Gonzaga

[Letter 46][10]

Jesus [and] Mary.

Illustrissime domine, domine, post humilem commendationem.[11] May the peace and blessings of Jesus Christ always be with Your Excellency, my most special lord. There are three things that a human being naturally desires. First, security and peace. Second, life, which is desired *non solum* by humans, *sed etiam omne animal.* Third, knowledge. *Unde, illustrissime Domine*, I do not truly care for the last two things, because I keep the life eternal in my mind. Nevertheless, while I am in this world, I have a great need for the first thing, that is, a quiet and a restful place without the tumult of the crowds. *Unde, illustrissime Domine*, knowing that this place is so good for my state of mind, I pray that You concede me this grace, not at all for the sake of the material things, but *solum* for the comfort of the place. *Et ideo*, I plead that You do not choose to remove my brother from the vicariate of this place that offers me rest.[12] The Lord will be Your Excellency's remunerator, and I shall always be obliged to pray to Christ Jesus to keep You in the state of happiness. *Pax vobis.* December 26 [ca. 1489].[13]

[Letter 47]

Jesus [and] Mary.

Illustrious Lord, my most special, etc. I have learned that Your Excellency has rotated his officials, which is a necessary and reasonable thing to do. My brother's vicariate here in Bigarello has also been vacated. Many may testify how well my brother has exercised Your Excellency's office. It is expected that You decide about Your officials according to Your wishes. Nevertheless, I pray Your Excellency that, for the love of God and love of me, You keep my brother in Your favor and do not abandon him, because I promise to pray to the Lord ardently for Your Excellency's salvation and happiness. I ask to be held always in Your favor, and, once again, I appeal to You and petition for Your mercy, knowing how much reverence and devotion Your Excellency has for the Holy Mother of Jesus Christ. *Pax vobis.* Bigarello, October 1, 1491.

[Letter 50]

Most Illustrious Prince. I have not wanted to burden Your Excellency in these tormented days, but a great need forces me [to turn to you] in the name of good Jesus. I have a brother who is in charge of his many children.[14] I am asking Your Excellency to provide him with an office of Your choosing. I ask to be held always in Your favor. Mantua, March 27, 1497.

[Letter 51]

Jesus [and] Mary.

My Most Illustrious Lord. My beloved spouse, Jesus Christ, the Lord, who sees and knows everything, knows that I pray every day that he in his clemency would keep Your Lordship from all evil and make You victorious in all Your actions. Most of all, I pray for the salvation of Your soul that it may pass from this realm to that of God and his eternal happiness. My Lord, I turn to You as somebody who loves Your Lordship and with all my heart I ask You to perform an act of charity, because I know that I myself am unable to help. Acts of charity are dear to the Divine Majesty. My Beloved Lord, I have been visited several times by the wife of Messer Giovanbattista Trevigno. She has been very anguished, and she has lamented her adverse fortune of having been left in the condition that is known by Your Lordship. Far from her relatives, she finds herself in the country where she is put in great need and where she only has the mercy of Your Lordship. I beg that in Your clemency You provide for her needs and show that You hold her in Your favor. Do that in *amore Dei* and in order to demonstrate to the public that Your ways are free, just as were those of Your predecessors. Therefore, My Lord, I ask You to provide her staple goods or provisions, or at least *victum et vestitum* for her pitiable brigade of children. Until now I have supported her, but I am presently unable to do so, because I do not have the means. I beg Your Excellency to have compassion for her. Please forgive me if I am tedious to Your Lordship. I ask You to hold her and myself in Your favor. *Pax vobis.* On the feast of All Saints [November 1], 1498.

[Letter 54]

Jesus.

My Most Illustrious and Beloved Lord, may the peace of the pacific sweet Jesus Christ be always with Your Illustrious Lordship. I am humbly pleading You to exercise Your usual clemency and mercy and to show Your favor to a poor man, Messer Pietro del Bruno, and his relative, who You have put in prison in Sermide. My Beloved Lord, Pietro del Bruno was brought up in our house and is a bailiff of one of my brothers. I ask You to hold him in Your favor, because that poor man is not the culprit. I am certain that he knows nothing. If it pleases Your Lordship, he will give good ransom and he will be constantly watched. I am pleading that Your Benign Lordship sees fit to exercise Your benign clemency and mercy. I ask to be held in Your favor, and I take it as my highest duty to pray that the Lord holds You in the state of greatest happiness. Amen. Mantua, December 9, 1499.

[Letter 56]

Jesus [and] Mary.

Most Illustrious Lord, beloved in the precious blood of Christ Jesus. May his peace and well-being be always with Your Excellency, etc. Even though I am aware of my condition and state, it is not appropriate to ask from Your Illustrious Excellency what I am ask-ing for my nephews and nieces in the enclosed supplication. However, they have been left to me as if they were my children to protect, and, knowing that they are at the age when they only con-sume and do not produce, I am afraid that poverty will lead them to evil.[15] Thus, might it be possible for You to provide dowries for the two young girls who wish to enter a monastery to serve God? The aforementioned necessities and constraints force me to ask if Your

Lordship could be graceful and exempt my nephews, mentioned above, for ten years, or for a shorter or a longer period, depending on what You see as fitting.[16] If I am presumptuous with my requests, I ask for Your Excellency's forgiveness. We throw ourselves at Your feet, but if your answer is no, may my request be as it would have never been said aloud. I ask to be enclosed in Your favor, and I am most obliged to pray to God that he keeps You *cum* the Illustrious Madonna, Your wife, in the state of happiness. *Pax vobis.* Mantua, March 21, 1500.

[Letter 64]

My Illustrious Lord in the precious blood of the Crucified Jesus. May his peace be always *cum* Your Lordship. I have already several times, Beloved Lord, asked You to give the castellany of Ostia to Jacomo de la Nova, my poor relative from Ostia, for whom I feel compassion and love. With Your usual clemency You promised me to fulfill this desire, and You said You were most pleased to do so. Now it is time to rotate the officials, and I blush to be reminding Your Excellency. I pray that Your Excellency finds it fitting to console me during these solemn festivities by fulfilling the above-mentioned promise and see that the above-named Jacomo will, in effect, receive the castellany mentioned above. I see the fulfillment of this thing as a special grace from Your Illustrious Lordship. As Your unworthy servant, I ask to be held in Your favor. Mantua, December 31, 1501.

[Letter 65]

Jesus [and] Mary.

My Most Illustrious and Excellent Lord, beloved in the precious blood of Christ Jesus. May the peace of Christ be always *cum* Your Excellency. My Dear Illustrious Lord, the pleas, cries, tears, sobs, and sighs of the poor daughters of Messer Jacomo de la Colomba have moved me to write to You. The daughters have again and again begged me or asked somebody else to beg on their behalf, but I have always turned them away and excused myself, because I have not wanted to act. But now they are forced by extreme necessity to find a living, and I cannot refuse them. My heart has been moved by pity and compassion to such a degree that it is no longer possible for me to stay away from writing. With heartfelt pity and tears in my eyes I am writing to Your Excellency, the most compassionate of all. How could these four daughters be married and given dowries if they do not have anything to live on? My Beloved Lord in Jesus Christ, I ask Your Pious, Most Merciful, and Sweet Excellency that, for the sake of the sufferings of the Crucified Jesus, You see it pleasing to give then a provision. I ask You to pardon me if I am causing displeasure with my letter. Even if my heart would be made of rock or iron I could not avoid being moved by pity. Their eyes are like fountains; so profuse are their tears. Thus, I am asking You indeed to hold them in Your favor. I myself am under infinite obligation to pray ardently that God keeps You in the state of happiness. Amen. Mantua, June 10, 1502.

[Letter 68]

Jesus [and] Mary.

My Most Illustrious Lord, beloved in the precious blood of Christ Jesus. May the peace of Christ be always *cum* Your Lordship. I have been moved by compassion, and, because it is the time for pardons by both the Celestial Lord *et etiam* the earthly ones, I want to satisfy the wishes of those people who have asked me to appeal to Your Lordship.[17] I am sending to You my messenger who carries a few letters and supplications that were given to me when Your Lordship returned from France.[18] Because Your Excellency said that You wanted to pay me, the unworthy one, a new visit, I did not send the letters to You before. With all my might I ask You to hold them in the favor of Your benign and merciful Lordship. *Similiter,* I am asking Your Lordship to be favorable to the son of Messer Gasparo Gonzaga, as well as to all paupers and prisoners. I ask Your Lordship to forgive me if I am too presumptuous in my requests or if I burden Your Excellency. It is my desire that Your Lordship and I meet in paradise. I ask to be held forever in Your favor. I ardently pray to the Lord and his sweet and most Holy Mother that they keep You *cum* the Illustrious Madonna Your wife and Your precious son in the state of happiness. Amen. Mantua, April 12, 1503.

[Letter 70]

Jesus [and] Mary.

Most Illustrious and Excellent Lord, beloved in the precious blood of the Sweet Jesus. The Most Illustrious Lady, beloved wife of Your Excellency, paid me a visit on the behalf of Your Most Merciful Excellency, and I learned from her that You are ill with fever. The news troubles and saddens me, and I pray for God's grace. I beg Your Lordship to let me know soon about Your state, as You told Messer Alessio You would do. I shall pray to the Lord and Our Lady that, if it pleases the Divine Majesty, Your Lordship's health will be restored. I ask to be held always in Your favor. *Pax vobis.* Mantua, June 20, 1503. I wrote in a hurry.

[Letter 71]

Jesus [and] Mary.

Most Illustrious and Excellent Lord, beloved in the precious blood of the Christ. I have received Your Lordship's letter.[19] The news that My Lord is well has given me such comfort that it is difficult to express it in speaking or writing. You have always been present in our prayers, even if they may not be of any special value. My Lord, beloved in the holy wound of Christ Jesus, I have said the prayers for You, and I have ceaselessly made sure that also other pious people have done so, because I cannot rely on my own. I am praying to the merciful Lord and his most Holy Mother that they provide Your Lordship with faith. If it pleases Your Clemency, please let me have frequent news of Your state of health. Your Lordship will never leave my mind. Our mothers in San Vincenzo[20] do not cease *cum* their ardent prayers. I have written to our Vicar General to order all the friars of all our monasteries to pray for Your Lordship. I ask to be held always in Your favor. *Pax vobis.* Mantua, September 1, 1503.

[Letter 72]

Jesus [and] Mary.

Most Illustrious and Excellent Lord, beloved in the precious blood of the sweet Jesus and his most devout and Holy Virgin Mother. My Beloved Lord, it seems like a million years since I have had news from Your Excellency. I pray and plead that You are favorable toward me and allow me know how You are, because I cannot think of any sweeter graces of God than knowing that You are well. I went today to pay my respects to the Lady Marchioness. The baby, Lord Federico,[21] and the princesses are well.[22] They, and I, Your unworthy servant, ask to be held always in Your favor. Mantua, September 15, 1503.

[Letter 74]

Jesus [and] Mary.

Most Illustrious and Excellent Lord, my most beloved. True peace [is in] the pure and sweet side of the immaculate Lamb, Jesus, where all the just and purged souls are united in his precious blood, etc. I have been deeply consoled by the honor that our Holy Father and the Romans have shown to Your Lordship.[23] May the Lord and his most Holy Mother be praised in all things. I pray that the Divine Majesty and the Sacred Virgin will grant Your Excellency a safe return. I beg that You write me in Your mercifulness Your news as often as possible. Your Lordship, please forgive me if I am presumptuous, but, My Beloved and Most Illustrious Lord, the love and dedication that I feel toward Your Excellency forces me to be presumptuous. I am not going to say more at this time, but I ask to be held in Your favor. Mantua, October 11, 1503.

[Letter 75]

Jesus [and] Mary.

My Most Illustrious and Excellent Lord, beloved in the precious blood of the crucified, sweet Jesus Christ. May his peace and salvation be with You. I have received a very dear letter from Your

Lordship.[24] It gave me a great consolation to receive it, but learning that Your Lordship has been ill, filled me with a deep sadness. I am quite distressed, My Dear Lord, and I am saddened by any displeasure that Your Excellency faces. I pray that the Lord and his most Holy Mother give You health and victory, and I have hopes that this will happen. The friars and the sisters pray intensely for Your Lordship. I am eternally grateful that Your Lordship finds it agreeable to write to me, an unworthy servant, and I ask to be kept always in Your favor. Mantua, October 17, 1503.

[Letter 76]

Jesus [and] Mary.

My Most Illustrious and Excellent Lord, beloved in the precious blood of the crucified, sweet Jesus. May the salvific peace of this Jesus always be *cum* Your Lordship, My Beloved and Illustrious Lord. I have written several letters to Your Excellency, but I have not received a reply since Your Excellency's letter from Agro Romano, in which I learned the painful news that Your Lordship is ill with fever.[25] I have since learned that, for the grace of the Lord and his sweet and most devout and Holy Mother, You are recovering well. The news filled me, Your unworthy servant, with extreme happiness and joy in Jesus Christ. More recently still we have learned that Your Lordship is well and prospering, even if You suffer from quite sinister pains. I pray that the supreme Lord will provide You in everything and that his most merciful Mother will give victory to Your Excellency. I hope that all this will happen by the virtue of Your mercy and clemency, and by the pious devotion that You have toward the merciful Mother, the most Holy Virgin Mary. You will be aided by the ardent prayers of a great number of servants of Jesus Christ who ceaselessly, *die et nocte*, pray that the merciful and compassionate Divinity will grant victory to Your Lordship and Your entire company. I have been asked by our fathers in Saint Dominic and mothers in San Vincenzo to send You their regards, and especially those of the father lecturer, who is writing to Your Lordship a letter of his own.[26] I ask to be held always in Your favor. Mantua, November 9, 1503.

[Letter 78]

Jesus [and] Mary.

My Most Illustrious and Excellent Lord, very beloved in the precious blood of Christ, etc. I am presently unable to pay a visit to Your Excellency, even though I anxiously desired to do so. My inability is caused by my sins. May the Lord be praised in everything. My Illustrious Lord, I am pleading Your Merciful Lordship for a favor. Our nephew, Fra Thomas, is going to sing his first Mass, and we are offering a feast to the fathers. If Your Lordship ever wants to show that You hold me in Your favor, I ask You to fulfill this one, that is, to sit with the fathers. This is not a big thing, and Your Lordship has done greater things for me. I ask to be held always in Your favor. Mantua. On the fourth [of January],[27] 1504.

Lucia Brocadelli:
Seven Revelations

Introduced and Translated by E. Ann Matter

Editor's Note: Among the *sante vive,* the early modern Italian "live women saints" studied by Gabriella Zarri,[1] Lucia Brocadelli (1476–1544) cuts a particularly tragic figure. At the turn of the sixteenth century Lucia was the official prophet of the court of Ercole I d'Este (Ercole il Magnifico) of Ferrara.[2] She came from a wealthy family of a small Umbrian town, Narni, and had been briefly married to a nobleman named Pietro of Milan before escaping marriage for a life dedicated to serving God.[3] While a Dominican penitent in Viterbo, Lucia made a name for herself as the recipient of visions and the stigmata; she attracted the attention of Ercole, who stole her away to Ferrara in an elaborate ruse. In Ferrara she established a new convent for a community of Dominican penitent women and named it, appropriately, Santa Caterina da Siena.[4]

In the following years Lucia inspired Ercole to publish a treatise praising female prophets at court. Ercole described a number of women who served the prophetic function in Italian cities: Osanna Andreasi in Mantua, Stefana Quinzani in Crema, and Colomba of Rieti in Perugia.[5] Ercole's defense of female prophecy reflects a concern to appear orthodox in the wake of the burning of his former spiritual mentor, Girolamo Savonarola, in 1498. The little book was elegantly printed with woodcuts from Albrecht Dürer's workshop

---

Note: This translation is based on the manuscript Pavia, Biblioteca Civica "Bonetta" MS II.112 (già B 12). The critical edition of the text, ed. E. Ann Matter, Armando Maggi, and Maiju Lehmijoki-Gardner, has appeared in *Archivum Fratrum Praedicatorum* 71 (2001): 311-44.

and was known throughout the German Empire as a confirmation of the stigmata borne by Catherine of Siena and other Dominican holy women.[6]

But Lucia's fame declined precipitously after the death of Ercole in 1505, especially after she was reported to have lost the marks of the stigmata.[7] For the following three decades she was isolated and strictly controlled, if not an out-and-out prisoner, in the very house that had been built for her. According to the single surviving manuscript, Lucia's revelations were written in 1544, the year of her death. A second hand in the manuscript records the date of transcription and describes the hand in which it is written as Lucia's own.[8] We have a few letters in Lucia's hand, part of a correspondence between herself and Ercole, especially leading up to the abduction, but until the recent discovery of the autographed manuscript of this book of revelations, we only had passing references to Lucia's visionary prowess.

Lucia's *Seven Revelations* is an important text for the study of women's religious expression in early modern Catholicism. The *Revelations* seem to have been preserved in the context of a female religious world, as is suggested by the elaborate manuscript cover featuring a scene of religious symbols in a mirrored landscape embroidered in pastel colors on a cream-colored silk.[9] Xenio Toscani dates the embroidery to the late eighteenth century, but it is also clear that religious symbolism such as this, centering around the disembodied Sacred Heart of Jesus and the Wounds of Christ portrayed as fragments of a human body, was common in emblems of the sixteenth century.[10]

If the cover is from the eighteenth century, it might well be from the first decade, when the relics of Lucia Brocadelli (including her left leg, separated in 1693 and taken back to her hometown, Narni, in 1720) were declared authentic and her official beatification was decreed.[11] Printed flyers from the pontificate of Clement XI (1700–1721) promise a plenary indulgence to all the faithful of either sex who visit the Church of Santa Caterina in Ferrara (Lucia's convent) to see the exposition of the earthly remains of the Blessed Lucia and hear a sung Mass and *Te Deum*.[12] Also preserved at Ferrara are lists of names and cures attributed to Lucia Brocadelli, dating from 1690 to 1748.[13] The triumphal nature of the design of the manuscript cover could, then, reflect this period of consolidation of Lucia's cult and date from some two hundred years after her death in 1544. Nevertheless, perhaps because of the disfavor in which Lucia lived for the last part of her life, the *Revelations* were never published and never became part of the Dominican spiritual tradition.[14]

Lucia Brocadelli's *Revelations* proceed according to a liturgical calendar, beginning on the feast of the Annunciation and continuing through Easter. The *Revelations* describe a series of guided tours of paradise, led by Jesus or (in the First Revelation) by the Virgin Mary or (in the Seventh Revelation) by Saint Paul. All three of the guides are significant. Lucia shows a devotion to Mary as the Queen of Heaven and encourages the Dominican prayer of the Rosary.[15] Mary shows great tenderness toward her, calls her "Luce" (Light), a pun on "Lucia."[16] Paul is also an interesting choice, probably related to the strong christological message of the book.

But it is clear that Lucia has the most emotional relationship with Jesus, whom she repeatedly calls "my sweet Jesus" or "my consolation." Jesus, in turn, habitually addresses Lucia as "daughter," often with accompanying adjectives such as "beloved," or "sweetest," and four times he is said to have called her by name.[17]

Lucia's paradise is, perhaps unsurprisingly, an old-fashioned one based in a traditional Christian apocalyptic cosmology and showing a medieval religious imagination. Her guides point out palaces, gardens, angels, maidens carrying cups, altars covered with cloths, and heavenly seats, often in groups of four or seven. What is revealed to her comes straight from a long line of Christian apocalyptic literature, beginning, of course, with the Apocalypse or Revelation to John, the last book of the New Testament. This apocalyptic material is mediated through a long history of exegetical and homiletic texts, including one by Lucia's fellow Dominican, the martyred spiritual and political leader of Florence, Girolamo Savonarola (d. 1498).[18] Like Savonarola, Lucia is graced with a vision of many saints, including the Holy Innocents, slain by Herod when Jesus was born,[19] and the nine orders of the angelic host, as described classically in the *Celestial Hierarchies* of Dionysius the Pseudo-Areopagite.[20]

Lucia's *Revelations* are not always easy to follow. The text contains repetition, imagery that is difficult to interpret, and even some unintelligible passages. Nonetheless, Lucia's text is also surprisingly theological, with a special emphasis, acted out in a different setting in each revelation, on the "humanity of the divinity," the mystery of the incarnation of Christ. It was an established part of medieval trinitarian theology that the Holy Spirit was the love, and therefore the unity, between the Father and the Son.[21] Obviously, Lucia Brocadelli never followed the path of Scholastic learning that included a compulsory commentary on the *Sentences* of Peter the Lombard; she may never have read this influential passage from the Lombard or the discussion in Augustine's *De trinitate* on which it is based, or any of the many Dominican commentaries that elaborate on it. Nevertheless, she is conversant with the rather sophisticated theological notion that the Holy Spirit is the love that binds together the Father and the Son.

Lucia takes immediate advantage of the praise for her suffering by likening it to the passion of Christ. She asks Jesus: "If it pleases and contents you, allow me to kiss your five wounds, for you know for how long I have desired this." Jesus replies that this is a big request, since even Catherine of Siena only kissed the wound in his side,[22] but he then grants Lucia's request. The passionate description of Lucia kissing the wounds of Jesus that follows matches the intensity of mystical language of any medieval woman visionary. This language is perhaps even closer to Franciscan devotion to the Crucified and may be a clue to a better understanding of the role of characters and ideals in the *Seven Revelations* that are specifically identified as Franciscan.[23]

The spirituality of suffering is also closely related to Lucia Brocadelli's Dominican heritage, worthy of a woman who was once the superior of a religious community named after Saint Catherine of Siena. Ascetic bodily mortification was a central part of the spirituality of Dominican penitents, and the incorporation of suffering into one's life was seen as a means to spiritual power. Although most of Lucia's bodily and spiritual sufferings, including her loss of authority, and presumably her toothaches, were not self-inflicted, they were nevertheless embraced as means for spiritual power.

As Gabriella Zarri has noted, Lucia's *Revelations* allow us to see her in the midst of her everyday spirituality. Zarri continues: "The *Liber* can also help to dispel one of the most serious accusations against the Dominican tertiaries: that they were women of little intelligence who allowed their more ingenious collaborators to construct the deceit of false stigmata. In her *Seven Revelations*, Lucia

Brocadelli appears not only intelligent and capable, but also rela-
tively cultured."[24] Also, we could add, blessed with a rich imagination able to make an original mélange of traditional visionary
imagery filtered through her personal experience.

Lucia Brocadelli: *Seven Revelations*

The Book of Blessed Lucia of Narni
written in her own hand
in the year of Our Lord 1544[25]

Jesus Mary

[First Revelation][26]

Venerable Father, these things were revealed to an unworthy
servant of Jesus on the night of the Annunciation to the sweet and
glorious Virgin Mary, her special advocate, beginning at midnight.
First the Virgin showed her four beautifully adorned crowns,[27] and
then the Lord showed four beautifully adorned chairs.[28] The first
crown was for her spiritual father, the second was for one of her
dear spiritual sons, the third was for a good father of the order of
Saint Francis, and the fourth was for herself, that is, for the one to
whom these things were shown, and for similar persons. The
above-mentioned chairs were for the praise of sweet Jesus, my own
love, my sweet solace.

This unworthy servant of Jesus was then led to a most beautiful palace, greatly adorned, and she found [Jesus] her sweet love,
who said to her these lovely words: "My beloved daughter." And she
immediately kneeled and said: "What does my sweet love command?" And then he said: "My daughter, come close to me and follow me."

And sweet Jesus went to a beautiful palace, and she followed him. And when he arrived, sweet Jesus immediately sat down on a chair of remarkable beauty. When he was seated, all the orders of angels[29] and saints[30] were in that palace; they were all dressed in colors that were different the one from the other. And all the angels genuflected, and they sang among themselves beautiful lauds,[31] each one of them different and similar. And then all the orders of all the angels were like ornaments to the throne[32] of the Lord, according to their spiritual and angelic form and nature, except for the order of the Thrones, and they were for the ornament of the crown.[33]

Then my sweetest Lord said to his unworthy servant: "Does it seem to you, my spouse, that I have a beautiful throne?" She answered: "My love, it is beautiful, of such remarkable pulchritude that it cannot be told." And with these words, all the saints sat down around the palace. Those sitting down did not appear in their chairs, that is, their own chairs, but many were seen to sit on the chairs. And all the martyrs and virgins were the ornament of all the other saints, that is, one martyr and one virgin for each.

And then our most sweet Savior stood on his feet before his throne, and immediately there appeared his beautiful mother Mary, Queen of the Heavens. The Lord sat on his chair, and then I commended my dear father to her and to her beloved Son, and with all my heart. And from the left side of our Lord there was as the ornament of his throne the Innocents who died for our Lord.[34] And all the virgin women and martyrs genuflected before the Lord and our Madonna, and they all praised with diverse lauds, and each one different. There were all the saints praising the sweet Queen of Heaven with similar lauds, and they were all in harmony.

When these lauds were finished, all the angels of all the orders moved, and they sang diverse lauds to our Lord, all different. When these were done, our sweet Lord made a gesture, which was immediately recognized by the order of the seraphim, who are superior to the others. And they went out of the palace, and after a short while they returned, each carrying a cup of gold covered by a paten.[35] And they sang marvelous songs. And, gathered at the door of the palace, suddenly the seven orders of angels began to play their instruments, and the order of thrones responded with the sweet melodies of their songs; and they harmonized their songs, that is, those strumming their instruments harmonized together with the different songs that they sang.

When these three lauds were finished, immediately the order of the seraphim came near to the throne of our most sweet Lord, and all were there around that cup in the hand of the three angels of the order of the seraphim. Then they all genuflected before these three angels of the order of the seraphim. They presented that cup to the Lord with marvelous and different lauds. Having received it, he immediately sat down on his throne, and an angel of this order of the seraphim went to the middle of the palace, placing a book on the lectern; and only he sang a song almost like the song of the Epistle.[36] He was heard as if all the heavens responded to him.

Then, since all the angels were at the steps of the chair of the Lord to give the cup to his Sweet Goodness, he was aware of that. He got up by himself and went up above the cup, since the angels were in procession to give it to the Lord.

And then that Sweet Goodness called this, his daughter, by her own name[37] and said: "Sweetest daughter, come to me." And she went before the presence of her Spouse, and she knelt down. And then sweet Jesus went above that cup and said to her: "Daughter, look in this cup." And, looking, she saw inside four liquids, which were these: the first was balsam, the second was oil, the third was liquid gold, the fourth and last was wine. And the divisions that separated these four liquids were of crystal.

And sweet Jesus said to his daughter: "I want to tell you, O most beloved daughter, what this cup is, and what these four liquids mean. So, daughter, know that this cup signifies my humanity. Balsam denotes my wisdom, that which is given to my soul. But, since balsam is superior to all other liquids in goodness and virtue, odor and medicine, so was the wisdom given to my soul superior to all created wisdom.

"Oil, dearest daughter, signifies the humility and meekness given to that soul and its action. This is because oil humbles everything on which it is placed and is good for many things. It is a peaceful liquid, just as my soul was peaceful. I know how to suffer every evil and torment, as I did at the time of my passion when I preached with all humanity.

218

"And gold signifies my divinity because, just as gold is superior to all other metals in beauty, in the same way my divinity is superior to all created things. And first this shows the humanity of the divinity[38] because the divinity conserves all created things and keeps those things lost by the flesh.

"The wine denotes my passion and the wine is more like me than other liquids because since wine is pressed by clogs,[39] thus did my blood flow out of my humanity by the great force of my torments. But since wine gladdens the heart of men [Ps 104:15], so is my blood a comfort to the human soul.

"And I want to tell you the meaning of the crystal divisions placed between the liquids in the cup. They signify this: as crystal is a fragile substance dividing these liquids, thus was the body that I received fragile and gentle. I placed my body as an ornament for the four properties that are signified by the four liquids I have told you about, which are there in that way as an ornament of the cup along with the crystal divisions."

And then sweet Jesus said to this his daughter: "My dear and sweet daughter, I want to tell you about that cover that you see. I want to tell you what the cover of the cup signifies, because I took it off personally when the angels came near me, coming up to the steps of my throne. This cover, my beloved daughter, means that you saw my human body as silver, adorned with jewels. Just as in the cup everything was covered by the paten, so indeed were all the properties of my body covered in light. And just as the cover of the cup was ornate with gems, even so was my body ornate with all kinds of virtue, and by all the good customs of exaltation and veneration of the cover over the cup. When the angels approached my throne, this meant the exaltation of my humanity. When my heavenly father came close to me, just as that cover of the cup was touching one thing, thus my exalted body is elevated above all things that are created and are still to be created.

"My beloved daughter, I want to tell you the meaning of my sitting in my chair when I had received the cup. It signifies the time I spent in the world up to the day of my ascension, and ascending into heaven in soul and body I joined with my divinity. Now I think that since I have sat in my chair, I have fulfilled all the mysteries for which I descended to earth.

"And now I want to tell you, dearest daughter, the meaning of these three angels who held the cup in their hands and who brought it to me. My dear daughter, they stand for the holy Trinity, in which the humanity took its rest. And just as all the orders of seraphic angels had their hands on the cup, in that way the hand of all men disgraced and reviled and poisoned my body. And further, the fact that the angels held the cup in their hands means that all the virtues of my body were changed for the good so that they could abandon it. These three angels holding the cup in their hands also mean three things worthy of memory, that is, humility, justice, and glory, which my celestial father gave to humanity.

"Furthermore, my sweetest daughter, I want to proclaim to you the meaning of that angel who stood in the middle of my palace singing. This one signifies my humanity, which I praised, magnifying the most high and holy Trinity by the mystery fulfilled by my incarnation, as was made perfect in that incarnation, passion, resurrection, and ascension. And that angel acted for the glory of all the angels, and for all the martyrs, and for all the angelic nature. The lectern on which the book was placed signifies my person, and the book on the lectern from which that angel sang is my divine wisdom, about which all things sang and should sing."

When the sweet Lord had said these things, immediately the angels who were there for the adornment of his throne, that is, the throne of our sweetest Lord, got up and processed before it. And he left that palace and went to another palace, in which the feast of the cup had been prepared, and did not appear again nor was he seen again. That one appeared in the face of my sweet love Jesus just as the face is seen, and is seen in the mirror of humanity.

Here ends the first revelation of the palace.

[Second Revelation]

Here begins the second revelation to the praise and glory of my sweet love Jesus, received by his worthless servant.

Our Lord was present when this was written by her in this second revelation. Being in holy prayer, I was called by my proper name by the sweetest love, who said: "Come with me, my dearest daughter."[40] And, hearing the sweet and soft voice of her dearest love, she went immediately and with great haste. And she saw him with all his company, that is, with all his celestial court. And they went to another most beautiful palace, different in beauty and in form from that other one, that is, from the above mentioned, which had three doors. And then the Lord came near the door of the palace, it seemed to me, by the space of eight arms. And all the company entered into the palace and came before our sweetest Lord and the order of the angels by one door of that palace, and they all, all, sat down at his right hand. And on the thrones they were in human form.

These three doors of the palace were separated one from the other by a space. And right then, at that time, the order of the thrones and the order of the cherubim entered into that palace all together with the orders of the angels and sat at the left hand at the entrance to that palace, and they were all in human form. And while the angels and the above-mentioned orders of the thrones and the cherubim sat themselves down on their chairs, the Lord came near the palace. And when our sweetest Lord was at the door through which the cherubim had entered, they all got to their feet. But, staying in their places, they all sang lauds with songs and marvelous melodies on their instruments, different from those played before, and symphonies, that is, more marvelous harmonies than the others. They were of such melodious sweetness that they could never be thought or told.

And when the Lord entered into the palace, that same order genuflected and ended its marvelous lauds, and then sang new lauds with songs and sounds on musical instruments. Then the sweet Lord went to sit on his chair, prepared in the middle of the right-hand door, through which all the other six orders had entered, and all the saints followed our sweetest Lord, and each of the orders sang different lauds among themselves. And then the first three orders, which had come in first, stopped their lauds but responded to the other six orders with their instruments. And their sweetness and harmony was such that it can never, ever be told or thought.

And at once our Lord sat on his chair, and immediately there appeared in the middle of that palace a beautiful palm tree, which had seven roots divided from one another by equal spaces. And those roots reached all the way to the walls of the palace, and there were as many branches of that tree as there were angels of all the nine orders, and each branch reached above the head of its angel. And the angels sat on those branches, and just as each angel moved, the branch moved. And then our sweetest Redeemer called me, the least of his servants, by name, saying: "My sweetest daughter, come closer to me." And she went at once and adored him as her dear Lord, and stood at his side.

And then that Lord said to her: "O, my dearest daughter, O my beloved, what do you think of the beauty of this tree and its branches and roots?" She answered: "My sweetest Spouse, it seems to me of such and so much beauty that if I had all the understanding of all the men of our world, and of all creatures, I would not be able to know how to tell it." My sweet Love, Jesus, answered: "You speak the truth, beloved daughter, unless it happened by my wish." And rising up after this speech, he stepped down from his throne and said to her: "My dear daughter, come with me, for I wish to show you still greater marvels than this tree." And so sweet Jesus took her by the hand, and kissed her sweetly, and went toward the tree. And coming near it, sweet Jesus leaned down and touched the root of the tree, saying to this his servant "Look, O my sweet daughter, my much beloved, at these roots." And she, looking, saw on each root a verse that said: "O God of love." And when she saw this, sweet Jesus said to her: "Dear daughter, now look well, first I want to open these doors so that you can see what is inside."

And just as soon as sweet Jesus had said these words, all the doors were opened with great and sweet sounds, and much wonder, so that all the heavens were heard, and sounds of marvelous harmony, in such a way that all the angels, and the saints major and minor, and all the blessed souls sang lauds, all according to their own eternal understanding. Sweet Jesus said to this his servant: "Tell me, O my beloved daughter, does this not seem a great thing?" She answered: "Domine mi, nihil est mirabile magne tue potentie." "My Lord," she said, "nothing is as greatly marvelous as your power" [cf. Sir 39:25].[41] To this sweet and good Jesus replied: "You speak truly, most beloved daughter, but human understanding is also marvelous."

And when these words were said, a kneeling damsel appeared inside each door. Each looked out at the tree, and each had her hands extended toward heaven as if praying, and their beauty could never be thought or told in human language. I saw a type of creature who had all of the created speculative intellect and ingenuity of the world all in herself.[42] And that damsel answered: "A thousand times more than in herself." And then that sweet Jesus said to this his servant: "I give you the grace, my beloved daughter, to look at this first damsel." And she looked and in her face she saw the faces of all the others, in spite of the fact that the soul of this damsel did not move from its place, a thing that seemed impossible to human understanding. But nothing is impossible in the Lord.

And at once that sweet and good Jesus entered into this first door of the tree, but holding his unworthy servant by the hand. And at once this damsel came inside, and good Jesus embraced her, and having embraced her, after this, that damsel did not appear, nor was she seen again. But looking at that sweet Jesus, she was seen in his divine face, as an image appears in the mirror. She was heard to sing a laud in the face of our Lord, saying: "Laudatus e magnificatus sit rex glorie, qui mortem tulit et pascionem per generis humani excupatio." "Praised and magnified," sang the damsel, "be the king of glory, he who takes away and has taken suffering and death for the reparation of humankind."[43] And she sang that laud with such harmony and sweetness that it is unthinkable and untellable.

Then I went close to the root of the tree, and there was so much light in that tree, and it had the same beauty as the door described above through which the sweet Lord had entered. And then suddenly the seven damsels were in triumph before the divine majesty, and were there in a minute. They were seen in his face as the first damsel had been, each one singing her different laud. Then that highest Goodness said to his unworthy servant: "Does it not seem beautiful to you, dearest daughter, that there is such beauty and wonder in this trunk and its root?" His servant answered: "My most sweet Lord, your beauties are not to be marveled at because you are the mirror and the form of all the children of men."

To which that sweet and highest Goodness responded, saying: "Sweetest daughter, since I know you desire it greatly, I wish to tell you what this tree is, and who are these seven noble damsels. This tree, my daughter, signifies the humanity of Jesus Christ, that is, my own humanity. And its roots, which are seven, denote the seven gifts of the Holy Spirit, by which my unity was ornamented.[44] The seven doors placed in the tree trunk are the seven different types of mercy I show to sinners, through that power that was given to my human nature. And note well, my dear daughter, that just as these seven doors were suddenly opened by the praises of my celestial court, so were these mercies opened when I was raised up on the cross.

"And know that these seven damsels who were above each of the doors, were without the virtues, the three theological and four cardinal,[45] these supreme virtues are prepared to come out so that they can lead sinners. It is good that they did not come out, since you saw the ones I will receive, and it is good for them finally to return to me with that thing that they always have in me. And I am the one who is and was this virtue, but I offer myself in all things so that they hear me and receive me according to their desire so that they can be saved. And just as these seven virtues are reflected in me, in the same way they should shine in each one who has the spirit and the intelligence, and having these virtues, and meditations and thoughts of me, and sees in me all the virtues through one virtue and every good appearance and good action that come from me.

"Again I want to tell you, beloved daughter, why the first damsel entered into me before all the others, and then all the others entered. This is the reason: because the first virtue is humility, which I had, humbling myself unto death on the most bitter cross, a very shameful death. And I have given my graces to the world in spite of the fact that every day they ignore my precepts and the gifts I have made. Daughter, I think the tree is when I completed the mystery of my incarnation and passion, and when I rose from the dead, and the mystery of my passion was more greatly known and told than it had been before, through which I can say that now all the virtues have returned to me, as I am recognized as man and God. And note well, my dearest daughter, that my bending down and investigating near the roots of the tree signifies when I humiliated myself wishing to be incarnate of the Virgin Mary, at which bending down, the seven doors were indeed opened with a marvelous sound, as when I was born into the world there was the most great sound of the angels praising and blessing in heaven and on earth" [Luke 2:9–15].

Then that supreme goodness said to his unworthy servant: "My dear daughter, so that you understand these things that are being said to you, lift up your eyes and look." Then she immediately lifted her eyes, and the tree appeared no longer. She saw sweet Jesus sit on his throne, and his servant remained at the side, kneeling before him. Then that Sweet Goodness said: "Dearest daughter, I wish to tell you why a branch of the tree reached over each of the angels; I mean, daughter, above the head of each angel. This denotes the glory that I gave to all the angels beyond that which they had before. First of all I added glory to them through my humanity, but then appeared above all their glory, just as the branches were above each angel. And just as the roots of that tree made up all the roof of the palace,[46] thus my humanity includes and takes up all things that are in heaven and in earth. And now I do not wish to say more, dearest daughter."

Here ends the second revelation.

[Third Vision]

Here begins, to the praise and glory of sweet Jesus, the third revelation shown to that same servant.

And the divine majesty said these words: "Dearest daughter, first I wish to tell and declare the meaning of those four chairs that I have shown and described above.[47]

"[First][48] The first is of our <u>father confessor,</u>[49] all covered in white, denoting his purity of heart and clean conscience. The fringes at the top and in the middle signify the charity that he had for his neighbor. And those precious stones in the chair are the contemplation he makes when he prays the Rosary of my mother.[50]

"[Second] The second chair is of the <u>dear son</u> given by his mother. Since it is totally covered with roses, it signifies his charity poured out for his neighbor, and especially for the health of souls. And the white fringes wrapped around that chair and the first chair denote his purity of heart, and the way of his consent, and the joys found there, which are the delight of those who love divine and spiritual things.

"[Third] The <u>third</u> chair you saw, the one covered with different colors, is that of our confirmed friar of the order of my beloved

225

Francis.[51] The different colors show how in diverse and various ways he came to my service, and his service to me gives me a great deal of pleasure. And for the great prayers you made to me at different times, which I have heard, know that I have already led him, ahead of you, to the benefits of my passion. And the adornments of his chair are his fervent and charitable sermons, and the preaching to souls done justly and with good zeal.

"[Fourth] <u>Yours,</u> daughter, all covered with silver and adorned with precious stones and beautiful jewels, denotes and signifies your pure and sincere purity of heart and your virginity,[52] practiced sincerely and with great difficulty and obstacles, for my love. And the ivory columns of the sides signify your great constancy and your great effort against the flesh, and against your nature, and against the senses when you turn to me. You have been, my dear daughter, in the heat of the fire, and then in combat with the waves of the stormy sea.[53] And the great ornaments of your crown and your chair signify the great alms and charity you have shown to the poor for my love. Your hands have been the cause of everything done for my love and the love of my mother, Mary. And they are even more adorned by various and different tribulations, and borne for us with such constancy and true patience, with such suffering and forbearance, for my love. And you have abandoned life, possessions, dignity, and the people who loved you so much, for my love.

"And I, the one who rewards good, think that you will certainly be well rewarded by me and given an infinite prize: my happy homeland. And you will live with me, your Spouse, in eternity. And the other adornments of your chair and your crown are the good deeds done for my love and the penitence and abstinence of so many years, and still yet the worthy meditations and contemplation and tears abundantly shed for my passion, and many tears of love that are pleasing to me. And those precious stones that adorn your virginal crown are the injuries and infamies borne for my love, in consideration of my disgrace and vilification. And they are yet more decorated, adorned, and magnified because of the fathers whom you have often told to make my flagellation at the column, and the father you told about my crown of thorns, contemplating with tears those fifteen thorns that reached even into my brain, and the other contemplations you did and acted out with love. Weep for what has been done to me, my daughter, and thus think about my bitter life and passion and death. And keep me as an immaculate angel before your eyes as an example."

And, when this sweet discussion was finished, <u>he went</u> to a beautiful castle, and he was followed by his glorious mother, the queen of heaven and earth, with all her court, all the company, and I went with them. All of the angels in existence were in that castle, and Lord Jesus, who was of marvelous beauty and of a different magnitude, entered it. Much of the palace was seen before us. There had been prepared a most beautiful and marvelous chair for his Divine Majesty, and another for his sweet mother, Mary, whose beauty was stupendous. They were different the one from the other. And there were also prepared innumerable other chairs for all the saints who were with that sweet Majesty. They were all of the greatest and most stupendous beauty, each different from the others. And I recognized those who were confessors.[54]

When the Divine Majesty entered that castle together with that company, at once they all sat down in their chairs before the eyes of Jesus. And the Divine Majesty and his sweet mother sat on their magnificent and high thrones, but the angels were all genuflecting on the roof of that castle, singing marvelous and beautiful lauds, each different from the others. And just as soon as all were seen to be seated on their chairs, the sweetest Lord was seen, all dressed in a garment so white that not one of the saints could recognize or understand it, except for his sweetest mother, Mary, and the apostles.

Now, all the other angels did not recognize that garment. But as soon as that sweet Empress of the Heavens had recognized that garment, she immediately descended from her throne with the apostles and kneeled before her sweetest Son, and the apostles did the same. Then all the angels of all the orders who were kneeling on the roof raised themselves in the air from that castle and made their dips and whirls, praising the Divine Majesty with diverse lauds, different from the previous ones. And they played sweet melodies on their instruments, singing harmoniously and softly that which was marvelous to think and to say. And just as soon as the sweetest Lord was dressed in that garment, all of the male and female saints who were not genuflecting on the roof of that castle where the angels had been previously, stood up. And each had a marvelous song of joy, each different from the other, according to the virtue and merit of each, according to which of their works done in the world were pleasing to sweet Jesus and had been rewarded, since those saints knew themselves to be before the Lord. And they held those songs of joy in their hands, but without knowing the reason why.

And then that Divine Majesty called this his servant, who knew this great thing, by her own name and said: "Dearest daughter, come close to me, your beloved Spouse, closer than you are," because his unworthy servant, constrained by fear, stayed some way off. She went and bowed before such great majesty on the first step of the throne of her Great Majesty and adored him with great fear and with every reverence. And this Sweet Goodness said to her: "Lift up your eyes, sweetest daughter, and look at me." And when she did this, immediately she looked at her Divine Majesty, and she understood everything about that throne and the white garment, and she realized that the Virgin Mary was kneeling before her sweet Son.

And then that sweet Jesus said to this, his servant: "Do you recognize me, my beloved daughter?" She answered with great reverence: "My sweet and dear Lord, of course I recognize you, and I thank your majesty and power." Then that Sweet Goodness answered with such sweetness and said: "My sweetest daughter, I want to tell you everything about this very marvelous and great garment I have on my person, which thing I will show and have shown to my celestial and triumphant court, even though they do not understand it, except for those already mentioned and named. But understand, dearest daughter, that this garment signifies the body of my humanity, which I show you in this glory and the great power given to said body by my celestial Father, by the virtue and power of the divinity that were given to him."

And when my sweet Love had said this, the Virgin Mary inclined herself before the form of our humanity and kissed the feet of the Lord. And when this was done, in the blink of an eye, all of the angels of all the orders kissed them, returning in a few minutes to the places where they were making lauds, each different from the other, and playing their instruments. And when this was done, the Empress of Heaven and Earth sat on the throne of her sweetest Son at his right hand. And as soon as she had taken her seat, she drew her Son to herself, his splendor and purity, in such a way that all could understand. And with that, they understood all the things that they did not understand before.

Then all the saints of paradise began the lauds for heavenly *Glorias*, each according to his own intellect and different from the ones before. And at once they knew the song of joy they held in their hands. And when the laud was finished, and knowing the cause of their song of joy, at once all these saints, those who came in the second act, returned to their places, kneeling where they were all in their own places. Sweet Jesus lifted his feet, and they knew this since they were in their places, and they gave thanks to the Lord in that moment with immense and divine lauds, each different from the others.

Then this sweetest Jesus called this, his servant, and said to her: "Does it seem to you, dearest daughter and my beloved, a marvelous and beautiful thing that they all recognize me according to their intellect, and that some thank me with their intellect and their merits, through which they are saved?" To which she replied: "Domine mi nihil est tibi peris quia omnia potes quecunque volis." "My Lord," she said, "nothing is marvelous in your presence, since you can do anything you want" [cf. Job 42:2; Wis 11:24]. Then sweet Jesus came down from his throne and, holding his sweetest mother, the Virgin Mary, by the hand, he said to this servant of his: "O my most beloved daughter, do you still see this castle?" And she, looking around, saw nothing of that castle, but she saw its outline, with all beauty, in the face of the Divine Majesty.

And he said to this his servant: "Dear daughter, I do not wish to say anything else; let us go to another place." Then all of his celestial court moved and went with the sweetest Lord and his unworthy servant, and followed him. Here ends the third revelation. Here begins the fourth revelation shown unworthily to her.

[Fourth Revelation]

Passing from this castle, our sweetest Lord went to another place of his realm. But, dear Father, I wish first to tell what happened to me on Good Friday.[55] In that night, our Crucified Lord appeared and said: "Look, and consider well, my dear daughter, how I, though innocent, have been treated by my creatures. And so, my dear daughter, bear your tribulations and persecutions with patience, whether they be from creatures or from demons. And if you wish to be content with whatever fortune, bear it for my love, as I have always done. Look what I have borne for your love. Persevere, dearest daughter. When you come to my heavenly homeland, dear daughter, you will have from me the reward for all of the many burdens you have borne and the numerous pains from our enemies. And I have allowed it all to happen for the sake of grace and glory. It has been very pleasing to me that you have willingly borne all of the pain you have had from the extraction of your four teeth from your mouth, and the four teeth that you had fall out.[56] And this is a great pain. Now, beloved, my daughter, tell the one you love that I am consoled."

And she said: "My love, I return infinite thanks to your Divine Majesty. I am confounded by all of the goodness and sweet words given me. I am so miserable, miserable above all your creatures. Indeed, my sweet Lord, I raise up my spirit to ask a great new grace. If it pleases and contents you, allow me to kiss your five wounds, for you know how long I have desired this."

And that Sweet Goodness replied: "Daughter, you ask a very great thing. My dear daughter Catherine of Siena only kissed the wound of my side, and you wish to have more than she had.[57] Nevertheless, I will not deny you this contentment, my spouse, because I like your great desire above that of all my servants." And so he allowed his unworthy servant to kiss him.

She began at first with his holy, beautiful feet, with tears, and then moved to his sweet side. And she stayed a long time at this holy side because she felt such delightful sweetness and softness that she could not take herself away. It was as if she were drunk. Then she went to his most holy hands. He bore this with great love, and when she had kissed all the wounds, he stretched out his sweet arm, blessed her, and disappeared. And here ends this apparition.

He went to a place of his kingdom. When he arrived, he lifted his hand and said: "Lift up your eyes and see." And when sweet Jesus had said this, there stood a beautiful and most marvelous city, full of blessed souls. And there was seen there the soul of my first confessor in great glory. And among all of these blessed souls were seen gardens, both small and large, and in the midst of that city there stood a great palace. In this palace there was a door, over which was written "This is the Palace of Divine Majesty." And the great Majesty was seen in that palace with all the company of the saints and the archangels. And they all looked at this unworthy servant, and they gave her a great welcome celebration. And I think this happened because for a long time now she has said her Office once every week.[58]

Now, returning to our story, that company came with sweet Jesus. Now he said to this his servant: "Now, my sweetest daughter, how does this city that I have created with a wave of my arm seem to you?" To which I replied: "My love, the city is admirable in size and beauty, and so greatly so that I could never know or comprehend it." There was prepared in that same palace the marvelous and high throne of the Lord, and that of his sweet mother, Mary, sweet with marvelous beauty. And once again there were the other chairs for each of the saints and for all the orders of the angels. And just as soon as the Divine Majesty was seen to sit down, three persons were seen sitting, who were then seen to be just one, that is, that same sweet Jesus. And then, quickly, all sat down; his sweet mother, Mary, and the apostles, and all the saints sat down.

And as soon as they were seated, the city, which had previously been hidden, was manifested to them who did not know it, that is, they took notice of it. *E statim* [all at once],[59] as soon as they recognized it, they kneeled down, thanking the Lord and his great power. When some lauds had been sung, sweet Jesus stretched forth his most holy hand over those aforementioned saints, and they sat down *ipso facto* on their chairs. And then the Divine Majesty called this his unworthy servant, who went with all reverence to stand before that Sweet Goodness, who said to her: "My sweetest daughter, look into my face." And she, with all patience, looked into the face of her sweetest love. And at once she recognized three persons in one essence, and she knew how the Holy Spirit proceeds from the Father and the Son. And when this was done, the Divine Majesty stood up from his chair onto his feet and gave witness to the Trinity in the unity and divinity of the Person of the Son, of the True Person of the Father, and of the divinity of the Holy Spirit.

And then all of those who had had witness of this mystery kneeled before him with lauds and marvelous songs, each one different from the others. And all the angels and the saints sang double lauds. They sang one laud to the divinity, and the other to the humanity, and they praised the whole Trinity with their instruments. And when the lauds and songs and sounds were done, the Divine Majesty sat on his chair, and immediately there appeared alone the humanity in the divinity. Then all the angels and saints sat down. Then that Divine Goodness called this, his unworthy servant, and said to her: "O my sweetest daughter, lift up your eyes and see." And she, looking around, no longer saw either the city or the palace, or all the angels there were *hinc inde* [in that place].

And that Sweet Goodness said to this, his unworthy servant: "Now, dear daughter, where is this city?" And he murmured: "*Io sum*[60] all of these things, and I humble myself to show you my own self before you in this form." And when this his servant looked at that Divine Majesty, she saw all of that aforementioned city in his breast. And then that infinite Goodness said to this, his useless servant: "My dearest daughter, to me very beloved, I do not wish to tell you more about this." The fourth revelation ends and the fifth begins.

[Fifth Revelation]

Being totally lifted up in the spirit, there was shown to her a marvelous and beautiful piazza, in which benches were all lined up for a celebration. Having departed from the above mentioned place with all the aforementioned company, the Divine Majesty went to another place as wide and large as a piazza, with benches all around to sit on, and these benches were covered with cloths of gold. And sheaves of wheat were extended as a roof over the piazza. On each bench was written where and in which place each one should sit down. As soon as the Divine Majesty placed his foot in that piazza, all the angels of all the orders and the male and female saints except that sweet Mary followed him to their benches.

And each one stood in the midst of his place, since places had been divided among them all, with an angel and a saint of all those who were in the company of the Divine Majesty. And when she went into the middle of the piazza, she could not understand it at all except for the fact that its splendor would not have been so great even had all created things been the sun. In this same mutation, sweet Jesus made all the saints and all the angels sit in their places. They were all singing songs, melodies, and lauds before the Divine Majesty. And when these were done, that sweet Jesus sat on a marvelous throne together with his sweetest mother. Before this time, I could not see that throne perfectly.

Then all the saints kneeled before the Divine Majesty with new songs and softest lauds. Then he gave each of them a new garment, and as soon as they saw themselves clad in it, they went before the Lord and kneeled down. That sweetest Lord stretched out his hand to them, and each angel placed his hand in the hand of the sweet Lord. And they all stayed like this. And then that Sweet Goodness said: "My daughter, look carefully at these things so that you can tell your confessor." And then he said to the angels "And what thing do you say about me?" And they answered, saying: "Lord, we say that your power is great and high." And when the angels had said this, the Lord made them all sit in their places, and they, seeing each one sit in his place, thanked the Divine Majesty for his great glory, each according to his intellect.

Then I saw my sweet Love raise his feet from his throne and say: "My sweet spouse, magnified are those in my realm who have done, and do, and will do my will." And, saying that, he was immediately recognized in human form, in which they knew the divinity and the most holy soul of our sweetest Lord. And they knew the mystery in which he was incarnate in that sweet Virgin Mary. They knew the glory of all the angels of all the orders, and the rejoicing they did among themselves. And all those angels knew this thing equally, and all the saints had it according to their intellect, except for five saints who knew only the humanity, and those praised the Lord according to the understanding of sweet Jesus that they had.[61]

When these lauds were finished, they all sat down on their chairs, and that Sweet Goodness, calling his unworthy servant, said to her: "My dearest daughter, you know me and you have known me." And she replied reverently and with fear: "My sweetest Spouse, yes, according to how it is pleasing to your benign majesty." And that Divine Spouse said again to her: "Dise pro quo vis me plus diligere: an per padre, an per filio, an per fratre?" "Tell me how you love me the best: as a father, or as a son, or as a brother? And you should know, beloved daughter, that when you love me as a father you will have part of my great power, and when you love me as a son you will have part of my glory, and when you love me as a brother, even more than a son, you will have part of my goods."

And then his unworthy servant answered, saying: "My sweet Love, I am ready in all ways to love you above all others. My beautiful Spouse, I wish to love you as a father, as a spouse, and more than father or son, as a brother." That infinite goodness replied: "According to your wish, daughter, I give you part of my goods in all things of mine." And he murmured, saying: "Beloved daughter, I wish to tell you the difference between father and son or brother; therefore, listen well, my beloved. The apostles, my daughter, loved me and were loved by me as a father, and this because of the miracles they performed, but it was I who gave them the power to perform miracles. The confessors loved me as a son, as they confessed my name and for this have had a part in my glory. But those who loved me as a brother are those of your human path, those who have loved me as a brother. The ones of this kind are neither very bad nor very good, but they give good thanks to me with their words and with the true recitation of my name as a brother."

And sweet Jesus murmured and said to me: "My dearest daughter, I wish to say something else to you, a thing that is not offered; that is, what it means to love me as Lord and King. And so I want you to know that to love me as Lord means to know me as the Lord of all things, and that I have the power of such pain and glory. And there are many others who love me because of high divine dominion, who fear the judgment of the Father and the justice that could be exacted of them. And this type of love carried to the Lord is not perfect. My dearest daughter, I do not wish you to love me out of fear but for love.[62] The one who loves me out of love always fears doing something that might displease me. But now I wish to tell you, my beloved, about the ones who love me as KING.[63] They are the martyrs who love me as KING and have prayed and who die bravely as though they were servants of a temporal KING, who search and struggle for the crown of justice of their KING, giving themselves to death for love of those. If it should be necessary for this manner and type of love, I do not consider any but these, who wished to spontaneously offer themselves for my name, espousing their bodies and souls. I wish to tell you this, sweetest daughter."

My Father, I will go back because I have not told the above properly.[64] The Lord said: "exposing their bodies and souls together to death for my name." Sweet Jesus said to this his most vile servant: "I wish to tell you, sweetest daughter, the meaning of the fact that I made all the hands of my saints in one of my hands, those far away as much as those close at hand. This means, my beloved daughter, that those who are in my glory are content by the small or the large amount they have of that glory. Thus both the one who has a moderate or temperate amount, and that one who has a lot, in that way are as quiet as all of the hands of my saints, who were all quiet, the far away as much as the close by. In that way, the one who has little glory is as content as the one who has much glory."

And when he had said this, the Divine Majesty immediately got up, saying to his worthless servant: "My dear daughter, lift up your eyes and see." And he looked around, and he said again: "My dear daughter, look well, lift up your eyes." And she, looking around again, no longer saw that piazza or its ornaments. But that Lord and his Divine Majesty moved with all of his court and went to another place. And turning to this, his unworthy servant, he said to her: "My most beloved, I wish to tell you why the place of each one was written on each bench, and why there were the cloths of gold on those benches. This means that the place of each one was written in the middle of the bench, and that there was a cloth of gold over each of those benches. Now take note, my daughter, that this means that each one who lives in my glory understands and knows the reason for which he was saved and the glory that is due to him, and just as the first, they all know the glory they can have, and the way in which they should be in my high and triumphant reign.

"And the benches that were covered with cloths of gold signify that my glory is prepared equally for each soul of those who wish to come, from the one who has [much] to the other one with less. But the cloths of gold that were laid out over the pavement of the piazza mean my bitter passion, which I undertook for each man equally. Each one can put his foot in equally, as much as he wishes, as if in a piazza, since the piazza of a city is known by all to be common. And just as it is public and for all, so in the same way is my passion. As all the saints then kneeled before their seats, so ought all who are in the world think about the piazza and come to the knowledge of my passion, and I think that all who are in the world are kneeling before their seats once again.

"I think I am in the midst of the piazza when they are at the point of death and know me to be the one who took away all of their weariness with my humanity, so that they might be able to come to those seats of theirs. And so, as those men now present in the world labor wearily, then they will ascend to the rest prepared for them after many labors. True rest is when they venerate me and rest in my glory, on those benches and resting in their seats. And notice, beloved daughter, the splendor they have: it is the glory that I give to them according to their merits, and they shall be rewarded according to their deeds, through which they are saved. And I do not wish to tell you more about this at the moment." The fifth revelation ends.

[Sixth Revelation]

I will tell you here, Father,[65] what I saw the night of the resurrection.[66] Your daughter, praying with great and ardent desire to see the sweetest Love when he came out of his holy sepulcher, was next to that sepulcher. I awaited with many tears to see my Love, Jesus the Nazarene. And as I was so situated, behold, he came forth singing sweetly with a red mantle covering his beautiful person, and the mantle was very high. He was so very lovely and beautiful and totally splendid that my tongue could never, never tell of it. And his unworthy servant adored him, adored all of him, and that Sweet Goodness said to her: "O my sweetest daughter, I have wished to satisfy all your great desires, so that you are granted no more than my love, and so you can be stronger and more constant in the great battles with your cruel enemies, so that they cannot prevail against you. I know how to bring good and just desires to pass, and I yield this to my servants.

"And come closer to me, my daughter, and you will smell the sweetest odor of my person."[67] And she went with true reverence, and came close to that Jesus, all softness and sweetness. What she smelled come out of that precious body would be impossible ever to tell, not ever, or to narrate it.

Thus present I was in fact taken up in the spirit, actually beyond all the senses. At once I heard a most sweet voice saying: "O Paul, my Apostle, quickly, lead this my spouse and your beloved to rest because she is worthy of such merit since from the solemnity of my birth[68] she has always hungered to have Jesus, and she has been greatly crucified by her false enemies. Some have broken her head, others the fingers of her hand, some have pulled her around and treated her badly, some have thrown her in the well, some have knocked out her teeth. And she has suffered all these things and great pain with true patience for my love."[69]

And she answered: "My sweet love, the patience and the strength that I have had in all of my pains and torments are the result of your abiding goodness; I could never have done such things by myself because I am very weak because of my great imperfection. Your help has been what has created such constancy in me." Having said these words, the Lord said no more to his unworthy servant. But he turned toward my beloved Paul and said: "Take my beloved spouse into that most beautiful garden so that she can see the celebration of the dressing of my sweetest mother. This will be for her pleasure, because she is her true mother." And my dear Paul said: "My Lord, well and willingly will I lead my dear beloved to such rest. Your majesty knows what I especially adore about her is her care for your mother."

And so, having said these words, he took me by the hand with great love and led me to his beloved with great joy. This his beloved first saw her sweetest love Jesus at the entrance to the garden. Seeing him lift up his feet with all of his company, that is, all of his celestial court, she followed him. They left this place and his servant went with them and with her beloved Paul, and she saw sweet Jesus enter in a most beautiful and much adorned garden, all surrounded by trees and leaves and plants known in this world. There were many others that were unknown, a great pleasure to see. These others were not known by men of the world. The other trees were divided by type so that there was a group of trees of the world, that is, known in the world, and another group the world did not know. And the big and little plants were divided in the same way.

Everything was all in flower, all the trees and the plants, and those trees had fruit, and some of the fruit was already ripe and some was not yet. And then the Divine Majesty said to all the saints: "Go through the garden and take my spouse with you, and know to praise the great things of this garden since there are different things in it." And turning to this his most vile servant, that infinite Goodness said: "O my most beloved daughter, see if you have pleasure and rest in this garden." And having said this, his Sweet Goodness went through the garden with his sweet mother, the Virgin Mary.

Oh, what pleasure it was to see them, my dear Father, and as we walked along, he said to this useless servant: "Dear daughter, watch carefully what I do now." And at once the Divine Majesty extended his most holy hand, or rather arm, and then all of the saints and holy souls of his kingdom were under the trees. Some were under the trees, some under the plants, and some under the leaves. Some were under one thing, some under another. And so all were under something, either a leaf or a plant or a tree.

And the angels stood in a circle, all those of each order made their own circle, and in this way they were all singing and playing their instruments. And all the blessed souls and all the male and female saints made marvelous lauds to the Divine Majesty according to what glory they expected. But it seemed to me that as soon as there were those harmonies and songs and sounds, that sweet Divine Majesty sat down on a marvelous and most worthy throne prepared there next to his sweet mother, sweet Mary, the divine soul. And as soon as her sweet Son was seated, then all the saints and the blessed souls, who were sitting under the above-mentioned things, leaves, trees, and plants, were seated on top of them. And they were all on top of the trees, and on top of the leaves, and on top of the plants. Then that Supreme Goodness said to this his unworthy servant: "My sweet daughter, I wish to tell you what this garden is. It is the thing that signifies that my saints were at first underneath and are now on top. *Antequam ulterius progrediar* [and before I go further], know, daughter, that this garden stands for my glory, and signifies the garden of my words which I left for the human race when I left this world. And the saints under the trees which you saw means when they are in the world, but when they are on top of the trees and the plants it means that they are seated on my words, through which they are now saved in the celestial choir. And from this they have glory, which glory, as you see, my sweet daughter, consists in seeing this my garden in which, resting, the delight in the harmony of their infinite singing."

And with his soft words, sweet Jesus rose up on his feet from his chair and immediately revealed himself in humanity and divinity, and I knew the Father in divinity and the Spirit in unity and the Son in humanity; and the one gave divinity to the other, and knew nothing less in his humanity. And I heard three Persons speak in one voice. There was no one else present except his sweet mother, Mary, and the apostles, and this his unworthy servant. Then, knowing this, the Queen of Heaven, our Mary sweeter than honey, kneeled down in front of her sweetest son, and that sweet Love of mine placed both of his hands on the head of that sweet and most worthy mother with great love, and keeping his face high and inclined toward the head of his sweet mother. And then immediately that sweet Mary of ours was prepared in the manner of a queen, and dressed in all splendor and great light, which gave to the angels and all the saints greater glory than before, and Mary was more resplendent than her son.

Then this sweet Mary turned to her unworthy daughter, saying: "O my daughter and spouse of my son, your name is Light because you are the daughter of the eternal light.[70] Do I not seem lovely and beautiful to you, daughter?" To this the unworthy daughter replied with all reverence, saying: "My sweetest Lady and Queen, we always see you beautiful and most lovely, more than any creature your sweetest son has ever created." And then my sweet Love replied to his unworthy servant: "Does it not seem to you, my daughter, that my mother is most beautiful and lovely?" She answered: "Yes, Lord." The sweet Lord said: "Now know that I could show her even more beautiful and lovely, but I rest here because your eyes would not understand it. Do likewise, my daughter, and act in this way, comporting yourself happily all your days so that you can come to this glory."

This is not well written, Father Confessor; I will go back again to say it better so that there will be passages where you can see in this glory as much as you can see it in its fullness, how the triumphs of heaven are marvelous and adorned above all things, and the one who does this will be blessed.[71]

And when the Divine Majesty had said this, all the angels moved and made a great reverence to the empress of heaven, with lauds, with sweet and high songs. Then the Divine Majesty took his mother by the hand and made her sit with him on his throne, saying: "Hec est regina da qua semper delectatus sum." "This is the queen of whom I am always pleased, even to the highest delight" [cf. Matt 17:5]. And as soon as sweet Jesus had said these words, all the blessed souls and all the male and female saints knew the beauty of sweet Mary, some more, some less. And sweet Jesus said to this his servant: "I would like you to know, my most beloved daughter, that my mother is always pure and beautiful and remains always in such beauty, but this cannot be known by all. I wished to spill out my grace on your eyes so that you could know. And I would like you to know, daughter, who are those blessed souls and saints that you saw underneath the plants and the leaves. They are those who in the world did not have great virtue but are saved in my faith because of works, or faith, or their contrition. But those who are seated on top of the trees are those who showed great virtue in the world, and for that reason they sit above the others in my kingdom. And those are above the trees who in the world had no contrition, and no information about them is given to the human race; they are those who believed in me more than not, and more than is written about me. And those who sat above the trees are those who in the world did not know (that is, about me). They did not have great information and glory since information was not given to the human race."

And when these words were finished, sweet Jesus lifted up his feet from his throne and, taking his sweetest mother by the hand, said to his unworthy servant: "My dearest daughter, what do you think this garden is? You should know, dear daughter, that I am the one who gives glory to each one according to his merits." And having said this, at once the garden no longer appeared, and everything appeared in our Lord in the manner of a mirror, adorned with all its beauties. Then the Lord said: "Daughter, I wish to tell you more about this garment." And here ends the sixth revelation shown by the Lord and about his mother.

240

[Seventh Revelation]

The night of his resurrection and of his beloved, Saint Paul,[72] I was led, unworthily and only through divine goodness, to a celestial and happy homeland, and before my eyes was my beloved Saint Paul, and indeed he. It was during Holy Week. He had led me to our homeland out of goodness and helped by a religious friar of the Order of Saint Francis.[73]

Because he was strongly tempted, God sent him a circle of gold as a remedy and the same for a spiritual mother of his. The Lord commanded them in holy obedience, and soon they were accompanied by his beloved Paul and by Signore Chieronimo, his most devout advocate.[74] And he found that Franciscan father, of the above-mentioned first name, in heartfelt tears with great devotion, before the sacrament. He prayed with devotion and worried that the enemy was in the form of that spiritual mother. She made the Sign of the Cross on his forehead and heart and comforted him saying: "Father, do not doubt that I am not the enemy, but I am the one sent to you by the Lord for your good and to give you something brought from heaven for your comfort and cure. Go to your cell and prepare yourself as a good religious with all honesty."

And thus having made the remedy for himself, he returned to his homeland with the same two saints. On Easter Tuesday, her beloved Paul yet once again led this his beloved to her old homeland for the good and the health of one of her brothers who had not confessed for three years and was a great sinner.[75] And her spirit was taken into his house, or rather his palace, and she said his name: "I have come on the part of the Lord to tell you that your soul is in a most wicked state. Confess all your sins soon, because God will soon send your death." And then he said: "I think you are the devil." And so then I said: "Brother-in-law,[76] you may be sure that I am not the devil but am your dear sister-in-law."[77] And he said: "I have no in-law in the world." And I said to him: "It is very true that I am no longer your sister-in-law, since it has been many years since I rejected your brother, who has lived a good life as a good servant of God. But you, poor thing, you live like the beasts. But listen carefully to what I want to tell you; a few words will suffice. You know well that you once wished to do a cowardly deed to me, since your brother was out of town, and you have never had enough goodness to confess your sin all these many years. Even if you did not do the deed, it is enough that you had the evil and perverse will, and your soul is corrupted more than your brother's. You suggested this to me, your soul thus committing a betrayal. I beg you on behalf of God that you confess this and your other great sins, because God is full of mercy. I am certain that he will forgive your sins, for the sake of your soul. Do it soon. Do not be troubled by what I tell you, my dear brother-in-law, because I say it for the good of your soul, and for your salvation, since I love your soul as much as my own. And God is my witness that he has sent me to you for your salvation, and I have had no part in these things I tell you, for you know them better than I do, and indeed, one could lament the evil company you have kept for many years. So leave this evil life and keep good company to your consort. Live as a good man, in the fear of God, because you cannot escape from his hands, either through justice or through mercy. Remember that you must die. Believe that all your deeds will be placed before the just judge. And these things I tell you are not fables but true things, and you must consent to them as soon as possible.

"What is heaviest is one other grave sin. I wish you to confess about those two sisters who are dead, who are damned because of you, that is, your daughter and your sister, to whom you sent word that you wanted them at once, and then you killed them, that is, you gave death, that is, the monastery, [since] they were there against their will.[78] And indeed you have more reason. Indeed, you must have compassion on human fragility. Oh, rise up, my dear brother-in-law, think about it, and do good deeds for this little time that you have left in this life. You are rich, so give alms, because, as water kills the fire, so do alms and penitence kill sins. At the point of death, nothing will help you a bit if you have no good deeds: not riches, not dignity, not children, not relatives, not friends, not one thing, if you have no good deeds."

And he said: "My dear sister-in-law, holy and full of charity, I am willing to go tomorrow morning to confess all my great sins. I pray you, pray to God that I make a good confession and have true contrition for all my sins, and that God gives me the grace that will save me. And then when I am confessed, I will come to visit you before I pass from this life. Then I will die contented."

And I said: "If you have not confessed well when you come to me, I will know it, because I believe God will reveal this secret to me. Now I leave you, my dear brother-in-law. Keep in mind these things that I have told you for the good of your soul, and give me […]."[79]

Appendix
Medieval Dominican
Penitent *beatae* in Italy

AA.SS.:
> *Acta sanctorum quotquot toto orbe coluntur*, 67 vols. (Paris: Palmé, 1643–)

Benvenuta Boiani of Cividale (1255–92)

The unmarried Benvenuta lived in her parents' home in Cividale. Her anonymous Latin *vita* was written probably between 1292 and 1294. Her cult was popularized by the Dominican Leonardo Mattei in the 1440s. She was beatified by Pope Clement XIII in 1765.

Sources: *AA.SS.* October XIII, 145–85. Italian translation *Della vita della beata & devotissima Vergine Benvenuta da Civivad d'Austria del Friuli*, ed. Munio Sforza (Ferrara: Vittorio Baldini, 1595), 1–153.

Studies: Andrea Tilatti, *Benvenuta Boiani: Teoria e storia della vita religiosa femminile nella Cividale del secondo Duecento* (Trieste: Edizioni LINT, 1994).

Giovanna (Vanna) of Orvieto (1264–1306)

Giovanna's parents died when she was a child. She remained unmarried and supported herself with her work while living at a benefactor's home. Her anonymous Latin *vita* was probably written during the first half of the fourteenth century. Her cult was popu-

larized by the Dominican Thomas "Caffarini" of Siena, who translated her *vita* into Italian in August 1400. She was beatified by Pope
Benedict XIV in 1754.

Sources: *La* Legenda *di Vanna da Orvieto*, ed. Emore Paoli and
Luigi G. G. Ricci (Spoleto: Centro Italiano di Studi sull'Alto
Medioevo, 1996), 137–76. Thomas of Siena's translation into
Italian in ibid., 191–236.

Studies: Enrico Menestò, "Giovanna da Orvieto: la santità tra
un fuso, un ago e un rocchetto di filo." In *Umbria sacra e civile*, ed.
Enrico Menestò and Roberto Rusconi (Turin, 1989), 125–34; and
Emore Paoli, "'Pulcerrima vocor ab omnibus et non Vanna': Vanna
da Orvieto dalla storia alla agiografia," in *La* Legenda *di Vanna da
Orvieto*, ed. Emore Paoli and Luigi G. G. Ricci (Spoleto: Centro
Italiano di Studi sull'Alto Medioevo, 1996), 3–75.

Margherita of Città di Castello (1287–1320)

The blind Margherita was a descendant of a noble family, but
her parents deserted her when she was a child. She remained
unmarried but found a home in a benevolent family in Città
Castello. Two anonymous fourteenth-century versions of her *vita*
survive. Her cult was popularized by Thomas "Caffarini" of Siena,
who translated the shorter version of Maria's *vita*, the so-called
recensio minor, into Italian in 1400. She was beatified by Pope
Clement X in 1675.

Sources: *Le* legendae *di Margherita da Città di Castello*, ed.
Maria Lungarotti (Spoleto: Centro Italiano di Studi sull'Alto
Medioevo, 1994).

Studies: Daniele Solvi, "Riscritture agiographice: le due 'legendae' latine di Margherita da Città di Castello," *Hagiographica* 2
(1995): 251–76; and Chiara Frugoni, "Su un 'immaginario' possibile
di Margherita da Città di Castello," in *Il Movimento religioso femminile in Umbria nei secoli XIII–XIV*, ed. Roberto Rusconi (Spoleto:
Centro Italiano di Studi sull'Alto Medioevo, 1994), 203–16.

Sybillina Biscossi of Pavia (1287–1367)

Sybillina became an orphan at a young age, so she quickly had to earn her own living as a servant. When she lost her sight, she withdrew from society to live as a recluse in a cell attached to the Dominican Church of Pavia. Her life was written soon after her death by the Dominican Thomas of Bozzolasto, but her cult did not spread outside her native town. She was beatified by Pope Pius IX in 1854.

Sources: *AA.SS.* March III: 67–71.

Studies: Anna Benvenuti Papi, *"In castro poenitentiae": Santità e società femminile nell'Italia medievale* (Rome: Herder, 1990), 396–400.

Villana Botti of Florence (1332–60)

Villana, a wife and a mother, was probably dressed in the Dominican habit only when she was buried in the Dominican Church of Santa Maria Novella, but she had numerous lifelong contacts with the Dominican friars and penitents in Florence. Her *vita* was written by Dominican Girolamo Giovanni in the 1420s, when her cult was popularized by her grandson Sebastian, also a Dominican. She was beatified by Pope Leo XII in 1824.

Sources: *AA.SS.* August V: 862–69.

Studies: Stefano Orlandi, *La beata Villana: Terziaria domenicana fiorentina dal sec. XIV* (Florence, 1955); and Anna Benvenuti Papi, *"In castro poenitentiae": Santità e società femminile nell'Italia medievale* (Rome: Herder, 1990), 171–203.

Catherine Benincasa of Siena (ca.1347–80)

Catherine took the Dominican penitent habit sometime between 1363 and 1368. As an unmarried woman she lived in the house of her parents, Lapa and Giacomo Benincasa, and in the homes of her fellow penitents. Her prophetic teaching and public mystical experiences made her a celebrity during her lifetime.

APPENDIX

Catherine's first *vita*, the so-called *Miracoli*, was written by an anonymous author from Florence during the fall of 1374. Raymond of Capua, Catherine's confessor between 1374 and 1378 and master general of the Dominican Order (1380–99), wrote her life, the so-called *Legenda maior*, between 1385 and 1395. Thomas "Caffarini" of Siena popularized Catherine's cult during the first decades of the fifteenth century. She was canonized by Pope Pius II in 1461 and declared a doctor of the church in 1970. She is the only medieval Dominican penitent woman of Italy who has been formally canonized.

Catherine's writings: Catherine of Siena, *Il Dialogo della Divina Provvidenza*, 2nd ed., ed. Giuliana Cavallini (Siena: Edizioni Cantagalli, 1995). In English, *The Dialogue*, trans. and intro. Suzanne Noffke (New York: Paulist Press, 1980). Catherine of Siena, *Le lettere*, notes by Niccolò Tommaseo, ed. Pietro Misciatelli, 6 vols. (Florence, 1970). In English, *The Letters of Catherine of Siena*, trans. Suzanne Noffke, 2 vols. (Tempe: Arizona Center for Medieval and Renaissance Studies, 2000, 2001).

Sources: Raymond of Capua, De S. Catharinae Senensis (the *Legenda maior*), in *AA.SS.* April III: 862–967. In English, *The Life of Catherine of Siena*, trans., intro., and anno. Conleth Kearns (Washington, DC: Dominican Publications, 1980). *I miracoli di Caterina di Iacopo da Siena di Anonimo Fiorentino*, ed. Francesco Valli, in Fontes Vitae S. Catharinae Senensis Historici, vol. 4 (Siena: University of Siena, 1936). *Il Processo Castellano*, ed. M.-H. Laurent, in Fontes Vitae S. Catharinae Senensis Historici, vol. 9 (Milan: Fratelli Bocca, 1942). Thomas of Siena, *Libellus de supplemento: Legende prolixe virginis beate Catherine de Senis*, ed. Giuliana Cavallini and Imelda Foralosso (Rome: Edizioni Cateriniane, 1974). Thomas of Siena, *Sanctae Catharinae Senensis legenda minor*, ed. E. Franceschini, in Fontes Vitae S. Caterinae Senensis Historici, vol. 10 (Siena: University of Siena, 1942). For letters concerning Catherine of Siena, see *Leggenda minore di S. Caterina da Siena e lettere dei suoi discepoli*, ed. Francesco Grottanelli (Bologna: G. Romagnoli, 1868), 253–390.

Studies: Articles in the *Atti del Simposio Internazionale Cateriniano Bernardiniano*, ed. Domenico Maffei and Paolo Nardi (Siena: Accademia Senese degli Intronati, 1982); Giuliana Cavallini,

Catherine of Siena (London: Geoffrey Chapman, 1998); Suzanne Noffke, *Catherine of Siena: Vision through a Distant Eye* (Collegeville, MN: The Liturgical Press, 1996); Karen Scott, "St. Catherine, 'Apostola,'" *Church History* 61 (1992): 34–46; and Karen Scott, "Urban Spaces, Women's Networks, and the Lay Apostolate in the Siena of Catherine Benincasa," in *Creative Women in Medieval and Early Modern Italy: Religious and Artistic Renaissance*, ed. E. Ann Matter and John Coakley (Philadelphia: University of Pennsylvania Press, 1994), 105–19.

Bibliographies: Lina Zanini, *Bibliographia analitica di S. Caterina da Siena, 1901–1950* (Rome: Centro Nazionale di Studi Cateriniani, 1971); and Zanini, *Bibliographia analitica di S. Caterina da Siena, 1950–1975*, ed. Maria C. Paterna (Rome: Centro Nazionale di Studi Cateriniani, 1985).

Maria Mancini of Pisa (ca. 1350–ca. 1431)

Maria died as a Dominican nun in the strictly encloistered monastery of San Domenico in Pisa, but for about three years (ca. 1375–78) this twice-widowed mother of eight lived an active life as a penitent. The Latin *vita* written by Maria's anonymous confessor has been lost, but Serafino Razzi, who wrote her short *vita* in Italian in 1577, claimed that he relied on the original *vita*. She was beatified by Pope Pius IX in 1855.

Sources: Serafino Razzi, *Vite dei santi e beati del sacro ordine d' Frati Predicatori, cosi huomini, come donne* (Palermo: Giovanni Antonio de Franceschi, 1605), 651–59.

Studies: Niccola Zucchelli, *La Beata Chiara Gambacorta: La chiesa ed il convento di S. Domenico, Pisa* (Pisa: Cav.F. Mariotti, 1914), 121–28.

Maria Sturion of Venice (ca. 1379–99)

Young Maria returned to live as a penitent in her parents' house when she was abandoned by her husband, Giannino della Piazza, soon after their marriage. She was formally dressed in the

Dominican penitent habit a month before her death in July 1399. The Latin *vita* of Maria was written by Thomas "Caffarini" of Siena in 1402. He translated the *vita* into Italian with some additions in 1403. Her cult has never been formally confirmed.

Sources: Thomas of Siena, *Legenda cuiusdam B. Mariae de Venetiis*, ed. Flaminius Cornelius, in *Ecclesiae Venetae Antiquis Monumentis*, 13 vols. (Venice, 1749), 7:363–420. Thomas of Siena's Italian translation: *La santità imitabile: "Leggenda di Maria da Venezia" di Tommaso da Siena*, ed. Fernanda Sorelli (Venice: Deputazione Editrice, 1984), 151–221.

Studies: Fernanda Sorelli, "Introduzione," in Thomas of Siena, *La santità imitabile: "Leggenda di Maria da Venezia" di Tommaso da Siena*, ed. Fernanda Sorelli (Venice: Deputazione Editrice, 1984), 3–143.

Margherita Fontana of Modena (1440–1513)

Margherita lived as a penitent in her aristocratic family's home. Her short *vita* was written in Italian by the Dominican friar Desiderio Paloni around 1585. Her cult never spread outside her native town, nor has it ever been formally confirmed.

Sources: Latin translation of Paloni's Italian *vita* may be found in *AA.SS.* September IV: 134–39.

Studies: Maiju Lehmijoki-Gardner, *Wordly Saints: Social Interaction of Dominican Penitent Women in Italy, 1200–1500* (Helsinki: Suomen historiallinen seura, 1999), 48, 82–83, 128, 131, and 135.

Magdalena Panatieri of Monferrato (1443/53–1503)

Magdalena lived as a penitent in her aristocratic family's home. Her life has been poorly documented and the first *vitae* were written only during the late seventeenth century. She was beatified by Pope Leo XII in 1827.

Sources: Domenico Maria Marchese, *Sacro diario domenicano*, 6 vols. (Naples: Giacinto Passano, 1679), 5: 408–13; and *AA.SS.* October, Auctaria, 168*–73*.

Studies: Maiju Lehmijoki-Gardner, *Wordly Saints: Social Interaction of Dominican Penitent Women in Italy, 1200–1500* (Helsinki: Suomen historiallinen seura, 1999), 48, 104.

Osanna Andreasi of Mantua (1449–1505)

Osanna lived as a penitent in her aristocratic parents' home. After the death of her parents, she helped to take care of her younger siblings, and later she lived with the families of her two brothers.

Osanna's letters written to the members of the ducal Gonzaga family have survived. The Dominican Francesco Silvestri of Ferrara and the Olivetan Girolamo Scolaro each wrote a *vita* within a few years of Osanna's death. Osanna's cult was popularized by Isabella d'Este and Francesco Gonzaga, who patronized the saint during her life.

In 1515 Pope Leo X granted the right for local celebration of Osanna's *dies natalis* or feast day. Osanna was beatified by Pope Innocent XII in 1694.

Osanna's letters: Giuseppe Bagolini and Lodovigo Ferretti, *La beata Osanna da Mantova, terziaria domenicana* (1449–1505) (Florence: Tipografia Domenicana, 1905), lxv-xcvj (appendix).

Sources: The Latin *vita* by Francesco Silvestri, *AA.SS.* June IV: 552–664; and Girolamo Scolari (Montolivetano), *Libretto de la vita et transito de la beata Osanna da Mantua* (Mantua: Leonardo Bruschi, 1507). For the Latin translation of Scolari's *vita*, see *AA.SS.* June IV: 601–64.

Studies: Giuseppe Bagolini and Lodovigo Ferretti, *La beata Osanna da Mantova, terziaria domenicana* (1449–1505) (Florence: Tipografia Domenicana, 1905); and Gabriella Zarri, *Le sante vive: Cultura e religiositá femminile nella prima etá moderna* (Turin: Rosenberg & Sellier, 1990), 87–163.

Stefana Quinzani of Orzinuovi (1457–1530)

Stefana was born in Orzinuovi, near Brescia, but spent most of her life in Crema and Soncino. As a daughter of a poor family she earned her living working as a servant. In 1519 she founded a penitent community in Soncino dedicated to Saints Paul and Catherine of Siena. Stefana's letters, which she wrote to the members of the Gonzaga family, have survived. Two records concerning her public imitations of Christ's passion document the late medieval fascination with Jesus' sufferings. Her cult was popularized soon after her death by the Dominicans Bartholomeo of Mantua and Battista of Salò, but their Latin *vitae* have been lost, and only a later Italian version that freely combines information from both texts has survived.

Stefana was beatified by Benedict XIV in 1740.

Stefana's letters: Antonio Cistellini, *Figure della riforma pretridentina: Stefana Quinzani, Angela Merici, Laura Mignani, Bartolomeo Stella, Francesco Cabrini, Francesco Santabona* (Brescia: Morcelliana, 1979), 176–93.

Sources: Paolo Guerrini, "La prima 'legenda volgare' de la beata Stefana Quinzani d'Orzinuovi secondo il codice Vaticano-Urbinate latino 1755," *Memorie storiche della diocesi di Brescia* 1930 (no. 1): 89–186. For Stefana's two imitations of Christ's passion, see Giuseppe Brunati, *Vita, o Gesta di santi bresciani*, 2 vols. (Brescia: Venturini, 1854–56), 2:55–64; and Antonio Cistellini, *Figure della riforma pretridentina: Stefana Quinzani, Angela Merici, Laura Mignani, Bartolomeo Stella, Francesco Cabrini, Francesco Santabona* (Brescia: Morcelliana, 1979), 194–97.

Studies: Antonio Cistellini, *Figure della riforma pretridentina: Stefana Quinzani, Angela Merici, Laura Mignani, Bartolomeo Stella, Francesco Cabrini, Francesco Santabona* (Brescia: Morcelliana, 1979); Vittorio Tolasi, *Stefana Quinzani: Donna, suora e beata (1457–1530)*; Inediti dell'epistolario Gonzaga e sintesi del processo di Beatificazione (Brescia: Tipografia di S. Eustacchio, 1972); and Gabriella Zarri, *Le sante vive* (Turin: Rosenberg & Sellier, 1990), 87–164.

Lucia (Camilla) Bartolini Rucellai of Florence (1465–1520)

Camilla Bartolini changed her name to Lucia when she and her husband Rodolfo received their Dominican penitent habits from the visionary reformer Girolamo Savonarola in 1496. Lucia founded a penitent community dedicated to Saint Catherine of Siena in Florence in 1500. Lucia does not have her own *vita* but is known from the documents concerning her conversion and her founding of the penitent house. Her cult has never been formally confirmed.

Sources: For Lucia's conversion and her penitent community, see Raymond Creytens, "Il Direttorio di Roberto Ubaldini da Gagliano, O.P., per le terziarie collegiate di S. Caterina da Siena in Firenze," *Archivum Fratrum Praedicatorum* 39 (1969): 127–72.

Studies: Luigi Passarini, *Genealogia e storia della Famiglia Rucellai* (Florence: M. Cellini E.C., 1861), 130–31; and Giuseppe Richa, *Notizie istoriche delle chiese fiorentine divise ne' suoi quartieri*, 10 vols. (Florence: Pietro Gaetano Viviani, 1709), 8:278–84.

Colomba Guadagnoli of Rieti (1467–1501)

Colomba took the penitent habit in 1486 and lived a few years as a penitent in her parents' home before she founded a penitent community dedicated to Saint Catherine of Siena in Perugia in 1490. Colomba wrote a short rule or *modus vivendi* for her community. Her cult was supported by the Baglioni family of Perugia. Colomba's confessor, a mathematician, Sebastiano d'Angeli Bontempi, wrote her *vita* a few years after her death. Colomba was beatified by Pope Urban VIII in 1627.

Colomba's rule: Giovanna Casagrande, "Terziarie domenicane a Perugia," in *Una santa, una città*, Atti del Convegno storico nel V centenario della venuta a Perugia di Colomba da Rieti, Perugia, November 10–12, 1989, ed. Giovanna Casagrande and Enrico Menestò (Spoleto: Centro Italiano di Studi sull'Alto Medioevo, 1991), 142–47.

Sources: *AA.SS.* May V: 150*–226*. In Italian, Sebastiano Angeli, *Legenda volgare di Colomba da Rieti*, ed. Giovanna Casagrande in collaboration with M. L. Cianini Pierotti, A. Maiarelli, and F. Santucci (Spoleto: Centro Italiano di Studi sull'Alto Medioevo, 2002).

Studies: *Una santa, una città*, ed. Giovanna Casagrande and Enrico Menestò (Spoleto: Centro Italiano di Studi sull'Alto Medioevo, 1991); and Gabriella Zarri, *Le sante vive* (Turin: Rosenberg & Sellier, 1990), 87–164.

Lucia Brocadelli of Narni (1476–1544)

Lucia ended her marriage with Pietro of Milan in 1494 when she took the penitent habit and lived in penitent communities in Rome, Viterbo, and finally in Ferrara, where Duke Ercole I d'Este donated a house dedicated to Saint Catherine of Siena for the use of penitents in 1501. In 1544 Lucia wrote *Seven Revelations*, a collection of her visions. Her Latin *vita*, which, according to tradition, was written soon after her death, has been lost. Serafino Razzi's late-sixteenth-century collection of a few testimonies remains the first hagiographic account concerning Lucia. Lucia was beatified by Pope Clement XI in 1710.

Lucia's book: E. Ann Matter, Armando Maggi, and Maiju Lehmijoki-Gardner, "*Le rivelazioni of Lucia Brocadelli da Narni*," *Archivum Fratrum Praedicatorum* 71 (2001): 311–44.

Sources: Serafino Razzi, *Vite dei santi e beati, cosi huomini come donne del sacro ordine de Frati Predicatori* (Florence: Bartolomeo Sermantelli, 1577), 152–54.

Studies: E. Ann Matter, "Prophetic Patronage as Repression: Lucia Brocadelli da Narni and Ercole d'Este," in *Christendom and Its Discontents: Exclusion, Persecution, and Rebellion, 1000–1500*, ed. Scott L. Waugh and Peter D. Diehl (Cambridge: Cambridge University Press, 1996), 168–76; E. Ann Matter, Armando Maggi, Maiju Lehmijoki-Gardner, and Gabriella Zarri, "Lucia Brocadelli da Narni: Riscoperta di un manoscritto pavese," *Bollettino della società pavese di storia patria* 100 (2000): 173–99; and Tamar Herzig, "The Rise and Fall of a Savonarolan Visionary: Lucia Brocadelli's

Forgotten Contribution to the *Piagnone* Campaign," *Archiv für Reformationsgeschichte/Archive for Reformation History* 95 (2004): 34–60.

Caterina Mattei of Racconigi (1486–1547)

Caterina was an unmarried penitent who supported herself with her handiwork, especially with silk weaving. Around 1523 the mystic was forced to desert her hometown due to accusations of sorcery. She settled in Caramango, where she remained for the rest of her life. Her *vita* was initially written by her two confessors, the Domenicans Domenico Onesto and Gabriele Dolce, then revised by her supporter Giovanni Francesco Pico della Mirandola, and completed by the Dominican Pietro Morelli. Caterina was beatified by Pope Pius VII in 1808.

Sources: Giovanni Francesco Pico and Pietro Martire Morelli, *Compendio delle cose mirabili della venerabil serva di Dio Catterina da Raconisio vergine integerrima del Sacro Ordine della Penitenzia di S. Domenico distinto in dieci libri* (Bologna: n.p., ca. 1680); and Serafino Razzi, *Vite dei santi e beati, cosi huomini come donne del sacro ordine de Frati Predicatori* (Florence: Bartolomeo Sermantelli, 1577), 108–35.

Studies: Gabriella Zarri, *Le sante vive* (Turin: Rosenberg & Sellier, 1990), 87–164; and idem, "Potere carismatico e potere politico nelle corti italiane del Rinascimento," in *Poteri carismatici e informali: chiesa e società medioevali*, ed. Agostino Paravicini Bagliani and André Vauchez (Palermo: Sellerio Editore, 1992), 182–87.

Notes

Munio of Zamora: The *Ordinationes*

1. On Munio of Zamora, see R. P. Mortier, *Histoire des Maitres Généraux de l'Ordre des Frères Prêcheurs*, 3 vols. (Paris: Alphonse Picard, 1905), 2:170–293; and Peter Linehan, *The Ladies of Zamora* (Manchester: Manchester University Press, 1997).

2. The expression *ordinationes* should be viewed in the context of Dominican legislative terminology. The term was synonymous with admonitions *(admonitiones)*, which the Dominican general and provincial chapters could pass as quasi-laws. See G. R. Galbraith, *The Constitution of the Dominican Order 1216 to 1360* (Manchester: Manchester University Press, 1925), 76–77, 104.

3. The manuscript containing the *Ordinationes* was described by Giuseppe Pardi in "Elenchi di mantellate senesi," *Studi Cateriniani* 2 (1924–25), no. 2: 44–49.

4. Gilles Gerard Meersseman, *Dossier de l'ordre de la Pénitence au XIIIe siècle* (Freiburg: Editions Universitaires Fribourg Suisse, 1961), esp. 143–56; William A. Hinnebusch, *The History of the Dominican Order*, 2 vols. (New York: Alba House, 1965) 1:400–404; and Raymond Creytens, "Costituzioni domenicane," in *Dizionario degli istituti di perfezione*, ed. Guerrino Pelliccia and Giancarlo Rocca (Rome: Edizioni Paoline, 1974–), 3:190–97.

5. Thomas of Siena, *Tractatus de ordine fratrum et sororum de penitentia Sancti Dominici*, ed. M.-H. Laurent, in Fontes Vitae S. Catharinae Senensis Historici, vol. 21 (Siena: Unversity of Siena, 1938), 37–44.

6. For a fuller discussion concerning recent approaches to the history of Dominican penitent rule, see the General Introduction, herein.

7. Latin: *sorores portantes habitum eiusdem ordinis* [the Order of Friars Preachers].

8. The notion that the breaking of the *Ordinationes* was not a sin but a human trespass that could be rectified through reconciliation and penance was directly from the constitutions of the Dominican Order (see Raymond Creytens, "Les constitutions des Frères Prêcheurs dans la rédac-

tion de S. Raymond de Penyafort (1241)," *Archivum Fratrum Praedicatorum* 18 [1948], 29).

9. Black and white were seen as colors of Dominican *conversi* and other lay associations. In the thirteenth century the black used by *conversi* and penitents had a shade of gray to it, but by the fifteenth century the Dominican *conversi* and other lay groups wore deep black (see Raymond Creytens, "Les Convers des Moniales Dominicaines au Moyen Age," *Archivum Fratrum Praedicatorum* 19 [1949], 26–27).

10. The two-layered habit of the penitents was modeled after the Dominican *conversi* (see ibid., 27).

11. The formula of this blessing of the vestments is identical with the blessing of the habit of the friars at their profession (see Creytens, "Les constitutions des Frères Prêcheurs," dist. I, chap. XV, p. 41).

12. It may be presumed that these sisters received a similar tonsure to the *conversi*, who shaved the nape of the neck. This tonsure differed from the crown-shaped tonsure of the clergymen (see Creytens, "Les Convers des Moniales Dominicaines," 28–29).

13. The taking of the habit signified the entrance to the Dominican penitential life. There were neither formal oaths nor a period of probation (novitiate).

14. Munio's *Ordinationes* perceived lay sisters as being under the direction of the local prior rather than under the master general, which was always the case with the friars and with the penitents from the fifteenth century onward (cf. The Dominican Penitent Rule, chap. 20).

15. Lay religious, including penitents of various orders and *conversi* and *conversae* of monasteries, were not expected to sing the Psalms of the Divine Office. Instead, they celebrated the Hours by reciting the *Pater Noster* and some other prayers.

16. The passage conflates two calendars. The *Quadragesima* of Saint Martin was a forty-day fast that began on the feast day of Saint Martin (November 11) and continued to Christmas. In the *Ordinationes* Advent is marked as the beginning of a second set of obligations in the middle of the *Quadragesima* of Saint Martin. Such a conflation of calendars suggests that the *Ordinationes* brought together two traditions, each of which was at some point followed by the penitents.

17. That is, Maundy Thursday.

18. During the thirteenth century the following Marian feasts were celebrated: the Annunciation (March 25), the Visitation (July 2), the Purification (February 2), and the Assumption (August 15).

19. The annual cycle of ten communions reflected the observances of friars, monks, and nuns, a fact that suggests that Munio saw penitent piety in semi-monastic terms. Typically, lay religious were expected to take communion only three or four times a year (cf. various rules for religious laity in Meersseman, *Dossier de l'ordre de la Pénitence*, 82–159).

20. Fasting in this context means eating only one meal a day, namely, lunch. It was eaten around None, that is, between 1:30 and 2:30 p.m.

21. The order wanted to control fasting and other forms of asceticism to avoid excess, which was associated with pride and individualism.

22. Dominicans practiced bloodletting, considered to be good for health (see Creytens, "Les constitutions des Frères Prêcheurs," dist. I, chap. VIII, p. 36).

23. The penitents often were a source of friction between the secular clergy and the mendicants. Munio hoped to appease the parish clergy with this stipulation and to clarify that even though penitent women were protected by the Dominicans, they did not enjoy full religious status and, accordingly, they were not exempted from ecclesiastical tithes.

24. The fact that the *vestitae* took the active role in seeking Munio's approval testifies to these women's involvement in their governance.

The Dominican Penitent Rule

1. See General Introduction, and the introduction to the *Ordinationes* of Munio, herein.

2. Martina Wehrli-Johns, "L'Osservanza dei Domenicani e il movimento penitenziale laico: Studi sulla 'regola di Munio' e sul Terz'ordine domenicano in Italia e Germania," in *Ordini religiosi e società politica in Italia e Germania nei secoli XIV e XV*, ed. Giorgio Chittolini and Kaspar Elm (Bologna: Società editrice il Mulino, 2001), 300–303; and Maiju Lehmijoki-Gardner, "Writing Religious Rules as an Interactive Process—Dominican Penitent Women and the Making of Their *Regula*," *Speculum* 79 (2004): 677–83

3. The complicated genesis of the formal penitent rule also makes it impossible to determine whether the person stating orders in the rule (Latin: *volumus et ordinamus*) was a Dominican leader, possibly master general, or the pope. The former was the case if the *Tractatus* contained the first full copy of the rule, but if the *Tractatus* copied the papal rule, the expression *volumus et ordinamus* used in the text refers to the pope giving the ordinances.

4. The Dominican Order was a centralized organization, within which members swore loyalty to the master general of the order rather than to the head of their local institutions, which was the case with many other religious orders. See G. R. Galbraith, *The Constitution of the Dominican Order 1216 to 1360* (Manchester: University of Manchester Press, 1925), 135–36.

5. On the penitent men of Venice and their role in the approval of the Dominican penitent rule, see Lehmijoki-Gardner, "Writing Religious Rules as an Interactive Process," 676–77, 680–82.

6. The expression "we demand and declare" (Latin: *volumus et ordinamus*) may refer either to the master general of the Dominican Order or to the pope as the giver of the ordinances (see note 3 above).

7. The terms "master" (Latin: *magister*) and "director" (Latin: *director*) were interchangeable expressions that referred to a Dominican friar who supervised a penitent group. On the appointment of the director/master, see chap. 20.

8. Latin: *fraternitas.*

9. It is not clear how a confessor's (Latin: *confessor*) tasks compared with the functions of the aforementioned master and/or director of the penitent group. He probably was the spiritual guide of the community, whereas the master and the director had more administrative responsibilities. The fact that the penitents were to draw their testament according to their confessor's advice, however, suggests that he offered practical advice as well.

10. Married women rarely joined penitent associations. Typically, penitent women were widows or unmarried women.

11. Black and white were the colors of Dominican *conversi* and other lay associations. See Raymond Creytens, "Les Convers des Moniales Dominicaines au Moyen Age," *Archivum Fratrum Praedicatorum* 19 (1949), 26–27.

12. The Dominican penitents wore two tunics, one of which was shorter than the other. The two-layered habit of the penitents was modeled after the Dominican *conversi* (see ibid., 27).

13. This rite is identical with that found in the *Ordinationes* of Munio (see chap. 3). It is also identical with the blessing of the habit of the friars at their profession (see Raymond Creytens, "Les constitutions des Frères Prêcheurs dans la rédaction de S. Raymond de Penyafort [1241]," *Archivum Fratrum Praedicatorum* 18 [1948], dist. I, chap. XV, p. 41).

14. The profession underscored the religious status of penitents, but it did not involve the taking of the three religious vows of chastity, poverty, and obedience, which were necessary for full members of reli-

gious orders. The *Ordinationes* of Munio had not required penitent profession. It is not clear when the Dominicans began to demand profession from their penitents, but it is probable that such practice arose only at the time of the writing of the formal rule. Raymond of Capua described in great detail in his *Legenda maior* (completed in 1395) the way in which Catherine of Siena took the penitent habit, but he did not make any reference to Catherine's profession. Had profession been practiced during Catherine's time, Raymond would certainly have underscored the fact that Catherine went through this formal rite. See Raymond of Capua, *De S. Catharinae Senensis* (the *Legenda maior*), in *Acta Sanctorum* April III (Paris: Palmé, 1866), 879–83 (chaps. 69–79). Translation in English: *The Life of Catherine of Siena*, trans. Conleth Kearns (Washington, DC: Dominican Publications, 1980).

15. The rite of the penitent profession was inspired by the same rite of the Dominican friars (see A. H. Thomas, "Profession religieuse des dominicains: Formule, cérémonies, histoire," *Archivum Fratrum Praedicatorum* 39 [1969]: 5–52).

16. This ruling was not yet mentioned in Munio's *Ordinationes*, but it was imposed on Dominican penitents of Siena in 1352 (see Siena, Biblioteca comunale, T.II.8.b., f. 3r.).

17. Many penitent women who could afford monastic dowries moved on to Dominican nunneries.

18. The canonical hours are Matins, Lauds, Prime, Terce, Sext, None, Vespers, and Compline. Matins and Lauds were commonly said together, around 1–3:30 a.m., depending on the time of the year. The last canonical hour of the day, Compline, was said around 6–9 p.m.

19. The *Ordinationes* of Munio did not require the saying of the *Ave Marias* at each canonical hour, but the formal rule placed the *Ave Maria* side by side with the more traditional requirement of saying sets of *Pater Nosters*. Such promotion of Marian prayers was connected to the Dominican Order's increasing emphasis on Marian piety during the fifteenth century. Toward the second half of the century this effort culminated in the Dominican promotion of the Rosary.

20. Six psalms begin with *Laudate*, and it is not clear which one is being referred to.

21. Penitents were not expected to sing the Divine Office, which was as a practice limited to the full members of religious orders and to the clergy.

22. Celebrated on November 1.

23. Matins was a nighttime office, celebrated around 1–3:30 a.m., depending on the time of the year. Unlike the *Ordinationes* of Munio, the

formal rule does not suggest that the penitents were to convene at a church for Matins (cf. the *Ordinationes* of Munio, chap. 7). It is implied that Matins was to be said at home.

24. It is not clear to what kind of office the term "prelate" (Latin: *prelatus*) refers. Was he the master or the director of the penitents, or the confessor, or a prelate from the local parochial church?

Frequent reception of the Eucharist was considered a privilege. Although religious laywomen's eucharistic piety was one of the most celebrated aspects of medieval mysticism, the church was in general opposed to laywomen's frequent communion, which the church feared burdened clergymen and led to the desacralization of the sacrament. See Joseph Duhr, "Communion fréquente," in *Dictionnaire de spiritualité, ascétique et mystique, doctrine et histoire*, ed. Marcel Viller (Paris: Beauschesne, 1953), 2:1234–92, esp. 1236–71.

25. Unlike full members of religious orders, the penitents were not exempt from ecclesiastical taxation.

26. Fifty days before Easter. The members of religious orders commonly began their Lenten fast at *Quinquagesima*, whereas the rest of Christianity waited until the *Quadragesima*, forty days before Easter, to begin their fasts.

27. Saintly penitent women were known for their extreme bodily austerities, but the rule discouraged unsupervised asceticism, and extreme ascetic acts were commonly regarded as signs of individuality and arrogance.

28. The Dominicans had chivalric, anti-heretic confraternities, but the penitent associations were intended as peaceful brotherhoods. On Dominican confraternities, see Gilles Gerard Meersseman, in collaboration with Gian Piero Pacini, *Ordo fraternitatis: Confraternite e pietà dei laici nel medioevo* (Rome: Herder, 1977), vols. 2 and 3.

29. That is, the Last Rites.

30. That is, within the period of eight days after Easter.

31. This annual rite of deciding about the term of the prior or prioress reflected the ideals drawn up in the constitutions of the Dominican friars. The constitutions allowed the community to limit the power of its leaders. In most religious orders the term of office of the priors or prioresses was not limited (see Galbraith, *The Constitution of the Dominican Order 1216 to 1360*, 122–24).

32. The penitent women's meeting was set to Friday (the day of penance), whereas penitent men could convene on any day of their choice.

33. Whereas the penitents following the *Ordinationes* of Munio were still considered responsible only to the prior of the local Dominican

convent (see the *Ordinationes* of Munio, chap. 7), the formal penitent rule placed penitents within the master general's jurisdiction. They were thus considered an integral part of the Dominican Order.

34. Breaking the stipulations of the rule was not considered a mortal sin, but rather a trespass that could be amended by doing penance. See Creytens, "Les constitutions des Frères Prêcheurs," 29; and I. M. Tonneau, "L'obligation 'ad poenam' des constitutions dominicaines," *Revue des sciences philosophiques et théologiques* 24 (1935): 107–15.

The Legend of Giovanna of Orvieto

1. For studies of Giovanna and her cult, see Enrico Menestò, "Giovanna da Orvieto: la santità tra un fuso, un ago e un rocchetto di filo," in *Umbria sacra e civile*, ed. Enrico Menestò and Roberto Rusconi (Turin, 1989), 125-34; and Emore Paoli, "'Pulcerrima vocor ab omnibus et non Vanna': Vanna da Orvieto dalla storia alla agiografia," in Emore Paoli and Luigi G. G. Ricci, *La* Legenda *di Vanna da Orvieto* (Spoleto: Centro Italiano di Studi sull'Alto Medioevo, 1996), 3–75.

2. Giovanna's cult was supported by a group of urban authorities in Orvieto. They issued a wax offering in her honor in May 1307, less than a year after her death. The ruling was renewed in 1314 and in 1350 (see Paoli, "'Pulcerrima vocor ab omnibus et non Vanna,'" 16–17).

3. Ibid., 5–16.

4. The first surviving version of Giovanna's *Legend* is possibly an abbreviated version of a lost, longer text (see ibid., 12–13). On the manuscript tradition of the text, see Ricci's introduction concerning the edition of the *Legend* in Paoli and Ricci, *La* Legenda *di Vanna da Orvieto*, esp. 88–91.

5. Munio of Zamora wrote his *Ordinationes* in Orvieto on the feast of Saint Ambrose (December 7) in 1286.

6. Thomas translated Giovanna's *Legend* in August 1400. He described the purpose of his translation in the following way: "La qual leggenda [of Vanna] fu volgarizata in Vinegna per uno frate Thomaso d Siena de' Frati Predicatori per consolatione et edificazione de le devote persone volgari, e spezialmente del decto abito." See *Leggenda della beata Giovanna (detta Vanna) suora dell'Ordine della penitenza di S. Domenico*, ed. Luigi Passarini (Rome: Tipografia Sinimberghi, 1879), 32. A facsimile of Passarini's edition of Thomas's translation may also be found in Paoli and Ricci, *La* Legenda *di Vanna da Orvieto*, 195–242.

7. Thomas wanted to emphasize Giovanna's Dominican connections and to represent her as an early example of a Dominican penitent (not merely as an institutionally ambiguous "bearer of lay habit" or *vestita*). Thus, he either translated *vestita* as "penitent," or he used the terms *"vestita"* and "penitent" side by side. A few times he also clarified that the original text's vague references to "the habit" or "sisters of the same order" referred respectively to the Dominican penitent habit and to the Dominican penitents. See *Leggenda della beata Giovanna (detta Vanna)*, 8, 13, 17, 27.

8. Within the text Giovanna is spoken of as a *vestita*, a bearer of the habit of Saint Dominic, rather than a penitent. The use of the term "penitent" *(soror de penitentia)* in the opening statement and in the table of contents reflects the terminological choice of a later author who replaced the lost first page of the original manuscript (the first page included the chapter titles and the beginning of the *Legend* up to the middle of the third chapter). On the manuscript and its replaced first page, see Ricci's introduction concerning the edition of the *Legend* in Paoli and Ricci, *La Legenda di Vanna da Orvieto*, 79–80.

9. On the use of the term "sisters of penance" or "penitents" in the text, see note 8 above.

10. During the thirteenth century Orvieto was involved in battles between the supporters of the papacy, the Guelfs, and the supporters of the Roman emperor, the Ghibellines (see Daniel Waley, *Mediaeval Orvieto: The Political History of a Italian City-State 1157–1334* [London: Cambridge University Press, 1952], 22–92).

11. On the tradition of viewing manual labor as a spiritual exercise that supported the life of prayer and protected one from the temptations that might enter an idle mind, see Christopher J. Holdsworth, "The Blessings of Work: The Cistercian View," in *Sanctity and Secularity: The Church and the World*, ed. Derek Baker (Oxford: Basil Blackwell, 1973), 67–70.

12. I have translated the term *sutor* as "dressmaker," but it is also possible that Giovanna was a cobbler. In the Middle Ages dressmaking and cobblery were considered lowly and sometimes even illicit professions (see Jacques Le Goff, "Licit and Illicit Trades in the Medieval West," in *Time, Work, and Culture in the Middle Ages*, trans. Arthur Goldhammer [Chicago: University of Chicago Press, 1980], 59).

13. The Latin word *hospitium* used here might refer either to a private home in which Giovanna received hospitality or a more institutionalized hospice.

14. It is not clear what *castrum* the *Legend* refers to, but we may presume that Giovanna moved at this point to Orvieto, which had one of the oldest Dominican convents in Italy, founded in 1220.

15. According to the Vulgate. Translation mine.

16. We learn later in the *Legend* that Giovanna died in 1306 at the age of forty-two. Thus, if Giovanna wore the habit for twenty-two years, she must have taken it sometime in 1284, when she was about twenty years old.

17. This collection of Giovanna's virtues reflects a practice of formulating stereotypical lists of virtues that emphasized simplicity, patience, humility, charity, chastity, and other virtues of self-restraint. These were inspired by a long tradition that began in antiquity and were seen in the "fruits of the spirit" in Paul's letter to the Galatians (5:22–23). Giovanna's virtues reflected this kind of predesigned pattern of virtues, and thus the passage offers little information concerning her individual characteristics (see Réginald Grégoire, "I libro delle virtù e dei vizi," *Schede medievali* 5 [July–December 1983]: 326–58).

18. Sext, the fourth canonical hour, was celebrated around noon. None, the fifth canonical hour, was celebrated around 1:30–2:30 p.m.

19. By this time, Giovanna might have already lived in the house of her prioress, Ghisla. On Ghisla, see note 23 below.

20. According to the thirteenth-century text "The Nine Ways of Prayer of Saint Dominic," this position was one of the ways in which Dominic prayed (see Simon Tugwell, ed., *Early Dominicans: Selected Writings* [New York: Paulist Press, 1982], 98).

21. The assumption of the Virgin Mary is celebrated on August 15.

22. The feast day of Saint Catherine of Alexandria was celebrated on November 25.

23. Ghisla (who later in the *Legend* is also spelled Ghiscila) was a wealthy woman from Orvieto. Ghisla and her husband, Ildebrandino Sperandei, patronized the Convent of San Domenico in Orvieto, and in 1292 the couple made a considerable bequest to the convent (see T. Mamachi, *Annalium Ordinis Praedicatorum* [Rome, 1756], appendices, cols. 184–86). Ghisla's husband was a full member of chivalrous Dominican confraternity, the *militia* of the Blessed Virgin Mary (see Domenico Maria Federici, *Istoria de' Cavalieri Gaudenti*, 2 vols. [Venice, 1787], 1:377). The full members of the *militia* lived communally in convent-like settings, which left Ghisla to pursue her own life of religion as a Dominican *vestita*. The *Legend* speaks of Ghisla as the prioress of the *vestitae* of Orvieto, but it is not clear how she was appointed to this position. It may be that Giovanna had earned her keep at Ghisla's place by working as a servant,

because twice Ghisla is introduced as Giovanna's matron (Latin: matrona). Ghisla was one of the main supporters of Giovanna's cult. Several testimonies come from her, and she was one of the key persons at the translation of Giovanna's remains to an altar in the church of San Domenico (see 82–83, herein).

24. The mention of brothers, or friars (Latin: *fratres*), as the recipients of the *Legend* suggests that the text was written for an audience of religious men, who could have been either Dominican friars or, more likely, members of a religious lay association.

25. The readers are again addressed in the masculine (Latin: *dilectissimi*), which may or may not include women. This address strengthens the hypothesis that the text was written to men, or, at least, not exclusively to women (see note 24 above).

26. Fra Giacomo Bianconi of Bevagna (1220–1301) was known for his healing miracles (see *Dizionario biografico degli italiani* [Rome: Istituto della Enciclopedia Italiana, 1968], 10:248–49). Giacomo was a prior in Orvieto during Giovanna's life, but his election took place in 1278, that is, six years before Giovanna may be presumed to have taken her Dominican habit. Thus, in 1278 she would not yet have had a prioress who is mentioned in the account as the recipient of Giovanna's prophecy (see Paoli, "'Pulcerrima vocor ab omnibus et non Vanna,'" 25–27). This chronological inconsistency might be seen as challenging the authenticity of the vision or, alternatively, Giovanna might have told about her vision to Ghisla, her prioress, before she actually took the habit but already knew Ghisla.

27. Francesco was from the powerful Monaldeschi family of Orvieto. Elected the bishop of Orvieto in 1279, he oversaw the building of the majestic Duomo of Orvieto. See Pericle Perali, *Orvieto: Note storiche di topografia e d'arte dalle origini al 1800* (Rome: Multigrafia Editrice, 1979), 76–85.

28. The passage probably refers to the turbulent transition of power from Ranieri della Greca's rule to that of the Councils of the Seven Arts in 1292 (see Waley, *Mediaeval Orvieto*, 59–83).

29. The fact that the devil took "the appearance of a religious woman" (Latin: *in specie religiose femine*) tells of the ambiguous status of religious laywomen. Religious laywomen were praised for their life of devotion and chastity, but their religious status was also seen as a facade for women who were seen to enjoy suspicious amounts of freedom. Cf. Francesco of Barberino, *Del Reggimento e de' costumi delle donne* (Rome: Stamperia De Romanis, 1815), 212–16.

30. The author seems to refer to Mark 4:20 or Luke 8:8, although the biblical version refers to bearing the fruit a hundredfold.

31. The emanation of various odors of flowers and other sweet fragrances from a corpse was seen as a popular sign of sanctity.

32. "Mixtorum aromatum et tritorum." I am not aware of the meaning of the "tritorum."

33. "Aromata trita et mixta et fervida."

34. The Latin inexplicably changes twice from the third-person singular into third-person plural. According to the text the virgin was called by the others (Latin: *ab aliis*), and she also replies in plural by saying "sisters" (Latin: *sorores*). However, the beginning and the rest of the story is written in third-person singular. This kind of inconsistency was probably created by the scribe who copied the text.

35. The lady in question must be Ghisla, with whom Giovanna lived at least for nine years (see note 23 above).

36. Emore Paoli has suggested that the saintly friar was possibly Nallo, who died April 9, 1348 (see Paoli, "'Pulcerrima vocor ab omnibus et non Vanna,'" 16). Nallo's saintly fame and miracles were discussed in Jean [Giovanni] Mactei Caccia's Chronicle of the Convent of Friars Preachers in Orvieto (see *Chronique du couvent des Prêcheurs d'Orviéto*, ed. A. M. Vieil and P. M. Girardin [Rome: Tipografia Agnesotti, 1907], 128–31). It is, however, impossible to determine whether the author indeed referred to Nallo or to another Dominican. In fact, the friar in question could also have been Nicola Brunati, who also enjoyed saintly fame in Orvieto. On Nicola, see note 44 below.

37. I wish to thank my father, Jorma Lehmijoki, M.D., for helping me in the translation of this passage, which involved such medically detailed terminology.

38. The "Order of the Continent" referred commonly to Franciscan penitents (Latin: *Fratres et Sorores Ordinis Continentium seu de Paenitentia Sancti Francisci*) (see Alfonso Pompei, "Terminologia varia dei penitenti," in *Il Movimento francescano della Penitenza nella società medioevale*, ed. Mariano d'Alatri [Rome: Istituto Storico dei Cappuccini, 1980], 15).

39. The matron in question must be Ghisla, Giovanna's prioress.

40. The reference to Giovanna's grave underground shared with other women is in conflict with the earlier statement that she was buried in a sepulcher that lay under a timbered canopy (see 78–79 herein). This peculiar passage seems to suggest an animated underground scene within which Giovanna was exposed to constant gossiping of deceased women buried close to her.

41. Ildebrandino of Clusio is mentioned in the Chronicle of Jean [Giovanni] Mactei Caccia as a papal penitentiary (see Caccia, *Chronique du couvent des Prêcheurs d'Orviéto*, 60 and 103). Ildebrandino died in 1310 on December 17 (see ibid., 85).

42. It was necessary to receive papal permission before moving a body to a new tomb. Thanks to Kirsi Salonen for this information.

43. Pietro (Petrus Bonaguida of Orvieto) was elected provincial prior of the Province of Rome in 1304 (or 1305), and he held the office until 1309. He died in 1313. See P.-T. Masetti, *Monumenta et antiquitatis veteris disciplinae ordinis praedicatorum* (Rome: Typographia Rev. Cam. Apostolicae, 1864), 1:299–302. He is mentioned in *La cronaca di S. Domenico di Perugia*, ed. Andrea Maiarelli (Spoleto: Centro Italiano di studi sull'alto medioevo, 1995), 21 (list of provincial priors), and 148 (index, which states that Pietro's position as prior began in 1305). See also Caccia, *Chronique du couvent des Prêcheurs d'Orviéto*, 86–87.

44. Fra Nicola Brunati (d. 1322), the prior of the Dominican convent in Orvieto, is mentioned in *La cronaca di S. Domenico di Perugia*, 43, 56–57, and 144. Nicola enjoyed a reputation of sanctity: "sepultus iusta hostium sacristie cum maxima difficultate propter pressuram gentium quia omnis turba querebat eum tangere ex devocione, dicentes plures ex illis quia virtus ex eo exibat ad sanandum infirmos, sicut et testimonio plurimum repertum est" (57).

45. The octave of Saint Martin was celebrated on November 19, that is, on the eighth day after his feast day on November 11. The year of Giovanna's translation was 1307.

46. That is, Ghisla, Giovanna's prioress.

47. It is not clear why Giovanna's habit was by her side, not on her. Being buried wearing the religious habit was considered a privilege, and it was usually granted to *vestitae*/penitents.

48. During the fourteenth century, the years in which the feast day of Saint Gregory (March 12) fell on Tuesday after the second Sunday of Lent were 1308, 1370, 1381, and 1392. The year of the miracle in question must have been 1308.

49. I have been unable to find any definition for *duragnum*, but the word seems to denote some kind of a hardening on or under the skin (Latin: *durus*, hard), possibly a tumor.

50. The members of the Berardino family were supporters of the Guelfs and allies of the Monaldeschi family (see Waley, *Medieval Orvieto*, 50–51).

51. The Latin form of Matteo's name is Matheus Crassus, which might not have been a proper name but rather a name referring to his big frame (Latin: *crassus*, "fat, big, or strong").

52. I thank Antti Arjava for his help with this passage.

53. The reference to giving a *solemn* vow (Latin: *cum fiducia votum emittens*) to Giovanna appears first here and will then be used in several cases below. The sudden appearance of references to the practice of a solemn vow might suggest that the remaining miracles of the text were added at a later point.

54. The miracle suggests that a version of Giovanna's life already existed and that it was seen as a relic.

55. Della Terza was a powerful noble family from Orvieto.

56. Sister Ghiscilla is introduced through her father, a fact that suggests that she was a *vestita* who was not married. Most *vestitae* were married or widowed women.

57. The conclusion was added later, when the manuscript was moved from Orvieto to Venice, where Thomas "Caffarini" of Siena was guiding the local penitent women and looking for material with which to illustrate the virtues of the Dominican religious lay life for these women (see notes 6 and 7 above).

The Miracoli *of Catherine of Siena*

1. The anonymous author of the *Miracoli* wrote that he was inspired to write an account of Catherine's life during her stay in Florence at the time of the meeting of the Dominican General Chapter in 1374 (May 21). The *Miracoli* seems to have been started while Catherine was still in Florence (she left Florence on June 29) and completed on October 10, soon after the day of the last recorded miracle in the text.

2. Scholars have always assumed that the author of the *Miracoli* was a man. However, some elements within the text have made me to wonder whether the author could actually have been a woman. Medieval religious women certainly wrote hagiographic texts, and, not unlike the author of the *Miracoli*, they typically expressed themselves in a vernacular tongue and avoided theological interpretation—a practice limited to clergymen. The facts that the author learned about Catherine from *pinzochere*, rather than from Dominican friars, that Catherine got invited to the author's home, and that the author wanted to "befriend" Catherine may also suggest a female author. The hypothesis that the author was a woman might, indeed, help to explain why the text was not used by Raymond, Thomas,

and other subsequent promoters of Catherine's cult. A vernacular text by a woman would not have been seen as authoritative or worthy of dissemination. I have not been able to determine where the manuscript containing the *Miracoli* was kept before it was bought by Senator Carlo Strozzi and in 1785 placed in collections of the Biblioteca Laurenziana of Florence (where it may be found under the code Strozzi XXXI). It is possible that the *Miracoli* was kept in a female monastery in Florence and there escaped the attention of the promoters of Catherine of Siena's cult. The texts of this manuscript (a copy of Catherine's book *The Dialogue, the Miracoli,* and a letter describing Catherine's death) were copied in 1485 into another manuscript that was intended for the nuns of the Bridgettine monastery of Paradiso, close to Florence, as may be seen in the identification found in the manuscript (Florence, Biblioteca Riccardiana, codice 1267, f. 190r).

   3. The original manuscript seems merely to suggest that the General Chapter convened because of the master general's orders ("Venne [Catherine] a Firenze del mese di maggio anni MCCCLXXIV, quando fu il capitolo de'frati Predicatori per comandamento del maestro dell'ordine, una vestita delle pinzochere di santo Domenico..." [Florence, Biblioteca Laurenziana, Strozzi XXXI. f. 177r]). Francesco Valli added in his edition a comma before the words "per comandamento," an addition that allows a reading that Catherine was summoned by the master general ("Venne a Firenze del mese di maggio anni MCCCLXXIV, quando fu il capitolo de' frati Predicatori, per comandamento del maestro dell' ordine, una vestita delle pinzochere di santo Domenico") (Francesco Valli, ed., *I miracoli di Caterina di Iacopo da Siena di Anonimo fiorentino,* in Fontes Vitae S. Catharinae Senensis Mistorici, vol. 4 [Siena: University of Siena, 1936], 1). My translation here relies on the text of the manuscript. For a critique concerning the claim that Catherine was summoned to appear in front of the Dominican General Chapter, see Timoteo Centi, "Un processo inventato di sana pianta," *S. Caterina da Siena—Rassegna di Ascetica e Mistica* 4 (1970): 325–42. I am grateful to Giuliana Cavallini for drawing my attention to Centi's article and to problems concerning Valli's transcription of the passage.

   4. It is not certain whether Raymond was appointed as Catherine's confessor by the Dominican General Chapter, or whether he and Catherine had already met, and their preexisting (but certainly still young) spiritual relationship received the order's approval in Florence (see Centi, "Un processo inventato di sana pianta," 338–42).

   5. Raymond of Capua, *De S. Catharinae Senensis* (the *Legenda maior*), in *Acta Sanctorum* April III (Paris: Palmé, 1866), 862–967. Translation in English: *The Life of Catherine of Siena,* trans. Conleth Kearns (Washington, DC: Dominican Publications, 1980).

6. For a biography of Raymond of Capua, see A .W. Van Ree, "Raymond de Capoue: Élèments biographiques," *Archivum Fratrum Praedicatorum* 33 (1963): 159–241.

7. On female audiences and their impact on the production of vernacular devotional texts, see Katherine Gill, "Women and the Production of Religious Literature in the Vernacular, 1300–1500," in *Creative Women in Medieval and Early Modern Italy: A Religious and Artistic Renaissance*, ed. E. Ann Matter and John Coakley (Philadelphia: University of Philadelphia Press, 1994), 64–104.

8. For parallels between the *Miracoli* and the *Legenda maior,* see Robert Fawtier, *Sainte Catherine de Sienne: Essai de critique des sources hagiographiques,* 2 vols. (Paris: De Boccard, 1921), 1:95; and idem, *La double expérience de Catherine Benincasa* (Paris: Librairie Gallimard, 1948), 47–76.

9. Tommaso della Fonte (d. 1390), Catherine's first confessor, wrote several booklets concerning her visions, deeds, and miracles. The booklets have been lost, but both Raymond and Thomas of Siena, chief promoters of Catherine's cult, made several references to Tommaso's booklets.

10. Raymond's version suggests that Catherine took her habit soon after the death of her sister Bonaventura (1362) and certainly before her father's death (1368) (see Raymond of Capua, *Legenda maior,* 879–80 [pars. 69–76]; cf. *Miracoli,* chap. 8, herein).

11. In 1374 the master general of the Dominican Order was Elias of Toulouse and the General Chapter met on May 21 in Santa Maria Novella, Florence. On the translation of this passage, see note 3.

12. The expression "a servant of God," not unlike "a friend of God," was used of persons who were venerated as saints by their contemporaries.

13. Religious laywomen were required to move in groups to avoid suspicious interaction with men and other laypeople and thus to protect their reputations as respectable women (see the *Ordinationes* of Munio of Zamora, chap. 11; and the Dominican Penitent Rule, chap. 13).

14. According to Raymond of Capua, Catherine went to visit her older sister, Bonaventura, and was accompanied by her brother, Stefano. Raymond's timing of the event differed slightly from that of the *Miracoli.* He wrote that Catherine was "around six years old" (see Raymond of Capua, *Legenda maior,* 870 [par. 29]).

15. The author's reference to Christian iconography as a matrix for Catherine's recognition of the vision's personalities offers a concrete example of the interrelation between Christian art and visionary experiences. See Millard Meiss, *Painting in Florence and Siena after the Black Death* (Princeton, NJ: Princeton University Press, 1951), 105–7. On the

relationship between Christian art and visions in general, see Chiara Frugoni, "Female Mystics, Visions, and Iconography," in *Women and Religion in Medieval and Renaissance Italy*, ed. Daniel Bornstein and Roberto Rusconi, trans. Margery J. Schneider (Chicago: The University of Chicago Press, 1996), 130–64; and Jeffrey Hamburger, *The Visual and the Visionary: Art and Female Spirituality in Late Medieval Germany* (New York: Zone Book, 1998).

16. The version of the vision in the *Miracoli* differs from Raymond's account. Raymond, for example, emphasized that Jesus appeared at the top of San Domenico, thus underscoring Catherine's affinity to the Order of Friars Preachers (see Raymond of Capua, *Legenda maior*, 870 [pars. 29–30]).

17. Raymond wrote about the same event, but he did not include a narration of Catherine's espousal to the baby Jesus as a child (see Raymond of Capua, *Legenda maior*, 870–71 [pars. 33–34]). Instead, he wrote that Catherine's mystical espousal happened when she was a young woman and about to return to the world after a three-year period of solitary life (see ibid., 883–84 [pars. 84–91]).

18. Cf. ibid., 871 (pars. 35–37).

19. The church was the Church of San Domenico. It was characteristic of the *Miracoli* not to emphasize Catherine's Dominican connections.

20. Catherine's father died on August 22, 1368.

21. The author of the *Miracoli* offers a psychologically convincing view of Catherine as a young girl who was torn between her desires to please her mother and to follow her religious vocation. By contrast, Raymond did not discuss Catherine's psychological tensions and her hesitation but rather represented Catherine's decision as a straightforward and jubilant deed of a saintly person who felt secure about her calling (see ibid., 871 [pars. 33–34]).

22. Raymond of Capua wrote that Catherine's life of solitude lasted only for three years (see ibid., 882–83 [pars. 82].

23. Cf. note 15.

24. The term in Italian is *sirocchie*, which was typically used in reference to biological sisters. In this context, however, the term might refer to two religious sisters who were probably members of a religious lay association. If the latter is the case, the negative reference to the sisters as embellished and disreputable provides an interesting testimony of negative associations concerning religious laywomen.

25. The author gives the Dominican habit a miraculous power to protect Catherine of Siena from the dangers of the world. A similar depiction may be found in *The Legend of Maria of Venice*, chap. 6, herein.

26. The author of the *Miracoli* tied together the vocations of Catherine and her mother, Lapa, a suggestion that is in striking contrast with Raymond's *Legenda maior*; in which Lapa is represented as the most vehement opponent of Catherine's religious calling. Lapa lost her husband in 1368, and thus it would not be surprising if she indeed took the penitential habit soon after.

27. Terce, the third of the day's canonical hours, was celebrated around 8 a.m., depending on the time of the year.

28. None, the fifth of the day's canonical hours, was celebrated around 1:30–2:30 p.m., depending on the time of the year.

29. The *Miracoli's* depiction of the meal as a shared, quasi-monastic ritual among penitent women differs from Raymond's emphasis on Catherine's participation in family meals. Raymond emphasized the domestic context of Catherine's daily life, whereas the *Miracoli* presented *pinzochere* as independent women sharing their religious way of life.

30. Catherine's public career as a peacemaker and Dominican reformer began only after the writing of the *Miracoli*, but the passage here suggests that she enjoyed a reputation as a locally known saintly advisor early.

31. Cf. Raymond, who specified that Catherine scourged herself three times a day: first, for herself; second, for the other people who were still alive; and third, for the dead (see Raymond of Capua, *Legenda maior*, 877 [par. 63]).

32. "Quotidie eucharistiae communionem percipere nec laudo nec vitupero" (Augustine, *De ecclesiasticis dogmatibus*, chap. 23, in *Patrologia Latina* 42: col. 1217).

33. The Lateran Council of 1215 stipulated that the laity should receive communion at least once a year (see *Conciliorum Oecumenicorum Decreta*, eds. J. Alberigo et al. [Bologna: Istituto per le Scienze Religiose, 1973], c. 21, p. 245).

34. Medieval churchmen were cautious about laypeople's frequent communion, a practice reserved for members of religious orders. See, Joseph Duhr, "Communion fréquente," *Dictionnaire de spiritualitè, ascétique et mystique, doctrine et histoire*, ed. Marcel Viller (Paris: Beauschesne, 1953), 2:1250–73; and Caroline Walker Bynum, *Holy Feast and Holy Fast: The Religious Significance of Food to Medieval Women* (Berkley: University of California Press, 1987), 57–59.

35. Raymond of Capua was cautious about reporting heavenly visions of this kind. Referring to 2 Corinthians 12:1–10, he explained that heavenly transportations should not be addressed in human language (see Raymond of Capua, *Legenda maior*, 912 [par. 201]).

DOMINICAN PENITENT WOMEN

36. I thank F. Thomas Luongo for allowing me to consult the manuscript of his upcoming book *The Saintly Politics of Catherine of Siena*, in which he argues that the revolt in question was probably the "Revolt of the Bruco" of 1371.

37. Medieval Siena was divided into seventeen *contrade*, urban regions, some of which were intensely hostile toward one another.

38. Probably the Hospital di S. Maria della Scala, located across the street from the Duomo.

39. The friar in question is William of Flete (d. 1382), an Englishman living as an Augustinian hermit in Lecceto. It is not certain whether Catherine met with William though. Bartolomeo Dominici claimed, in contrast with the *Miracoli*, that Catherine and William had been friends since 1368 (see Bartolomeo Dominici's testimony in *Il Processo Castellano*, ed. M.-H. Laurent, in Fontes Vitae S. Catharinae Senensis Historici, vol. 9 [Milan: Fratelli Bocca, 1942], 307). William became one of the first persons to promote Catherine's cult. He wrote a letter to Raymond of Capua in which he defended Catherine and other women's prophetic roles. See Robert Fawtier, "Catheriniana," *Mélanges d'archéologie et d'histoire* 34 (1914), fasc. 1–2, pp. 76–85.

40. Cf. Raymond of Capua, *Legenda maior*, 918–19 (pars. 228–30).

41. Agnes of Montepulciano, a Dominican nun, died in 1317. Raymond of Capua was the spiritual director of Agnes's foundation between 1363 and 1366. Inspired by his stay at Montepulciano, he wrote Agnes's life (see Raymond of Capua, *De S. Agnetis de Montepolitano*, in *Acta Sanctorum* April II [Paris: Palmé, 1866], 789–815).

42. The *Miracoli* suggests that Catherine went alone, or, probably, with her female companions, to Montepulciano before her trip to Florence in May 1374. By contrast, Raymond emphasized his own role as the arbiter of the visit, which he stated took place in the fall of 1374, that is, after Catherine had already been in Florence (Raymond of Capua, *Legenda maior*, 942–44 [pars. 324–29]).

43. The church in question was San Domenico.

44. Cf. Raymond of Capua, *Legenda maior*, 895–96 (pars. 134–38).

45. Cf. ibid., 897–98 (chaps. 140–41). The *Miracoli* represents Catherine's brothers as the opponents of her generosity, whereas Raymond discussed Catherine's largess and her father's reactions.

46. Siena was hit by plague in the summer of 1374.

47. Catherine's brother, Bartolomeo Benincasa, died in August 1374.

48. This friar is probably Raymond of Capua, who in the *Legenda maior* related the same account in the first person singular (see 925–26 [pars. 254–55]).

49. The second friar is probably Bartolomeo Dominici (cf. Raymond of Capua, *Legenda maior*, 926 [pars. 256]).

50. Matteo di Cenni di Fazio was a nobleman from Siena who was chosen as the rector of the Hospital of Santa Maria della Misericordia in September 1373.

51. Raymond also wrote in the *Legenda maior* about the miraculous healing of Matteo. He relates that he himself was the messenger between Matteo and Catherine (see ibid., 923–24 [chaps. 245–48]). Thus, it is possible that the "devout religious" mentioned in the *Miracoli* was also Raymond.

52. Marian feasts, especially the feast of the Visitation (July 2) and that of the Assumption (August 15), were important civic feasts for the Sienese, who regarded the Virgin as the town's protector and patron saint.

53. That is, the Nativity of the Virgin Mary, celebrated on September 8.

54. Raymond discussed the event in a great detail and he referred to the *pinzochera* as Andrea (see Raymond of Capua, *Legenda maior*, 900–903 [pars. 154–64]).

55. The unique, and, perhaps, unintentional, coexistence of Catherine's two betrothals in the *Miracoli* (for the first one, see chap. 3) suggests that in the 1370s there existed two versions of Catherine's betrothal. The first version of Catherine's espousal as a young girl was perhaps copied from Tommaso della Fonte's booklet or circulated by other *pinzochere*, whereas the story of the second espousal came from another source, which the anonymous author heard of only after he had completed the main body of his text. Raymond too related the story of Catherine's drinking of the pus, but in his version Christ rewarded Catherine with a crown of thorns, not with a ring (see Raymond of Capua, *Legenda maior*, 903 [pars. 163–64]).

Thomas of Siena: *The Legend of Maria of Venice*

1. For these texts, see *The Legend of Giovanna of Orvieto*, translated in this collection; and *Le Legendae di Margherita da Città di Castello*, ed. Maria Cristiana Lungarotti (Spoleto: Centro Italiano di Studi sull'Alto Medioevo, 1994). On Thomas's hagiographic writings, see Fernanda Sorelli, "La produzione agiografica del domenicano Tommaso d'Antonio da Siena: esempi di santità ed intenti di propaganda," in *Mistiche e devote*

nell'Italia tardomedievale, ed. Daniel Bornstein and Roberto Rusconi (Naples: Liguori, 1992), 157–69; and Oriana Visani, "Nota su Tommaso d'Antonio Nacci Caffarini," *Rivista di Storia e Letteratura Religiosa* 9/2 (1973): 277–97.

2. *Sanctae Catharinae Senensis Legenda minor*, ed. Ezio Franceschini, in Fontes Vitae S. Catharinae Senensis Historici, vol. 10 (Siena: University of Siena, 1942).

3. Thomas Antonii de Senis "Caffarini," *Libellus de supplemento*, ed. Giuliana Cavallini and Imelda Foralosso (Rome: Edizioni Cateriniane, 1974).

4. *Il Processo Castellano*, ed. M.-H. Laurent, in Fontes Vitae S. Catharinae Senensis Historici, vol. 9 (Milan: Fratelli Bocca, 1942). The testimony gathered at this inquest underlay Catherine's canonization half a century later, in 1461.

5. Thomas of Siena, *Tractatus de ordine fratrum et sororum de penitentia Sancti Dominici*, ed. M.-H. Laurent, in Fontes Vitae S. Catharinae Senensis Historici, vol. 21 (Siena: University of Siena, 1938).

6. On the history of the penitent rule, see General Introduction, herein.

7. Fernanda Sorelli, "Imitable Sanctity: The Legend of Maria of Venice," in *Women and Religion in Medieval and Renaissance Italy*, ed. Daniel Bornstein and Roberto Rusconi, trans. Margery J. Schneider (Chicago: University of Chicago Press, 1996), 165–81.

8. Fernanda Sorelli, *La santità imitabile: "Leggenda di Maria da Venezia" di Tommaso da Siena*, in Deputazione di storia patria per le Venezie, Miscellanea di studi e memorie 23 (Venice: Deputazione Editrice, 1984), 102–17; and idem, "Per la storia religiosa di Venezia nella prima metà del quattrocento: inizi e sviluppi del terz'ordine domenicano," in *Viridarium Floridum: Studi di storia veneta offerti dagli allievi a Paolo Sambin*, ed. Maria Chiara Billanovich, Giorgio Cracco, and Antonio Rigon (Padua: Antenore, 1984), 89–114.

9. Sorelli's thorough introduction and careful annotation have been of invaluable assistance as I prepared this translation.

10. Thomas of Siena, *Legenda cuiusdam B. Mariae de Venetiis*, in *Ecclesiae Venetae Antiquis Monumentis*, 13 vols., ed. Flaminius Cornelius (Venice, 1749), 7:363–420.

11. "Our order is known to have been founded initially for the sake of preaching and the salvation of souls" (see "The Early Dominican Constitutions," in *Early Dominicans: Selected Writings*, ed. Simon Tugwell [New York: Paulist Press, 1982], 457).

NOTES

12. In other works, Thomas places his arrival in Venice late in November 1394. The Dominican friary of Santi Giovanni e Paolo is also known as San Zanipolo, the Venetian dialect conflation of the names of the two saints to whom it is dedicated, John and Paul. Thomas, a native of the Tuscan city of Siena, uses the Tuscan form.

13. At the end of the fourteenth century, under the leadership of Giovanni Dominici and with the support of Thomas and others, Venice had become the leading center of the Dominican observance. Like other expressions of the observant movement, which brought reform and fresh vigor to all the major mendicant and monastic orders in the late fourteenth and fifteenth centuries, the Dominican Observants called for a return to the strict observance of their order's rule in all its pristine rigor. See, in general, Francis Oakley, *The Western Church in the Later Middle Ages* (Ithaca, NY: Cornell University Press, 1979), 231–38; and Mario Fois, "L'Osservanza come espressione della 'Ecclesia semper renovanda,'" in *Problemi di storia della chiesa nei secoli XV–XVII* (Naples: Edizioni Dehoniane, 1979), 13–107. On Venice in particular, see Venturino Alce, "La riforma dell'ordine domenicano nel '400 e nel '500 veneto,'" in *Riforma della chiesa, cultura e spiritualità nel Quattrocento veneto*, ed. Giovanni B. Francesco Trolese (Cesena: Badia di Santa Maria del Monte, 1984), 333–43.

14. That is, *Tractatus de ordine fratrum et sororum de penitentia Sancti Dominici.*

15. The history of the convent of Corpus Domini and of the devout women who lived there was recorded by one of their number, Sister Bartolomea Riccoboni, *Life and Death in a Venetian Convent: The Chronicle and Necrology of Corpus Domini, 1395–1436*, ed. and trans. Daniel Bornstein (Chicago: University of Chicago Press, 2000).

16. Most penitents in Venice were women. The fact that the group had a few male members represents a rare exception within the history of the Dominican life of penance.

17. Thomas quotes Raymond of Capua's letter of authorization in *Tractatus*, 34–35. Raymond's successor as master general of the Dominican Order, Thomas of Fermo, confirmed Thomas in this office on May 25, 1401, in a letter quoted in *Tractatus*, 35–36.

18. The Sturion belonged to a legally defined class peculiar to Venice known as the *cittadini originali*. They tended to be merchants or professionals, often (like Maria's father) quite well-to-do, but in social and political terms ranking below the nobility, who held the exclusive right to sit in the Great Council of Venice. One sign of Nicolò Sturion's economic standing is that he married a woman from an important family, though not

a Venetian one; Maria's mother came from the Servidei family of Verona, prominent members of the ruling class of that mainland city. See Sorelli, *La santità imitabile*, 103–8.

19. Again, Thomas seeks to enhance Maria's stature by exaggerating the social and economic status of the circles in which she moved. The Piazza family were reasonably well-off merchants, though perhaps not quite so well off as the Sturion. Maria's father-in-law seems to have owned a cheese shop. In this respect, as in so many others, Maria seems not to have made a good marriage. See Sorelli, *La santità imitabile*, 108–9.

20. Relations between Francesco Gonzaga, ruler of Mantua, and Giangaleazzo Visconti, duke of Milan, had been tense since 1393 and erupted in open warfare in 1397. Since Maria was born around 1379, Giannino's departure should be set in 1394 or 1395.

21. The allusion is to Philippians 3:8. Thomas uses two terms, *convertito* and *converso*, both past participles of the verb *convertire* (to convert), to hint at the parallel between Maria and the *converso:* a lay person who donned the religious habit and entered the service of a monastic institution, though without taking the monastic vows of poverty, chastity, and obedience.

22. Of the many epidemics of the plague that struck Venice in the second half of the fourteenth century, Thomas is presumably referring to the one in 1397. Being in mourning for her siblings justified Maria's adoption of a more sober style of dress. In the Latin version of this text Thomas takes this opportunity to suggest that Maria's decision to cut the ornaments from her clothing rather then pass them on to her sisters was prophetically inspired: she knew that they would have no use for them. Thomas of Siena, *Legenda cuiusdam B. Mariae de Venetiis*, 371.

23. The allusion may be to a passage in Raymond of Capua's *Legenda maior* of Catherine of Siena, which describes how Catherine guarded herself against Satan's attacks by constructing for herself a mental cell (Raymond of Capua, *De S.Catharinae Senensis* [the *Legenda maior*], in *Acta Sanctorum* April III [Rome: Palmé, 1866], 874–75 [par. 45]). Translation in English, *The Life of Catherine of Siena*, trans. Conleth Kearns (Washington, DC: Dominican Publications, 1980). The reference may also be to a passage in one of Catherine's letters (see Catherine of Siena, *Le lettere*, notes by Niccolò Tommaseo, ed. Pietro Misciatelli, 6 vols. [Florence, 1970], 3:198).

24. The last sentence of this paragraph, with its suggestion that Maria's display of exceptional piety initially provoked some snide comments, is not found in the Latin version. The first three sentences of this

paragraph, like the aside about her manner of dress in the previous one, are also additions made by Thomas in the Italian version.

25. Catherine's severely penitential life is described in Raymond of Capua, *Legenda maior*, 876–80 (pars. 57–76). In this respect, as in so many others, Thomas presents Maria as an example of how Catherine of Siena's heroic virtue and extravagant austerities might be adapted and moderated, making her an easily imitated model of comportment suitable for decent women and of a piety that did not overstep (as Catherine's did) the bounds of propriety. Note how often Thomas acknowledges in passing (as he does here) the limits to Maria's asceticism and credits her with the good intentions to make some sacrifice that she ended up not fully performing— often on his insistence that she not be so hard on herself.

26. Ibid., 883 (par. 82).

27. In the Latin version this chapter concludes with a passage in which Thomas reiterates that Maria performed all these bodily austerities with joy and good humor, without any sighs of hypocritical sorrow.

28. This sentence begins a long digression on sin and confession that is not found in the Latin version. Thomas draws liberally on the standard theological sources, the *Sentences* of Peter Lombard and the *Summa theologiae* of Thomas Aquinas, paraphrasing them loosely rather than citing them exactly. His intent is clearly didactic: Thomas repeatedly calls on the devout reader to note this or that point, as he classifies the various ways in which one can offend God or one's neighbor and teaches how to confess these faults properly. The entire passage betrays a certain carelessness, whether on the part of Thomas or his copyist; here, for instance, a phrase or line about sins of locution has been dropped, producing the puzzling definition of cogitation as speaking aloud rather than as unvoiced thought.

29. "I confess my guilt to God and blessed Mary and blessed Dominic and to all the saints and to you, father, for I have sinned greatly in thought, speech, deed, and omission; I beseech you, pray for me or absolve me."

30. This concludes Thomas's long digression on sin and confession, which is not found in the Latin version. He now returns to Maria where he left her, confessing fully yet concisely.

31. Thomas omits here a few lines from the Latin version, attesting to the efficacy of Maria's prayers and to her success in winning her parents' support for her devotional activities.

32. As a married woman, Maria's body belonged exclusively to her husband, just as his belonged to her. In order for her to swear to live chastely, he would have had to renounce his rights and grant her permission—and he wasn't around to do that.

33. Saint Dominic's readiness to be martyred "bit by bit, mutilating my limbs one by one, then gouging out my eyes, then leaving my truncated body half dead, wallowing in its own blood" is mentioned by all his early biographers, including the source of this quotation: Jean de Mailly, "The Life of St. Dominic," in Tugwell, *Early Dominicans*, 55.

34. The question of individual and communal property was a hotly debated issue within the Dominican Order. One of the contributors to this debate was Giovanni Dominici, who wrote on the subject a brief treatise, *An liceat fratribus predicatoribus in communi vel in particulari possessiones habere*, just a year or two before Thomas wrote this passage (Raymond Creytens, "L'obligation des constitutions dominicaines d'après le B. Jean Dominici, O.P.," *Archivum Fratrum Praedicatorum* 23 [1953]: 195–235).

35. Very little—not even the name of her husband—is known about the widow Caterina, daughter of a certain Master Guglielmo Marioni, who was the first to receive the habit of the Sisters of Penance and apparently died of plague not long thereafter.

36. That is, the smaller friary of San Domenico of Castello and the larger one of Santi Giovanni e Paolo.

37. This paragraph does not appear in the Latin text. In its place are found two sentences not included here, to the effect that Maria also avoided contact with all priests other than her parish priest, whom she saw only at the established times for receiving the sacraments and always after consulting with Thomas.

38. The works of mercy, both corporal and spiritual, are typically seven in number, though there is some slight variation in how they are defined. In one little handbook of Christian doctrine prepared in the middle of the fifteenth century for the instruction of laymen and laywomen, the seven corporal works of mercy are defined as feeding the hungry, giving drink to the thirsty, clothing the naked, sheltering pilgrims, visiting the sick, visiting those in prison, and burying the dead. The seven spiritual works of mercy are defined as giving counsel, instructing the ignorant, admonishing sinners, consoling those who are troubled and suffering, forgiving offenses, bearing troubles patiently, and praying for the living and the dead (see *Libretto della dottrina cristiana attribuito a S. Antonino arcivescovo di Firenze*, ed. Gilberto Aranci [Florence: Angelo Pontecorboli editore, 1996], 66). This popular text, reprinted frequently in the second half of the fifteenth century, was ascribed to Antonino Pierozzi, who entered the Dominican Order in 1405 under the inspiration of Giovanni Dominici and ended his long and distinguished career as archbishop of Florence (1446–59).

39. This passage draws on Thomas Aquinas, *Summa theologiae*, 2a2ae, 44, 7, and more directly on Thomas Aquinas, *De perfectione vitae*

spiritualis, in his *Opuscula theologica*, vol. 2, *De re spirituali*, ed. R. M. Spiazzi (Rome, 1954), XIII, 129–31.

40. Thomas Aquinas, *Summa theologiae*, 2a2ae, 184, 2, and Thomas Aquinas, *De perfectione vitae spiritualis*, XIV, 131–34. As one might guess from the way he promises three ways and delivers only two, Thomas's rephrasing of Aquinas here (as elsewhere) is loose to the point of being careless and confusing. He first blurs the clear logic of Aquinas's treatment of extension, which steadily widens from friends and acquaintances to include strangers and even enemies, and then collapses Aquinas's second and third characteristics—intensity and effect—by turning effect into affect.

41. This verse is also quoted by Aquinas in his discussions of this question (*Summa theologiae*, 2a2ae, 26, 2 and 44, 2). The Latin text treats this question at greater length and with greater learning, invoking the authority of Gregory the Great's *Moralia* and Bede's scriptural commentary, along with other passages from the Bible.

42. In fact, the fraternity of painters met in this church dedicated to Saint Luke, the patron saint of painters.

43. Thomas promoted reverence for Catherine of Siena by distributing images of her as well as by writing texts about her, so a painter could well have thought he would be interested in receiving another.

44. The habit of the Dominican Order of Penance, the crucifix, and the proffered heart are all motifs typical of the iconography of Catherine of Siena.

45. Here Thomas echoes Psalm 116:15: "Precious in the sight of the Lord is the death of his faithful ones."

46. "Sweeter than honey and honeycomb," an echo of Psalm 19:10 and Sirach 24:20.

47. The Latin version mentions Niccolò's father instead of his brother, though both were apparently physicians: "frater Niccolaus fuerat filius cuiusdam magistri Iohannis in medicina doctoris eximii." A vivid profile of Margherita Mussolini can be found in the necrology of Corpus Domini (Riccoboni, *Life and Death in a Venetian Convent*, 71–72). Thomas elsewhere refers to the mother, Lucia, as belonging to the Franciscan Third Order rather than the Dominican Order of Penance (Tommaso "Caffarini" da Siena, *Historia disciplinae regularis instauratae in coenobiis Venetis ordinis praedicatorum nec non tertii ordinis de poenitentia s. Dominici in civitatem Venetiarum propagati*, in Cornelius, *Ecclesiae Venetae Antiquis Monumentis*, 7:182 and 205).

48. Thomas gives a lengthy portrait of Niccolò in *Historia disciplinae*, 203–18. Giovanni Dominici's writings about him are reported there, 218–25, with some additional mentions in Giovanni Dominici,

Lettere spirituali, ed. M.-T. Casella and G. Pozzi (Freiburg: Edizioni Universitarie Friburgo Svizzera, 1969), 102 and 188–89.

49. This injunction, with slight variations, is cited by Jesus in all three Synoptic Gospels: Matthew 22:37; Mark 12:30; Luke 10:27.

50. The Latin version includes here a sentence comparing Maria's fervent love of God to the ardor of the seraphim, as described in Book 7 of Pseudo-Dionysius the Areopagite's *Celestial Hierarchies.*

51. She (or Thomas) is echoing Paul (Phil 1:23): "My desire is to depart and to be with Christ, for that is far better."

52. The stages of charity as described here derive from Thomas Aquinas, *Summa theologiae,* 2a2ae, 24, 9, which includes the same allusion to Philippians 1:23. The term *dilezione,* translated here "delectation," refers to a constant spiritual love, especially that which unites human beings in charity. The same root gives Thomas his standard term for Maria: *diletta.*

53. This sentence introduces a long digression—Maria's profession to God of her love for him, as imagined by Thomas—that is not found in the Latin version. The words Thomas puts in Maria's mouth are obviously far more his than hers: the use made of writings by Peter Lombard and Thomas Aquinas shows his Scholastic training, just as the rhetorical organization of the entire passage around a set of key terms (heart, soul, mind, strength) derived from a verse of scripture reflects his experience as a preacher.

54. As so often through this passage, Thomas is here following Aquinas, who uses "elicited act" *(actus elicitus)* to mean an act from and in the will itself, as distinguished from an act commanded by the will but in another power *(actus imperatus):* Thomas Aquinas, *Summa theologiae,* 1a2ae, 1, 1.

55. The vesting of these women occurred in 1398. Little is known about these women. Astrologia Verzoni's family probably moved to Venice from Ferrara in the latter part of the fourteenth century.

56. *Historia disciplinae,* 198.

57. The feast of Saints Peter and Paul is June 29, placing this encounter on the morning of June 28.

58. Antonio Soranzo belonged to one of the wealthiest and most distinguished families in Venice. A close friend and associate of Giovanni Dominici, he was deeply engaged in promoting the Dominican Observant movement. In 1397, he formed part of the party sent by Dominici to Forlì to investigate the miracles attributed to the recently deceased Brother Marcolino of Forlì. On the contrasting interpretations of Marcolino's life and miracles advanced by Observants and Conventuals, see Daniel Bornstein, "Dominican Friar, Lay Saint: The Case of Marcolino of Forlì," *Church History* 66 (1997): 252–67. The following year, Soranzo accompanied

Giovanni Dominici, Thomas of Siena, and others on a preaching tour of central Italy that inspired a number of dramatic conversions and convinced several women to enter the Venetian convent of Corpus Domini: see the biographies of Sisters Piera of Città di Castello, Onesta dei Marchesi, and Tommasa of Città di Castello in Riccoboni, *Life and Death in a Venetian Convent*, 91–94 and 98. In 1399, Soranzo joined Dominici in organizing and leading a religious procession in defiance of a governmental prohibition, and as a consequence shared Dominici's sentence of banishment from Venice (though for just one year rather than Dominici's five). On this episode, see Daniel Bornstein, "Giovanni Dominici, the Bianchi, and Venice: Symbolic Action and Interpretive Grids," *Journal of Medieval and Renaissance Studies* 23 (1993): 143–71. Soranzo's wife, Marina Contarini, came from an equally prominent family, and one that was similarly linked with Giovanni Dominici and his work of religious reform; like her husband, she too became a Dominican penitent.

59. Vespers, the sixth of the seven canonical hours of worship, is celebrated in late afternoon or early evening. Maria and her friends had spent the entire day running around Venice in the midsummer heat: from her home in the parish of San Giuliano (in the heart of the city, between San Marco and the Rialto) to the nearby Santi Giovanni e Paolo, then to Corpus Domini (on the present site of the train station), to Santa Maria della Carità (now incorporated in the museum of the Accademia), and then back across the Grand Canal (for the second time) to her starting point.

60. None, the fifth of the seven canonical hours of worship, is celebrated mid-afternoon.

61. The Mocenigo family was one of the most important in Venice. Its vast network of marriage alliances has been studied in detail by Bianca Betto, "Linee di politica matrimoniale nella nobiltà veneziana fino al XV secolo: Alcune note genealogiche e l'esempio della famiglia Mocenigo," *Archivio Storico Italiano* 139 (1981): 34–64; and Stanley Chojnacki, "Patrician Women in Early Renaissance Venice," *Studies in the Renaissance* 21 (1974): 180–203.

62. As it turned out, Maria died exactly a month later, on July 28.

63. Zanetta dalle Boccole died in 1427, after living more than thirty-two years in the convent of Corpus Domini. Her life is summarized in Riccoboni, *Life and Death in a Venetian Convent*, 96–97; Riccoboni confirms what Thomas says here: "She was a widow; she was 22 years old when she converted, and with great fervor she left two children to God's keeping and entered as a nun here inside."

64. Thomas's phrasing refers literally to the inner and outer man: "giocondità e festa dell'uomo dentro e di fuore."

65. The feast of Mary Magdalene is July 22, placing this encounter on July 21.

66. In the Latin version, Thomas writes at somewhat greater length about this figure, Bianco da Siena (or Città di Castello). A follower of Giovanni Colombini, the founder of the Gesuates, Bianco was well known as a composer of devotional lyrics (Fernanda Sorelli, "Per la biografia del Bianco da Siena, gesuato: una testimonianza di Tommaso Caffarini [1403]," *Atti dell'Istituto veneto di scienze, lettere ed arti: Classe di scienze morali, lettere ed arti* 136 [1977–78]: 529–36).

67. From the end of the fourteenth century the Dominican friars of Santi Giovanni e Paolo and of San Domenico in Venice, like the Dominican sisters of Corpus Domini, adopted the custom (already practiced by their fellow Dominicans in Chioggia, Lucca, Pisa, Rome, and Siena) of celebrating the anniversary of the death of Catherine of Siena with some solemnities on the first Sunday after the feast of Saint Peter Martyr (April 29) (M.-H. Laurent, "Introduzione," in Laurent, *Il Processo Castellano*, vi–vii).

68. Fernanda Sorelli has searched the Venetian archives for the testament supposedly redacted by Maria, but without success (Sorelli, *La santità imitabile*, 203 n. 73).

69. The testament of Nicolò Sturion, dated August 27, 1400, and containing as specified a bequest of three hundred ducats to the convent of Corpus Domini, is published in Sorelli, *La santità imitabile*, 233–34.

70. Perhaps an echo of Luke 3:21, when at the baptism of Jesus "heaven was opened."

71. There is no mention of the death of Madaluccia Morosini in the admittedly incomplete version of the *Historia disciplinae* published by Cornelius.

72. Both Isabetta di Bartolomeo di Michele Moccindente and her husband, Gherardo Burlamacchi, belonged to wealthy and politically prominent families from Lucca. When a rival faction took power and banished the Burlamacchis from Lucca, the couple took refuge in Venice. Isabetta's will, dated September 27, 1397, and published in Sorelli, *La santità imitabile*, 220–30, confirms her involvement with the same spiritual circles in which Maria moved. She left bequests to the Gesuates, the Observant friars of San Domenico in Venice, the friars of Santi Giovanni e Paolo, and the convent of San Domenico in Pisa, and she named as one of her executors the priest Leonardo Pisani, a close friend and supporter of Giovanni Dominici who (like Antonio Soranzo) was sentenced to a year in exile for his leadership of the religious procession organized by Dominici in 1399.

73. The chapel of Saint Ursula, adjacent to Santi Giovanni e Paolo, was home to a lay devotional confraternity dedicated to the virgin martyr Saint Ursula.

74. Chiara Gambacorta (1362–1420) had close ties to the admirers and followers of Catherine of Siena and played an important role in the reform of the Dominican Order. In 1382 she entered the convent of San Domenico of Pisa, which had been built for her by her father, Pietro Gambacorta, ruler of the city of Pisa until his death in October 1392. Her convent provided the model and inspiration for Corpus Domini in Venice, which in turn was taken as a model for Dominican convents of strict observance elsewhere in Italy, further extending Chiara Gambacorta's influence.

75. Matins, the first of the canonical hours of prayer, is celebrated between midnight and dawn.

76. Terce, the third of the canonical hours of prayer, is celebrated mid-morning.

77. The church militant comprises those Christians on earth who are engaged in a continuous war against evil and the enemies of Christ; the church triumphant is composed of those Christians in heaven who have triumphed over evil and the enemies of Christ.

78. Thomas uses the term *veste*, meaning "garments," "clothing," or (by extension) "the body," which clothes the soul. Given his (or perhaps her) obsessive focus on her habit, the use of this ambiguous term may not be entirely accidental.

79. This delightful odor was a phenomenon frequently observed at the burial of people who died with a reputation for sanctity, such as (to offer one example especially close in time to this and linked to the same devotional circles) the Dominican friar Marcolino of Forlì (Bornstein, "Dominican Friar, Lay Saint," 256–57).

80. Sister Bartolomea Riccoboni describes Sister Onesta dei Marchesi as "the daughter of the marquis of Monte Santa Maria, and thus a woman from a great lineage, very elegant and notoriously worldly," who was converted by the preaching of Giovanni Dominici and his fellow friars and entered the convent as a twenty-three-year-old widow (Riccoboni, *Life and Death in a Venetian Convent*, 93–94).

81. Thomas later says that the mother of this Sister Maria was named Cataluccia or Madaluccia, but since the necrology of Corpus Domini doesn't identify any of the various nuns named Maria as being the daughter of a Cataluccia or Madaluccia, there is no way to be sure which of them is meant. Since she was ill at the time of this vision in the summer of 1399, it might be Sister Maria Rizzi, who died on April 12, 1401. The convent necrology says of her: "She was 20 years old and a pure virgin. She

was one of the women who entered on the first day the convent was enclosed, and she lived in the order for six years. She was a very obedient woman and remained ill for a long time" (Riccoboni, *Life and Death in a Venetian Convent*, 67).

82. In 1399 the feast of Corpus Christi fell on May 29, so its octave was June 5. The Church of San Pietro was the seat of the patriarch of Castello, the primate of Venice.

83. That is, July 24, the day before the feast of Saint James the Apostle.

84. The hesitancy in Thomas's phrasing suggests that Orsa was not actually on her knees but lying in bed with her knees drawn up "as if she were kneeling."

85. The scene recalls depictions of paradise in paintings of the Last Judgment, on which see Alberto Tenenti, "L'attesa del giudizio individuale nell'iconografia del Quattrocento," in *L'attesa dell'età nuova nella spiritualità della fine del medioevo*, Convegni del Centro di studi sulla spiritualità medievale 3 (Todi: Accademia Tudertina, 1962), 171–93. On the ways in which paintings and visions shaped each other in the Italian context, see Chiara Frugoni, "Female Mystics, Visions, and Iconography," in Bornstein and Rusconi, *Women and Religion in Medieval and Renaissance Italy*, 130–64.

86. On the emergence of the concept of purgatory, see Jacques Le Goff, *The Birth of Purgatory*, trans. Arthur Goldhammer (Chicago: University of Chicago Press, 1984). On the way it entered into calculations of good works, charitable bequests, and penitential sufferings, see Jacques Chiffoleau, *La comptabilité de l'au-delà: Les hommes, la mort et la religion dans la région d'Avignon à la fin du Moyen Age (vers 1320–vers 1480)*, in Collection de l'École Française de Rome 47 (Rome: École Française de Rome, 1980).

87. July 22 is the feast of Saint Mary Magdalene; July 29, the octave, is the feast of Saint Martha. Mary and Martha of Bethany were taken to be models of the contemplative and active lives, respectively, based on the passage in Luke 10:38–42, and Mary of Bethany was conflated with Mary Magdalene by Pope Gregory the Great. On the complex formation of the medieval image of Mary Magdalene, see Katherine Ludwig Jansen, *The Making of the Magdalen: Preaching and Popular Devotion in the Later Middle Ages* (Princeton, NJ: Princeton University Press, 2000). On the use of Martha and Mary as personifications of the active and contemplative lives, see Giles Constable, *Three Studies in Medieval Religious and Social Thought* (Cambridge: Cambridge University Press, 1995), 97–130.

NOTES

88. Raymond of Capua describes how the five-year-old Catherine would kneel and recite an *Ave Maria* at each step when she went up or down stairs (*Legenda maior*, 869–70 [par. 28]).

89. "Jesus Christ, Son of God, have mercy on me."

90. I have translated these verses from Thomas's loose rendering into Italian.

91. The Church of San Giuliano is right in the heart of Venice, between the Rialto Bridge and Piazza San Marco. The priest mentioned here must be Andreas Violante de Tuderto, whose name is the only one that appears between 1378 and 1420 in the series of parish priests of San Giuliano compiled by Cornelius, *Ecclesiae Venetae Antiquis Monumentis*, dec. IV–V, p. 339. Thomas uses the standard Italian name for the church rather than the Venetian dialect one by which it is commonly known, San Zulian; after nearly a decade in Venice, he remained a Tuscan outsider.

92. Thomas was unsure of the exact date and left it blank. The necrology of Corpus Domini supplies the date, though it seems to be confused about the year: "In that year [1400] Sister Marina Ogniben passed from this life on June 20 at the hour of compline. She was twenty-two years old and had lived in the order for five years and was consecrated. She was a young woman of holy life and great fervor, and entered the convent with a younger sister, without the permission of her mother and her relatives. She fell sick and remained ill for a year, bearing it with very great patience; a few days before her death a voice was clearly audible singing very sweetly and devoutly in the infirmary where she lay ill, which one can only believe was some holy angel that came to visit the bride of Christ. When she received communion she remained almost rapt from herself, with her face so joyous that it seemed to radiate light" (Riccoboni, *Life and Death in a Venetian Convent*, 65).

93. On the enduring tradition of the virago ideal—a virile mind in a feminine body—see Barbara Newman, *From Virile Woman to WomanChrist: Studies in Medieval Religion and Literature* (Philadelphia: University of Pennsylvania Press, 1995).

94. Thomas uses the term *grazia* throughout this chapter to mean the reverence, esteem, honor, and deep affection bestowed on a person in recognition of her spiritual character. Though he speaks in this preamble of how gracious and considerate Maria was toward everyone, the chapter itself details how gracious everyone was to her—which Thomas takes to be evidence of the special merit they discerned in her.

95. There is no record that Giacoma ever entered the Dominican Order of penance.

96. The two bulls of Boniface IX (1389–1404) are dated January 18, 1401 *(Humilibus et honestis)* and April 27, 1402 *(Sacre religionis)*. Thomas incorporates portions of them in his *Tractatus*, 29 and 37.

97. "From his descendants the Lord brought forth a godly man, who found favor in the sight of all and was beloved by God and people, Moses, whose memory is blessed" (Sir 45:1).

98. August 22, the octave of the feast of the Assumption on August 15.

Thomas of Siena:
The *Libellus* concerning Catherine of Siena
(Part One)

1. For a more detailed biography of Thomas of Siena (d. 1434), a Dominican friar and a promoter of the Dominican Order of Penance, see the Editor's Note to *The Legend of Maria of Venice*, herein.

2. Part One, translated here, consists of two treatises that focus on Catherine's childhood and youth and on her visions. Part Two of the *Libellus* consists of seven treatises: the first five concern Catherine's visions, prophecies, and miracles; the sixth focuses on her eucharistic devotion; and the seventh offers a treatment of and sermons concerning Catherine and other saints' stigmata. Part Three of the *Libellus* is divided into six treatises: The first four address Catherine's death; the fifth finds fifteen parallels between Catherine's death and that of Christ; and the sixth promotes the writings of fifteen leading supporters of Catherine.

3. For a general introduction to the *Libellus de supplemento* and its relation to Raymond of Capua's *Legenda maior*, see Imelda Foralosso, "Introduzione," in Thomas Antonii de Senis "Caffarini" (Thomas of Siena), *Libellus de supplemento*, ed. Giuliana Cavallini and Imelda Foralosso (Rome: Edizioni Cateriniane, 1974), pp. xxiv–xxvi; and Oriana Visani, "Nota su Tommaso d'Antonio Nacci Caffarini," *Rivista di Storia e Letteratura Religiosa* 9/2 (1973): 286–89.

4. Thomas may have begun his book as early as 1400–1401, when he received two letters from Matteo Guidoni, prior of the Camaldolite hermitage Santa Maria degli Angeli in Florence, and one letter of an anonymous Camaldolite monk, forwarded to Thomas by Stefano Maconi, a disciple of Catherine. The writers voiced their dissatisfaction concerning Raymond's decision to exclude some of Catherine's miracles and visions

(see Thomas of Siena, *Libellus*, 2–8). For the chronology of the writing of the *Libellus*, see Foralosso, "Introduzione," xxvi–xl.

5. Thomas outlined his conception of the history of the Dominican Order of Penance in his *Tractatus*, written between 1402 and 1407. His *Historia disciplinae*, also written between 1402 and 1407, set the Dominican penitential movement within the context of the history of the Dominican Observant Reform. See respectively, *Tractatus de ordine fratrum et sororum de penitentia Sancti Dominici*, ed. M.-H. Laurent, in Fontes Vitae S. Catharinae Senensis Historici, vol. 21 (Siena: University of Siena, 1938); and *Historia disciplinae regularis instauratae in coenobiis Venetiis ordinis praedicatorum nec non tertii ordinis de poenitentia s. Dominici in civitatem Venetiarum propagati*, in *Ecclesiae Venetiae Antiquuis Monumentis*, ed. Flaminius Cornelius, 13 vols. (Venice, 1749), 7:167–234.

6. Thomas pushed Raymond of Capua to complete the *Legenda maior*, and, according to Thomas's own testimony, Raymond even dictated some parts of the book to him (see Thomas of Siena, *Libellus*, 403; and *Il Processo Castellano*, ed. M.-H. Laurent, in Fontes Vitae S. Catharinae Senensis Historici, vol. 9 [Milan: Fratelli Bocca, 1942], 32). The *Legenda maior* was completed in 1395, but during the 1410s Thomas continued to produce and collect more texts concerning Catherine. He wrote the *Libellus;* organized a diocesan collection of testimonies concerning Catherine's sanctity, the so-called *Il Processo Castellano* in Venice (the testimonies were collected between 1411 and 1416); and even produced two reductions of an abbreviation of Raymond's *Legenda maior*, known as the *Legenda minor* (done between 1412 and 1416–17) (see *Sanctae Catharinae Senensis legenda minor*, ed. Ezio Franceschini, in Fontes Vitae S. Caterinae Senensis Historici, vol. 10 [Siena: University of Siena, 1942]).

7. Thomas returned to the theme of Catherine's miraculous writing in his testimony in *Il Processo Castellano*, 58. For critique concerning the claim that Catherine wrote some of her own letters, see Robert Fawtier, *Sainte Catherine de Sienne: Essai de critique des sources*, 2 vols. (Paris: De Boccard, 1921), 1:47–48 and 2:354.

8. The second treatise of Part One differs from other sections of Thomas's *Libellus*. For instance, the repeated reference to Catherine's desire to die after her mystical experiences or her expressions of frustration in trying to explain mystical experiences in ordinary language do not appear with the same frequency and consistency elsewhere in the *Libellus*. Also, the repeated identification of the visions through the places in which they happened (at home, in church, and so forth) that characterizes this section is not apparent in other sections of the book. Moreover, this section emphasizes the role of Tommaso della Fonte as confessor and witness

of these events. For a summary of the arguments in favor of the claim that the section was copied from Tommaso della Fonte's booklets, see Foralosso, "Introduzione," xlvii-xlix. A passage in Raymond of Capua's *Legenda maior* offers further support to the claim that the second treatise of Part One of the *Libellus* was copied from Tommaso della Fonte's notebooks (see Raymond of Capua, *De S. Catharinae Senensis* [the *Legenda maior*], in *Acta Sanctorum* April III [Paris: Palmé, 1866], 911 [par. 199]). Translation in English: *The Life of Catherine of Siena*, trans. Conleth Kearns (Washington, DC: Dominican Publications, 1980). In this passage Raymond wrote that for lack of space he was unable to use all Tommaso's accounts concerning Catherine's visions and ecstacies, but he offers a short summary of the kinds of visions he had been forced to exclude. These characterizations are brief and vague, but they seem to refer to the same visions that are reported in the second treatise of Part One of the *Libellus*.

9. Thomas offers a biography of Tommaso della Fonte and lists his writings in *Libellus*, 376–79. Raymond of Capua made several references to Tommaso's booklets (see *Legenda maior*, pars. 82, 142, 162, 164, 181, 186, 189, 199, 202, 210, 230, 244, 260, and 283).

10. Thomas organized a *scriptorium* that focused on copying and promulgating texts written by Catherine or concerning her, and a good part of the earliest surviving documents relating to her were produced and copied in this *scriptorium* (see Eugenio Dupré Theseider, *Epistolario di Santa Caterina da Siena* [Rome: Istituto storico italiano, 1940], li–lvi; E. Messerini, "Lo scriptorium di Fra Tommaso Caffarini," *S. Caterina da Siena* 19 [1968], 1:15–21).

11. Thomas of Siena, *Libellus*, 1–9.

12. Thomas refers to the *Legenda* several times in his *Libellus*. The *Legenda* in question is Raymond of Capua's life of Catherine, the *Legenda maior*.

13. Raymond of Capua was chosen as the master general of the Dominican Order in May 1380, only a few weeks after Catherine's death, and he held the position until his own death on October 5, 1399. On Raymond, see A. W. van Ree, "Raymond de Capoue: Éléments biographiques," *Archivum Fratrum Praedicatorum* 33 (1963): 159–241.

14. Giuliana Cavallini has suggested that Catherine's book was, in fact, written over a period of a few months, probably between late 1377 and early 1378 (see Catherine of Siena, *Il Dialogo*, 2nd ed., ed. Giuliana Cavallini [Siena: Edizioni Cantagalli, 1995], xxiv–xxx; translation in English: *The Dialogue*, trans. and ed. Suzanne Noffke [New York: Paulist Press, 1980]).

15. Catherine of Siena, *Le lettere*, notes by Niccolò Tommaseo, ed. Pietro Misciatelli, 6 vols. (Florence, 1970). For ongoing translation in English, see *The Letters of Catherine of Siena*, trans. Suzanne Noffke, 2 vols. (Tempe: Arizona Center for Medieval and Renaissance Studies, 2000, 2001).

16. For a collection of letters to and concerning Catherine of Siena, see *Leggenda minore di S. Caterina da Siena e lettere dei suoi discepoli*, ed. Francesco Grottanelli (Bologna: G. Romagnoli, 1868), 253–390. One of Thomas's ways to promote Catherine's cult was to solicit letters testifying about her sanctity. He copied these letters in various passages of his *Tractatus, Libellus,* and *Historia*. One of the most influential of these letters was that of Stefano Maconi, written in 1411 (see *Epistola Domni Stephani de gestis et virtutibus S. Catharinae*, in *Acta Sanctorum* April III, 969–975). A testimony of Catherine's life is offered also by the Sienese notary Cristofano Gano Guidini, published as "Memorie di Ser Cristofano di Galgano Guidini da Siena, scritte da lui medesimo nel secolo XIV," *Archivio Storico Italiano* 4 (1843): 25–47. This testimony presents a touching portrayal of the ways in which Catherine influenced Gano Guidini's personal life.

17. Though Thomas does not mention names, among these "trustworthy persons" must have been penitent women who were often present during Catherine's ecstasies and shared their experiences with Raymond, Tommaso, Thomas, and other followers of Catherine.

18. Thomas of Siena, *Libellus*, 8–9.

19. Thomas does not, in fact, discuss the topic at the beginning of Part Three of his *Libellus*.

20. The complete *Legenda* (Latin: *legenda prolixa*) in question is Raymond's *Legenda maior*, whereas the abbreviated legend refers to the *Legenda minor*, Thomas's abbreviation of Raymond's work.

21. Thomas frequently referred to treatises and chapters within Raymond's *Legenda maior*. However, his references rarely match the version of the *Legenda maior* that has survived. It might be that Thomas was using a lost version of the *Legenda maior*, or that he referred to implicit parallels between themes rather than to direct dependence between the individual stories (see, Foralosso, "Introduzione," xlvi–xlvii).

22. Cf. Raymond of Capua, *Legenda maior*, 869–70 (par. 28).

23. Cf. ibid., 870 (chap. 29). This vision is included also in the *Miracoli* of Catherine of Siena, chap. 2, herein.

24. Cf. Raymond of Capua, *Legenda maior*, 875 (par. 53).

25. Repeated accounts of Catherine's entrance in the wound and her reception of the penitent habit from the wound presented Thomas with divine authorization of Catherine's penitent vocation.

26. Raymond of Capua, *Legenda maior*, 961 (par. 403). The chapter may be found, in fact, in the sixth treatise of the third book.

27. Catherine often used a tree as a spiritual metaphor in her writing (see Giuliana Cavallini, *Catherine of Siena* [London: Geoffrey Chapman, 1998], 51–66).

28. This image of the tree surrounded by a hill of chaff is not from the *Legenda maior*, but, instead, from Catherine's book *Il Dialogo*, 112–15 (chap. 44). Translation in English: *The Dialogue*, trans. and intro. Suzanne Noffke (New York: Paulist Press, 1980), 89–91 (chap. 44).

29. Raymond of Capua, *Legenda maior*, 888–89 (pars. 106–9).

30. Sinoper was red ink.

31. According to Thomas's testimony later in the book, the Dominican penitent sisters in Venice had Catherine's mantle, one of her teeth, one of her fingers, and one of her arm bones as relics (see Thomas of Siena, *Libellus*, 406). See also his testimony in *Il Processo Castellano*, 58.

32. Thomas claimed that Catherine's letters, which in today's collections are numbered 371 and 372, were personally written by the saint (see *Libellus*, 269 and 274). Catherine said that she personally wrote letter 272 and another unspecified letter (see Catherine of Siena, *Le lettere*, vol. 4, no. 272).

33. Raymond indeed discussed Catherine's letters to him at the beginning of Part Three of the *Legenda maior*, but he did not suggest that these letters were personally written by the saint (see *Legenda maior*, 946 [par. 337]). Raymond wrote that Catherine learned to read miraculously, but he did not claim that Catherine learned to write (see *Legenda maior*, 890 [par. 113]).

34. Cf. Raymond of Capua, *Legenda maior*, 890–91 (pars. 114–15). Raymond emphasized the Virgin Mary's role in Catherine's mystical espousal, he included more holy figures in the scene, and his depiction of the ring differed from that of Thomas.

35. Thomas underlined his dependency on the *Legenda maior*, but the second treatise of Part One cannot, in fact, be traced back to Raymond's work. Raymond did not narrate the kinds of events that are discussed in this treatise, and his conception of Catherine's christocentric spirituality was indeed quite different from the heavenly visions offered here. The second treatise is a particularly valuable document to understanding the development of Catherine's cult, because, as has been sug-

gested in the Editor's Note above, the treatise seems to be a fairly direct copy of the now lost notebooks of Tommaso della Fonte.

36. Catherine burst into a mystical singing of joy and praise of God, *iubilus*, which is associated with the mystical state of ecstasy. This singing was common among medieval female mystics (see Bernard McGinn, *The Flowering of Mysticism: Men and Women in the New Mysticism, 1200–1350* [New York: Crossroad, 1998], 39–40). Mystical singing may also be viewed as one way that women were able to teach (see Carolyn Muessig, "Prophecy and Song: Teaching and Preaching by Medieval Women," in *Women Preachers and Prophets through Two Millenia of Christianity*, ed. Beverly Mayne Kienzle and Pamela Walker [Berkeley and Los Angeles: University of California Press, 1998], 146–58).

37. Ecstasy was seen to be manifested as death from the world, seen in such physical signs as bodily rigidity, missing pulse, and insensitivity to touch.

38. The second treatise contains frequent references to Catherine's desire to die after her mystical experiences. This refers to ecstasy as a sensation of bodily death and to the related theme of mystical death (Latin: *mors mystica*), an annihilation of the mystic's soul as it comes into union with God. Raymond of Capua discussed Catherine's mystical death, but he avoided describing what Catherine might have seen in paradise. Instead, he focused on the effect that Catherine's "mystical death" had on her apostolicism (see *Legenda maior*, 914–15 [pars. 213–18]).

39. Catherine lived only a few hundred feet away from the Church of San Domenico in Siena.

40. Cf. Raymond of Capua, *Legenda maior*, 891–93 (pars. 118–25).

41. Raymond too told a story concerning Catherine's mystical vestment, but Raymond wrote that Catherine received a vestment of blood from Christ as a token of his gratitude for the assistance she gave to a pauper (see ibid., 896 [chap. 137]).

42. Catherine's refusal to share her vision with her companion underscored her commitment to her confessor's guidance and the direction of the hierarchical church.

43. Mary Magdalene was one of the heavenly protectors of the Dominican Order and one of Catherine's personal patron saints. She was venerated as a symbol of penance and preaching. On the cult of Mary Magdalene among the Dominicans and other mendicant orders, see Katherine Jansen, *The Making of Magdalen: Preaching and Popular Devotion in the Later Middle Ages* (Princeton, NJ: Princeton University Press, 2000).

44. "Postea videbatur sibi videre Christum et quod haberet unum nevum in facie et quod constringeret eam in tantum quod semper vide-

batur sibi tangi ab ipso[…].” It is not clear why the specific mention of the birthmark on Jesus' face is made. I thank Antti Arjava for his help with this passage, especially with identifying the little-used term *nevum* as a birthmark.

45. “Aliquando habuit infirmitatem sanguinis ex utraque parte et hoc habuit propter violentiam quam ipsa faciebat sibi propter abundantiam dulcedinis et suavitatis bonorum Dei, quia trahebatur ita a Deo quod non poterat sustinere et ita patiebatur magnam corporis infirmitatem.” It is difficult to determine to what kind of “illness” or “wounds” the passage refers, in part because the expression “ex utraque parte” refers to two sides, but the illness is discussed in the singular *(infirmitas)*. It is also confusing that *hoc*, which clearly refers to *infirmitas* (f.) is masculine. The confusion may arise from Tommaso della Fonte's text or from Thomas of Siena's careless copying of Tommaso's text. I thank Juhani Norri for his help with this section.

46. One of Catherine's letters was directed to Sister Maddalena di Alessa from the Monastery of Santa Bonda (see Catherine of Siena, *Le lettere*, vol. 3, no. 220).

47. Sleeping on a plank was one of the monastic disciplines, followed also by the mendicants.

48. It is not clear why the reference to the date is made. January 11 was perhaps emphasized because it was part of the octave of the Epiphany.

49. Probably December 13.

50. The saint in Catherine's vision is not identifiable.

51. Margaret of Antioch, whose feast day was celebrated on July 20.

52. It is probable that Raymond wrote about this vision in the *Legenda maior* when he stated that he learned from Tommaso's booklets about one of Catherine's visions that happened on the feast day of Saint Margaret in 1370. While the text above stated merely that Catherine's heart ached, Raymond used this event to elaborate on Catherine's mystical exchange of hearts with Christ (see *Legenda maior*, 908–9 [par. 186]). This passage offers an exceptional opportunity to see in concrete terms how Raymond might have focused on an unspecified detail in Tommaso's texts (in this particular case heartache) and weaved it into his teachings concerning Catherine's christocentric mysticism (in this particular case, Catherine's mystical exchange of hearts with Christ).

53. Contrary to Thomas's claim, almost none of the visions discussed in the second treatise of Part One of the *Libellus* appears in the *Legenda maior*.

NOTES

Stefana Quinzani's Ecstasy of the Passion

1. For an edition of Stefana's *vita*, see Paolo Guerrini "La prima 'legenda volgare' de la beata Stefana Quinzani d'Orzinuovi secondo il codice Vaticano-Urbinate latino 1755," *Memorie storiche della diocesi di Brescia* 1930 (no. 1): 89–186. Stefana also features as one of the early modern "living saints" in Gabriella Zarri, *Le sante vive: Cultura e religiosità femminile nella prima età modern* (Turin: Rosenberg & Sellier, 1990), 87–164. Stefana's life and the process of her beatification are described in Vittorio Tolasi, *Stefana Quinzani: Donna, suora e beata (1457–1530)*, Inediti dell'epistolario Gonzaga e sintesi del processo di Beatificazione (Brescia: Tipografia di S. Eustacchio, 1972).

2. Stefana's letters to the Gonzagas are edited in Antonio Cistellini, *Figure della riforma pretridentina: Stefana Quinzani, Angela Merici, Laura Mignani, Bartolomeo Stella, Francesco Cabrini, Francesco Santabona* (Brescia: Morcelliana, 1979), 176–93. See also Tolasi, *Stefana Quinzani*, 24–62; and Adriano Prosperi, "Spiritual Letters," in *Women and Faith: Catholic Religious Life in Italy from Late Antiquity to the Present*, ed. Lucetta Scaraffia and G. Z. Howard (Cambridge, MA: Harvard University Press, 1999), 117–21.

3. At Osanna's death, Stefana wrote a laud of her virtues in a letter to Isabella d'Este (see Cistellini, *Figure della riforma pretridentina*, 180–81.)

4. In her letters Stefana several times asked for financial support from the Gonzagas (see Cistellini, *Figure della riforma pretridentina*, 188–90).

5. *Early Dominicans: Selected Writings*, ed. Simon Tugwell (New York: Paulist Press, 1982), 98. On Giovanna, see *The Legend of Giovanna of Orvieto*, chap. 5, herein.

6. For the history of the Stations of the Cross, see Herbert Thurston, *The Stations of the Cross: An Account of Their History and Devotional Purpose* (New York: Burns & Oates, 1906). I thank Christopher K. Gardner for drawing my attention to the parallels between Stefana's passion and the Stations of the Cross.

7. The original has been lost, but the authenticity of the first surviving copy, done in the late sixteenth century, is confirmed by Domenico Codagli in his *L'Historia orceana* (Brescia: Gio. Battista Borella, 1592), 153–54.

8. The testimony of Giovanni Antoni of Terno, following the document, shows that the exact day of this vision was February 17, 1497 (Giuseppe Brunati, *Vita, o Gesta di santi bresciani*, 2 vols. [Brescia: Venturini, 1854–65], 2:58).

9. Stefana stayed in Crema between 1473 and 1500. She worked as a servant first in the family of Giovanni Sabbatini, a doctor, and then in the family of GianFrancesco Verdello.

10. A *marcello* was a Venetian half lira, minted first in 1473 during the rule of Doge Nicolò Marcello and named after him.

11. The conflicts to which Stefana alluded were probably those between the papacy and the Dominican visionary and preacher Girolamo Savonarola, who was excommunicated in 1497 and burned as a heretic in 1498. Savonarola's visionary spirituality and call for moral reform had a great impact on Stefana (see Guerrini's introduction in "La prima 'legenda volgare,'" 76–78; on Savonarola and women religious in general, see Lorenzo Polizzotto, "Savonarola, Savonaroliani e la riforma della donna," in *Studi savonaroliani, verso il V centenario [Savonarola 1498–1998]*, ed. Gian Carlo Garfagnini [Florence: Galluzzo, 1996], 229–40; and Tamar Herzig, "The Rise and Fall of a Savonarolan Visionary: Lucia Brocadelli's Forgotten Contribution to the *Piagnone* Campaign," *Archiv für Reformationsgeschichter/Archive for Reformation History* 95 (2004): 34–60.

12. "Deinde per tutti li ordeni in generali he per tuta la chieresia. Et maxime per li predicatori acio posseno far fructo ne le lor prediche, subiungendo, se non farano fructo signor non restera per loro ma per li cori di peccatori indurati." It is unclear what the passage refers to.

13. Stefana's comment suggests that she did not see the Dominican penitent life as a popular vocation. It is impossible to offer an estimate of the number of the Dominican penitents at the turn of the sixteenth century. However, at this time an exceptional number of Dominican penitent communities were being founded in Florence, Pistoia, Perugia, Milan, and other central and northern Italian towns. Thus Stefana's claim is rather surprising; it may be that she is referring to a low number of Dominican penitent women in her own town.

14. "Be your name praised in everything, O Lord. Through the person of Stefana in the fragile sex you have shown us in our time your great and marvelous, and almost incredible, works, both to those who see and those who do not see."

15. The text is followed by statements of twenty-one men, all of whom witnessed the event and confirmed the narration. Some of them were high-ranking clerics, two belonged to the Dominican Order, several were doctors of both canon and civil law, one was a medical doctor and another a public notary, one was a Franciscan tertiary, and a few men signed their testimony without specifying their profession. The statements of twenty-one witnesses show that Stefana's passion was observed by an audience of well-educated men whose words gave legitimacy to Stefana's

extraordinary imitation of Christ. Although women were apparently not seen as important witnesses of Stefana's passion, they might have sat in the audience. Stefana's other public imitation of Christ's passion took place on July 16, 1500, at the house of Paola Carrara, and was attended by Isabella Gonzaga, Osanna da Mantova, and several other Mantuan women (see Brunati, *Vita, o Gesta di santi bresciani,* 2:62–64).

Osanna of Mantua:
Letters to Francesco Gonzaga (a selection)

1. Similar requests on behalf of the poor and troubled were done by many other persons of saintly reputation. Cf. Stefana Quinzani's letters to the Gonzagas, in Antonio Cistellini, *Figure della riforma pretridentina: Stefana Quinzani, Angela Merici, Laura Mignani, Bartolomeo Stella, Francesco Cabrini, Francesco Santabona* (Brescia: Morcelliana, 1979), 176–93. See also Vittorio Tolasi, *Stefana Quinzani: Donna, suora e beata (1457–1530),* Inediti dell'epistolario Gonzaga e sintesi del processo di Beatificazione (Brescia: Tipografia di S. Eustacchio, 1972), 24–61.

2. Bagolini's and Ferretti's *La beata Osanna da Mantova, terziaria domenicana* (1449–1505) (Florence: Tipografia Domenicana, 1905) is still the best introduction to Osanna's life. Gabriella Zarri offers an excellent study concerning the prophetic roles of Osanna of Mantua and other late fifteenth-century female saints in *Le sante vive: Cultura e religiosità femminile nella prima età moderna* (Turin: Rosenberg & Sellier, 1990). For one of the key articles of the book in English, see Gabriella Zarri, "Living Saints: A Typology of Female Sanctity in the Early Sixteenth Century," in *Women and Religion in Medieval and Renaissance Italy,* ed. Daniel Bornstein and Roberto Rusconi, trans. Margery Schneider (Chicago: The University of Chicago Press, 1996), 219–304. See also Gabriella Zarri, "Osanna da Mantova," in *Il Grande Libro dei Santi,* ed. Claudio Leonardi, Andrea Riccardi, and Gabriella Zarri, 3 vols. (Turin: San Paolo, 1998), 3:1528–30; and A. L. Redigonda, "Osanna Andreasi," in *Dizionario biografico degli italiani* (Rome: Istituto della Enciclopedia Italiana, 1961) 3:131–32.

3. For Osanna's letters to Isabella d'Este, see Bagolini and Ferretti, *La beata Osanna,* xcviii–xcix (I: letters 85–90).

4. E. Ann Matter, "Prophetic Patronage as Repression: Lucia Brocadelli da Narni and Ercole d'Este," in *Christendom and Its Discontents: Exclusion, Persecution, and Rebellion, 1000–1500,* ed. Scott L. Waugh and Peter D. Diehl (Cambridge: Cambridge University Press, 1996), 168–76; and Tamar Herzig, "The Rise and Fall of a Savonarolan Visionary: Lucia

Brocadelli's Forgotten Contribution to the *Piagnone* Campaign," *Archiv für Reformationsgeschichter/Archive for Reformation History* 95 (2004): 34–60.

5. Valentino Brosio, *Francesco II Gonzaga: Marchese di Mantova* (Turin: G. B. Paravia, 1938).

6. Girolamo Scolari (Montolivetano), *Libretto de la vita et transito de la beata Osanna da Mantua* (Mantua: Leonardo Bruschi, 1507), Lib. I, chap. lxcv: "Fu da tutti meritatamente honorata si come corpo sancto e matre de la patria."

7. Isabella d'Este began organizing a collection of documents pertaining to Osanna immediately after Osanna's death on June 21, 1505. Isabella's letter to Sister Laura Boiarda, written only three days after Osanna's death, shows that the promotion of Osanna's cult was already well on its way (see Bagolini and Ferretti, *La beata Osanna*, cii-ciii [letter II: V]).

8. Francesco Silvestri, *Beatae Osannae Mantuanae de tertio habitu Ordinis Fratrum Praedicatorum vita*, in *Acta Sanctorum* June IV (Paris: Palmé, 1867), 552–664; and Scolari, *Libretto de la vita et transito de la beata Osanna da Mantua.*

9. Bagolini and Ferretti, *La beata Osanna*, 288; see also cxxviij-cxxx, which includes a copy of Leo X's letter.

10. The numbers of the letters refer to the numbering used in Bagolini and Ferretti, *La beata Osanna.* Bagolini and Ferretti present a collection of Osanna's letters addressed to Girolamo of Mantua, her confessor (forty-three letters); Frederico Gonzaga (two letters); Francesco II Gonzaga (thirty-four letters); and Isabella d'Este (six letters).

11. Osanna wrote in Italian, but she frequently used Latin phrases. I have kept the Latin expressions in the translation in order to preserve the flavor of Osanna's style.

12. One of Osanna's younger brothers, Antonio, was Francesco's vicar in Bigarello, close to Mantua, from ca. 1485 to ca. 1492 (see Bagolini-Ferretti, *La beata Osanna*, 131–32).

13. Osanna ended her letters by signing her name as "Suor Osanna Andreasi, unworthy servant of Christ and His Excellency [Francesco]."

14. Possibly Osanna's aforementioned brother Antonio, or perhaps Giovanni Buono (d. 1499).

15. Osanna's brother Antonio died in 1498 and Giovanni in 1499, and both of them left large families behind. Some of them joined the Dominican Order, including Fra Tommaso, who is mentioned in letter 78.

16. It is not clear whether Osanna asks her nephews to be exempted (Italian: *esenzione*) from military service or from taxes.

17. Osanna's letter was written in Easter week (Wednesday). Her reference to the freeing of prisoners that week was probably inspired by the biblical reference that such a practice existed at the time of Jesus (see Matt 27:15).

18. In 1503 Francesco served as a *condottiere* in the army of the French king, Louis XII (see Frederick J. Baumgartner, *Louis XII* [New York: St. Martin, 1994], 132–33).

19. Francesco wrote to Osanna from Bologna on August 30, 1503, to ask her to pray for him. For the letter, see Bagolini and Ferretti, *La beata Osanna*, cj (letter II: III).

20. San Vincenzo was a monastery of Dominican nuns in Mantua.

21. Federico was born in 1500, and he was to rule Mantua after his father's death in 1519.

22. Francesco and Isabella had two daughters: Eleonora was born in 1493 and Margherita in 1496.

23. Francesco met with Pope Pius III, who had been elected on September 22, but whose brief reign was to end on October 18, soon after Osanna wrote her letter.

24. Francesco wrote to Osanna from Grottaferrata in Agro Romano on September 29, 1503, to ask her to pray for him. For the letter, see Bagolini and Ferretti, cj (letter II: IV).

25. See letter 75.

26. Possibly Francesco Silvestri, Osanna's confessor and future hagiographer, who had been appointed as the lector at Mantua's San Domenico in 1498.

27. The letter mentions the day of its writing, but not the month. Bagolini and Ferreti date the letter to January and suggest that Thomas possibly celebrated his first Mass on Epiphany (January 6) (see Bagolini and Ferretti, *La beata Osanna*, 189).

Lucia Brocadelli: *Seven Revelations*

1. Gabriella Zarri, *Le sante vive: Cultura e religiosità femminile nella prima età moderna* (Turin: Rosenberg & Sellier, 1990).

2. For details of Lucia Brocadelli's life of prophecy, see E. Ann Matter, "Prophetic Patronage as Repression: Lucia Brocadelli da Narni and Ercole d'Este," in *Christendom and Its Discontents: Exclusion, Persecution, and Rebellion, 1000–1500*, ed. Scott L. Waugh and Peter Diehl (Cambridge: Cambridge University Press, 1995), 168–76; Tamar Herzig, "The Rise and Fall of a Savonarolan Visionary: Lucia Brocadelli's

Forgotten Contribution to the *Piagnone* Campaign," *Archiv für Reformationsgeschichte/Archive for Reformation History* 95 (2004): 34–60; Edmund G. Gardner, *Dukes and Poets in Ferrara: A Study in the Poetry, Religion, and Politics of the Fifteenth and Early Sixteenth Centuries*, 2nd ed. (New York: Haskell House, 1968); and Adriano Prosperi, "Brocadelli (Broccadelli), Lucia," in *Dizionario biografico degli italiani* (Rome: Istituto della Enciclopedia Italiana, 1972), 14:381–83.

3. These details are from Giacomo Marianese, *Narratione della nascita, vita e morte della beata Lucia di Narni dell'ordine di San Domenico, Fondatrice del monastero di Santa Caterina da Siena in Ferrara* (Ferrara: Vittorio Baldini, 1616).

4. Many documents from this house are found in Ferrara, Biblioteca della Curia Arcivescovale, Cartelle 25–26.

5. Letter of Ercole I dated March 4, 1500 (Modena, Archivio di Stato, Iurisdizione Sovrana, Santi e Beati 430 A), printed as *Spiritualium personarum feminei sexus facta d'amiratione digna* (Nürnberg, 1501), a tract of twelve unpaginated leaves (six in Latin, six in German).

6. For example, the story of Lucia, the Dominican penitent with the five wounds of Christ, was known to the German chronicler Johannes Trithemius, *Joannis Trithemii Sponheimensis…Annalium Hirsaugiensium Opus* (Monastery of St. Gall: Joannes Georgius Schlegel, 1890). Thanks to Gabriella Zarri for this information.

7. Lucia Brocadelli's role in the disputes between Dominicans and Franciscans about whether or not Catherine of Siena, or indeed any woman, could bear the stigmata of Christ has been discussed by Gabriella Zarri in the joint article of E. Ann Matter, Armando Maggi, Maiju Lehmijoki-Gardner, and Gabriella Zarri, "Lucia Brocadelli da Narni: Riscoperta di un manoscritto pavese," Bollettino della società pavese di storia patria 100 (2000): 173–99, esp. 189–99.

8. Pavia, Biblioteca Civica "Bonetta" MS II. 112 (già B12) (see Xenio Toscani, *Catalogo dei manoscritti della Biblioteca Civica "Bonetta" Civici Istituti di Arte e Storia Pavia* [Pavia: Tipografia del Libro, 1973], 79–80). I am grateful to Professor Toscani for his generous help, particularly in the early days of the discovery of the manuscript. The title is written on the flyleaf in an eighteenth-century hand, but the hand can be shown to be Lucia's through comparison with autographs of letters she wrote to Ercole (Archivio di Stato di Modena, Giurisdizione Sovrana, Busta 430, "Lettere autografe e copie de lettere della Beata Suor Lucia da Narni)." I would like to thank Gabriella Zarri for help in locating these documents. For reproductions of Lucia's hand in manuscripts in Modena and Pavia, see Matter et al., "Lucia Brocadelli da Narni," Fig. 3 and Fig. 4. We do not know

when or how the manuscript came to Pavia, but the text designated as the *Liber* of Lucia Brocadelli appears as number 127–B 12 in Renato Soriga's list dated December 1910 (see Pavia: Museo Civico di Storia Patria, *Registro degli oggetti arrivati nel Museo*, quaderno 18 [1908–27]).

9. For the cover, see Matter et al., "Lucia Brocadelli da Narni," Fig. 1 and Fig. 2.

10. See, for example, Georgette de Montenay, *Emblemes ou devises chrétiennes* (1571); Benedetto Haeften, *Schola cordis* (1629); and Francesco Poma, *Cardiomorphoses sive ex corde desumpta emblemata sacra* (Verona, 1645). Among modern studies, see Armando Maggi, *Identita' e impresa rinascimentale* (Ravenna: Longo, 1998); and Giovanni Pozzi, "Schola cordis: di metafora in metonimia," in *Sull'orlo del visibile parlare* (Adelphi, 1993). My thanks to Lucia Miodini and Maria Antonietta Tovini for their help in the analysis of these symbols.

11. "Sac. Rituum Congregatione Eminentiss., & Reverendiss. D. Card. Ferrario Ferraien. Beatificationis & Canonizationis B. LUCIAE DE NARNIA Monialis ordinis S. Dominici Fundatricis Monasterij S. Catharinae Civitatis Ferrariae. POSITIO SUPER Dubio. An Sententia dar. mem. Cardinalis Macchiavelli super cultu ab immemorabili praestito erga Beatam sit confirmanda, in casu, & ad effectum, etc." (Rome: Typus Rev. Camerae Apostolicae, 1707). This document and others concerning Lucia Brocadelli's cult and relics are found in Ferrara, Biblioteca della Curia Arcivescovale, Cartelle 25 and 26.

12. "INVITO La santità di N.S. Papa Clemente XI concede Indulgenza Plenaria a tutti li Fedeli Christiani dell'una e l'altro sesso, che veramente pentiti, confessati, e communicati visitaranno la chiesa delle MMRR Madri di Santa Caterina da Siena nel dì 9 Giugno, in cui si esporrà alla pubblica venerazione il Sacro Corpo della B. LUCIA DA NARNI, che fù Fondatrice di detto Monastero, e si cantarà la Messa Solenne, con il Te Deum in Musica, in rendimento di grazie a SD Maestà, per quella ricevuta sopra il culto immemorabile della sudetta BEATA, in Vigore del Breve della santità sua, conformatorio del Decreto della Sacra Congregazione de' Riti, Perciò s'invita ogni fedel Christiano a volere intervenirvi pregando SD Maestà per li presenti bisogni. GIO: BATTISTA BOCCARDI VICARIO GENERALE EPIS. In Ferrara, Per Bernadino Pomatelli. Impressore Vescovale." Ferrara, Biblioteca della Curia Archivescovale, Cartella 25.

13. Ferrara, Biblioteca della Curia Arcivescovale, Cartella 26.

14. Although Marianese's biography claims to incorporate no-longer-extant eyewitness testimony, the earliest printed biographical notice of Lucia Brocadelli is Serafino Razzi, *Seconda parte delle vite de' santi*

e beati dell'ordine de' frati predicatori nelle quale si raccontano le vita, & opere, di molte Sante, e Beate Donne del medesimo ordine (Florence: Bartolomeo Sermartelli, 1577), 152–54. Razzi's account is also based on contemporary narratives, including that of Lucia's confessor, Marcheselli, and Antonio da Ravenna, the elderly prior of the Dominicans of Ravenna, who had known Lucia and her confessors.

15. The confessor who is assigned a chair in the Third Revelation prays the Rosary; later in this revelation she is praised by Jesus for two mimetic devotions that are equivalent to the second and third sorrowful mysteries: the flagellation and the crown of thorns.

16. See the Sixth Revelation, in which the Virgin Mary says "your name is Light because you are the daughter of the eternal light." This is the only specific mention of Lucia's name (but see note 17).

17. Lucia relates that Jesus called her by name (but without actually mentioning her name) once in the First Revelation, twice in the Second Revelation, and once in the Third Revelation.

18. On Savonarola, see Roberto Ridolfi, *The Life of Girolamo Savonarola*, trans. Cecil Grayson (New York: Knopf, 1959). For the cults that surrounded Savonarola, see Patrick Macey, *Bonfire Songs: Savonarola's Musical Legacy* (Oxford: Clarendon Press, 1998).

19. Matthew 2:16–18. Savonarola's *Compendion of Revelation* was known in Italian and Latin (see Girolamo Savonarola, *Compendio di rivelazione*, ed. Angela Crucitti [Rome, 1955]). All references in this translation will be to the English translation by Bernard McGinn in *Apocalyptic Spirituality* (New York: Paulist Press, 1979), 192–275; for the passage in question, see 230.

20. See the English translation of the *Celestial Hierarchies* by Colm Luibheid, *Pseudo-Dionysius: The Complete Works* (New York: Paulist Press, 1987), 143–91. The parallel scene in Savonarola's *Compendium* is in McGinn, *Apocalyptic Spirituality*, 256–64.

21. Augustine, *De trinitate*, Bk. 8; and Peter Lombard, *Sentences*, Bk. I, dist. XVII, par. I, cap. 1.

22. Catherine of Siena, *Il Dialogo*, ed. Giuliana Cavallini, 2nd ed. (Rome: Edizioni Caterinianae, 1968), 26. Translation in English: *Catherine of Siena: The Dialogue*, trans. and ed. Suzanne Noffke (New York: Paulist Press, 1980), 64.

23. There are a puzzling number of references to Franciscans in the text. In the First Revelation the third chair is for "a good father of the order of Saint Francis"; in the Third Revelation the colors of this chair are related to the "diverse and various ways he came to my service"; a Franciscan friar also appears in the Seventh Revelation and is actually

saved from temptation by Lucia's intervention. The role of Franciscans in this text is a very interesting topic for further study.

24. Matter et al., "Lucia Brocadelli da Narni," 190.

25. Pavia, Biblioteca Civica "Bonetta" MS II. 112 (già B12). The title is written on the flyleaf in an eighteenth-century hand.

26. All of the titles in the text are rubricated marginal notes, written in the manuscript by a second hand. They are indicated here in brackets.

27. In Savonarola's *Compendium*, the visionary, led by Saint Joseph, sees one triple crown (see McGinn, *Apocalyptic Spirituality*, 242–47).

28. In Savonarola's vision the crown is quickly followed by a throne designated the throne of King Solomon (see McGinn, *Apocalyptic Spirituality*, 247–55). In Savonarola's vision the throne of Solomon has a series of steps related to a spiritual ascent.

29. The nine orders of the angels (seraphim, cherubim, thrones, dominions, virtues, powers, principalities, archangels, and angels) derive ultimately from the *Celestial Hierarchy* of Dionysius the Pseudo-Areopagite. For the Savonarolan parallel, see McGinn, *Apocalyptic Spirituality*, 256–64, where the visionary is shown a similar scene.

30. In Savonarola's revelation the orders of saints are spelled out: confessors, virgins, doctors of the church, martyrs, apostles, prophets of the Old Testament, and the angels who protect the people of Florence (see McGinn, *Apocalyptic Spirituality*, 249–54). Lucia seems to be following this loosely: virgins and martyrs are mentioned below.

31. The word *lauds (laude)* has, besides the generalized meaning of "praise," a technical meaning of a vernacular hymn of the sort sung by the confraternities of late medieval and early modern Italy, especially those related to the cult of Savonarola (see Macey, *Bonfire Songs*).

32. At this point, the word for the chairs seen in the vision changes from "sedia" (which I translate "chair") to "catedra" (which I translate "throne").

33. Lucia Brocadelli seems to be playing here on the two meanings of *throne*—the seat and the angelic order.

34. That is, the Holy Innocents killed in Bethlehem when Jesus and his parents escaped to Egypt (Matt 2:16–18).

35. A paten is the ceremonial plate on which the bread of the Eucharist is placed during the Mass (see Elizabeth Parker McLachlan, "Liturgical Vessels and Implements," in *The Liturgy of the Medieval Church*, ed. Thomas Heffernan and E. Ann Matter [Kalamazoo, MI: Medieval Institute Publications, 2000], 369–429).

36. It is not clear to what text Lucia refers with the "song of the Epistle."

37. As mentioned above (note 17), this is the first of five times Lucia says that she is called by name in the visions. The first four times the speaker is Jesus; the final time, the only time her name is actually recorded in the text, the speaker is the Virgin Mary.

38. One of Lucia's many references to the human nature of Christ, a focal point of her devotional theology (see especially Revelation Three).

39. A reference to the stamping out of wine by feet.

40. Lucia here breaks into first-person singular, which she uses also in a few other places in the text.

41. Lucia answers Jesus in Latin and translates into Italian for the sake of the reader. This happens frequently in the text and reflects Savonarola's Italian version of the *Compendium*, where quotations from the Bible and liturgy appear in Latin.

42. "Tuti li creati intelecti spiculativi e inzegni de mondo." A phrase like "created speculative intellect" suggests that Lucia had some knowledge of Scholastic theology.

43. This seems to be a liturgical citation, but I have not been able to place it. This time, a figure in the vision speaks in Latin; once again, the visionary translates it.

44. The reference here is to the seven gifts of the Holy Spirit: wisdom, understanding, counsel, fortitude, knowledge, piety, and fear of the Lord. This patristic and medieval commonplace ultimately derives from a Christian interpretation of Isaiah 11:2–3 but has a long tradition in Christian allegory, especially connected to the liturgy (see E. Ann Matter, "The Pseudo-Alcuinian 'De septem sigillis': An Early Latin Apocalypse Exegesis," *Traditio* 36 [1980]: 122–23).

45. The three theological virtues are faith, hope, and charity. The four cardinal virtues are prudence, justice, fortitude, and temperance.

46. "El solaro del palacio." *Solaro* may mean "attic"; I translate it here as "roof."

47. Visions of thrones in heaven are found in Franciscan literature, for example, *The Mirror of Perfection*, chap. 60, trans. Leo Sherley-Price, in *Saint Francis of Assisi Writings and Early Biographies: English Omnibus of the Sources for the Life of Saint Francis*, ed. Marion A. Habig (Chicago: Franciscan Herald Press, 1983), 1185–86; and *The Writings of Leo, Rufino, and Angelo, Companions of Saint Francis*, chap. 23, ed. and trans. Rosalind B. Brooke (Oxford: Clarendon Press, 1970), 128–31.

48. A second hand has added the indication of the four seats in the margin (indicated here in brackets) and underscored the owner of each seat in the manuscript, as I do here.

49. We are not sure about the identity of the father confessor to whom this narrative is told. Two possibilities, Martino of Tivoli and Arcangelo Marcheselli, are discussed in Matter et al., "Lucia Brocadelli da Narni," 197–99. The personal pronouns in this section are confusing.

50. Although Dominican tradition claims that the Rosary was promulgated by Saint Dominic in the thirteenth century, it is generally agreed by modern scholars that the devotion (including the legend attributing it to Saint Dominic) derives from Dominican circles at the end of the fifteenth century, not much before the date of this manuscript (see Marina Warner, *Alone of All Her Sex: The Myth and the Cult of the Virgin Mary* [New York: Alfred A. Knopf, 1976], 305–9; and Anne Winston-Allen, *Stories of the Rose: The Making of the Rosary in the Middle Ages* [University Park, PA: Pennsylvania State University Press, 1997]).

51. The fact that a friar of the Franciscan Order, not the Dominican Order, is mentioned here may be another indication of details from the last years of Lucia's life.

52. Lucia's virginity is emphasized here. Lucia was briefly married to Pietro of Milan, but the marriage was possibly never consummated. Lucia meets her former brother-in-law in Revelation Seven.

53. This may be a reference to Lucia's sufferings after the death of her patron, Ercole I d'Este of Ferrara.

54. Confessor is a category of sainthood that is usually attributed to men who did not die as martyrs but whose exemplary Christian life is deemed worthy of sainthood.

55. This is the first of a number of personal interpolations that have more to do with Lucia Brocadelli's earthly life than with her visions.

56. This intimate personal note does not seem to have theological or allegorical implications but is instead a clear reference to Lucia's life and physical sufferings.

57. Noffke, *Catherine of Siena: The Dialogue*, 64.

58. It is clear here that this means once a week, but it must be noted that one would expect a Dominican penitent to say some version of the Office, at least an abbreviated one, every day!

59. Once again Lucia uses a Latin word, this time in the midst of an Italian sentence. This happens below with the words *ipso facto* ("at once") and *Io sum* ("I am"—a mixture of Italian and Latin), and in the Fifth Revelation.

60. A possible reference to God's description of himself to Moses on Mount Horeb: "I AM WHO AM" (Exod 3:14).

61. This is a puzzling passage. It is hard to understand what saints could know Jesus only in his humanity.

62. This is a common theme in Catherine of Siena's *Dialogue.*

63. "RE" (king) is capitalized and written with different ink.

64. Here Lucia breaks from her narrative and directly addresses the father confessor to whom she is writing, explaining that she must amend what she has said.

65. Once again, Lucia addresses her confessor directly.

66. That is, the Vigil of Easter. The First Revelation began on the night of the Annunciation to the Virgin Mary, March 25, a date that always falls in the Lenten period. The revelations, then, have moved through Lent to Easter.

67. The perfume of God is a common theme in Christian mystical and spiritual literature, with a source in the Vulgate text of Canticles 1:3. Here it emphasizes the special gift given to Lucia. Note that the third-person account changes to first person at the end of the description of the perfume.

68. That is, from Christmas to Easter. The choice of Paul as a guide at this point is fitting, since Paul is the most important biblical theologian for the humanity and divinity of Christ.

69. This may be testimony to physical abuses of Lucia Brocadelli after the death of her patron Ercole I d'Este. We have no record that Lucia was ever tortured by the Inquisition, although this passage might suggest it.

70. "Tuo nome Luce perchè sei fiola de la eterna luce," an obvious pun on the name Lucia. This is the only time a version of the name is actually given in the text.

71. Once again, Lucia breaks off the narration of her visions to speak to her father confessor metatextually about the way in which she is relating them.

72. The narrative seems to continue temporally through the night of Easter. The reference to Saint Paul the Apostle is hard to understand, since the feast of Peter and Paul is June 29.

73. Once again, Lucia seems more connected to the Franciscans than to members of her own Dominican Order.

74. It is not clear who Lucia means here, since Gerolamo (also spelled Hieronymo, or, as she has it here, Chieronimo) was the Christian name of Savonarola. But he, of course, was a Dominican.

75. From this point on, Lucia's narrative crosses over from the spiritual realm of her heavenly journeys to the world of human life, so that her spiritual actions are for the good of those still on earth. The encounter with her brother-in-law is remarkable for the personal details of her life.

76. This unnamed relative seems to be the brother of Lucia's husband, Pietro of Milan.

77. Notice that in what follows Lucia Brocadelli speaks in the first person and seems to refer to an attempted rape. There is no record of such a story between Lucia and her brother-in-law in the hagiographical materials.

78. This passage is not altogether clear, but the main point seems to be that the brother-in-law's sister and daughter were forced into the "death" of monastic vows.

79. The text ends in the middle of the next word, at the bottom of f. 30v of the manuscript. It seems that the text was nearing an end, especially because the tone has shifted to a more personal level. It would not be surprising if seven revelations were the original intention of the author, since seven was a significant number of completion in medieval symbolism. But, of course, we have no way of knowing for sure whether Lucia intended to, or actually did, write more revelations than those surviving in this manuscript.

Selected Bibliography

This bibliography contains selected publications concerning Dominican penitent women and other religious lay groups in the Middle Ages. For sources concerning particular Dominican penitent women, see the Appendix.

Bagolini, Giuseppe, and Lodovigo Ferretti. *La beata Osanna da Mantova, terziaria domenicana.* Florence: Tipografia Domenicana, 1905.

Benvenuti Papi, Anna, *"In castro poenitentiae": Santità e società femminile nell'Italia medievale.* Rome: Herder, 1990.

Boesch-Gajano, Sophia, and Odile Redon, "La Legenda maior di Raimondo da Capua, construzione di una santa." In Maffei and Nardi, *Atti del Simposio Internazionale Cateriniano Bernardiniano,* 15–36.

Bolton, Brenda M. "Mulieres Sanctae." In *Sanctity and Secularity: The Church and the World,* edited by Derek Baker, 77–95. Oxford: Basil Blackwell, 1973.

——. *The Medieval Reformation.* London: Edvard Arnold, 1983.

Bornstein, Daniel E., and Roberto Rusconi, eds. *Women and Religion in Medieval and Renaissance Italy.* Translated by Margery J. Schneider. Chicago: The University of Chicago Press, 1996.

Bynum, Caroline Walker. *Holy Feast and Holy Fast: The Religious Significance of Food to Medieval Women.* Berkeley and Los Angeles: University of California Press, 1987.

Cain, James R. "Cloister and Apostolate of Religious Women." *Review for Religious* 27 (1968), 2: 243–80, 3: 427–48, 4: 652–71, 5: 916–37; 28 (1969): 1: 101–21.

Casagrande, Giovanna. "Il movimento penitenziale nei secoli del basso medioevo: Note su alcuni recenti contributi," *Benedictina* 35 (1988): 475–507.

——. "Terziarie domenicane a Perugia." In Casagrande and Menestò, *Una santa, una città,* 109–59.

——. *Religiosità penitenziale e città al tempo dei comuni.* Rome: Istituto storico dei cappuccini, 1995.

Casagrande, Giovanna, and Enrico Menestò, eds. *Una santa, una città*. Spoleto: Centro Italiano di Studi sull'Alto Medioevo, 1991.

Cavallini, Giuliana. *Catherine of Siena*. London: Geoffrey Chapman, 1998.

Cistellini, Antonio. *Figure della riforma pretridentina: Stefana Quinzani, Angela Merici, Laura Mignani, Bartolomeo Stella, Francesco Cabrini, Francesco Santabona*. Brescia: Morcelliana, 1979.

Coakley, John. "Friars as Confidants of Holy Women in Medieval Dominican Hagiography." In *Images of Sainthood in Medieval Europe*, edited by Renate Blumenfeld-Kosinski and Timea Szell, 222–46. Ithaca, NY: Cornell University Press, 1991.

———. "Gender and Authority of the Friars: Significance of Holy Women for Thirteenth-Century Franciscans and Dominicans," *Church History* 60 (1991): 445–60.

———. "Friars, Sanctity, and Gender: Mendicant Encounters with Saints, 1250–1325." In *Medieval Masculinities: Regarding Men in the Middle Ages*, edited by Clare A. Lees, 91–110. Minneapolis: University of Minnesota Press, 1994.

Cox, Ronald J. *A Study of the Juridic Status of Laymen in the Writing of the Medieval Canonists*. Washington, DC: The Catholic University of America Press, 1959.

Creytens, Raymond. "Il Direttorio di Roberto Ubaldini da Gagliano, O.P., per le terziarie collegiate di S. Caterina da Siena in Firenze," *Archivum Fratrum Praedicatorum* 39 (1969): 127–72.

d'Alatri, Mariano, ed. *Il Movimento francescano della penitenza nella società medioevale*. Rome: Istituto Storico dei Cappuccini, 1980.

Elliot, Dyan. *Spiritual Marriage: Sexual Abstinence in Medieval Wedlock*. Princeton, NJ: Princeton University Press, 1993.

Fawtier, Robert. *Sainte Catherine de Sienne: Essai de critique des sources hagiographiques*. 2 vols. Paris: De Boccard, 1921.

Ganay, M.-C. de. *Les bienheureuses dominicaines (1190–1577) d'après des documents inédits*. Bar-le-Duc: Imprimerie Comte-Jacquet, 1926.

Gill, Katherine, "Open Monasteries for Women in Late Medieval and Early Modern Italy: Two Roman Examples." In *The Crannied Wall: Women, Religion, and the Arts in Early Modern Europe*, edited by Craig A. Monson, 15–48. Ann Arbor, MI: University of Michigan Press, 1992.

———. "Women and the Production of Religious Literature in the Vernacular, 1300–1500." In *Creative Women in Medieval and Early Modern Italy: Religious and Artistic Renaissance*, edited by E. Ann Matter and John Coakley, 64–104. Philadelphia: University of Pennsylvania Press, 1994.

————. *"Scandala:* Controversies Concerning Clausura and Women's Religious Communities in Late Medieval Italy." In *Christendom and Its Discontents: Exclusion, Persecution, and Rebellion, 1000–1500,* edited by Scott L. Waugh and Peter D. Diehl, 177–93. Cambridge: Cambridge University Press, 1996.

Goodich, Michael. "Ancilla Dei: The Servant as Saint in the Late Middle Ages." In *Women of the Medieval World: Essays in the Honor of John F. Mundy,* edited by Julius Kirshner and Suzanne F. Wemple, 119–36. Oxford/New York: Basil Blackwell, 1985.

Grundmann, Herbert. *Religious Movements in the Middle Ages: Historical Links between Heresy, the Mendicant Orders, and the Women's Religious Movement in the Twelfth and Thirteenth Century, with the Historical Foundations of German Mysticism.* Translated by Steven Rowan. Notre Dame, IN: University of Notre Dame Press, 1995.

Guarnieri, Romana. "Pinzochere." In *Dizionario degli istituti di perfezione,* edited by Guerrino Pelliccia and Giancarlo Rocca, 6:1721–49. Rome: Edizioni Paoline, 1980.

Herzig, Tamar. "The Rise and Fall of a Savonarolan Visionary: Lucia Brocadelli's Forgotten Contribution to the *Piagnone* Campaign," *Archiv für Reformationsgeschichter/Archive for Reformation History* 95 (2004): 34–60.

Hinnebusch, William A. *The History of the Dominican Order,* 2 vols. New York: Alba House, 1965.

Kieckhefer, Richard. *Unquiet Souls: Fourteenth-Century Saints and Their Religious Milieu.* Chicago: The University of Chicago Press, 1984.

Kienzle, Beverly Mayne, and Pamela J. Walker, eds. *Women Preachers and Prophets through Two Millenia of Christianity.* Berkeley and Los Angeles: University of California Press, 1998.

Kleinberg, Aviad M. *Prophets in Their Own Country: Living Saints and the Making of Sainthood in the Later Middle Ages.* Chicago: The University of Chicago Press, 1992.

Lehmijoki-Gardner, Maiju. *Worldly Saints: Social Interaction of Dominican Penitent Women in Italy, 1200–1500.* Helsinki: Suomen Historiallinen Seura, 1999.

————. "Writing Religious Rules as an Interactive Process—Dominican Penitent Women and the Making of Their *Regula,*" *Speculum* 79 (2004): 660–87.

Leonardi, Claudio, Andrea Riccardi, and Gabriella Zarri, eds. *Il Grande Libro dei Santi,* 3 vols. Turin: San Paolo, 1998.

Linehan, Peter. *The Ladies of Zamora.* Manchester: Manchester University Press, 1997.

Lungarotti, Maria, ed. *Le legendae di Margherita da Città di Castello*. Spoleto: Centro Italiano di studi sull'alto medioevo, 1994.

Maffei, Domenico, and Paolo Nardi, eds. *Atti del Simposio Internazionale Cateriniano Bernardiniano*. Siena: Accademia senese degli Intronati, 1982.

Makowski, Elizabeth. *Canon Law and Cloistered Women: Periculoso and Its Commentators 1298–1545*. Washington, DC: The Catholic University of America Press, 1997.

Mason, Mary Elizabeth. *Active Life and Contemplative Life*. Milwaukee, WI: Marquette University Press, 1961.

Matter, E. Ann. "Prophetic Patronage as Repression: Lucia Brocadelli da Narni and Ercole d'Este." In *Christendom and Its Discontents: Exclusion, Persecution, and Rebellion, 1000–1500*, edited by Scott L. Waugh and Peter D. Diehl, 105–19. Cambridge: Cambridge University Press, 1996.

Matter, E. Ann, Armando Maggi, Maiju Lehmijoki-Gardner, and Gabriella Zarri. "Lucia Brocadelli da Narni: Riscoperta di un manoscritto pavese." *Bollettino della Società Pavese di Storia Patria* (2000): 173–99.

McDonnell, Ernst. *Beguines and Beghards in Medieval Culture, with Special Emphasis on the Belgian Scene*. New Brunswick, NJ: Rutgers University Press, 1954.

McGinn, Bernard. *The Flowering of Mysticism: Men and Women in the New Mysticism, 1200–1350*. New York: Crossroad, 1998.

McNamara, Jo Ann. *Sisters in Arms: Catholic Nuns through Two Millenia*. Cambridge, MA: Harvard University Press, 1996.

Meersseman, Gilles Gerard. *Dossier de l'ordre de la pénitence au XIIIe siècle*. Freiburg: Editions Universitaires Fribourg Suisse, 1961.

Meersseman, Gilles Gerard, in collaboration with Gian Piero Pacini. *Ordo Fraternitatis: Confraternite e pietà dei laici nel medioevo*, 3 vols. Rome: Herder, 1977.

Menestò, Enrico. "Giovanna da Orvieto: la santità tra un fuso, un ago e un rocchetto di filo." In *Umbria sacra e civile*, edited by Enrico Menestò and Roberto Rusconi, 125–34. Turin: Nuova Eri-Edizioni RAI, 1989.

Mooney, Catherine M., ed. *Gendered Voices: Medieval Saints and Their Interpreters*. Philadelphia: University of Pennsylvania Press, 1999.

Mulder-Bakker, Anneke. *Lives of the Anchoresses: The Rise of the Urban Recluse in Medieval Europe*. Trans. Myra Meerspink Scholz. Philadelphia: University of Pennsylvania Press, 2005.

Noffke, Suzanne. *Catherine of Siena: Vision through a Distant Eye*. Collegeville, MN: The Liturgical Press, 1996.

Osheim, Duane J. "Conversion, *Conversi*, and the Christian Life in Late Medieval Tuscany," *Speculum* 58 (1983): 368–90.

Paoli, Emore. "'Pulcerrima vocor ab omnibus et non Vanna': Vanna da Orvieto dalla storia alla agiografia." In *La* Legenda *di Vanna da Orvieto*, edited by Emore Paoli and Luigi G. G. Ricci, 3–75. Spoleto: Centro Italiano di studi sull'alto medioevo, 1996.

Pazzelli, R., and L. Temperini, eds. *Prime manifestazioni di vita comunitaria maschile e femminile nel movimento francescano della penitenza (1215–1447)*. Rome: Commissione Storica Internazionale T.O.R., 1982.

Pennings, Joyce. "Semi-religious Women in Fifteenth-century Rome," *Medelingen van Het Nederlands Institut te Rome* 47, n.s. 12 (1987): 115–40.

Polizzotto, Lorenzo. "When Saints Fall Out: Women and the Savonarolan Reform in the Early Sixteenth Century," *Renaissance Quarterly* 46 (1993): 486–525.

———. "Savonarola, Savonaroliani e la riforma della donna." In *Studi savonaroliani, verso il V centenario (Savonarola 1498–1998)*, edited by Gian Carlo Garfagnini, 229–44. Florence: SISMEL edizioni del Galluzzo, 1996.

Ree, A. W. van. "Raymond de Capoue: Éléments biographiques," *Archivum Fratrum Praedicatorum* 33 (1963): 159–241.

Rusconi, Roberto, ed. *Il Movimento religioso femminile in Umbria nei secoli XIII–XIV.* Spoleto: Centro Italiano di Studi sull'Alto Medioevo, 1994.

Scaraffia, Lucetta, and Gabriella Zarri, eds. *Women and Faith: Catholic Religious Life in Italy from Late Antiquity to the Present.* Cambridge, MA: Harvard University Press, 1999.

Scott, Karen. "St. Catherine, 'Apostola.'" *Church History* 61 (1992): 34–46.

———. "Urban Spaces, Women's Networks, and the Lay Apostolate in the Siena of Catherine Benincasa." In *Creative Women in Medieval and Early Modern Italy: Religious and Artistic Renaissance*, edited by E. Ann Matter and John Coakley, 105–19. Philadelphia: University of Pennsylvania Press, 1994.

Simons, Walter. *Cities of Ladies: Beguine Communities in the Medieval Low Countries, 1200–1565.* Philadelphia: University of Pennsylvania Press, 2001.

Sorelli, Fernanda. *La santità imitabile: "Leggenda di Maria da Venezia" di Tommaso da Siena.* Venice: Deputazione Editrice, 1984.

———. "Per la storia religiosa di Venezia nella prima metà del quattrocento: inizi e sviluppi del terz'ordine domenicano." In *Viridarium floridum: Studi di storia veneta offerti dagli allievi a Paolo Sambin*, edited by Maria Chiara Billanovich, Girogio Cracco, and Antonio Rigon, 89–114. Padua: Editrice Antenore, 1984.

————. "Imitable Sanctity: The Legend of Maria of Venice." In Bornstein and Rusconi, *Women and Religion in Medieval and Renaissance Italy*, 165–81.

Temperini, Lino. *Carisma e legislazione alle origini del terzo ordine di S. Francesco*. Rome: Editrice Franciscanum, 1996.

Thompson, Augustine. *Cities of God: The Religion of the Italian Communes, 1125–1325*. University Park, PA: Pennsylvania State University Press, 2005.

Tolasi, Vittorio. *Stefana Quinzani: Donna, suora e beata (1457–1530)*. Inediti dell'epistolario Gonzaga e sintesi del processo di Beatificazione. Brescia: Tipografia di S. Eustacchio, 1972.

Vauchez, André. *The Laity in the Middle Ages: Religious Beliefs and Devotional Practices*, edited and introduced by Daniel E. Bornstein, translated by Margery J. Schneider. Notre Dame, IN: University of Notre Dame Press, 1993.

————. *Sainthood in the Later Middle Ages*. Translated by Jean Birrell. Cambridge, England: Cambridge University Press, 1997.

Visani, Oriana. "Nota su Tommaso d'Antonio Nacci Caffarini." *Rivista di Storia e Letteratura Religiosa* 9/2 (1973): 277–97.

Wehrli-Johns, Martina. "L'Osservanza dei Domenicani e il movimento penitenziale laico: Studi sulla 'regola di Munio' e sul Terz'ordine domenicano in Italia e Germania." In *Ordini religiosi e società politica in Italia e Germania nei secoli XIV e XV*, edited by Giorgio Chittolini and Kaspar Elm, 287–329. Bologna: il Mulino, 2001.

Woods, Richard. *Mysticism and Prophecy: The Dominican Tradition*. Maryknoll, NY: Orbis Books, 1998.

Zarri, Gabriella. *Le sante vive:* Cultura e religiosità femminile prima età moderna. Turin: Rosenberg & Sellier, 1990.

————. "Living Saints: A Typology of Female Sanctity in the Early Sixteenth Century." In Bornstein and Rusconi, *Women and Religion in Medieval and Renaissance Italy*, 219–303.

————. "From Prophecy to Discipline, 1450–1650." In Scaraffia and Zarri, *Women and Faith: Catholic Religious Life in Italy from Late Antiquity to the Present*, 83–112.

————. *Recinti: Donne, clausura e matrimonio nella prima età moderna*. Bologna: Il Mulino, 2000.

Index

Other Volumes in This Series

Other Volumes in This Series

Other Volumes in This Series

Other Volumes in This Series

Robert Bellarmine • SPIRITUAL WRITINGS
Safed Spirituality • RULES OF MYSTICAL PIETY, THE BEGINNING OF WISDOM
Shakers, The • TWO CENTURIES OF SPIRITUAL REFLECTION
Sharafuddin Maneri • THE HUNDRED LETTERS
Spirituality of the German Awakening, The •
Symeon the New Theologian • THE DISCOURSES
Talmud, The • SELECTED WRITINGS
Teresa of Avila • THE INTERIOR CASTLE
Theatine Spirituality • SELECTED WRITINGS
'Umar Ibn al-Fārid • SUFI VERSE, SAINTLY LIFE
Valentin Weigel • SELECTED SPIRITUAL WRITINGS
Vincent de Paul and Louise de Marillac • RULES, CONFERENCES, AND WRITINGS
Walter Hilton • THE SCALE OF PERFECTION
William Law • A SERIOUS CALL TO A DEVOUT AND HOLY LIFE, THE SPIRIT OF LOVE
Zohar • THE BOOK OF ENLIGHTENMENT

The Classics of Western Spirituality is a ground-breaking collection of the original writings of more than 100 universally acknowledged teachers within the Catholic, Protestant, Eastern Orthodox, Jewish, Islamic, and Native American Indian traditions.

To order any title, or to request a complete catalog, contact Paulist Press at 800-218-1903 or visit us on the Web at www.paulistpress.com